ZIP ZAP

For Judge Lee West,
who has been here and
done this in the biggest
way. all the best,
Tom Word

ZIP ZAP

*The True Story of
a Dog and a Dream*

MIKE GADDIS

STACKPOLE
BOOKS

Published by
STACKPOLE BOOKS
5067 Ritter Road
Mechanicsburg, PA 17055
www.stackpolebooks.com

Printed in the United States

First edition

10 9 8 7 6 5 4 3 2 1

Library of Congress Cataloging-in-Publication Data

Gaddis, Mike.
    Zip zap : the true story of a dog and a dream / Mike Gaddis.— 1st ed.
      p. cm.
    ISBN-13: 978-0-8117-0196-9
    ISBN-10: 0-8117-0196-4
    1. English setters—Training. 2. Pointing dogs—Training. 3. Field trials. I. Title.

SF429.E5G33 2006
636.752'6—dc22

2006005290

Dog days—
a Season of Joy, a Season of Pain,
all for the Treasures we find between

PROLOGUE

SEVENTEEN YEARS, SEVEN MONTHS, AND SEVENTEEN DAYS.

The symmetry of her life is almost as preoccupying as the wonder of it. And I wonder still. I will always wonder. For there was, from its dawning seconds, no moment less than remarkable, no minute less than intriguing, no hour bereft of inspiration. Sixty-three revolutions of this peripatetic planet have taught me the value beyond measure of a brilliance so rare, dogs and people alike.

But on that December day, her time had lapsed—though how could it be?—and there was nothing on God's earth I could do to unend that. I, who had been granted the gift of her, the incredible blessing of her. I, alone, who had been permitted the privilege of her destiny.

We stood limply under an ancient gray cedar tree on the last day of the year, Loretta and I, in the gathering dusk, only sparsely sheltered from the cold, pouring rain. Stung equally by certainty and disbelief, caring of nothing beyond the moment. For there *was* nothing beyond the moment, nor for many others to come. Our world had stopped, and it would be a long time before it turned on. Tears streamed down our faces as profusely as the raindrops, and both spattered somberly against the wet, muddening mound of a newly turned grave.

The very last thing I had wanted to do on New Year's Eve was dig a grave, and most especially this one. It had been solemn from the break of light that day, dismal and uneasy, prayerfully quiet, as if the heavens were presciently in mourning.

We found her peacefully at rest that afternoon, still warm, in her kennel house.

"It must be done today," I said to Loretta. "I cannot face it on the first of another year, and expect to go on living."

And now the rain beat down on her remains, and ours. There was a great part of me buried there with her, and a part of me, because of her, that will carry on boldly for the rest of my days, until I'm with her again.

"We grow so unaccustomed to perfection," Loretta said, closing to my side, her eyes swollen and red, "that it must be shown to us. We never really achieve it on our own."

So it was. Something greater than the nick between Johnny Crockett's John and November's Calling gave us Pat that providential May morning of 1976. Something greater than five generations of blue-blooded English setters, something greater than the biological pairing of genes on chromosomes. Something magical. Something unknown. And it had lasted seventeen years, seven months, and seventeen days.

As dreaded as her passage, it was not unanticipated. Her frail and weary body, so alien to her mien, could no longer answer the fire of her spirit, and her spirit, as ever, yearned for freedom. So she had simply lain down without a whimper, and died as gracefully as she had lived.

Her spirit, in life or in death, is indomitable. I know, because I knew her. It burns on, and day after day, I find it in a dozen places. A little of it to see me through in a troubled time. A little of it to remember on a mellow November noon. A little of it looking up at me through the eyes of Molly, her latest granddaughter. Asking me if I'm carrying on.

"Yes," I assure her quietly, and vow each time anew.

For we were a team, she and I, and once upon a time . . . we were invincible.

It seems so long ago, and as fresh as yesterday.

~ CHAPTER 1 ~

"IT'S GONNA BE TODAY," LORETTA PLEDGED INTUITIVELY, A TWINKLE IN her eye, that gone a-glimmering May morning twenty-nine years ago. I had seen that look before. Our daughter was born later that evening during a prime episode of *Gunsmoke.* Old Doc was in attendance, though my wife was subsequently hands-down on the idea of naming her Kitty. And I had seen that dimple in my wife's eye again, and again, just before parturition of a half dozen of her friends.

Now, just as the sun climbed out of bed, here she was, freshly back from running Melanie to school and a trip to the kennel—with Cindy trooping by her side, waddling along as stylishly as her distended abdomen would allow—reporting the equivalent of an order for hot, boiling water.

I reappraised our mama-to-be. She looked no different, I thought, than the other two dozen times I had examined her in the past week, at the tag end of an interminable wait that had gathered suspense from its conception, sixty-one days ago. But I had learned better than to doubt.

"I'm bringing her in where we can watch her," my wife announced. "You'd as well call in to work."

"That sure, huh?" I said.

She gave me a winsome look.

My erstwhile gunning companion, meantime, had spun precariously but thrice around, plopping down dead center of the braided rug. I walked over and dropped to my knees beside her, caressing an ear. She was as lovely as ever, tricolored with a full mask, except sprawled broad as a barn. She looked up at me with labored hazel eyes, like she was looking for someone to blame.

She did seem to be breathing a bit heavy.

"What say, old girl," I inquired, "things pullin' close?"

Her tail beat the rug.

"Get a temperature?" I asked my better three-quarters.

"No need," she declared, pulling a bag of broiled liver from the refrigerator and emptying the contents into the small warming pan rattling rhythmically from heat convection on the stove burner.

"It's gonna be today. Any time maybe."

"So don't go wanderin' off somewhere," she admonished sternly, "where we can't find you if we need you."

Women.

They must learn this from the womb, how to affix just enough guilt and probability to keep a man around.

She dumped the liver summarily from the warming pan into a food bowl, trekked over, and set it in front of Cindy. I kissed her teasingly on the neck, and she slapped me away.

"Watch," she remanded.

We had been giving Cindy the liver twice daily for the past three weeks as a prenatal supplement, on the promise of an old-time breeder and trainer that it would bolster the vitality of the litter. Normally she devoured it in a heartbeat.

The setter heaved herself upright at the expense of a tortured and protracted groan, took a few tentative sniffs, and declined. She stood apathetically over the bowl, a trace of anxiety in her eyes.

"See," Loretta reiterated.

I shook my head in surrender. "I'll be just downstairs," I submitted, "in the basement."

I had left a box of number nine shotshells uncompleted on the reloading bench the evening before. Already looking ahead to the next dove and woodcock season. I'd go down and finish up.

Almost before I reached the bottom of the stairs, Loretta was shrieking. Without heraldry, Cindy had migrated to the living room sofa, crawled up, and graced the world with pup Number One, and then Two, his oldest sister. Five minutes later, she gave birth to Three, their younger brother. All were the favor of their mama, beautiful white, black, and tan tris—little wet, blind, squirming, joyous whimpers of puppydom. Begging to be loved.

"Good girl, Cindy," I whispered.

I stood there in a trance, lost at the wonder of them. How ardently we had waited for this moment. Nothing of life thrills me more than the happening of little puppies. Nothing.

"Thanks, girl," I said.

Then, as always, I ran suddenly hot and nervous. Cindy, like each of the matrons before her, had begun frantically fussing over first one and then another of the pups, rolling and licking them roughly until they cried, kicking and stomping them around, until I was scared she would mother them to death in their first half hour.

"Look out," my wife ordered brusquely, back with a bowl of warm water to help clean up.

I happily stepped aside, my brow soaked, my palms sticky, my pulse racing like a Chinatown taxi meter. Thinking . . . a man's got no place in a birthing barn nohow.

"A little past eight thirty," Loretta mused, wringing the washcloth for the third time.

I nodded.

"You okay?" she asked, smiling.

"Yes," I lied, wondering how close I was to faint.

"How could you know?" I asked feebly. "I mean, be so sure?"

"Mamas just know," she replied, capsulating one of life's great truths, the gleam of mystery in her eyes.

There appeared, after several uneventful minutes, to be a lull in the maternity ward. Mama's breathing had calmed a bit; she had grown less frantic, and the three pups were beginning to look like somebody, drying out a mite. Mama's belly, however, was still swollen tighter than a seed tick.

"That can't be all," I said.

"Ohhh, no," Loretta agreed, then issued a second general order: "Help me get everybody out to the kennel house."

Gone and back again, she unlimbered a laundry basket and a light blue flannel blanket. Hastily, she arranged the blanket into the basket, then picked up each pup, examining it for a tender moment, and depositing it into the makeshift nest. Rapidly, all three wadded together, swaddled by the blanket.

"Here," she urged, handing them to me, "you carry this."

"Gladly," I complied.

Cindy was up and whining, worried and rocking uncertainly on the edge of the sofa, balanced like a penny on a pencil tip, all four feet gathered closely under her. Her attention was riveted to the muted noises from the basket. She was piercing me with fretful eyes.

"Just following orders," I submitted meekly.

"C'mon, girl," Loretta coaxed, tempting her off the couch. "Just five minutes, then a reunion." Cindy floundered on the mushy footing of the cushions, before grunting arduously to the floor.

Dogging the basket to the back door, she pushed past at the invitation to go outside, bounced less than buoyantly a few yards, looked back, and squatted to pee. Beneath the folds of the blanket, there were tiny whimpers.

Life was in order.

With the other inhabitants of the kennel at an inquisitive crescendo, we trooped in a small procession the fifty yards to the whelping house, which in those more austere but infinitely happy days of our subsistence amounted to a small, white box frame of wallboard and two-bys. Modest would have been an understatement. At plumb, hardly eight feet square to the rafters, it incorporated a simple shed roof, one meager window, and a door. But inside, it was warm, tight, and dry. On the floor at its center had been arranged a spacious whelping box complete with puppy baffles and a clean bed of newspapers, and above its plebian threshold was proudly inscribed "November Setters," the family marquee. By either side of the whelping box there was just enough room to squeeze in a couple of Lilliputian chairs, and in the corner was barely breathing room for a small table. On the table were fresh, fluffy towels and a half dozen washcloths; an assortment of tinctures, salves, and ointments; a box of Kleenex; a bottle of hydrogen peroxide; a small spool of waxed linen thread; a pair of scissors; a box of matches . . . and Dr. Louis Vine's book on home veterinary care. Finally, from the ceiling was suspended a heat lamp to kill the morning chill.

I passed the basket to Loretta and switched on the heat lamp. It bathed the little bassinet with warm orange light. One by one, Loretta transported the first three puppies from the folds of the blanket to the whelping box, unable to resist a bit of baby talk along the way.

"Lookat t-h-at f-a-c-e," she cooed, hoisting the firstborn female, pup Number Two, for me to see. The pup was exquisite, all marked up like a calico kitten.

"Beda," she pronounced, choosing a name offhand from our lengthy list of probables. "This will be Beda . . . little *warrior maiden.*"

"But we might not keep her," I said.

This was, foremost, a litter of field trial prospects, and I had promised myself to be painfully selective. Which is exactly the word—painful—when you think about separating yourself from little puppies you've seen into the world . . . after their hearts have beat in time with yours for eight weeks, or eight hours even. But I was dying for a dog or dogs for horseback pointing-dog trials. I had read Nash Buckingham and Horace Lytle, and Er Shelley, an' Henry Davis, and Bill Brown—worn the covers off *American Fields*—till I was blue in the face. I wanted it for real, wanted it bad.

"We'll keep her," she vowed.

Maybe. Hopefully.

She placed her carefully in the center of the whelping box, set the basket on the floor, picked up Number One, and cradled him lovingly against her cheek with both hands before lowering him to a berth beside his sister. The she dug out Three, with the full black mask and tan cheeks, and braced him up Buddha-like in the palm of her hands. There was a cute little what-sit at the height of his ample belly.

"Such a cute woodle sing," she babbled mischievously.

I smiled, uncertain of her reference.

She added him to the pile. All three snuggled into a knot.

Cindy piled in, lay down beside them, but was abruptly up again. She was growing restless once more. At ten forty-five, she groaned and heaved anew, and Number Four was born, another little boy, with a black left ear and right eye patch. His mama licked him clean of the placenta and clipped the umbilical cord neatly with her teeth.

We watched nervously, tempted to help; sometimes the slip of a canine tooth can sever the cord too closely, resulting in a rupture. But we abstained, for the better, allowing nature its means.

Mama took another lengthy sabbatical then, appearing reasonably comfortable and absent of distress. Glistening white beads grew at the nipples of her swollen breasts; on cue, her milk was coming. We sat in unceasing admiration of our second generation of November Setters—November, for I loved the month as dearly as I would love these puppies—guessing at how bountiful it would ultimately be. Talking of their rearing and training, of the greatness we hoped ahead, praying for each little life a safe and happy journey. So many things could flounder when fate overwhelmed destiny. The best you could hope was that they tracked in harmony.

"Please, God," Loretta whispered.

A bit before lunch, Cindy was anxious again, whining, straining once, then again, and in a squishy whoosh, Number Five was born. Black patches on both ears, a half mask, and another cute "woodle sing" at the summit of his abdomen. When he was clean, he immediately set on the arduous adventure to his siblings a foot and a half away, trembling and tottering and falling back time and again as he tried to navigate Mama's foreleg, righting himself and stubbornly trying once more. Pups One through Four refused to wait, mounting their maiden search for dinner.

Mama remained fidgety, whining softly and licking at herself.

Thirty minutes afterward, at precisely twelve twenty, a tiny female squeezed herself into the world, except for size no more conspicuously at first than any of the others. Immediately, she was the pride of her mother's pain . . . but such a tiny, determined little thing . . . with tiny paws clawing for purchase, each slighter than the smallest of my wife's fingernails, contesting her mother's lavish attention with an unconquerable will to prevail.

Loretta's notes, on a tattered yellow notepad, are replete with our first impressions:

> #6, 12:20 p.m., Female. Patch above L. ear.
> Spot next to R. ear. Rump patch.
> Giving Mama a fit.

For as long as I live, a Number Six debut and a rump patch will be my foremost measures of a newborn pup.

Almost on her heels, another sister appeared. Seven, now. Wearing two black ears, trapped and crying bloody murder for a time between Mama's hind legs. Finally I bent over and rescued her, for Cindy was finding greater and greater necessity for dividing her time. Abruptly, the pup hushed and was given to travel, with small thought of the annoyance that had detained her. Life is spontaneous with dogs, to the last moment. Enviably, I believe, for foresight is not always a gift.

Number Eight was right behind, a struggling little boy wearing a half mask that shadowed the better part of a left eye and ear, and a rich black patch at the base of his tail. He seemed for a time slightly weaker than the rest, and we watched him anxiously, relaxing a mite when he gained his bearings and struck out for the milking parlor.

Number Nine, a wriggly little girl sporting black ear muffs, followed expeditiously, fussing at the discomfort of eviction. Cindy scrubbed her down, washed face and ears, and proclaimed her fit for company with the eight others now in a desperate scuffle for table space at her breast. I noted with satisfaction that the little Number Six female was fastened to a rear spigot, fighting aside the rough-and-tumble conquests of her bigger brothers.

'Twas a time before Number Ten came along, five hours in fact, and we had about decided the litter was complete. Lo and behold, at seven forty, another strapping male was emancipated, about as easily as pouring water out of a boot. A looksome young man, this restless lad, the biggest of the bunch, with two black ears and a left eye patch, and a smudge of tan at the corner of his mouth that looked suspiciously like a tobacco stain. A few minutes later, he had bulled his way into the feeding frenzy, bumped a brother off a teat, and locked on for dear mercy. When we pried him loose six days later, it seemed, he was already scaling a hefty two pounds, ten ounces on the baby scales.

When Number Eleven hit the ground, however, two hours junior, he proved the equal of his predecessor—poundage, plumbing, and persuasion. A half hour later, a rivalry had sprung between the two that waxed red hot the length of their affiliation. So dashing and debonair was this latest young chap with the knock-'em-dead markings that according to Loretta, he favored slightly her movie idol, John Derek.

"Thisun'll make the ladies swoon," she predicted lyrically.

"He'll have to have a special name, something with brass, class, and charisma. Maybe somethin' from my romance novels."

"Wonder if he'll point a bird?" I sighed.

Mama was persevering bravely, though her plight was compounding by the minute, nearly a dozen suckling mouths and umpteen prickly little toenails increasingly dependent upon her patience. After more than twelve hours of labor, she was tired and gaunt. You could see the dent of fatigue in her soft brown eyes. But there was the glint of devotion there, too, and pride.

"I know, girl," Loretta offered sympathetically.

We had hoped she was through at eight, avoiding the strain of a larger litter. But eight was history. Now we wished, fervently, for eleven to be all.

It was . . . until ten thirty-five, when little Miss Grace emphatically arrived, chastely white, with a hint of ticking and a distinctive dab of mascara at her right eye. Fourteen hours after the first, she completed a gorgeous dozen.

The box, however, was a mess.

"We've got to change these papers," Loretta declared.

In a series of tiny smacks, I pried loose the pups from eight swollen nipples, gathered up the four sleepers on the perimeter, folded aside the blanket, and deposited them one by one into the basket. This time there was a wad.

"Take 'em outside a minute," my wife suggested. "See if Cindy won't follow you."

She did, watching my every move. In the dark, under the stars, while Loretta quickly changed and smoothed the papers, I considered the twelve little lives wriggling under the blanket. What grand things lay ahead, I hoped.

"Okay," she said.

A few minutes later, after a grueling contention of twelve hungry mouths over a table of eight settings, a puddle of puppies lay about the warmth of their mother's breast, twitching and sleeping. I searched among them for the little Number Six female. Noticeably smallest, she had wormed her way snugly between the considerable bellies of her two biggest brothers, and died to the world.

Ten days later, precocious from the start, she was the first to open her tiny blue eyes and look at me. As she rested in the cup of my palms, blinking demurely, she simply stole my heart away and never gave it back. It was in no way, understand, an act of surrender. Maybe on my part, but not hers. There was a major independent essence she never relinquished. And I never asked. It had to be that way. Boldness stems from confidence, and without it there cannot be brilliance. There would be times when the fire flamed too high, that would hurt us, and more often when it would lift us the height of a dream.

A few notions hence, still a trifle of a thing at three weeks old, she was struggling in the restraint of my hand, while Loretta tried desperately to dab some Furacin on a moving spot of staph. Suddenly there was a diminutive little rumble, and Retta withdrew in astonishment.

"The little rascal's growling at me," she exclaimed, staring blankly, her eyes large and bright.

"Growlin'!" she repeated.

I laughed, as amazed.

So she was. No less certainly than when she registered her disgust at a dose of Nemex with a first worming. Her undiluted reaction to tribulation was defiance, not so much aggression as determination, with narrow limits for compromise. Physically, as well, she was unyielding. At fifteen days, she was toddling, with astonishing spurts of agility that portended an incredible lifelong athletic ability. With unflagging courage, she threw herself at every challenge.

Among her siblings, life was to be largely on her terms, it was decided in the next few weeks. Though unassertive in a dominance sense and thoroughly playful, she was volatile as a blasting cap and not to be stepped on. Grittiest of the band, she was undeterred by any obstacle or any adversity. Slow down, back up, or quit was never in her constitution. Many's the moment the nastiest of her brothers would feel the speed and wrath of her temper, and those needle-sharp teeth.

Life was a wonderful affair. The air was fresh with puppy breath, and a dozen carefree little personalities were emerging, each with appeal. We would watch them for hours. Number One was bold, the first to actually play with *us*. He was an explorer, striking off into the unknown to the daring distances of twenty and thirty yards, tail stuck jauntily up over his back and canvassing every crevice. Never crying or whimpering when temporarily he was lost. His faith was constant; sooner or later, Mama would come to the rescue. Most like the Number Six female, who was ever his kin in adventure, though *she* never cared much *where* Mama was. Number Two kept tumbling out of the puppy house every time we opened the door to clean. I think she did it for the attention. She was a mischievous little bit, sneaking up behind her sisters and brothers and nabbing a hunk of hide, then retreating quickly, barking, backing, and spinning like a wind-up toy.

The Number Three male had a strut in his stride. Cocky he was, always trying to impose himself on somebody . . . anybody, that is, except the Number Six female. But then, his "woodle sing" was cuter than ever.

Four was a sweetheart. He never picked fights, and he was polite with his sisters, deferring to his brothers. Roly-poly and affectionate, sitting before first one and then the other of us, he'd look up with pleading eyes and wag that little twig of a tail, begging us to pick him up. Barking impatiently after a time if we didn't. Five, contrarily, was a scrapper—sneaky— always pouncing on somebody in an unsuspecting moment, sidling stiff-legged around anybody who bucked him, with his baby hackles roached high, waiting for the slightest advantage. When tiny tempers flared, he was hell in a handbasket, chastening all but Numbers Six and Three. With these he provoked a face-off, but sidestepped a tangle, putting on his best bluff, puffing up and swaggering off in a face-saving retreat.

The Number Seven female with the two black ears was a teeny treasure, buoyant and sweet, fast on her feet. She was Melanie's early favorite; Melanie called her Patty. Where the name came from, I have no idea. Just out of the blue one day. At the little puppy stage, Patty was almost as fleet as Number Six, though less agile. She was a bit of a shrinking violet sometimes in the rough and tumble of things, preferring to avoid the conflict. She could look pitifully lonesome sometimes, off on the fringes of puppy-dom by herself, looking on. She gained a lot of lap time that way.

Eight was a glutton, making up perhaps for the weak start he was given to life. He now surpassed all but his biggest brother in size and heft, though the distribution of it rested a mite more pudgily on the hanger. He pestered his mama unmercifully, forever draggin' at a tit, until she would crawl up in my lap to get away from him. He'd fuss and fuss, trying to convince somebody he was starving.

Sister Nine was jaunty, ballerinalike. A little shaky on her feet, yet, for jetés, but showing the promise. More than the rest, she'd whirl and spin, scamper and chase her tail, jump and dance out of pure exuberance. She tickled me with her prep-school antics. We called her Suzy-Q.

Ten and Eleven were big, rough, and burly farm boys, good-natured, blustering and buddying around together, trying to outdo each other, wrestling and running. The former was happy-go-lucky, one bounce ahead of easy, sensitive and slightly shy—a lot like Hoss Cartwright. The latter was lay-'em-out gorgeous, sexy and sophisticated, with an unmistakable air. One day of many when he had his brother handsomely tangled into a full nelson, boldly straddling him, bristling and puffing—the swashbuckling adventurer—Loretta momentarily lowered a Harold Robbins book to her lap.

"Dax," she said.

"What?"

"*Dax*. I've finally found it. That's the name," she replied.

"That's the name for him. It's right," she said.

"Dax."

I had to admit—it was dead on. Kinda like Rhett, or Derek, or Dirk. But better. Suddenly I felt a little inadequate.

"Mike's nice, too," my wife said to me, smiling faintly.

"Yeah," I thought.

And then little Miss Twelve wandered up. What a beauty. A debutante in need of a ball. Every bit the distaff equivalent of Number Eleven, she was perpetually happy and congenial, chic as silk and stunning as a snowflake.

"Hey, Linda," I chirped, holding out my fingers. Immediately, she stopped to chew on them.

"Whad'id you call that puppy?" Loretta demanded.

"Linda."

"Linda?"

"Linda Evans." I smiled smugly. "You know, like in *Those Calloways* and *The Big Valley*."

She blew through her mouth. "You wish," she said.

I laughed, relishing the reckoning.

$\backsim$ CHAPTER 2 $\backsim$

AT EIGHT WEEKS, WE BEGAN TAKING THE PUPS FOR SHORT ROMPS afield, through the woods behind the house, past the great adventure of the creek, to the frogs in the pond on the hill and the winged things—grasshoppers and butterflies—in the meadows beyond. They'd scamper and tumble, rollick and play, hunt themselves sleepy finally, and drop in place. We'd end up carrying a few back in the laundry basket Loretta brought along for the cause.

Each time out, we toyed with the estimation of them, which offered the character we sought. Boldness, grit, charisma, desire. Style. Hunting instincts. Bird sense. We loaded them into the truck at twelve and sixteen weeks, took them for progressively longer jaunts, evaluating objectively as our hearts would allow the traits of each. Charting to memory the things we found pleasing, and for consideration as well, aspects that seemed either latent or absent. The trick was knowing which. For a pup at sixteen weeks, even, is just that—a pup—and some blossom very handsomely as adolescents, well past their first year.

I played with them with a bird wing on a string, then a live, harnessed quail. Considered them on butterflies—which they loved most of all—and sparrows. All showed the requisite pointing instinct and class on "game," locking up perfectly sight or scent. A fathomless miracle, really, a few-weeks-old toddler pledged nose and soul to an ounce of feathers. Far too wondrous, it seemed, to be a matter of expectation, though it really was . . . a promise of the genes. But then again, there was the mystery of life. All you could look for was that superordinary, burning, white-hot desire, mirrored by individual degree in the fire of their eyes and the trembling intensity and expressiveness of their stand. Sometimes it flamed so high so early that you discovered it yourself, and sometimes when it was banked, only later, when it was fed and fueled, would it be revealed to you. Always, there were elements of the unknown that could be disclosed only by test and time.

At twelve weeks—three months—rightly and wrongly, we thought most promising as horseback dogs Numbers One, Four, Six, Eleven, and Twelve. Had we sold the balance of the litter at that point, we would have kept Number Six, but gifted to someone else two of the most exciting setters I have known in a forty-year campaign for the best.

Fortunately, we didn't. We had committed from the beginning to keeping them all a full year. We weren't professional breeders, just "a litter every few years" folks, for our own accord. The economics of the proposition were of minor thought. Their papa was the son of a national champion, the last setter to win at Grand Junction; their mama was a cracking good grousewoods gun dog. They'd throw some good pups. Our foremost concern was that we keep them long enough that we didn't overlook the best of them.

At four months old, individual enough they belonged to have call names, we held a christening. Loretta dug out the file; for years we had kept a standing list of possibilities, accessioning others occasionally we ran across and especially liked, from a song, a book, or a whim. It was a serious piece of business, coming up with a lifelong name for a pup, one that suited and would launch it into the world laudably. We never approached it with less than purpose, spending hours, even weeks, at the task. Until we had for each a name as distinctive as the persona, one that still rolled off the tongue sharply enough for a field summons.

A couple stood from prior order. Beda, by Retta's proclamation, old English for "warrior maiden," stuck with Number Two. Dax continued to be the overwhelming favorite for swashbuckling Mr. Eleven. Suzy-Q merely grew up to Suzy. Surprisingly, however, Melanie had switched allegiance some time before, transferring from Seven to the precocious Ms. Six the adornment of Patty. Perhaps it had something to do with Melanie being six herself, or maybe more that Six was the smallest and liveliest, and she and Melanie, slight and lively alike, had become great buddies by simple osmosis. Though I really wanted something more fiery, for the sake of our daughter we let it stand, clipping it to Pat for field cadence. Without surprise, Linda was tabled for Number Twelve by Madam Chairman, with nominations solicited anew from the floor. Lea, Rani, and Storm were put to vote. Storm won by popular acclaim.

Old business out of the way, we continued with the consideration of each of the others, stumbling for a length on cocky Number Three, opting at last for Thane, another intrepid Old English forename. In after years, some of my field-trialing friends had a habit of abusing it teasingly to "Thing," in which instance I could never avoid the association with "cute woodle," managing a chuckle each time, however serious the stakes might be. By an equally protracted process, each other name was decided, until finally, by order of birth, one through twelve, there was Hank, Beda, Thane, Joe, Jake, Pat, Jill, Ben, Suzy, Luke, Dax, and Storm.

Long before we were ready, they grew to an addled essence. The boys were big and gangly, still looking for themselves, the girls lithe and light, coming into their own. None more astonishingly than Pat, the Number Six female.

Her tender life almost ended there. The dark hand of Fate clutched at her on a hot afternoon in early September, and only the inexplicable summons of an archangel, and the quick wit of Dr. Danny Allen, saved her. I came home at noon from work, why I cannot say to this day. I had no special reason. Something called me there, from the midst of other pursuits more expedient. And still I had no way of comprehending the urgency of its message. I walked into the kitchen, snatched some bread from the bin, slathered on the Miracle Whip, and built a tomato sandwich from the fresh fruit of the garden. I sat down at the table, lifted the sandwich, and it called me again, to the back door this time, and beckoned that I take a glance at the kennel. And I got up without ever taking a bite, and stepped to the porch.

The dogs were up and barking. Beda, Pat, and Thane were yet kenneled together at that point, and my eyes swept the yard, drawn to their run. Beda and Thane reared against the fence, raising a fit. Strangely, Pat was not with them. I watched for a moment, uneasiness swelling in my chest. There was nothing of her.

I started for the kennel, my pace quickening the nearer I got and the emptier it seemed, and then I saw her. She was lying inertly on the ground. It stopped me dead. I stood for a terrified moment, staring. There was no sign of life. Time stopped and my heart lodged in my throat. Fighting, fumbling with the latches on the gate, not wanting to take my eyes off her, I rushed inside. To my utter relief, she was breathing . . . shallowly . . . but her body was completely limp, comatose or deep in shock. I searched quickly for a wound, a bite, anything—but could find nothing. I scooped her up in my arms. Her eyes rolled back in her head, and she drooped limply off either side. It was then that I prayed.

I ran, ran as hard as I could for the truck, flung open the door, and eased her onto the front seat. As I spun out of the drive in reverse, she was flung forward by the momentum. I jerked a hand off the wheel to steady her, and the truck careened violently left, slamming into a tree. I never stopped, simply downshifted and scraped my way free. Our old '71 Chevy still wears the scar. It was, fortunately, less than two miles and several stop-lights to Dan Allen, our vet, friend, and an Alpha Zeta brother at North Carolina State, there off Western Boulevard in Raleigh. I don't remember stopping. I can't remember cutting the ignition. Scary minutes later, the truck skidded somehow to a grinding halt in the gravel parking lot of Boulevard Animal Hospital, and I jumped out with Pat dangling over my forearms and rushed into the reception lobby, praying Dan was there.

Marcy was at the desk. She looked up and her eyes widened.

"Danny," I uttered urgently.

She wasted no time with foolish questions. I shall always appreciate that. She got up immediately and hurried to an examination room in the hallway. When quickly she returned, Danny was with her. Gwynne Tenneson, his chief clinical tech, followed closely behind.

One look at Pat, and you could see the gravity cloud his face.

"I found her this way, Dan," I stuttered, "in her kennel."

I was scared, real scared. I wasn't sure she was even breathing any longer. We already worshiped her. You had to, for her grit if nothing else, and there was far more. I could feel the despair rising, my hopes vanishing, my eyes welling with tears of desperation.

Danny raised an eyelid, listened momentarily to her heartbeat and respiration, then examined her hastily overall. She was still draped unconsciously over my arms.

Withdrawing the stethoscope from her chest, Dan glanced at Gwynne. "Let's get her to the back," he ordered. "Quick."

"Set up an IV. Glucose. Epinephrine. Antihistamine. Prednisone." He was spouting instructions to Gwynne as he ushered me along.

"Quickly," he reiterated.

"It's some kind of prophylactic reaction," he explained. "My guess is a sting—a bee or a wasp. Or a spider."

I listened in a daze, afraid to ask the question. My heart was beating through my chest.

When we reached the surgical ward, Gwynne was there and ready. I laid Pat on the cold stainless steel of the table. I could see no breathing at all now. She looked so small and drawn, her eyes glazed and unblinking.

Danny said nothing, filling a syringe from a small inverted bottle. While Gwynne found a vein and started the IV, I watched as the liquid from the bottle trickled slowly into the clear barrel of the syringe. It seemed to take forever. When the dose was complete, Danny immediately pushed the needle into the shoulder of the little setter and depressed the plunger. Almost instantly, he was filling another, quickly administering a second antidote as well.

"If we're not too late, this should do it," he said.

Numb with fear, I could offer nothing in return. I just looked at her, and prayed.

I had asked Marcy to call Loretta. She rushed in about that time, looking first to Pat, then me, and last, Danny. Sensing the solemnity, she stood, tears welling, her hand nervously at her lips.

For a short time there was no change, and then rapidly our sixth puppy started back to us. Blinking several times, she stirred slightly. The color was seeping back into her gums. She raised her head, struggled feebly, wanting to be up. Danny laid a hand on her side, calming her.

"Easy, sweetheart," he said softly to her. "Just rest there a minute longer. You were a long ways out.

"What was it . . . you get crossways with a bumbler bee?"

Limp with relief, we reveled in the consolation of our old friend's words. Once again, when all of hope seemed forsaken, we had felt his hand at our shoulder, drawing us back from the brink of a grave.

"Thanks, Dan," I said, past the burn in my eyes.

He smiled gently. "Too early to let her go," he assured me. "I got to shoot a bird over this un."

"That you shall," I promised.

"Was that really what happened?" Loretta asked. "A bumble bee?"

"Just a guess," Dan offered. "Some sort of varmint walloped her. It was a scare. We could have lost her."

Pat was up and on her feet now, prancing around on the table, tail popping. Toenails clicking. Like nothing had happened. Gwynne was trying to pull the IV. It was amazing, how dramatic the change.

Dan drew a final syringe, pumped in a bolt of steroid.

"God, I'll never hold her down now," I observed happily.

"Insurance," he exclaimed.

Our eyes caught for a minute, and I thanked him again without speaking.

"Doves, Saturday?" I requested, lifting Pat off the table.

"And supper afterwards," Loretta followed. "Bring Betty."

Dr. Dan had turned to the sink, scrubbing up. He threw up the back of a hand.

Then Pat drug me out of the clinic to the truck, and I rejoiced the whole way there, with a brand new leash on life. I opened the door and let her clamber up onto the seat, then closed it again.

"We *almost* lost her," I said gravely, turning to Loretta, alongside. "I thought we had."

Her face was tight. Tears were welling again. She reached across and rubbed the little setter's ear through the partially open window. "We *didn't*, thank God," she said.

I told her about coming home, not knowing why.

"Somehow, it wasn't meant to be," she mused, ". . . losing her. Her life wasn't finished."

I nodded.

"See you home," I said quietly, opening the door and nudging the puppy back.

She nodded.

Pat was trying to push past me. Grabbing and blocking, I managed to hold her at bay until I could climb in and hurry the door shut. Settling against the back of the seat, I gazed at her, truly considering her again for a time. Her eyes were ablaze, and she was sky high on the edge of the seat. Overwhelmed, I closed my eyes in thanks. Picking up a turn of the check cord still snapped to her collar, I studied it for several moments, thinking of what had happened. Thinking that it rested in a hand much greater than mine.

Next day, she was setting the grass afire again, pointing butterflies with aplomb, performing electrifying jetés and pirouettes, and chastising her nasty brothers. Destiny tumbled on.

∾ CHAPTER 3 ∾

SUMMER LAPSED, AND AT LAST AUTUMN WAS AT HAND. OCTOBER rushed by, and I tried to slow it down, but almost before I knew it, November was half spent. We'd had a frost or two; the cover was dwindling. Scenting conditions had been bettered with the cool, dry air. With spring puppy trials only a couple months away, I was growing ever more anxious and excited.

We were taking the bunch regularly to the field. We had wild quail then in Carolina, enough for encouragement. Now seven months, the pups were beginning to run and hunt ambitiously on their own, a natural range beginning to emerge. Joe, Jake, Ben, Suzy, and Storm were close and birdy, laying out at a comfortable gun-dog distance, shaping up nicely as foot-hunting companions. All were quick and classy. Hank and Dax were stretching it out pretty good, but not always as forwardly as desired. Jill was traveling, too, albeit with a surplus of looping. Some of that could be worked out with a horse, probably not all. Luke was a question still—nice, lovely on point, but sporadically in and out on the ground. The most delightful disclosures had been Beda and Thane. They had emerged from the shadow of the pack and were gathering a lot of attention. Beda was showing the determination and desire of Sister Six, though unblessed with comparable physical prowess and stamina. What I liked most was, given the limitation, she forever tried so hard to overcome it. That would carry far. She was gorgeous on point, forward on the ground, running bigger each time out. I was liking her a lot. Thane I admired as well. He was cocky as ever, bold, certain of himself. A man's man. Marvelously put together, he could run and he did, out there, and he looked mighty good doing it. I wasn't sure how level he was on the top story yet, but he was sure enough a comer.

Throughout, however, the littlest pup remained brilliantly and indomitably to the fore. Headstrong and fiery, front-running, lofty and free, she was abruptly becoming too much to handle from foot. Her small frame was becoming hard and compact, remarkably muscled, her way of going superbly athletic. She was blistering on the ground—incredibly fast— exploding off the check cord and driving ever forward with a high, tight, rhythmic lick. Bigger every time. You *had* to look at her. Every bounce was thrilling, a passion of poetry.

I knew I had a horseback dog. I knew she had a nose. She was finding birds, and when she found them, she was dazzling, pointing straight up and swelling to her toes, then coming loose and jumping square in the middle of them, taking them out just as prettily. Moreover, she had an exceptional tolerance for heat. Not many setters do, not at the extremes. If she had superlative ground intelligence and game sense as well, I would have a field trial dog. In my wildest dreams, maybe even three.

Come December, we started putting the field trial contenders—Hank, Dax, Pat, Beda, Thane, and Storm—in front of the horse, first in the roading harness. I'd lead the mare from the ground, control the pace and procession, see that nobody got tangled or doubled back under hooves. Loretta would walk out front, offering an enticement. They took to it eagerly, leaning hard into the rope and harness against the horse, bounding and bucking at first against the resistance, then gearing down into a steady, grinding haul, hindquarters knotted and digging for traction. Roading was important. Much like aerobics and strength training for human athletics. It would build the muscle, sinew, and wind to sustain the nothing-less-than-best necessary to win, from the twenty-minute puppy warm-ups, through the half-hour derby stints, to the sometimes hour-plus endurance demands of the top shooting dog and all-age contests that would follow.

Soon they were doing it with the pure joy of escape and challenge, me in the saddle and Loretta now rooting from the rear.

The grit of the little female was spellbinding. She never faltered, never quit—from harness-on to harness-off—straining against the drag of the horse with all her might, muscles bunched and strutting like they were cut in stone. Panting and digging, digging . . . digging. You could see the uncompromising resolve in every driving step. The blaze of it brought tears to my eyes. Only Thane could match it, and they battled each other, will against will. Beda had the fire. She tried so hard, working as consumptively as the other two in shorter, desperate sprints. But she was not gifted the stamina and would falter, ease back for a brief rest and breather, then throw herself against it again. It was electric, the three of them, nothing but puppies then, straining powerfully shoulder-to-shoulder. Awesome.

Neither Dax, good looks and all, Hank, nor Storm could sustain the same intensity over a twenty-minute haul. Each would stall and idle periodically, flagging not so much from exertion as from diminishing enthusiasm. It was more a matter of constitution than compromise. All three were very exciting young dogs. Their promise as class gun dogs was outstanding. But as field trial prospects, none embraced eagerly enough either the challenge or the competition of the roading drills. Their spark stopped one bellows short of a flame. It told much of the prospects for success in a field trial campaign. A talented field trial contender must have the heart and spirit of a warrior. There can be no less.

We worked along with them for a while, reaching back into the litter anew for someone else we might have underestimated, continuing the search for the supreme. Jill looked very good for a stint, sharp and snappy, except for her ground pattern. So did Joe. But neither would drive as consistently forward as a trial dog must do, and try as I might, I could not encourage it into them. I quit trying after a time, letting gun dogs be gun dogs, letting them quarter and ramble where their bird sense told them to go. There was honor enough in that alone.

It was hard, the choosing. For all were valiant in their own way. And all were lovely. And all were loved.

"Twelve little setter pups, each with a destiny," Loretta mused wistfully. "I want to be a part of every one, and can't."

That was the hell of it, raising puppies. There was no way, of course, we could keep all twelve, we thought then. I'd hate to face the same decision today.

"We're keeping at least six," she declared, as time kept edging toward our one-year ultimatum.

"We shouldn't," I said. "We're looking for field trial dogs, remember?"

"Gun dogs, too," she reminded. "Two at least." She was arguing deliberately, I realized, for something I had suggested.

"I suppose," I agreed, trying to capitalize.

As ever we tried to narrow it down, it kept turning full circle. Back to Beda, Pat, Hank, Dax, Storm, Thane, and Jill. But it was the devil's dilemma, from there. I kept retrieving us to center, to the field trial question. I just couldn't give up on Dax, Storm, or Hank. At times, each would flare brilliantly. With spring trials posted now in the fixtures of the *Field,* we forced ourselves to five, and finally to four. Then there were three.

Pat, Beda, and Thane it would be, as the trial hopefuls. That, at last, seemed preordained. Hank and Jill, or Storm and Dax we'd keep as gun dogs. Maybe. Things kept changing . . . with Suzy and Ben, Luke, Jake, and Joe . . . to confuse the issue. The thought of parting with any one of them was painful.

We settled in earnest then into the readying of our three trial prospects for the first of the juvenile stakes, almost at hand. The back pressure of the roading regimen, puppies though they were, had conditioned them to explode from the cord when released to run at will. And they would fly. I worked them half-and-half, roading and running, whetting the edge, always giving them less than they desired. Picking them up when they showed the slightest sign of fatigue. Which was never with Pat in a thirty-minute workout. Thane, ditto. Beda I had to watch more carefully, particularly in the heat. Gradually I worked them up to a zinging forty minutes.

They were looking great. To me at least. I wasn't strong into horseback trials for pointing dogs then. I had ridden a few. Mostly I was fresh off the back-pasture gun-dog circuit, where dogs are handled from foot. I knew horseback puppies had to run. These pups were running, larger than any I had worked before. I knew they needed to hunt a little, display the potential for going on to derby and shooting-dog stakes. These puppies were hunting. Whether enough, I was anxious to know.

Christmas turned by, and a New Year was born. The spring trialing season was afling in both Carolinas. The time was at hand. Yet I was hesitant, apprehensive I guess. One thing you have to learn in competitive dog trials is to get past the intimidation. I had beat the fear long ago with the walking stakes, but the horseback events, amateur or open, were a cut above, not so easily conquered. So I kept honing, and honing, pushing the pups higher.

Until a second time the keen blade of Fate came sizzling maliciously past, and once again, it almost cost us Pat.

We were boarding horses at the time at a stable off Penny Road near Raleigh. Behind the stable were some six hundred acres of farmland, woodland broken by carelessly harvested fields of beans and corn. It was home to four bevies of quail. I had been working the pups there for a time. It was big enough for a horseback heat of about thirty minutes, when they were laying out well, and handling. There was a long edge or two where they could stretch and places where the cover closed down tight enough they had to come back on their own. It had been adequate until that day. I usually had no trouble with Beda and Thane. They were running pretty good, Beda at that stage a deal wider than Thane—who was still awkwardly looking for top gear—but neither so ambitious nor independent as Pat. She had been getting bigger and bigger, and ever more a handful to keep up with, even horseback. It had reached the point I kept the horse in a running walk just to maintain contact, to "keep her on the string." On the far back side of the farm was State Road 1010, a paved rural road that was a well-traveled, east-west crossway on the south end of the city. I hadn't really worried much about it before; there was a fair margin of safety as long as I had the dogs in ken. But I was beginning to. Beda and Thane were still handling and coming back on their own well enough for comfort. Pat was becoming a gamble.

Even so, she knew the grounds and had been swinging on the back corner, coming around to complete the familiar circle back to the stable. But she was doing it faster and faster, and a bit more stubbornly each time. Not really out of hand intentionally, just afire with desire. Whatever, I really needed to wean her to bigger grounds. Our intention that afternoon was to train at a friend's farm an hour north in upper Granville County, but I had been detained by a work conflict. The only place left in the time we had was the stable round.

To make matters worse, the pups had gone for three days without a workout. Normally, I never let it lapse past two. Training for field trials, you don't miss workouts . . . you don't! . . . not if you are honest with yourself about winning. Like an Olympic regimen, it can be nothing short of a total commitment, because it must result in a total performance. But this time there had been unavoidable contingencies. Things I just couldn't keep out of the way. The dogs were jacked sky-high, and I was edgy and frustrated.

"Maybe you ought to wait till Saturday, for the Dean Farm," Loretta argued. "You keep telling me how big Pat's going now. We know it's safe there."

"It's been too long," I replied stubbornly. "They need running. And we need to take them to a trial—soon."

"Surely two days can't make that big a difference."

"It can when you're trying to be the best," I said, too adamantly perhaps.

"I just don't want to regret it," she said.

We almost did.

I put Beda down first. I was more concerned about Pat than I admitted. She was beginning to scare me. Beda I was confident about. She'd be hot, but she'd handle. Well, maybe. At the whistle, she exploded, scorching down the edge of the first big field. She was beautiful in her own right, buoyantly gaited and merry-going. It was a good three hundred yards to the woods gap on the far end. Usually she broke off somewhere about the three-quarter mark, pausing, glancing over her shoulder to check for me. Today she took the entire length of it without a stitch, sailing out of sight through the gap into the woods and beyond. I squalled at her, partly out of jubilation and partly to remind her I was back there, and scrubbed my horse into a gentle canter. When I broke out of the woods gap into the next field, she was already two-thirds of the way to its end, rolling on.

"*Eaahhyyeeah!*" I hollered, calling on her again at the corner.

This time she swung left around the upper edge, and darted into the woods toward the little head the first covey called home. Yes. Yes! I pulled the horse down to a running walk, jamming my closed fist into the air and jerking it back, hollering again out of sheer exhilaration. It's what a nicely going dog, puppy or all-age, does to you when he's really cooking. It's what puts people on a horse, for the privilege of keeping up.

When I reached the site of her departure, I cut onto an old log path and rode the short distance to where I expected her to be. She was wildly birdy, bouncing like a gazelle, whipping back and forth with her nose in the air, searching for scent. I suspected a wreck. She was flash pointing then, like the rest. That was about all. I had made no concerted effort yet to staunch them. I guessed that she had found the birds at home, which was good, and that she had momentarily rung the doorbell, then stormed the door down.

Suspicions were confirmed when a single got up wild along the next logical edge. By then, the little warring maiden had settled into a nice ground
race of pleasing puppy proportions, though not as large and thrilling as the
first ten minutes. Her pace had fallen to the degree that we would not make
the third, and last, big field. I steered her loosely for home, picking her up
near our starting point behind the stable at the thirty-minute mark, roading
her the rest of the way in.

Thane tore away as exuberantly, sprinting the distance to the first gap
in jig time. Difference was, when I yelled, he turned a split second to say
"ten-four," then dashed away on. He was still a mite gangly, hadn't learned
to get all four feet under him yet. But it was coming. When he finally collected himself, he was going to be one hard-driving, snappy piece of
dogflesh. I liked him a lot. He was getting a little bigger each time, lining
out a little better. In manner of going, really, it was hard to say which of the
three looked the better on the ground. Under motion, all were sheer class,
as animated and compelling as pointing dogs get. Whatever else we might
lack, we had that.

The male pup had taken the left side of the second field when next he
was in my watch, hanging the edge, then rimming the hedgerow dividing
the two fields. I saw him whip into the little lespedeza pocket that usually
attracted covey number two that time of day. I hoped they were there. But
too soon he shot out the back side into the bottom end of the big field. I
could just make him out through the trees. Grabbing the off side of the
hedgerow, he took it to its finish, then caught the turn and arced back
toward me. I lost him a few seconds, before he broke again into sight. I
turned the horse, smiled as he took the cue. Coming around and regaining
the front, he lined out perfectly through the short block of woods that doubled back in a crescent to the stable. He broke out into the high end of the
pasture ahead of me, glancing back to see if I was there. These pups were
learning.

Far before he was ready, I harnessed him, letting him stop by the pond
on the way in for a drink. He was proud as a kid with a toy. He knew he'd
done well.

I gave Retta the report.

"Cute woodle sing," she chirped, pulling the harness off, rubbing him
down and lavishing him with praise.

I watched them absently, dawdling with the cinch on the saddle. Then I walked over and picked up the harness, hung it back on the saddle ring.

It was wearing late. The sun was on the downhill drag. Still, I stalled a little longer. There was daylight enough.

"Well, it's Pat," I said finally. I had delayed and anticipated it as long as I could. Nervous and excited, my palms were sweaty.

"You're sure," Loretta pressed.

I wanted to turn Pat loose and I didn't.

"Yep," I said sternly. She gave me a taut look.

"You want to turn her loose for me?" I requested, climbing on the horse.

"No," she said.

"Just do it," I said.

Loretta led Thane to the truck, opened a dog box door, and got him in. Organizing the check cord back into an easy coil, she reached for the latch on Pat's box. The sixth pup was up and whining now, eyes blazing, every muscle cocked. She could see me on the horse, knew it was finally her time. For so fierce a dog, she had an amazing ability to relax, right up to the moment she knew she was to run. Beda would wear herself out before she ever ran, it seemed, straining and barking and fretting on the chain. Thane would work himself into a trembling frenzy. Many dogs will. But then, and even afterward, at the very height of her competitive years, Pat had the gift of repose . . . the facility of sluffing the pressure . . . until it counted. While beneath the facade, she was capped dynamite.

Loretta cracked the door to the box and grabbed for her collar in the same motion, hanging on as the little female burst out onto the tailgate. There was a momentary struggle as Loretta tried to snap on the cord.

"Wait, Pat . . . Pat, wait!" she begged stiffly, grunting in exasperation as she tried to hold the pup and get the snap on the collar at the same time.

"You need help?" Just as I started to get down, she successfully managed the connection.

"No," she declared breathlessly, her face etched with worry.

"Just in case," I said, checking the saddlebag for the walkie-talkie, "take the truck around the road to the other side. Park along the shoulder there somewhere, stay on the CB, and watch."

"What do I do if . . .?"

"Whatever you can. I'll be somewhere close. On the radio."

She looked at me, hesitantly. Started to say something more, but lost the chance.

Pat shot off the tailgate, throwing herself against the cord with all her might, digging her way to me. Dragging Loretta along. I rode up a piece, away from the truck. Loretta finally got her stopped, in front of the horse, unsnapped the cord, and ran four fingers under her collar. The pup was trembling nose-to-toes now, hindquarters knotted and bunched under the rump spot. My hand was trembling also, as I fingered the whistle. Then Pat cut her eyes up at me; in them flashed the white-hot augury of detonation, a jagged bolt of lightning before a clap of thunder. In a half century around hundreds of intrepid sporting dogs, as hunter and judge, gun dogs to major stakes champions, I've never encountered its equal. It would be her trademark, the rest of her life, in every trial we ever ran.

In the next instant, Loretta glanced up at me also, imperatively, with the question.

I took a deep breath and hit the whistle. It was like throwing gas on a fire.

A lot of dogs are fast. And then there are the very few so blistering they defy the physics of biomechanics and synergy. It's a consummate fusion of supreme athleticism and uncommon desire—so incendiary it overwhelms all logic—a combustion so powerful it's compounded by mystery. It's ultimate physiology, neuronuclear, binding soul, cell, and synapse into a single stroke of motion. And inexplicably it's something more. The result is incredible speed. When you see it, it's breathtaking.

Pat broke away so explosively that afternoon it was incomprehensible. Instantly I pushed the horse into a brisk running walk, and for several moments it seemed that I, along with the rest of the world, was locked wildly in reverse. Her hindquarters were lost in a blur and a cloud of dust, and the hundred yards to the corner of the field evaporated under her momentum so promptly that the second hand of my watch forgot to turn. By the time I reached the same spot, she was a streaking blur through the woods gap at the top end. I glanced back for Loretta. She had watched the initial sprint, was now running for the truck.

I kicked my horse into a canter. I had to stay in touch. The first few minutes were critical.

"Yeeeaaahhup—yeaah-oh."

I was singing to her, hoping she was listening. I made the woods gap, whipped through, broke into the second field. In the same moment, I saw her shoot out of the little lespedeza corner, gobble up the rest of the hedgerow, then hang the bottom edge of the third field. She was flying. Beautifully.

It scared me to death. I don't think it had been five minutes since we left the stable. I could see her now, far to the front on the long edge of the biggest field, a white dot at light speed. The third field was normally the last leg on our round, before we circled back. I began to curse myself. That's what you got for running one set of grounds too often. The dogs learn every bush, every covey haunt, begin to run the milk route. Forget where you are. But it was more than that. She was wound sky-high. I was overwhelmed. In a lot of years, I'd never had a dog like this.

"Pat! Heyye!"

"Heyyye!"

I squalled at her, once, twice, asking her to check back. I only heard my head roar. She was already three-quarters of the way up the far edge, going away.

"Paat!"

I could see the little setter check, way out ahead, on the edge. Not for me. Birds, maybe. Slowing, she had doubled back, whipped into the woods. This was my chance to catch up. I slapped Dolly with the reins, asking for more. The mare broke into a gallop.

It took forever, it seemed, to get up there. When I did, I reined the mare into the woods. Riding a quick, wide circle through the broken pines and light brush, I saw nothing of Pat, but as suspected, rode up a couple of singles. God. She would be cranked up now.

We flew to field edge again. Just as we broke from the woods, I saw her. At the upper corner of the field, beating back and forth in wild figure S's. About the same time, she straightened away, drove ahead to the last block of woods, two hundred yards of pines that spilled into one last field before the highway.

In desperation, I yelled at her.

"Pat! Heyyye! Pat!"

She stopped momentarily, looking. I whirled the horse around, rode fast away. It works often with puppies, before they've been fully command trained, after they've learned to stay in front of the horse. They see you going away, want to catch up, get back out front.

Not this time.

I looked over my shoulder. She had turned away, tore on.

I jerked the rein. The mare spun. I kicked her hard again into a flat-out gallop. She was blowing a bit, beginning to lather. This needed to be over. I was really worried now. It was hardly three hundred yards across that last field to the road. I had to get there!

I reached around with my right hand, kept the reins with the left. Fumbling with the bouncing buckle on the saddlebag flap, I dug out the walkie-talkie, turned it on with my teeth.

"Loretta!"

There was a rush of static, a stint of silence, then, finally, a voice.

"Yes."

"Where are you?" I stuttered, in broken breaths and aggravated words. Dolly was laid flat-out.

"1010, just past the church."

"She's heading for the road. Get there, now! Hurry!"

"Stop her!" the radio ordered frantically.

"I'm *tryin'!*" I screamed.

I jammed the radio back into the bag just as we reached the woods. They were thick. Hardly slowing, I sent the horse through, dodging trees. A limb slapped me hard in the face, knocked my hat off. Then another banged stiffly into my shoulder. I ducked a third, then dropped my head and chest close against the horse's neck, pulled my legs in tight, quit steering. Just gave the mare her head.

She busted through, out of the woods into the field, still at a dead run. Remarkably, I was aboard, in one piece. Jerking myself back to consciousness, I glanced anxiously for Pat. She was well across the field, streaking straightaway.

"*Pattt!*" Once more I squalled, as loud as I could.

She didn't heed. It wasn't so much obstinance as desire . . . the desire to run and hunt, blazing white-hot. Though now it carried the same danger.

No more than a hundred yards ahead of her lay the long, ominous ribbon of the highway. It was vacant for the moment, God knows how long.

I looked for Loretta. The truck was nowhere in sight. Almost in the same instant the radio crackled, the message unintelligible. The saddlebag was bouncing wildly. It took precious moments to get the unit out.

"Ye-a—h!" I hollered into the transmitter.

"There's a truck coming, there's a truck coming!" Loretta shrieked. *"I can't get there!"* I saw our green pickup emerge from behind the screen of trees to the east, flying, and in the same instant, the omen of death arise from the west. It was a six-wheeled hauling van, and it was screaming, its driver oblivious yet to our presence. I could hear the high whine of the spinning tires, the frenzied roar of the engine. The little setter was scorching also, directly for its path, less than fifty yards from the road now.

"Nooo!" I heard Loretta cry before the radio bounced from my hand. Now there was the blaring drone of a horn. Loretta, approaching but still too distant to intervene, had jammed it to the steering column.

The mare was giving her absolute all. But it was impossible; I could feel her beginning to labor with fatigue, blowing, pounding. We'd never make the road in time. My heart was blocking my throat. I was hot with fear. I could scarcely breathe. I was pleading, "Please don't let it end here . . . please . . ."

I was still fifty yards from the road, yelling madly at the driver of the truck, when all in the same hopeless instant time collided with temerity. Pat reached the highway and shot across in front of the van, jerking its driver violently to consciousness. Two horns blared insanely, six wheels screamed a death chant against the asphalt, and the mare shied wildly sideways, pitching me headlong into the dirt. As, miraculously, the setter veered left in an explosive burst and by inches dodged the sliding front wheels!

Only her astounding speed and agility had saved her. The instant I recovered, I struggled to my feet, dread clutching my chest so tightly I could barely breathe, expecting surely to see her small body lying bloody and broken on the roadway. But my eyes darted here and there, discovering nothing of her. It was seconds later, with incomprehensible relief, that I finally found her—streaking on—sailing happily across the next field toward the opposite woods line.

The driver of the van had brought the vehicle to a halt at last, pulling onto the shoulder. Loretta had pulled over as well, to the other side. The driver of the van was offering something to her through his open window. I could not wait to hear. I ran over to the blowing horse, grabbed the reins, clambered up onto her back. Urging her anew with my heels, we crossed the road in a stiff clop, and took in again after Pat.

"Sorry, Dolly," I said, but this thing was not yet over.

Not until thirty minutes and a half mile later at the apron of Bell's Pond, when finally I snapped the check cord onto the little setter's collar, getting down on my knees and drawing her up hard against my chest, and thanking the good Lord as humbly as I knew how for sparing her. Then I apologized to the mare—much more comfortably, I was certain, than I would to my wife.

I learned a valuable lesson that day, and have betrayed it little over the years. To keep a seat on the saddle, a man needed to be a hair less headstrong than his dog.

∼ CHAPTER 4 ∼

THAT VERY EVENING, I ENTERED PAT AND BEDA IN THEIR FIRST FIELD trial, an amateur puppy stake near Chesterfield, South Carolina. With the breath of Fate so unpredictably at our neck, I would wait no longer.

Thane I decided to hold out for a time. He was closing fast, but still a-ways from Cincinnati, a little more erratic in ground pattern than his sisters. It wouldn't be long. When he got himself uncorked, he was strong as Pat, though not quite as fast, and the equal of either female in looks. He could win, I thought, but we'd give him a spell.

Part of the decision was financial. It was usually Friday and payday before we had more than a couple of pennies to rub together. Fortunately, then, you could run a puppy for eight bucks. At today's rates, hardly out the gate, we would have gone bankrupt. So, early on we decided to field the best two dogs each trial, the two that had emerged most impressively from workouts. For the first three events, that was Beda and Pat.

Looking back, it's amusing how really green and poor we were to the horseback game. Our entire stake, when nothing was lost or misplaced, summed less than a few hundred dollars. We had scratched up a utilitarian horse trailer, a small two-stall tagalong, open on three sides so the weather could come in, with a dent or two. This, when the standard among the regulars was a roomy, closed-in dog-horse combination that would accommodate a herd of horses and four braces of dogs, with a tack room and maybe even sleeping quarters. But our trailer had both hubcaps, thank you, and on each was emblazoned the name "Gore," which then was one of the best, and when the wheels turned, the logos would blur and whir round with a sexy purr. Most ironically, it was painted pure stock gold.

To the trailer, we were able to add a Buena Vista saddle, a blanket pad and a bridle, a grooming and shedding brush, a hay bag, a check cord or two, three roading harnesses, two gallon-size orange juice containers that, when hung from a saddle ring, doubled nicely as water jugs. And for our six-year-old Chevy truck . . . a homemade dog box, a tin camper shell, and a scrap foam mattress for overnighting. Luckily, we already had Dolly, a four-year old chestnut walking horse mare, a gift from my dad. Thrown in for good measure when it was fully loaded—all we had left—were three fearless setter pups and ten gallons of faith.

But everywhere we went, we found, there was a Samaritan, some kind and caring someone who took us in hand and tried his best to make us welcome and pulled aside some of the blinding that makes horseback pointing-dog stakes so outwardly discouraging. At field trials, as everywhere, there are people, we found, and people come in a mix of assholes and aristocrats. There are always enough of each to go round, and it takes little more than the first half hour to distinguish the two. Doing so has little concern with money or property. There's a crusty old-timer in overalls in Virginia we came to love who has next to nothing beyond four dogs and a stubborn will, and a former state bureaucrat in chinos we came to despise who has most everything and four *dozen* dogs. Simply, we discovered, the assholes are the ones who have won a lot and want everybody to know it. The aristocrats are the ones who have won a lot too; it's just that, unlike the assholes, they have as much class as their dogs. Once you figure this out, and meet the aristocrats halfway, you can shed the pomposity like flushing the commode, concentrate on running your dogs, having a good time, never being embarrassed, and winning when you can.

His name was Bob Lindler, the Samaritan at that first Chesterfield trial. We pulled onto the grounds about sunup after a three-hour, predawn run from home, a little tired and a lot nervous. There were a host of other rigs scattered round, most bigger than ours, some with tethered horses standing lazily by on three legs, some with folks milling around them, all with a few dogs tied out—some with a lot—mostly English pointers and setters, a Brittany or two, one red setter. I could feel the heat prickle my neck. I steered our homebody truck and trailer around and bashfully off to the side, took a breath, and turned off the engine. When it died, I realized for final we were there and really got scared.

Watching, and stalling, I sat there a few minutes. Melanie was asleep on the seat between us.

"They just look like dog folks to me," my wife, who never knew a stranger in her life, observed lightly. "Can't be so bad."

"Uh-huh, and I'm the one on the board to handle the dogs," I thought.

We climbed out and undertook the first task, getting the mare off the trailer, which was a damn sight easier than getting her on, for she was as unaccustomed to hauling as we were to trialing and balked like a mule at loading. In my mind, every eye in the place was on us, seeing us for what we were . . . green as a gourd. Off in the distance, I heard the shrill blast of a whistle, and momentarily a handler singing to a dog. The first brace of the morning was under way. My stomach tightened. Being green was tough on a man's pride. From the first slap on the behind, no male likes to seem a fool. He'd rather take a lick in the nose. It was bothering me a lot more than Loretta.

"Shouldn't we ask somebody something?" she inquired demurely, while everybody on the place watched the horse bang off the trailer and I got her tied.

Inside, where she couldn't see, I grimaced, fussing with the knot on the lead.

"The puppies are supposed to run after the derbies," I replied, like I knew something. "The derbies must be out now." I hoped so. At least, that was what the trial chairman had promised by phone the night before.

She looked skeptical.

"Why don't you check the pups?" I suggested.

She was right, of course; I *ought* to ask somebody something. But I dreaded like hell doing it. I was too embarrassed to ask much. I didn't *know enough* to ask much. And my pulse was bangin' like a bass drum.

So I fooled around a bit more and ran a brush over the mare, then went about saddling her and hanging the dog gear aboard.

"Pat and Thane are fine." Loretta said, reporting in. "Beda's car sick, but whinin', wantin' out."

"How 'bout Mely?" I asked.

"Sleeping."

"We got to get 'em out and lead 'em around some," I declared. "They've been in the box a long time." That much I did know.

"Melanie, too?" she smiled.

The comment loosened me a bit. I smiled back.

"Well, Beda for now. I'll get Pat and Thane in a minute.

"Then Mely."

Before she turned, she glanced delicately over the grounds again, a subtle feminine hint. I could delay only so much longer. Discreetly, I checked around. Of the few people about, nobody seemed to be looking any longer. Most were probably out following the trial. I searched for someone minimally threatening, maybe capable of compassion.

This was ridiculous. Just do it, I told myself. Find somebody and do it! I was going to, and then I saw him, on the way over. He was a big man, with distinction, kindness on his face and some silver in his hair, on the comfortable side of middle-aged. He carried himself easily and wore an unmistakable air of confidence. A man at ease with his surroundings. He was neatly attired in khakis and boots, but lacked riding chaps, I noticed. He walked up and stuck out a hand, offered a smile.

"Bob Lindler," he allowed.

I responded in kind, introducing myself and Loretta.

"Beautiful mornin' for a field trial," he surmised. "Where you folks from?"

"Carolina, the one north of here," I replied, trying to shake aside the nerves.

He chuckled.

"I told Dub, I hadn't seen you-all before," he said. I wondered who Dub was.

"No, this is the first South Carolina trial we've been to," I volunteered. I didn't tell him it was the first gosh-to-goodness horseback trial we'd been to, period. Not at first. I didn't have to. I guessed he knew.

"Believe I saw your name on the puppy board," he recalled.

"Yes," Loretta declared warmly. "Did you notice when we were running?" I cringed at the ease of her audacity. A male thing. I would have checked on my own.

"Well, the one I remember was the sixth brace," he recollected. "A little dog named Pat?"

My heart did a somersault. The sixth pup in the sixth brace. Couldn't be bad.

He glanced at Beda, surging against the check cord, jerking Retta off balance.

"Is this her?" He reached down and brushed Beda's ear and shoulder with a gentle hand.

"No," Retta advised. "Her sister. One of twelve."

I knew what was coming next.

"How many did you keep?"

Loretta looked at me and grinned. "Twelve," she said.

"All twelve," he mused, a twinkle in his eye.

"We wanted to be sure of what we had," I said in defense.

"That's the way to do it," he agreed.

"And you're runnin' how many?" he added.

"Two."

"Any derbies?"

"No," I said, "just puppies."

"I love runnin' puppies," he said. "I don't get as much out of the older dogs anymore, but I love the pups. All that brass, sass, and fire."

Bob Lindler was easy, and I was beginning to relax a bit, about the time he was ready to leave.

"Well, I'd best be gettin' back over," he supposed. "Just wanted to come over and say howdy."

"Welcome to South Carolina," he finished, sticking out a hand a last time. "Luck to your pups. If I can help you in any way, holler."

He turned and started to leave.

"Thank you," I said sincerely.

"Ask him when we run," Loretta prompted, nudging me with anxious eyes. He heard her, turned and hesitated.

"Oh, you're in good shape," he advised. "It'll be a couple o' hours. Last brace of the shootin' dog's out now, then the derbies. You'll ride some, won't you?"

"Yes," I said.

"Well, you can kinda keep track of the derby braces as you go along. The puppies'll start right after the last brace of derbies. The braces are posted on the clubhouse wall."

He turned, starting off again.

"Mr. Lindler," I called. Nothing ventured, nothing gained.

He paused and turned once more. We closed the distance in equal steps.

"I don't know a lot about puppy stakes," I said, after he waited past a moment of hesitation. The rest of my ignorance he read between the lines. "I want to help my dogs all I can."

His face softened with the last remark.

"Oh, I imagine you know more than you think," he said. "'Bout runnin' dogs, anyhow."

It was a magnanimous thing to say, and it sat me more at ease.

"I know a little about foot-handled dogs," I replied.

"A class dog's a class dog, horse or foot," he said. "Horseback dogs need to go a little bigger. Are your pups runnin' pretty good?"

"I think so," I said. "One a good bit more'n the others, but pretty good, yes."

"This is actually the first horseback trial I've run them in," I confessed.

"Do you have anybody to scout?" he inquired.

"No-o," I said. I wasn't totally sure what a scout was supposed and supposed not to do. Or what liberty the judges allowed a handler and scout working together. A scout was pretty foreign to foot trials back then.

"We'll get you one," he pledged. "A good scout's at least half the battle."

"If the other handler's dog has a find, while we're runnin', what exactly do I do?" I asked uncomfortably.

Now he knew how really green I was.

"Nothing," he said, smiling. "Not in puppy stakes. If it happens, it'll be an accident. Well, sometimes not altogether an accident, but not part of the judging. Just go on with your pup. Try to keep him out front, on the course and huntin'. Puppies aren't run on birds in horseback trials—that is, they're not expected to do anything but maybe flash point, not back or anything like that. You want 'em to show a little hunt, handle a little, stay out front, but not the manners. It's strictly on potential.

"So you can forget that," he said, motioning to the blank pistol on my belt.

"A puppy needs to be fast, wide, handsome and hunting. You got that and you're going to win some."

Maybe he was right. Maybe I did know a little more than I thought.

"Ride the first couple o' braces," he suggested. "Just watch. It'll come quick enough. See somethin' you don't understand, ask somebody."

"I will," I said, smiling weakly. Well . . . maybe I would.

"Well, I got to go," he said, excusing himself. I had kept him longer than I should have. I felt a rush of gratitude.

"Obliged, Mr. Lindler," I called in Southern as he left. He threw up a parting hand.

Credit to Bob Lindler, I was feeling a good sight better about myself. Beginning to subdue the apprehension and engage the excitement.

"There's usually somebody," Loretta observed gratefully, still struggling with Beda, who was happily here and there against the cord.

"Yes," I said with thanks.

I was anxious to get Pat out. When I opened the box, she was curled into a ball as usual, utterly relaxed. Like it was just another workout. Until I snapped the cord on and she blasted past, dragging me several feet. Simultaneously, a rider came by roading a pair of dogs, and the little setter went berserk, whining, trembling, and straining after them. To be so small, she was unbelievably powerful, putting absolute mind and matter into every notion. She weighed thirty-three pounds and I one-ninety, and I could lean my entire weight against her and still she would pull me along.

She drug me around for five minutes, and then I put her back in the box, got Thane out, and showed him Paris. He liked what he saw, and now I wished we were running him too. 'Cause he was cranked higher than a heifer on a hot wire. I'd try to road him, at least, somewhere here before we left. Build the stamina and strop the "want to" even more. Maybe next time, he'd beat the girls out for a berth. He jacked up against a half dozen bushes—he'd recently learned how—scratched cockily off a time or two. Looked at me impatiently over his shoulder.

Now I was feeling sorry for him, guilty even.

"Put y'ur brass in y'ur dash, and it'll git your name on the list," I told him. He cocked up on another bush.

I collected him up and stuck him back in the box with Pat, then helped gather up Beda as well. By now, she had worn Loretta to a frazzle.

It would become a ritual, the first order of business at every trial, uncorking the dogs after several hours' incarceration in a traveling box. Doing everything possible to see they were comfortable and to optimize in every incidental way their condition for running.

I reached into the truck for the tie-out chain, and through the back window, I could see that Melanie was awake. Sorta. I could just see her head over the backseat. She was studying me, her face still soft and puffy with sleep, a while away from a smile. Going around to the passenger side, I opened the door, inviting her into my arms. She slid slowly across the seat, and climbed into my embrace. I shifted her to the crook of an elbow, brushing the silky blond locks into place about her temples. She folded against me, snuggling her head beneath my chin. She smelled clean and fresh, like little girl. My little girl.

"Are we here yet?" she asked weakly.

I laughed. "Yes, Sweetie, we're here. See the trailers and the horses, and the dogs?"

"Where's Patty?"

"In the box, waiting for you."

"Has she run yet?"

"Not yet."

"Will I get to see her?"

"Uhhh-huh."

"When?" she asked, lifting her head, her voice rising to an imperative.

"Soon. Are you hungry?"

"No," she said, returning her head to the cleft of my neck. I held her a moment longer, then handed her to her mother, close by my shoulder.

Wonderful years, those next six. The three of us, closely together, the dogs and Dolly, the old truck, tumblin' around like prairie weeds to field trials in several states. Gone now . . . twenty-five years gone.

I retrieved the tie-out chain that first day, staked it off to one side, pulled the pups out again, and tethered them to the drop stations. They were sky-high, up on their toes, tails popping, wild-eyed and barking, gathering in all of interest. Setting out the water bowls and lugging over a five-gallon jug, I filled them fresh and clean from the home well. Pat and Thane grabbed a lap between barks; Beda as usual was too wound up to bother. She always did this—stood there slavering, yapping, and dehydrating, and refusing to drink. It worried me no end, for it spelled deficit when she ran. Something more to overcome, and one of the principal reasons she wilted so readily in the heat. Thank God it was cold that day.

I heard a small voice. "Hey, Patty." Melanie had joined me. Pat was clamoring for her, rearing against the chain.

Melanie went to her, and the sixth puppy put her paws on my daughter's small shoulders, bathing her face and cleaning the remnants of a strawberry Pop-Tart from the corners of her mouth with a warm, wet tongue. The little girl wriggled and squinched, giggling. Loretta and I exchanged a smile, and Retta snapped a picture. It's over my desk now as I write, and how, dear Lord, I'd like to step back into it, just as we were.

"I'm going to check the board," I told Loretta. "Back shortly."

I found my way there. There were few people around. Annoyingly self-conscious, I nodded at a couple who were. One tipped an accord, one didn't. By the time I got back, the queasiness was returning. Loretta looked at me.

"Seven braces total. We've got the third and the sixth. Beda, then Pat."

"Pat *is* in the sixth," Retta mused, fascinated.

"Yep."

"Good sign," she said.

"Let's hope."

"Relax," she admonished.

"I'm trying. I'm gonna ride a derby brace, try to loosen up. You want to ride? If you do, I'll see if I can find a horse."

"No, you can put Mely on double with you later if Dolly's behavin'." She got up from her folding chair. "Think we'll walk over and watch the breakaway, though."

Melanie was playing with the puppy still, the two of them loading dirt on a toy dump truck. At Retta's beckon, she threw the small shovel down and ran to her mother. Pat immediately pounced on it, something new to chew.

"Paaat," I teased her, wrestling it away. She gave me a dirty look.

"Win today and I'll buy you several of 'em," I whispered, stroking an ear. She mouthed my hand, biting playfully.

Beda was frothing at the mouth, absolutely wearing herself out on the chain. Thane was occupied with a metallic green beetle, pawing and fussing at it. For safety's sake, since we were all leaving temporarily, I decided to put them back in the box. To try and conserve them. I knew Pat, at least, would unwind.

The mare was about as green as we were. She was strung tight, wall-eyed, fidgeting and whinnying. Dubiously, I put one foot in the stirrup, waited until she settled a moment, then quickly swung aboard. She bounced a time or two, crow-hopped several yards. I slapped her soundly on the neck, reined her toward an idle field back of the grounds, then gave her her head. Immediately she jumped into a canter. I pulled her back into a fast, flat-footed walk and held her there for most of three hundred yards, then swung her on a loop to the trailer. By the time we got there, she had come down a little. Enough, I hoped.

When we reached the breakaway point at the head of a sprawling bean-field, the dogs were just coming to the line, a gallery of a dozen or more horses and riders beginning to assemble to their rear. Dolly and I pulled up alongside. A couple of folks pulled off a riding glove, a rite of courtesy, stuck out their hands, and introduced themselves. I reciprocated. Now the judges were approaching, returning from the preceding brace. You could feel the electricity in the air, the swell of excitement portending the break-away.

It was a mixed brace, a lithe and leggy liver-and-white pointer that looked like Fast Delivery blood, and a cleanly made, purely white setter that could have been Grouse Ridge stock. Each was accompanied on the ground by someone kneeling on one knee, likely a scout, who was stroking and styling them into the facsimile of a pointing pose. Behind them were the mounted handlers, on horses sweaty and lean. I noticed the water jugs clipped to the saddle, made a mental note not to forget our own. A pair of tall, weathered, and saddle-born riders were sitting loosely on a bay and a black to one side, conversing quietly; they wore the air and ease of professional trainers. Gilbert Barkley and John Ray Kimbrell, I would learn, men I would come to admire and respect. Men who, at one time or another, would lay aside their regimentary bearing to give a greening amateur a leg up on handling a dog. That day, Gilbert had a stake in one of the two dogs that were to run, as trainer. But since it was an amateur stake, the owner was handling and Barkley was simply a spectator.

The Amateur Field Trial Clubs of America, or AFTCA, sanctioning body for the amateur events, made permissible the running of a professionally trained dog in either amateur or open money stakes under an amateur handler, but strictly prohibited the pros from handling or scouting in ama-

teur proceedings. It was a condition, though long-standing, that made it
doubly tough for an amateur off the sand lot, training and handling his own
dogs, to successfully compete. You knew up front you were going against
professionally trained dogs, dogs that by the time they reached their shooting-dog or all-age form knew the ropes so well they could traverse a field
trial course virtually on their own, orienting on their handler's horses and
the natural drift and scent of the course. Some were so savvy Grandma
Moses could have "handled," could she have yodeled a little, gotten off the
horse, flushed birds, and fired a gun. But all in all, it augmented the game,
sharpening the quality of both the dogs and the people who pursued it.
There were also some very, very good amateur handlers around, like Bob
Abric and Doc Nitchman and Billy Blankenship, who could hold their own
with the best of the pros most days of the week. These I would strive to
emulate.

Of course, you could always profit from watching the pros, the Kim-
brells and the Barkleys, the Harold Rays, Arthur Beans, Thelmer Pages,
Henry Carusos, the John Rex Gateses, Bert Robinsons, Gerald Tracys, and
Larry Moons.

I glanced for Loretta and Melanie, could see them away to my right,
Melanie wide-eyed and Retta engaging another lady with smiles and prat-
tle. I envied that in her, that easygoing amiability that endeared her at once
to most everyone she met. While they tried to whether my relative wariness
as arrogance or reserve.

Now the two judges were up, pulling in behind the two handlers and
their dogs. Both were adorned with a dignity that suited their occasion, and
each was seemingly aloof from the surroundings and attendant to nothing
beside his charge. The larger of them, a big man, wore a simple baseball cap
with a Purina logo on its face; the smaller, older, and most distinguished
rode dapperly beneath a Stetson Open Road. The gent under the Stetson
flipped a page in a small notebook, showed it momentarily to his companion, then both checked their watches.

"Ready, Gentlemen?" I heard one say, dimly, above the stomp and blow
of horses and the shift and creak of saddle leather, and close afterwards
something else that sounded faintly like ". . . aloose."

Then two whistles blasted shrilly, horses jumped, the dogs shot away in
a dead-out sprint, plumes of dust trailing their heels, and the entire gathering shifted rapidly into an urgent procession behind the judges. I urged

Dolly up somewhere near the front, which wasn't any kind of a chore, a
respectful distance behind the judges, where we could see and follow the
dogs. They were already halfway down the first long edge now, still hooked
competitively in tandem, neither with the edge on leg. The handlers had
separated slightly, were riding briskly, beginning in rhythmic, extended syl-
lables their handling songs. Now, at once, the two dogs split, the setter cutting suddenly lateral, bouncing into cover, the pointer hanging the field
edge on to its corner, then shooting right and away, a blur of white gliding
the far front. Within moments, the setter emerged ahead, at the field corner,
quickly taking the path of the pointer before him, no longer in sight.

Breaking out of a thin strip of woods and into another huge field, you
could see a small billow of dust along its left edge two hundred yards distant and then the pointer, at a slight angle ahead of it, flying, the setter a bit
handier, but hunting crisply through a jutting hedgerow on the opposite
side of the course.

"Wright's dog's gittin' it done."

From a rider beside me came the fervent exclamation, from his compadre a quick and fervent vow of affirmation, and at the top end of the
field, almost in the same heartbeat, the rangy pointer checked suddenly, slid
one-eighty to its belly, gathered up in a few crisp steps, and blew loftily into
point. A murmur ran through the crowd, the handler spurred his horse into
a hard gallop to reach his dog, and one of the judges broke away into a canter to follow. Close behind him pressed an excited gallery, me and the mare
among them. The setter meanwhile had hunted through, was scorching
down the opposite edge, on a path that would take him directly to the
pointing dog. His handler, riding hard out to intercept him in time—the
other judge in tow—would barely make it. Just as his dog hesitated, showed
a momentary inclination to honor, then moved ahead, he anchored the
longhair in place with a stern "Whoa!"

Now both dogs, youthful and fiery, stood beautifully under judgment,
handlers alongside, the gallery pasted tightly into a semicircle around them.
A shiver of exhilaration ran my spine. This was what brought people to
field trials.

Quickly the forward handler moved ahead of his dog to flush, and had
taken only a few steps into the small head of jack pines, black oaks, briers,
and broom grass when a precisely nailed bevy of wild birds sputtered
abruptly away in a dozen directions. Both dogs, hiked high as a kite and

loosened by the momentum of the birds, took a couple of stabbing steps to follow, met instantly by an equally stabbing succession of "Whoas!" The pointer slammed on brakes while the setter ignored orders, to the considerable consternation of his handler, breaking past to follow the birds. In the midst of the momentary chaos, the salutary shot was fired for the pointer, which this time stood firmly, earning a swell of appreciation from the gallery.

A nice derby find, it seemed. I looked to the judges for an expression of approval, so that I might better evaluate it, but both faces were duly impassive.

The pointer was swiftly collared, his handler clapping the dog's side in praise and leading him out of the cover. Returned to the hands of the scout, he was ushered rapidly forward, away from the immediate area of the find and back onto the course, while his handler mounted and hastened to proceed. Pushing his horse abreast of the straining derby, he again hit the whistle. Inflamed, the pointer flashed away anew. It was forever a race, a race to the birds. You could feel it, relentlessly, in the tension of the pace.

To emphasize the point, the setter broke cover ahead of the surging pointer, and immediately the two locked up again, tearing away to the gap at the next woods line. For the remaining fifteen minutes, the two traded blows, the setter finishing with three nice finds, though not as advanced in manners as the two of the pointer. Throughout, the latter was clearly the more attractive and forward on the ground.

From the gallery gossip back to the trailer, it appeared the pointer was the one to beat. My stomach was churning again. He had run pretty big, and had looked good doing it. Would our pups do as well? One of those fields, particularly, was immense compared to those we trained on at the stable. My confidence was tottering again.

When I rode in, Retta was tying up a hay bag for Dolly, and Mely was tucked into a chair sipping a Mountain Dew. There was a big, wet halo around her mouth, and she was grinning at me. I snapped the tether rope to the mare's halter; she already had her nose buried in the hay.

"How'd the pointer run?" Retta inquired.

I made a false swipe at Mely's Mountain Dew. She pulled it away and frowned. "Mine's," she said.

"Pretty big," I said emphatically to Loretta.

"He looked like he could," she submitted.

"I hope our dogs do as well," I said, with a hint of doubt.

"They will," she assured. "Surely you haven't forgotten Thursday afternoon."

"No, hardly, but the grounds are bigger here, particularly the second field."

My stomach was squirming.

"What's the matter?" she asked intuitively.

I shook my head. She laid a gentle hand on my cheek. I let my face rest comfortably against it, for a moment a little boy needing reassurance.

"Those pups aren't worried about who's here," she said, "or who they are, or what they came here in, or what they brought, or any of the ten things else you're bothered about.

"They just want to run, and they will. And they're dependin' on you to help 'em with the ropes . . . help 'em do their best. Do that, and it's all you can do.

"It'll be enough," she asserted.

She was right, a hundred-plus right. I'd not let it shake me. I'd not be intimidated. It was my job to stay together, and help my dogs. They were countin' on me, and I'd be there for them. We'd do our best, and the devil take the rest.

Still, it was daunting. It always is, even now. You look around and you see all the big, fancy rigs, and you think about who's there: the pros, the money, the people so obviously comfortable with the role play—people that have been at it so long it comes second nature—the dogs with the heavy reps, the ones with titles in front of their names. But then, gradually, the parable of the assholes and the aristocrats holds true with the people, and you find the fortitude to push through. In a thirty-dog stake, first this thing happens and then the other, and one dog after another eliminates itself or is compromised, titled and untitled alike, and suddenly near the end of the trial, you find your own have held up pretty damn well, maybe even are in it, and each time you gain a little more grit, to get you through the next . . . a little better than the last.

I didn't know all that then. There was a lot I didn't know then. But I promised myself something, right there in Chesterfield, South Carolina, at that very first trial before I took another step, something I have never betrayed and never will. In the end, it was about my dogs . . . not the people, not the money, not the status, not who's running what . . . but the heart, courage, and class of my dogs. Our wherewithal for trialing would usually be barely more than the money for entry fees and the gas to get there; I couldn't send them to Canada for the advantage of the prairies, I didn't have training access to a multithousand-acre plantation in Alabama, but we'd work like hell on the back forty. I'd field the best dogs we could, dogs I knew, come what may, would give me back in performance what I'd given them in training. Together, we'd be the very best we could be. Sometimes it would be enough; other times it wouldn't. But regardless of what happened, ever, in a trial, to keep us from winning, or that caused them to come up short on a given day—their fault, my fault, fate, whatever—I'd never be embarrassed over my dogs. And the people—well, that was simple enough. I'd treat them like they treated me.

I needed something to break the jitters. I'd seen folks roading dogs behind the gallery during the derby brace I had just ridden. So I hauled Thane out, much to his delight, put him in the harness, climbed back on the horse, and roaded my dog. When we got back, we all felt better.

A short time later, there was a whistle blast, and a halloo. The derby stake was concluded, and the winners were about to be announced: first, second, and third . . . three places normally, in a sanctioned trial. I wanted to walk over and find out who won, but the puppy stake would start immediately afterward, and I needed to ride the first brace to familiarize myself with the course and get a feel for the competition. On top of that, beat it back as I might, nervousness was re-encroaching as time neared.

From the board a few minutes later, on the way to the puppy breakaway, I found that the pointer, indeed, had won. Having watched him, I had a better idea of what it took—derbywise, anyhow.

The first two pups down were both pointers. Neither really got uncorked. One, while a pleasantly moving dog, never got farther than fifty yards from the horse, it seemed, more like the foot dogs I was used to. Its bracemate was in and out a lot, never lining out forwardly enough and consistently enough to take advantage of the course. Though happily, it ran with a dead tail carried well below its back. Not the merry, over-the-hips, flicking flagstaff you like to see. Neither one stirred much excitement, I thought. The judges looked to be riding nonchalantly. Our pups would be better, I believed. Also, as I suspected, the second and largest field was a part of the course. It would take a strong cast, like the derby pointer's, to carry its edge. Pat might do it. I wasn't sure of Beda; she might break off partway. The twenty-minute heat went by in a hurry.

The tension was growing, but before I started back to our trailer to get ready with Beda for the third brace, I took a minute to watch the next pair away. There was a lanky orange-and-white pointer named Jim that broke hard and fast and never let up until the far end of the first field. Then he made a loop back, before lining away again. A pretty nice pup, it appeared.

When I got back to the trailer, I did a quick mental check of the saddle gear while Retta tried in vain to get Beda, still wound tight, to drink a dab of water. Roading harness, rope, water jug, extra check cord . . . all were in place. I reset the saddle blanket, repositioned the saddle, tightened the cinch securely. Checked for the whistle around my neck. Gave the mare some water. She had settled in now, was doing great. No more rodeoing. All was ready.

I kept watching the minutes by on my watch. With each one, the pressure was building. Five minutes to spare, we'd get Beda out and head over. Loretta would turn her loose for me.

"When does Patty run?" Mely complained.

I pulled her up on my knee. "Beda first, and then Patty," I replied. "You're runnin' Patty, right?"

She looked at me for a moment. "No, you," she said, stabbing me with a finger and sliding to the ground.

"But she's your puppy," I argued.

"You," she repeated, with the finger again, smiling this time. I grabbed her by the seat of the pants and she spun away, giggling.

"You," Retta mimicked, including the finger.

I couldn't relax. I got up again, checked my watch. Fidgeted. Only another minute or two. From a vantage of thirty years, I look back now and wonder, since the glamour and the pressure's all with the derby, shooting-dog and all-age stakes, the classics and the championships, at all the nerves over a weekend puppy stake. Except that it has never changed. Right down to the one we ran only this spring with our latest litter of contenders. Patty's triple-great-grandkids. If it ever does, I'll quit.

It was time. I got Beda out of the box, slavering, digging and straining against the cord. Handing the end of the rope to Retta, I held on until she'd dug in, gained control. She and Melanie started with the puppy toward the breakaway point, while I trailed close behind on Dolly.

Beda was a strikingly made setter, doubly so leaning against the restraint of the cord, hindquarters knotted and pumping every jump. Classically tricolored with an eloquent carriage, she turned heads simply with her beauty.

Though frequently the brunt of mishap—at three weeks old, the one perpetually falling out of the back of the puppy house every time we opened the back flap to clean—it never dampened her spirits. A mischief in the kennel, she was forever into something, would run up and nip you playfully on the heels, then do fly-bys at a hundred miles an hour. She was a love, and the thing I loved most still was that in the toughest of times, gifted less raw physical power or stamina than either Pat or Thane, she tried so hard.

We got her to the line, and after some difficulty, Loretta got her stopped, then got down on a knee and wrapped her arms around the pup's shoulders to hold her. Melanie squatted importantly beside them. Our little warrior maiden was trembling all over, wanting to go, glancing tightly here and there at the people and the horses as the gallery gathered.

Her bracemate was brought up, a finely made, China-doll pointer female, black on white with a right shoulder patch. She was happy, not nearly so wired as Beda, but eager, her tail clicking sharply to and fro. When she saw Beda, she tried to gambol over but was pulled stiffly away. Beda cut an eye at her, trembled all the more, began to pant with anticipation. Loretta was gently stroking her sides in an ineffectual attempt at calming her. The pointer, meantime, was set into place, the two dogs standing closely side by side, Beda left, the pointer right. Cocked and ready, they waited before the course.

Glancing around for the judges, I met the eyes of the other handler, leaned over and clasped hands, wished him good stead. Just a little bit less than myself, I hoped.

Another man rode over, drew close, also offered a hand, and a smile to go with it.

"Cleg Kerns," he said. "Bob Lindler said maybe you could use a little help. I'm back here if you need me."

I felt a run of relief. I wasn't all that sure how to use him, except if Beda got out of ken, but I felt better that he was there.

"Thank you," I said earnestly. I looked around for Lindler, didn't see him.

Abruptly, the judiciary was up and into position behind us, the tension thickening. The two men exchanged terse pleasantries with members of the gallery, as a gaggle of butterflies flapped about my stomach. Fingering the whistle, I waited intently for their salutation, the nod to be off. But now there eventuated a considerable delay while we waited for one of the handlers from the previous brace to catch a puppy that wanted not to be, and that had lapped the course just ahead, rooting a legion of meadowlarks from the broomsedge. I worried that Beda would trip the edge at all the waiting.

Finally the overjoyed miscreant was apprehended and led aside, and the way stood clear. There was a creaking of saddle leather as lenient riders shifted their weight to center, gathered up reins, pulled loafing horses to attention. You could feel the moment charging, the voltage loading into the impending lurch to excitement. The judges rode a few feet closer, pulled to a stop, made a quick check of the brace. My heart was thumping. Beda made a stab at freedom. Loretta held on. The pointer pup bucked also. A moment of disorder ensued while they were set back in place.

"Beda?" the nearest judge asked, addressing me, and looking to the pup on the left.

"Yes."

"And Missy?" inquired the alter judge of the opposing handler, who nodded.

"Okay, Gentlemen," they said in unison, "turn 'em aloose."

Before the words ended, a whistle shrieked sharply, and the pointer dashed away. It caught me off guard, and I was late with my own, a mistake I would never make again. Beda was bucking and squirming to follow, and Loretta was fighting to hold her.

"Turn her loose!" I yelled. "*Turn her . . .*" And she did, and I hit the whistle as hard as I could.

Beda went away like the hurry in a hurricane. By the time she reached midway of the first field, she had overcome the fleeing pointer, and now they challenged, fading together and away to the far corner and swinging hard across the front. At the woods gap, both cast laterally for several seconds, darting oppositely left and right, then the pointer suddenly checked and looped back to locate her handler. When, momentarily, she found him, he frantically urged her on, riding forward, hitting the whistle. She whipped around and tore off anew. Beda, meantime, had shot forward through the gap and out of sight, straight up the course. She was right on the beam, high and happy, and I could feel the rush in my chest as the exhilaration imploded.

"*Yeaauuup, yeaaaupp, yeahey!*" I sang to her, letting her know I was there.

The little pointer bitch made the gap now also, catching the path, driving ahead. A minute or so passed as we negotiated the neck of woods. Behind were the huff and clop of fifteen horses and riders, but I heard nothing but the intermittent calls and commands of the contending handler and the voice growing inside that said I needed to see my dog. Ahead the woods were thinning, and I could begin to see a portion of the huge second field but could not find Beda. I rode along singing, hoping she would show. There's an adage, old as field trialing. You can win with almost any dog sometimes, except a *lost* dog.

Then we broke swiftly into the bottom of the great field, and I saw her break cover onto the far-right edge, a hundred-fifty yards out, turn and go hard away, her flag whipping with the happy rhythm of her gait. I could feel the surge of adrenaline, the nerves melt away like ice on a stove burner. I wanted to holler, "Yes! Yes!" as loud as I could. I was prickly hot, just with the sheer thrill of it. The pointer had taken the right edge, was looking good too, bearing quickly forward. Halfway to the extreme end of the field, they were neck and neck, left and right, flying. And then inexplicably, both pups looped off the edge and turned back, closing to us. My heart sagged. Urging the mare, I rode swiftly several yards ahead . . . the other handler likewise . . . seeking to turn them. But they continued back, keying on one another, reversing only when they were almost to us. Now both were ahead again, but then not quite so powerfully, choosing instead to stab laterally, hunting more diligently.

In a horseback hunting party, it would have been a small thing, an admirable thing even, but in a field trial, there is a fine line between hunt and run. Again and forever, a field trial is a race to the birds, and to prevail, a dog, and especially a pup not yet judged on birds, I found, must both hunt and run, with emphasis on the run. In ground pattern, they must carry consistently forward, the more fleetly and deliberately the better. The ability from puppydom for a dog to naturally catch and hold the front at horseback range, to drive consistently forward—to line out, in the parlance—is a rare and treasured trait, seemingly innate. You can encourage it in other good pups that have it in portion, when they're young, and many learn to stay the course well enough to frequently win. But it is the dog driven to push independently fast and forward, able to orient almost instantly on its handler, sight or voice, from the far-flung front—the dog that turns on, and wins going away—that puts the electricity in field trials.

Beda had it in good portion, and I had encouraged it constantly in training, and for the first ten minutes, she had flung herself forward against the course. Looking great doing it. She was "getting it done," as the man said. But as I feared, the tremendous edge was a stretch for her, and at a point, she had lost the certainty inside herself and doubled back to find it, to regain her bearings. Once she had, she was out and away again, though not so ambitiously. I'd remedy part of it; we'd find bigger training grounds.

But now the fat was in the fire. I'd help her best I could.

She was ahead at a modest range, cutting laterally in and out of the cover, always turning forward but digging in a bit much for a good front-going race. The pointer was doing the same.

I touched her with the whistle. *"Go aheeaadd!"* I urged, prodding her.

She rallied, quickened her pace and dug away, more directly again. The pointer pup caught sight of her and followed. Reaching the end of the field, bracemate abreast now, she stretched on into the last five minutes of the course, which opened again into a broad pasture after another neck of broken piney woods. Then she started digging in once more, and closing down some, not taking full advantage of the ground, before leaning away again into a pretty decent cast in the last sixty seconds. And then, almost as abruptly as it had started, it seemed, there came the hail of "Pick 'em uuuppp!" from the judges, and the twenty minutes was spent.

I rode quickly to Beda, well ahead, calling to her. She heeded, slowed and stopped, turned back toward me when I whoaed the horse and stepped to the ground. I got down on my knees, waiting for her, caught her in my arms, patted and praised her. Gave her some water. Seconds later, and with relief, I had her safely in the roading harness. She had done proud the first time down, whether enough to win anything I didn't really know—I wished she had been a little more strongly forward—but the first half had been good, the finish tolerable, and there had been the exceptional beauty of her going, as always.

A couple of riders from the gallery came by, one on a big chestnut gelding with a white blaze and three socks.

"A nice pup there," he said. "Pretty on the ground."

"Thanks," I returned. "Could have been a bit stronger," I added insecurely.

"Pretty nice, nonetheless, were I judging," he offered as they rode on.

"Thanks," I said again, beaming at my Number Two pup and rubbing her flanks. I was proud of her.

At the trailer, Loretta was waiting anxiously for the story. Melanie was playing in an anthill.

"If she looked as great overall as the breakaway, it had to be pretty respectable," Retta said as I rode in, Beda hard against the harness. Mely left the ants and ran to the pup.

"Unfortunately, she didn't," I replied, "but not bad either. Pretty nice really." Dismounting, I explained from beginning to end, while Retta pulled off the roading harness and exalted her pup. Mely had her arms around Beda's neck, receiving puppy kisses.

"Do you think we won?" Loretta asked.

"I don't know. Not yet, anyhow. Not over yet."

"Little warrior maiden," Retta cooed. I looked at her and shook my head.

"You're gonna spoil that dog."

"So?" she said.

"When does Patty run?" Melanie asked again.

"Before you know it, Sweetie; 'bout as soon as we can get her out of the box and get ready."

"Can I lead her to the getaway?"

"Breakaway, Sweetie."

"Breakaway," she repeated.

"You and Mama."

I returned Beda to the box with a final bit of praise, checked on Pat. She was curled into a ball, apparently unaffected. She raised her head and looked at me with sleepy eyes. Though she seemed totally calm, I knew well enough now that beneath it her spirit raged. She knew she was going to run. The anticipation seethed. Unlike Beda, she bottled it, as if she grasped the value of conservation. While the pressure grew and grew, ever more volatile, toward the moment it was granted freedom to explode. I was careful to say nothing, yet, to ignite it.

"Want some water, girl?"

She lapped at it readily. Good. One more boost to the equation. As I closed the box, she circled twice and twisted into a limp ball again.

"Minutes, Pat," I said, looking at my watch, "minutes."

The nerves were creeping out of the closet, back into the pit of my stomach. Running Pat was ever an adventure, and this time it was for real. I was still a little undone from the stable incident. No roads threatened. If I just didn't lose her. Walking back to the mare, I redid the saddle gear, checked the cinch. Then joined Retta, dropping into the chair beside her, fingering the check cord in my hands, watching Melanie coax a Slinky toy down the fender of the trailer.

"Maybe you'd better lead Pat to the line," Loretta said. "I'm scared to death I'll lose her, let her loose."

I though about it a moment. Probably she was right. Better safe.

"All right."

"Don't lose her out there," she begged, mirroring my mind.

"Pray God," I agreed.

"She can do it, Retta," I declared. "Maybe. If I can just get her around." I was far from certain what it took. But I believed in my dog.

"Bring her back safely," my wife said, "that's all I ask."

"And *win,*" I added, one eye on my watch.

"If we can do it safely," she conceded. "Pat's what's important."

"It's time," I said, getting up and unfurling the check cord. Time for the Number Six pup in the number six brace.

"Patty, Mely."

I brought Dolly up, handed the reins to Loretta, undid the latch on Pat's box. Still reposed, she looked at me inquisitively. Reaching in, I snapped the cord onto her collar.

"Let's do it, Pat."

She was out of the box and on the ground like a shot, jacked high on all fours, eyes darting this way and that, tail popping. She whirled in place twice, then again, asking direction, and when I grabbed for the mare's reins, Pat hit the end of the cord so hard it crucified me between horse and dog. Dolly bunched and jumped under the rein pressure, almost landing on top of me. Loretta jumped to pull Melanie away—for a moment, chaos reigned—then the procession was jerked into line again by the surging puppy, down and digging now with all her might for progress. Following, hanging on to the reins on one end and the cord on the other, using the mare for ballast, I steered her for the starting line.

You can dampen the stubborn aggressiveness of a dog like that by bringing her to heel beside you, or by looping a half hitch around her waist and enforcing subservience. I never did, all the years, because when you do, you're tampering with desire. What you take out, even a modicum, you can never put back. In field trialing, fortune, fortitude, generations of both people and canines are spent in attempting to breed dogs with an uncommon desire to run and hunt, and only one in a thousand comes gifted so extraordinarily as Pat. Brilliance is like perfection; it flares only with freedom. In a pointing dog, the proclivity to point at the sight or scent of birds—the urge to hunt—is instinct. Desire that is bespoken of awe is innate and inexplicable, God-given. I'd ask certain things of necessity from Pat later, and Thane and Beda, curbs on instinct like manners on game and a degree of handling response—but win, lose, or draw, I'd do any little thing I could never to blemish their soul.

When we got to the line, a small gallery had gathered, and there was already a man and dog waiting there: a tall, lanky, middle-aged man with a weathered face and a cowboy stance, and a big, rawboned, riprap pointer pup with enough leg to lap Kansas. I pulled Pat to a halt left and abreast of them. She stood straining hard against the cord, hindquarters locked and toenails dug in. The relax was completely out of her. I gave the mare to Loretta, pulled myself hand over hand up the cord until I reached her, got down beside her, and gathered her up more loosely. She was quivering now, against my arms. Twice she bunched and lurched, wanting away.

"Looks like that one's ready to go," the tall man remarked in a voice pitched slightly higher than his persona, grinning broadly. There was an ever so thinly slivered suggestion of ascendancy in his tone. Obviously, by now, he was the opposition.

"She's ready," I concurred.

He stuck out a big, hard hand. "Dub Watkins." I reached over and shook it firmly.

"Well, don't be too hard on my dog," he laughed. I smiled a bit self-consciously, stroked Pat's sides ear to flank. Watkins broke away, engaging someone else standing by on a fidgety, martingaled gray.

"Do it, Pat," I whispered under my breath. "Do it."

Several more riders were arriving, joining the swelling gallery, hoping to see a hot puppy. Everybody loves the fire and joy of a good pup. I hoped we would show it to them. On the periphery, I recognized Bob Lindler, on a well-made bay. I smiled and acknowledged, receiving his in return. Gratefully, as well, on the other flank I found Cleg Kerns. With the crisp tip of his finger, he signaled his convenience, should I need him.

Off to the right, still at some distance, I could see the judges approaching.

Dub Watkins handed the lead to the pointer to a friend, I guessed, turning for his horse. The friend picked up the pointer and set him down squarely facing the course, rubbed and styled him prettily into the semblance of a point. The big pup stood there proudly, almost as if he were afraid to move, but shivering. He had been here before. He was a good fourteen months old if he was a day.

I made no attempt to style Pat. She never did it well at the line, the anticipation too binding, the power in her wound up tightly as a mainspring. Then, or afterward, I never worried much about it. It's nice, but unessential. It's what happens when the clock trips that counts, and what happened with Pat was a lot.

Trusting my puppy now to Loretta, I relinquished my hold only when I was sure my wife was down in place with a firm grip on Pat's collar. Gathering up the horse, I stepped into the stirrup and swung into the saddle. There were a number more people here than before. The judges were working their way now, through them, the horses giving way side to side, the customary deference and salutations extended. Wildly the butterflies fluttered, all dozen at once, a wave of queasiness breaking like a raw egg and trickling down the walls of my stomach.

"Pat . . . Pat." I called softly to her until she looked at me, giving her a bearing. She glanced up and back, and in her eyes the fires raged.

I fingered the whistle to hand, locked it between my index finger and thumb. I'd be ready this time. This time there'd be no surprise. I'd told Loretta, "The instant . . . the very instant . . . you hear my whistle, *any* whistle, cut her loose!"

"Sixth brace," announced the judiciary appraisingly. "Let's see, on the right we have Mr. Watkins and . . . Duke; left Mr. Gaddis and . . ." after a hasty check of the book ". . . Pat."

There was a slight pause while one of the two restored his running order to pocket, then . . . "All right, Gentlemen, any time you're ready."

That was all I needed to hear. On the "y" in ready, I hit the whistle as urgently as a battle order. Pat exploded like powder in a flash pan, a virtual blur, and the pointer was right there with her. Down the left edge of the first field they tore in a blistering scorch, each committed body and soul to conquering the other. They took half its length, a hundred yards, in less time than it takes to tell it. I could see Pat—half the size, half the stride of the big pointer—digging into herself, her legs blurred into an illusion, the thrust and gather of her shoulders and hindquarters so abbreviated and violent between power strokes the muscles jumped and bunched like the drive train of an engine blown redline. It was impossible . . . *impossible* . . . for flesh and blood to combust so swiftly. Behind us, the gallery was barely off the line; you could hear the first muted exclamations of excitement, and the two dogs, neck and neck, had already taken the entire field and were rolling into its terminal corner.

They flashed around the turn of the field so fast they were knotted indistinguishably into one speeding streak of white, and in the space of an instant had shot across the front and through the woods gap going away.

Watkins spurred his horse to a short canter, squalled at his dog to break off, cursed. I followed suit.

He looked over at me, his face contorted with ire. "They're gonna lock up and run clean out of the damn country," he sputtered.

It can happen, two dogs so indomitably given to sovereignty they will not relent, locking into a ground race and going at breakneck speed as far as the country will carry them, taking themselves from judgment until they're exhausted or have squandered the better part of the time allowed for the

heat. You don't win that way. It can't be all run; you gotta have some hunt,
even in a puppy stake.

"*EEyyeeee, now! Yeaaaah! Yeeaaaah, Duke!*"

"*Yeeaaahp, Paaat! Heyyee! Eyyyeeoh!*

Both of us were clamoring now, trying to regain our dogs. Neither
came back. Watkins cursed again, spurred his horse to a gallop this time,
made for the woods gap. I kicked the mare into gear, gave him no ground.
We burst out of the gap into the huge second field. The two pups had
bested almost half its throw, racing furiously side by side yet down the
sprawling right half of the field, a quarter off the edge, flying!

We both squalled to the top of our lungs at the same instant, and like a
sliver of white paper torn evenly and smoothly into halves, pointer and setter peeled suddenly left and right to the edges. Searing, driving, going hard
away.

We had galloped a quarter of the way up the big field.

"We've got to wait for these judges," Dub spurted, reining his lathering
horse back.

He was right. I pulled back the mare, and in the same now-you-don't,
next-you-see-'em breath, both judges broke abreast from the woods gap
corner, in a brisk canter, the gallery pasted close behind.

Both pups were hunting a little now. Pat checked quickly, sliding to a
stop, dust billowing, retraced a few yards, testing the air, then corrected as
abruptly, spun and dug away. On the rival edge, Duke disappeared into a
finger encroaching the cover, tarried several moments, then appeared hard
and fast away again, grabbing ground. Down the respective sides of the field
they flew, two hundred yards apart and four distant, still at a dead draw. Pat
was driving with the tight, quick, light-on-her-toes lick that was her trademark, poetry to watch, plume twelve-high over her back and clicking like
an overwound metronome. A quarter century and a lot of dogs later, she
remains the fastest, most eloquently animated dog on the ground I have
ever seen. I was inebriated with the rush of it, proud to my collar buttons. I
could feel the pulse pounding in my neck; in my chest, the oxygen debt was
so urgent I was coming light-headed.

The pointer pulled up hard again, almost flash pointed, then dashed on.
Pat grabbed the half-moon cut of a deep inset off the edge, head up and

questioning the air like a shooting dog, around it so swiftly she looked like a small, white ball slung round on the end of a string.

"Yeeaaaahup! Yeeaah, now! Go aheeaaad!"

I sang to her, encouraging her, but wanting her to remember I was there. Watkins was exhorting the wound-up pointer now too, pressing him for an advantage.

Fleetly, far ahead, they closed on the finish of the great field . . . left and right . . . coming to its completion and crossing momentarily at its head like a salute of sword points. Five minutes to go in the heat.

Then, in a heartbeat, the pointer had reversed and was speeding away beyond the broad field into the forward and final stretch of the course, and Pat had disappeared as immediately as if the ground had swallowed her up.

I rode on with Watkins, lagging, calling, waiting anxiously for her to reappear . . . a precious minute, then two . . . three . . . I knew we had it going, needed to be out front again, quickly. We rode the broken patch of pines, came into the broad pasture. The pointer was well ahead, on course, looking strong. No Pat.

"Yooooaahhh, Paaaat!" I was on the edge of despair. Then, suddenly, I remembered! Cleg Kerns. If ever you'd use a scout, this must be it! I swung quickly in the saddle, searched desperately through the gallery to find him, could see him nowhere . . . only the judges, who seemed to be pressing, pressing, right on my heels. Then one of them called to me.

"Mr. Gaddis, your scout's out, back in the corner of the last field."

"Thank you," I said shakily, and turned back front, urging the mare forward. I glanced nervously at my watch. Less than thirty seconds. And then there was Pat, off my left shoulder, and she was whipping left and forward into the pasture from the woods, driving again, flying, digging away at light speed, and there were tears in my eyes, because like wildfire she was closing the gap to the pointer. I caught the figure of Cleg Kerns, melting his horse gently back into the edge cover. And right then and there, I learned for all eternity the enormous value of a good scout at a field trial.

She was almost there, almost to him, and I was alongside Watkins again, and then seconds too quickly the clock ran dead.

"Pick 'em uuppp."

We both broke hard and away to catch them, Dub Watkins right, me left. Both pups were still cranked up and reaching. We caught them at opposite ends of the pasture about the same time. I called to Pat stiffly, and she slowed, turning and looking for me. I kicked away the stirrups and slid down off the horse, kneeled and met her with open arms. Burying my face in the silky hollow between her ear and neck, I caressed her, thanked her, and there where no one could see, wept briefly with joy. In the next ten years, she would give more than another occasion to do it again.

As I was working her into the harness, Cleg Kerns rode up, a big smile on his face.

"Thanks for that," I said, getting up and shaking his hand.

"She's a hell of a puppy. Thought I'd kill my horse catching her. There was a woods path back there off the left corner of the field. That's what happened. She was to hell and back in there before I ever gathered her up. She was givin' Lindler's dog where-to-go 'fore that."

"You mean Watkins's dog," I asked.

"Well, Bob Lindler owns the dog. Dub runs him."

Once again, Bob Lindler had earned my respect, for facilitating a scout like Kerns against his own dog.

"That dog's leading for Puppy of the Year right now."

"The Duke dog?" I said.

"Yeah."

"He'll probably win it. He's a pretty nice puppy."

"But so's yours," he said, as he took his leave.

"Thanks again, Cleg," I offered.

"Pleasure," he said, tipping his hat.

We started back, the three of us, Dolly, me, and pup Number Six, rather proudly, I'll add. Pat was happily straining into the harness, barely tested it seemed. Along the way, there were compliments from several of the kind folks who had ridden the brace. It felt good.

The past twenty minutes had been, by a distance, the most exhilarating experience of my life, the siren song for twenty years to come of passionate horseback trialing up and down the Eastern Seaboard. A calling so consummate, enthralling, and demanding that for the extent of it, there was little more of life that I wanted, and at its end, little more to it I could give.

Melanie saw us coming and ran pell-mell to meet us. I can still see the eagerness in her eyes, the long, blond tresses billowing every bounce.

"Did Patty win?" she asked breathlessly.

"I don't know, Sweetie," I told her. "We'll have to wait and see." She looked perplexed.

"Maybe." I honestly didn't know. I wanted to hope.

Mely ran happily alongside Pat to the trailer. There, she dropped to her knees, inviting the pup into her arms. Not missing a beat, Patty pushed past her outstretched hands, rearing and planting a paw on each of her slender shoulders, and pummeling her face with kisses. Delighted with the giggles and shrieks, she pressed her advantage, until Melanie was wriggling and squealing under her on the ground. Finally, I stepped in and separated them, a puppy by the harness in one hand, a daughter by the overalls in the other. Overwhelmed, Mely wiped the slobber off her face with the backs of both small hands.

"Yuck, Patty," she complained.

Now it was Loretta's turn. This time I had to rescue Pat, pulling her out of the roading harness and putting her on the tie-out chain.

"She scared me to death the way she left," Loretta exclaimed. "I didn't know whether we'd see her again."

"Pretty nice," I concurred.

"How did it go?"

"I wish you could have seen it," I said, "all the way through."

"Better than Beda?"

"Yeah . . . stronger . . . bigger. Way bigger. Solid all the way . . . except for an absence in the back corner of the second field. That we could have done without."

"How long?"

"Five minutes maybe . . . a long time in a twenty-minute puppy stake."

"Does either of them have a chance?"

"Hard to say." Again, I was honest. Still, I was hoping.

"They will . . . this day or another," I said. I believed that. They were too nice.

We liberated Beda and Thane from the dog box, snapped them alongside Pat on the chain. They were glad to get out. All three rolled and wallowed, pulled themselves around in tight circles, the caress of the ground soothing against the soft of their bellies.

I had slid the saddle off the mare, was grooming her, when a whistle blew. Guessing it signaled the results of the puppy stake, we ambled over. Prickled by anxiety, I listened as the Trial Chairman read off the winners.

"Third . . . Betty . . . Jack Sievers." A pointer gyp from the fifth brace, which I hadn't ridden. Advancing, the handler accepted the third-place trophy and a yellow ribbon, shook hands with the Chairman, and thanked the judges.

"Second . . . John . . . Sim Carver." Smiles all around. An enthusiastic hand from the several of us. Another pup I hadn't seen, from the brace before Beda's. Sim Carver stepped forward, receiving the trophy and a handshake. Then others. I looked enviously at the red ribbon in his hand as he wound his way back to the rear. My hopes were starting to sag. We definitely wouldn't have both in there, which had been too much to wish anyhow, I guess. But that's the way we went to every trial, trying.

"And First Place, Amateur Puppy . . . ," the Chairman announced boldly, reaching for the blue and pausing for effect—I held my breath— "Duke . . . Dub Watkins." My heart sank. There was a loud round of applause as Dub strode up, hat, boots, and grin, to gather the rewards.

Loretta cast a disappointed look at me. I acknowledged with my eyes, then returned to an attempt at impassive. Dub was busy shaking a dozen hands. I walked over and added mine. He accepted it matter-of-factly, with nothing beyond a smile. I was expecting a word, maybe, about my dog. It wasn't exactly a runaway for Duke, you know. Stepping back to Loretta and Melanie, I felt Mely's hand at my sleeve. She looked up at me with empty eyes.

"Patty didn't win," she wondered.

There were things, then as now, that I couldn't begin to explain to a six-year-old vested in the unshakable surety of love and faith, innocent yet to the ambiguity of fortune. Things I can't, oftentimes still, explain to myself. Over the years, I guess I quit trying. Sometimes you wince and often you wonder, and eventually you come simply to weather the wrong, and rejoice at the right, with the trust that in the greater sum of things, the latter will prevail. In any endeavor, there are dues to be paid.

"Not this time," I told her.

But then there was an outstretched hand beneath my gaze, and I looked up to meet the eyes of a gentleman with a comfort.

"I enjoyed your pups," he said sincerely. "Very, very nice."

And when he stepped aside, there was another, just behind.

"They won with me," he said, "particularly the last one."

I could feel the assurance surging back, the believing.

"Another Samaritan," I thought gratefully.

We had hardly gotten back to the truck, were casually getting things together to leave, when Dub Watkins and Bob Lindler walked up.

Dub tipped his cowboy hat to Loretta, stuck out his big, rough hand.

"That was a nice pup you ran," he said to me squarely.

I felt a surge of pride, the kind you feel only rarely, when your toughest adversary bows momentarily and bestows an astonishing word or two of respect.

I smiled. "Yours as well," I said honestly. "Cleg Kerns told me he's ahead for Puppy of the Year," I added, "at the end of our brace."

"Well, there's a ways to go yet," Dub said confidently, "but we'll see."

"Glad I didn't know that at the beginning," I laughed.

"Naww," Dub drubbed, "wouldn't have mattered.

"Let me tell you somethin'," he said. "You always want to run against the best dog. The better the other guy's dog is, the better yours will be."

"They push each other," Bob added. "You get the best out of both, if they're the right kind."

"Competitive," Dub explained, "and any good one is."

It was a thing I guess I knew, but never had it been emphasized so dramatically by word or action. It was the luck of the draw, of course, except in training, but an item I would remember.

"Thanks, Bob, by the way, for Cleg Kerns," I mentioned, "against your own dog."

Lindler nodded. "Almost regretted it," he gulped, obviously in jest.

"This the one?" Watkins asked, walking over and stopping in front of Pat. Pat was locked into a puppy point, prior to an acrobatic pounce on a bug.

"Yes."

"Little thing," Watkins mused.

"'Bout thirty-four pounds worth," I said.

He and Lindler stood studying her for a minute.

"Does she always run like that?" Bob Lindler inquired.

"Yes," I said.

"The other one runs nicely, too," he remarked, referring to Beda. "Not quite as strong as this one."

"No, not usually," I admitted.

"What about the other one?" Bob asked, pointing to Thane.

"A littermate brother," I explained.

"Does he run as big as the rest?" Lindler surmised.

"Pretty strong," I answered.

"You didn't run him?"

"Not this time," I said. "Soon."

"They're good-lookin' pups," Bob Lindler observed. "And they're out of?" he continued.

"Crockett and Rebel dogs," I said.

"There were twelve in the litter," Loretta offered.

"And you kept these three?"

"Well, actually, we still have all twelve," Retta finished. There was a look of surprise on Watkins's face.

"We want to be sure of what we have," I declared, "so we decided to keep them all for a year . . . until we know."

"That's the way," Watkins agreed.

"Are there any of the others that run as good as these?" Lindler wanted to know.

"Not quite," I responded. "Not at this point."

"They're what . . . ten months old?" he asked.

"Eight."

"Just eight," he remarked with interest. I nodded.

Watkins and Lindler stood quietly for a minute or so, studying the dogs, especially Pat, occasionally trading an inaudible comment. Then Bob Lindler turned to me anew.

"Would you consider selling her?" he asked.

I looked at Loretta, meeting her glance. We smiled.

"Our trailer maybe, our house . . . the good silver," I chided, "but not the dog or the horse."

Lindler smiled, amused, but clearly earnest in his bid. As others would be.

"No, we couldn't. Thanks for the offer, but she's fam'ly and we enjoy her too much. She's really Melanie's dog, anyhow," I said, indicating our daughter, who was standing shyly by, but listening raptly.

"Well, should you change your mind, let me know."

"Doubtful," I warned.

We shook hands again, I thanked Bob once more for the scouting assist, and they walked away, with a comment between them after a few paces I would liked to have heard. They knew a good dog, no doubt, and I knew we had a commodity on our hands. Here people were, coming up and offering me money, me green as a Georgia gourd to the horseback trick, for a homebred setter pup born in the backyard. It was complimentary, to say the least. All thanks to Pat. And Beda, too.

A half hour later, we had loaded the mare without calamity and were pulling out of the grounds onto the dirt road back to the highway. I opened the throttle on the Chevy, urging it along towards home and contemplating the trial. Melanie lay across the seat between us, her head resting in Loretta's lap.

"Bob Lindler's a nice man," Retta remarked, "and Dub was too . . . really everbody was but the guy with the . . . , but I wish we could have beaten his dog."

"You sound like a field trialer," I said, grinning.

"Guess I am.

"It would have been nice to have won," she said, "particularly with folks like Dub Watkins and Lindler and the like. Nobody took us seriously."

It *would* have been nice, I thought. Probably, we should've had second or third. But be as it was, the pups had done themselves proud. Served notice.

I smiled, tipped my head in mute satisfaction.

"They knew we were here," I said.

~ CHAPTER 5 ~

THE FOLLOWING MONDAY WAS BROTHER'S DAY, NOT A PROCLAMATION of siblings, but a congress of friends—Roy High, myself, and Ed Boyette—the one day of every week we nooned at Jimmy Russo's Brother's Pizza Palace, across from NC State on Hillsborough Street in old Raleigh. There, in due course and sequence, we would have a garlic bread salad, a hamburger steak, a side order of spaghetti, and a ponder at the State of the Union. Roy and Ed were coworkers at the Office of State Personnel downtown, and invariably, within the space of a week, the three of us had assembled an agenda of sufficient notoriety for a convention. Once the quorum was established and proceedings opened, topics could be floated in order of personal imperative, without table limits—save politics and women—considerations of such complexity, unchecked, as to inexpeditiously exhaust the lunch hour. Each issue was wrung dry in the progression of its priority, and barring the occasional filibuster, normally concluded within the session. Now, however, a chasm yawned.

For three consecutive weeks, the secondary agenda had been stymied by a bill before the floor soliciting fitting registered names for two English setter pups. There would have been three, but you will remember that Beda, aka Warrior Maiden, was titled at whelp by a higher authority. Which was as well, since the stipulations called for a formality boundaried not only by the three words and twenty-one letters of the American Field Dog Stud Book, the body of auspices, but moreover by the sophistication and personality of the applicants. Coming up with the two, forbid three, had proven so formidable a task as to deplete list after list of possibilities by all parties to the proceedings. Already of precedential urgency due to delay, the matter had become all the more prodigious given exploits of the yet-to-be-christened, the one in particular, at Saturday's Chesterfield Trial.

Now Chairman Boyette waited politely as Jimmy Russo personally delivered the iced tea and salads, tarrying ex officio to relay the price of potatoes in Denmark, before gaveling the assembly to order.

So tediously entrenched was the issue that an introduction was superfluous.

"How about Double Time," he proposed forthrightly, dispensing of parliamentary palaver.

"Or Double Quick," Roy High augmented.

"Or Lickety Split," Ed jinked, rebounding.

"Well . . . pretty go-o-od," I allowed with the hesitancy of doubt. "Lickety Split's too coarse."

"Fast Pitch, then," Roy spurted. Roy was an ingrained sports fan.

"Raceaway!" Ed proclaimed.

"Better," I decided. Still with reservation.

"Flash Dance. Quicksilver. Grass Fire." Ed spurted appellations like machine-gun fire. Roy listened silently, a glint in his eye.

"Uhhmmn . . ." None of them bowled me over.

"Good grief," Ed sighed mournfully, dazed and baffled for the dozenth time. He joined Roy in silence, took a bite of garlic bread.

"Won't work," I concluded.

The waitress arrived with the hamburger steaks and spaghetti. The dishes lay cooling on the table, though no one ventured to eat. Ed finally lifted a fork. It dangled over his plate in suspension, waiting politely for an opening. Roy and I were still latched to the purpose, like a bulldog that won't leggo of the bull. Roy was up to something. I could tell. Thirty seconds drug by, the two of us deep in thought. Ed Boyette still held hopefully to the fork.

"Speed Deed," Ed gambled desperately, glancing at his spaghetti.

I shook my head. Ed rolled his eyes. "What month is this?" he moaned.

Roy leaned suddenly across the table, fixing me with his eyes.

"Just how fast *is* this dog?" he asked.

As suddenly, I jerked my attention left, staring.

"Did you see *THAT!*" I shouted.

"See what?!" both sputtered at once, searching vainly. Ed's fork clattered to the floor.

"*That's* how fast," I said calmly.

Roy grinned. Ed glowered, picking up and examining his fork, hailing the waitress for another.

Reaching inside his coat, Roy withdrew a folded piece of notepaper. Neatly he undid it, making a production of palming out the wrinkles over the table. I knew he'd been holdin' out. He sheltered the paper for a moment with one hand, then discreetly reversed it and pushed it slowly toward me with the index finger of the other. At the top of the page was a single name: Zip Zap.

Zip Zap . . . *Zip Zap!* It was perfect . . . *forever* perfect.

"Hallelujah!" Ed exclaimed, stabbing the fork into his spaghetti.

"*Where'd* you come up with that?" I asked excitedly.

"Deep left field," Roy exclaimed, as excited as I was.

"There was this left fielder in the thirties, played for the Dodgers, like zip . . . zap—could steal a base. Drove the pitchers crazy. Held the League record for something like six years runnin'."

"It's great," I marveled. It was Pat. Up the near side and down the further.

"Great," I repeated. Roy radiated triumph.

"Now come up with somethin' as good for Thane," I challenged. The grin on Ed's face wilted to a horseshoe.

"Well, maybe I will," Roy declared. "There's this rookie quarterback makin' news with San Francisco. You can book it he'll do big things. Name of Joe Montana."

"Bingo!" He'd done it. Again.

"Right on," Ed proclaimed, ladling in another round of spaghetti.

Roy leaned back, beaming, smug as a mouse in malt. I was tickled pink. Ed forked in another huge mouthful of spaghetti.

"Hot dog," the Chairman murmured, his mouth stuffed. "Next week we can plow anew. What'll it be? Floor's open."

"How about Connie Gentry?" I suggested.

Roy grinned. "Second," he submitted soundly.

Visions of a heavenly body orbited the table.

"Uhhhuuhhmmm," the Chairman warned, swiping his mouth with his napkin, "we may have to suspend the clock for that one."

"What the hell," he decreed. "We need a holiday."

Three weeks later, before the same quorum, I presented the Registration Certificates warranting Zip Zap, Warrior Maiden, and Joe Montana as duly accepted and recorded upon the august scrolls of the Stud Book.

A hail and toast, and November Setters launched officially its first trilogy of field-trial contenders.

~ CHAPTER 6 ~

OF THE SEVERAL REVELATIONS OF THE CHESTERFIELD TRIAL, NONE loomed more imperative than the need for bigger and more diverse training grounds. The little loop behind the boarding stable had been fine for beginnings, but we had outgrown it now, and if we were to propel ourselves onward and upward, new grounds were essential. Immediately the search was mounted. Even twenty-five years ago, finding horseback grounds for developing class dogs was a tall order. The basic bill of lading called for at least a thousand private acres, largely unfenced, remote and free of major roads, apportioned advantageously between fields and woodlot, a long sprawling edge or two to push a tired dog onto, to ask him to reach down inside himself and stretch to a strong finish. Enough cover and cropland to hold birds and encourage some hunt with the run. You needed laid-out weed fields here and there, tawny in autumn and hoary in winter, thicketed hedgerows, and ragged, briery heads. Shaggy country, but not so copious as to prompt stickiness or self-hunting, the propensity of a dog to become overly birdy and prone to loiter, or in addition, to discover the handling immunity proffered by heavy cover and lapse increasingly careless of its handler. Both were traits that could sometimes be turned to advantage in a gun dog, but never in a field trial competitor, which must forever and quickly carry the front. And if these criteria were insufficiently formidable, the proprietor of such an elusive estate must be willing to suffer hoofprints upon his property twice a week and the handling noise, not to mention an occasional renegade derby among his laying hens.

Public powerlines on backroads could do in a pinch, and did. A new roadway in progress could suffice, one initially graded to an extensive corridor. But neither was adequate, except for purely running and conditioning, since there were no birds. We did what we had to, for a time, but we required better. Soon.

Meanwhile, the puppy wars raged on. Chesterfield had smitten me mightily. I was panting for another field trial. Almost the minute we made home, I had pored through the new *Field*, looking for the next. It happened the coming weekend, the Princeton Club, not fifty miles from home. We had a good workout the Wednesday before on some huge pastureland I had acquired sudden access to on a farm up-county called Oak Hill. It was a working cattle ranch, plenty big enough for a puppy to unravel, but bereft of croplands and quail. Pat toured it royally, Beda and Thane near as well. I was pleased, especially with Thane. I'd have to run the rascal before long; he was looking better and better. But not this time. This time we entered the girls as before, and they were ready.

The trial of the Princeton Hunt Club proved an awakening too. Of odds. Contrary to Chesterfield, the grounds were small and thickly wooded, "tight," as they say. Too tight for a class puppy stake. This wasn't solely my feeling at the time, but that of other handlers as well. Who was I then to know? I was having a hard enough time yet with the nerves. But given the supposition, I could readily tell the difference.

Surprisingly, I kept the handle on Pat but lost Beda for too precious minutes. Pat blistered the course, hunting as she went, and was on the way around again when I caught up to her after pickup. With my skin tingling and my heart in my throat. I slid off the horse, and when I caught her, I hugged her. Beda, however, dug in halfway, caught a woods trail and ran slap out of ken, showing up a holler late and a finish short. I worried over it, that it was my fault. I hadn't sent the scout fast enough, maybe. Or been alert enough to turn her when I should.

"You're the handler," Bob Lindler had said. "You've got one job—to help your dogs."

Still, my spirits were bright as a Christmas morning. Because after riding every brace this time, and believing more unequivocally, then, in faith and fair, I was certain Pat had won.

Loretta was cautious. "We thought maybe at Chesterfield, you remember?"

"This time I know," I said.

But when the whistle shrieked and we hurried over to hear the decision, our sixth pup was not among the winners. She didn't place, even second or third, and there was little rhyme or reason that I could see to the ones that did. The ribbons fell to the tight little clique of people and dogs I had watched in a hivey cluster the entire stake, and that was that. Right or wrong, good or bad, in field trialing there's no practical appeal to the decision of the judges. I've never felt more downtrodden, nor so much the outsider. It was my first taste of petty trialing politics, like upchucking a sudden, bitter spurt of bile, that burns and bites and has to go back down eventually the way it came up. If you don't believe it happens, you've never been to a field trial. You find soon enough that least said the better, to "go on down the road" and chalk it up to dues. Occasionally, you find, the scales balance your way and you win one you didn't know you did.

From the few Samaritans that day, we got a blessing of heartening comments, and I bit my lip and stuck them in the vault.

The thing I couldn't brush aside was the cloud of disappointment on my young daughter's face. "You said Patty had won," she said, the trace of a tear on her cheek.

There is the old adage of speaking too soon. Until that day, I had no idea of its origin. Surely it was born at a field trial.

I would live with that for a while, that and the writhing injustice at the pit of my stomach that an honest dog had been deprived of recognition. But neither would last much longer. The clouds were about to part, and through them the sun would break.

First it snowed. Just a few inches, but we forgot field trials and anything more serious for a day, emancipating every pup in the dozen for a romp in a blanketed meadow with the flakes whispering down. The pups, Patty included, stayed hardly more distant than our shadow, happy at burrowing under the icy mantle of grass like moles, snorting and wallowing, and rooting out the sparrows that flitted between the drifts. Emerging ice-spangled and triumphant, they exalted when the rout erupted into an open chase. While Melanie made snow angels, Loretta and I rolled a snowman with stick arms and named him Parson Brown. But we told him we were already married, thank you, so there was nothing left to do in town, and proved it with a kiss as provocative as the tingling prickle of the flakes against our faces. Afterwards, we wandered in a peripatetic caravan past huddled green cedars and crystal creeks and bright red holly berries, frolicking the afternoon away. By dusk, fifteen spirits were clean as the newfallen snow.

Snow wasn't the only thing that fell from the sky that day. Later that evening, out of the blue, I got a call from Arthur Bean. Arthur was a professional trainer of renown, also of Carolina—High Point, an hour or so west of home—which was in the lapse and tag of the nineteenth and twentieth centuries, incidentally, a mecca of southern quail hunting and field trialing that drew luminaries, dogs and people alike, far and wide. Near there, the great English pointer bitch Mary Montrose, later to be the first triple National Champion, got her early schooling, and there, in 1889, the redoubtable pointer Rip Rap first appeared in a derby stake of the old Eastern Club. And, well, I had seen Arthur Bean a few times at trials, spoken to him only casually, always liked him. He was a large man, a contemporary of Paul Long, and Paul Walker, the celebrated Tarheel Hall-of-Famer of Fast Delivery and Spacemaster notoriety. Imposing, Bean, except that he had a plump cheeriness about him, an antediluvian air like Hobart Ames or Er Shelley or Horace Lytle, and the gentility to go with it. The first time I saw him, in the early sixties, he had just climbed off a big, mahogany gelding with a white blaze. He had on lace-up, leather riding boots to the knee, a canvas coat, and a tie. A latigo flushing whip dangling from his belt. I believe maybe a Stetson, the old felt hat that sat his head. Like I said, I liked him. His call that evening, however, was about as unexpected as four leafs on a clover.

"A friend tells me you're looking for a place to run your young dogs," he said. "There's a place an hour north of you, just in Virginia. I go there some.

"Elm Hill, they call it."

Aside from a few pleasantries, and encouraging me about my dogs, that's about all he said. But it was far more than enough, more than I thanked him for. Because Elm Hill, at the time, would come close to a dream. On top of that, just as he hung up, almost before I could lift my hand from the phone, it rang anew. Bennie Yates up in the Blue Ridge, who kenneled Johnny Crockett's John, the sire of our pups, was calling with a shooting invitation at grouse. I was too Southern to turn it down.

When blessings arrive like that, in a bunch, you don't need a postmark to presume the source. Though fortune has failed, to this day, to disclose the friend who told Arthur Bean I needed a little help along then. Just another angel, I suppose.

Two days afterward, first I could, I begged a reprieve from work, loaded the mare, and drove an hour north to Virginia. It was aptly named, the hill of great elms that crowned the highest promontory of the rolling thirteen hundred or so acres that overlooked the Roanoke River just below the town of South Hill. The remains of an old mansion still haunt that hill, even now; in its day, it was the lord's manor for a working plantation of field crops: grains and legumes, tobacco, and even rice. You can sit horseback by the old house at the advent of evening, one hill over, with a mist growing on the river and the first yellow pinpricks of light sprinkled distantly about the rising dusk, and imagine. Imagine who laid the huge, old hand-fashioned, oven-kilned brick in the great double chimneys, east and west. Chimneys covered now with gray-green moss and creeper. Imagine that the land runs suddenly summer green, that the rotting, peeling clapboards over the tired, old frame of the house are abruptly bright and whitewashed again, that the dilapidated roof and palisades of the porch stand as firmly as Virginia militia. See the gay lights of the ballroom through the window, smell the wisteria, hear the multitudinous murmur of blissful voices, the clop of prancing horses as carriages approach in succession up the fading tawny avenue between the grand, old trees. Chords of welcome. The strike of a fiddle.

There's the silhouette of Colonel Hambelton and Major Tredlock, their ladies, on the veranda. His daughter, the young woman of your wishing, waits alongside. There's a boast of Confederate gray about the yard and grounds. Smooth the lapels of your uniform, set your hat, straighten your sash and saber. Spur up your horse. Proudly now, you're Jeb Stuart Cavalry. It's time. Time to ride smartly in.

It was like that for me when first I saw Elm Hill. More so when later I would ride the National Championship over the Ames Plantation at Grand Junction; the storied old Continental Trial about Dixie, the Livingston holding near Monticello; the South Carolina Shooting Dog and Derby Classics at the venerable Belmont Estate near Savannah; the National Amateur Shooting Dog Free-for-All over Sedgefields, in the black-ground of

Alabama; and the fabulous wild bobwhite holdings of Blue Springs, Pinebloom, and Ichaway in the old-line Thomasville-Albany-Bainbridge plantation belt of south Georgia, the "bird-dog capital of the world." Each has a story, a captivating tale of passion, grace, and glamour. Spun from the saddle of an easygoing walking horse on the heels of a hard-going bird dog. A story that continues today. Fabled and haunting, the natural affinity and century or so that bind pointing-dog trials and antediluvian holdings, particularly through the Old South. Not only a quintessential piece of field-trialing heritage, but perhaps the most alluring. For it was that genesis, a classic morning just after the Civil War, when an avid coterie of sportsmen from the Volunteer State gathered on the old Greenslaw Plantation near Memphis to amicably wager their best plantation shooting dogs.

It was easy to forget for wistful moments that first day at Elm Hill that the plantation had lapsed over 120 years to a state game management area, and that game commission trucks, not horse-drawn carriages, now traveled its paths. In compensation, its contemporary purpose had been given largely to field trialing, and the grounds were planted and managed not only to steward the wild game that descended on, but to perpetuate quality pointing-dog trials as well. From a hub below the old mansion, three one-hour shooting-dog courses had been described, each traversing a meandering loop over and about the rolling hills or long river bottom before returning to its point of origin. Within the sprawl of each course were different circumstances of terrain and travail, ready to test not just the bird-finding acumen of canine competitors, but equally their handling response and fortitude, and to that objective each presented a slightly different challenge. The difference would become the luck of the draw, the random lottery that before every trial determines which two dogs and their handlers will be paired as a brace. Brace by brace the dogs are run, and a fickle congress of performance and fate determines the outcome. In addition to the number of smaller stakes contested over its grounds each year, Elm Hill showcased Virginia's flagship renewal, the Eastern Open Shooting Dog Championship.

By the state of Virginia's applaudable foresight, quite atypically and aside from trial dates, the Elm Hill grounds were also available to dog training. When I left that evening for home, the reverie of the old homeplace on the hill a dying silhouette against the purple of twilight, I was dizzy as a wish in a whirlwind. 'Cause it was all coming true. Good fortune was handing us the means over the mountain. A place to pair hard work and a dream.

We trained there for the first time within the week. Loretta packed a picnic basket, and we staked the dogs out under the elms by the old house. Dolly and I ran them one by one, for each was too much dog now for a coupling, and emboldened by the throw of the grounds, they threw themselves splendidly against it. Tit for tat, Beda and Thane reached into themselves and were thrilling. Beda a stanza of animation as she flashed about the rolling sprawl of the high ground, showed on the next hill, then the next, and rolled on. Thane, in a brass-and-class charge to the summit of the long, ascending knoll across the lake east of the old tenant cabin, was lost ahead and away along a distant edge of cedars, appeared next upon the cap of the hill, then shot into and out the far end of an expansive low-ground depression shaped like a bowl. Pretty nice.

At noon, Loretta spread a checkered tablecloth under the trees. Set out and opened the basket, handed me a sandwich. She was as taken by then with the place as I had been. She and Melanie had wandered what was left of the yard and gardens, loitered and peered about the old mansion. It was an idyllic day for early February, springlike, sun streaming down from a bell-clear sky. Here and there, daffodils were springing up through the moist black soil, the hint of a blossom-to-be swelling the color of a ripening banana upon a tender green stem.

"Imagine when first they were planted," Retta said.

"Generations and a century ago," I suggested. "They carry on. Longer than the people.

"Don't move off or die away."

"There's still jasmine about the colonnade," my wife added. "How lovely it must have smelled on a summer's evening," she wished, "jasmine and gardenia and lilac and sweet Betsy."

"Ummmhn."

The mare was loosely ground-tied, munching the scattered clumps of emerging green grass and onions. Melanie was pulling sprouts and Indian-giving them to her, afraid for her fingers. Wiping them on her T-shirt. She'd reek of onions, but who cared?

"Hold them in the flat of your hand," I instructed, "like this."

"That way she won't chomp you."

My daughter did as told, squealing gleefully as the soft lips of the horse nuzzled and gathered the grass, tickling her palm.

After a lazy lunch, I ran Pat. I had waited anxiously for this. I had saved the river bottom, a part of Course Two. It was near a half mile long, and Pat reached, faster and further than ever she had before, blazing to its limits, rimming the distant gray edge, a white speck against infinity. Coming around on her own, catching the closure of the land, she dashed on through the chute into the Silo Field, whirling and flash-pointing abruptly, then colliding with a small covey of quail on the hedgerow before I could get there.

It was by a sum the best workout we had ventured; it and the ones to follow would catapult us aptly into contention. With each, my faith in our dogs soared. They had the stuff. I had seen just enough dogs to know. The greatest challenge, I knew, was mine. Did I have what it would take, for Pat particularly, to groom them to peak and finish, to put a patent on the patina?

∿ CHAPTER 7 ∿

AT FOUR TWENTY SATURDAY MORNING, WE LOADED UP AND LEFT
again for South Carolina, the puppy stake of the Sumter County Shooting
Dog Association. Mill Creek Park was a pretty place to run a dog. It was a
midstate mix of mostly pines over low grass and sedge; heads of lesser hard-
wood that broke intermittently to open, sandy farmland; and scattered
stately live oaks spangled with Spanish moss. There were a few palmettos
sprinkled around, and through it all ran the small watercourse of the same
name that kept it alive. We pulled onto the grounds about sunup. The pale
yellow rays were just breaching the pines, spilling through in long, low
shafts, coaxing tendrils of mist from the forest floor. Through the open window, I could hear from a distance the plaintive *wheowwh-wit* of a single
quail. The morning was cool. Round and about you could see on the air the
gentle breathing of horses waiting tack and groom, the steam rising lazily
from fresh manure. Hear whinnies offered and answered, stiff words to a
paint gelding that was fidgeting and fretting. People were pulling dogs off
trailers, the excited canines collared and crow-hopping on hind legs the several feet to stake-out chains. I recognized Bob Lindler and Dub Watkins, to
one side, a couple of others from Chesterfield I couldn't put a name with. I
threw up a hand and got one back.

Melanie was waking, forcing herself off Mama's lap and rubbing her
eyes with her fists, her face pouty and red.

"Morning . . . glory," I teased.

She gave me a useless look and collapsed into Loretta's arms.

After I untrailered the mare, we checked the board. Beda had the first
brace, Pat the last. We were still redshirting Thane. I looked for Duke, found
him in the third.

The people were fresh and friendly. We first met Ed and Ingrid Turner there. They were a pleasant young couple close our age, in love with their dogs as nearly. Ed was tall and lanky, a natural cowboy. Ingrid was beautifully Scandinavian, the height of her husband, with long, lovely, straw blond hair. They were running pointers, derbies then, I believe. Our meeting would be fortuitous. Ed would scout occasionally for me over the next few years, I for him when Ingrid couldn't. We'd help each other any way we could. Bert Robinson and Gilbert Barkley were there, on hand from the open stakes concluded the day before. Bert was a young man then, already professional, but not at all snooty with it. I enjoyed his acquaintance. Gilbert I remembered from Chesterfield. Between us a few more words grew.

I was saddling the horse back of the trailer, Melanie and Loretta having breakfast in the cab of the truck, when I heard approaching footsteps, the whispery swish of chaps.

"Ready to sell that pup yet?"

Bob Lindler.

"'Bout the time Dub Watkins moves to Red China," I said.

He guffawed.

"Where's the daughter and missus?"

"Breaking a biscuit in the front of the truck. Have one?"

"Nawthanks."

"There're a few burrs around," he warned. "Might want to braid up your horse's tail."

He showed me how. Looked pretty neat; somebody might think I know something this time, I thought.

"Need a scout?" Bob asked.

"Think I have one. Much obliged." Ed Turner had offered, I explained.

"Well, Dub roaded Duke all week, he ought to be ready." If it was a comment calculated to make me uneasy, it worked.

"Yeah."

"We like to road the few days before, save the running for the trial."

We were doing the opposite, running our dogs mostly, roading more occasionally. I hadn't noticed yet that it was hurting us. It would leave me wondering, but not for long. The answer would come shortly.

"Well, good luck," he offered, turning to leave.

"Same," I said, and meant it mostly.

My wife and daughter joined me. "Saw Bob Lindler," she said.

"Uh-huh. Still wants Pat."

Melanie was bright awake now, quick and clever.

"Mine's," she said.

Only a few minutes before the breakaway. I led the horse around, let her relax and exhale, tightened the girth. The pups were up on their toes, raising a fuss, ready to go. Beda was panting and trembling, fighting the chain. She drove me crazy with that.

Loretta kneeled between Beda and Pat, consoled her warrior maiden, told both pups something secretly.

"It'll happen today," she said, regaining her feet.

I looked at her with the question. She tendered nothing but the gleam in her eye, smiled, and walked away.

Ten minutes later, Beda left the breakaway like she was needed in Newark, sailed through the sparse pines of the opening two hundred yards, and hung the edge of the first big field like she was tacked to it, speeding hard and away. Her bracemate, a lemon pointer, was trailing, yipping sharply of frustration and desire. Elm Hill had helped. Beda carried the long edge three-quarters of the journey before looping off laterally into the open field.

"Whuup, hey!" I hollered at her, hit the whistle, and she whipped back onto the edge. This time to the end, before hitting the next woods block and fanning left and right as she began to hunt. She was holding a nice handling distance, ranging forward, patterning beautifully through the pines. They must be liking her, I was thinking, feeling higher by the moment. I let her take it on, on her own, for the pace was brisk and she was doing great. But then the demanding final quarter of the course asked her spirit for more than her body could give, and she began to tire and shorten a bit, still laying out and going nicely, but with a little less than the punching drive a challenging puppy needs. Her finish was pleasing but not commanding.

She came to me happily. Hassling heavily. She tried so hard. Knowing now what I didn't then, Beda was shaping up a better derby than puppy. She had style to spare, and the hunt, and most enough run. Best of all, she was biddable. I would be able to keep her later, maintain contact and control, when Pat would sometimes be too hot to hold on the invisible string of rapport that coupled handler and dog in the fever of a fiercely contested heat. The puppy trials would lay the groundwork.

Loretta and Melanie were waiting as I roaded her in. Loretta dropped to folded knees and welcomed the puppy into her arms. "Little warrior maiden," she teased, hugging her close and squeezing. Looking up, her eyes were questioning.

"Pret-t-y nice," I said.

"Enough?" she asked.

"Don't know," I answered honestly. "Maybe needed to be a little stronger at the finish. You know how it goes. We'll see."

"Patty hadn' run yet," Melanie reminded.

"You're right, Sweetie, she certainly hasn't."

There was a setter in the next brace, a pup from the string of Sim Wright, that did a creditable job as well. Maybe shaded Beda a hair in the last minute of the heat. I had seen Sim's name in the *Field* a lot. Figured he ran a good dog.

Then Duke was along in the third, took Watkins's whistle and never looked back. I could concentrate on his race this time, riding with Bob in the gallery. He was a big, powerful, piston-driving dog that ate up the course in great, gobbling strides. He made it look easy. At a distance, when a dog goes really well, gait efficient and flying, he appears to literally glide over the ground. He's cast so smoothly, the rhythm of his beat so faultless, that there's no perception of pumping feet, just the blur of his body over the turf as if it's traveling on air. Duke had the beat and the bounce to go with it, and it was easy to see why he had been so formidable all season. His bracemate was hanging tough, but hopelessly outdogged. I looked over at Lindler midway through the heat; there was a Madonna-like smile on his face.

The intrepid pointer conquered the throw of the big fields about as easily as if they'd been five-acre garden plots, broke the edges only when hunting logic suggested, navigated the tight spots with aplomb, and flung himself into an ambitious finish that roached your neck hackles. When the judges asked him up, there was little doubt. He'd set a mark.

"Impressive, Bob," I granted.

Lindler squinched his eyes and nodded, smiling confidently. He'd earned the right.

My stomach had lost its hold on gravity, was floating around in sickening aerials. You watch a dog go out like that and set the high-water mark for a stake, and you're yet to run, it does that to you. Pushes you to the wall and punches you hard in the gut. Tells you you're less than you are. You have to fight it. Kick it back in the balls, never stop believing in yourself, or your dogs. Unfettered with the human frailty of pride, the dogs would do what they were born to. I kept telling myself that, but still I couldn't check the nerves. I almost wished I were elsewhere, not putting myself through this, somewhere peaceful and unrepressed. Almost. But this is what we had worked for. You can never know what you're made of until you truly ask.

Then I thought of Pat's name for really the first time, when it counted. Zip Zap.

I led Pat to the breakaway, my stomach in knots but an augury on my lips. "Look out, Lazarus, here we come."

I whoaed the sixth pup at the go line, handed Loretta the check cord, and climbed onto the mare. First thing I did was look for Ed Turner. He was ready, three horses over. He acknowledged with a nod. Our bracemate was led to place, another stilt-legged pointer. It was the standard, it seemed. The judges were up, but there was a short delay and a moment of bedlam while the opposing handler disciplined a recalcitrant mount. The gelding reared against the reins and shied. Pat looked back and away from the commotion with a jerk, then leaned to the front, her body quivering to go. I could see the scare in my wife's eyes that she was going to lose her. She had a death hold on the puppy's collar. Melanie was standing alone, a few feet away from her mother, tense and still, hands balled to her lips. Small, scared, and lonely. Finally the horse was steadied, the handler aboard and stationed behind his dog.

There was a ripple of loose jokes about a rodeo.

"Okay, Gentlemen, last brace, puppy stake," a judge announced cordially. "We're waitin' on you."

Not for long. I had learned. I hit the whistle flat-out.

Pat was gone like the last glimpse before doom. In the doubled four-beat of a walking horse, she was a blur, tearing through the skim of pines, stretching for the first big field. By the time we got there too, she was a click-a-lick speck burning the long edge, three-quarters to its end. Her bracemate caught up once, five minutes on, when the little setter whipped laterally into a corner to check a fragrant breeze. After that I never saw the pointer again. When Pat next appeared, it was far to the front. She paused, checking for me, caught my halloo, and hurled hard away. The only thing in her wake was a cloud of dust.

Another turn of pines—I lost her for a time. When we broke through, she was a fading paragon of motion, eclipsing another great field, pressing its end. If only I could hang on to her.

I caught Ed Turner at the periphery of my vision. He was riding the flank, glued to her like a hawk, ready to go at first summons.

"*EEEyeahh-now!*" Urgently, I called on her. Pretty as a pearl on a string, she swung the distant corner, flared across the front, poured it on into the next head of woods.

"*Yes.*"

My heart was slamming my chest. I was overexcited, riding too boldly ahead of the judges. I reined the horse back, trusted my dog, just let her roll. She was on course, keeping the ten-to-two-o'clock front, bouncing off all the corners. Hunting and reaching.

It was Pat and it was brilliant.

At time she was blistering the far gray edge, chewing up the shreds of the course, her flag snapping in rhythm with my pulse as she drove power-fully home for more.

"*Pick 'em uuupp.*"

Turner had to ride up and tell me. I was conscious only of my dog, taken with the trance of her.

"*That* little dog can stroll," Ed sputtered ahead of a big smile. "I was sure hopin' I didn't have to go after her."

"Unless you're goin' around twice, you prob'ly ought to pick her up," he followed.

Still it hadn't registered. I was watching for my puppy, out of ken again in distant pines.

"Time!" he called, stabbing at his watch.

Jerked to the moment like I'd hit the end of a check cord, I grinned sheepishly and spurred my horse to a gallop, racing away. My only thought to gather Pat safely to hand. Quickly Ed pulled alongside, his gelding matching the mare stride for stride.

"The land swings right past those pines," he yelled; "likely she did too. There's a woods path, in the corner," he motioned, his words broken by the jolt of the hoofbeats. "It'll break into the open beyond the trees, 'bout where I'm guessing she'll be."

We pressed that way, hauling up as we got closer. Only seconds of hesitation and Ed found the path, checked his horse, and shot through. The mare was hard on his hooves. Almost as quickly, Ed reined violently, jerking the gelding to his haunches, into a sliding halt. As brutally, I had to put the brakes on the mare; still, she almost ran over him. When the chaos subsided, there stood Pat in the middle of the path ahead, happy as a jaybird. Ed had almost run over her. I was happiest of all—that the calamity had been averted, of course, but more that she was on her way back to find me. That she wasn't just running wild, but cared, in a proper moment, where I was.

I got down and gathered my puppy, thanked Ed again, and slipped on the roading harness. "Good job," he said as he rode away.

It had been good. Real good. I was still sky-high, heart pounding in thudding beats against my chest. When Ed was swallowed by the pines, I got back down on my knees and thanked Pat for that, sharing secret words that she was the sun and the moon and the bridge between. Then I climbed on the mare, and we all pranced proudly back to the barn.

Loretta read immediately the elation in my eyes, but the presumption passed silently between us, for we were afraid to speak of it. Fate rode a fickle horse in field trialing.

Melanie, however, was undaunted.

"Patty won?" she said. It was more dogma than query, as in the moment before jubilation. I hadn't the heart to refute it.

"Yes, Sweetie . . . Patty won." Regardless.

Minutes later, it was fact, though not before a press of uncertainty, for after the whistle had shrieked and the small coterie had gathered, third place had been announced and only the two remained.

"Second place, Amateur Puppy," the Trial Chairman called boldly . . . pausing a lengthy second as he dropped his eyes to confirm again the name on the judge's slip . . . "*Pat,* Mike Gaddis." There was a rousing round of applause and I was stepping forward to accept a congratulation and a trophy, and when I stepped back, my little daughter was hitched by one hand to Mama's pant leg, grinning widely, and Loretta's eyes were bright and wet with joy. And the one and only thing wrong with the moment was that my puppy wasn't there to share it. I handed the trophy to Melanie. She reached for it and clutched it like a favorite toy.

"First place . . . Duke, Dub Watkins." It mattered, but it didn't. The first hand from the gallery was Bob Lindler's, and Zip Zap had her first win.

It mattered less moments later when, as we walked back to the trailer, one of the judges took the trouble to add a comment to his accord. "Mr. Gaddis, you might know . . . it was close, very close."

Then Dub himself, in his inimitable way, submitted an allowance.

"I watched your dog," he said, "to see if she was just runnin' or huntin' some too."

"She was huntin'," he admitted.

The sixth puppy turned a lot of heads that day, and a lot of hearts. When we pulled out for home, Melanie was tottering on the seat between us, at the brink of sleep. Still clinging to the trophy.

"Want me to take it, Sweetie?" I offered. "We can put it here on the dash, where you can see it."

She looked at me with doubtful, droopy eyes. "Mine's," she said, clutching it more tightly.

~ CHAPTER 8 ~

MOMENTUM'S A FUNNY THING. ONCE IT FINALLY WRESTLES GRAVITY to the ground, it's a formidable force. A week later, Pat won again, this time against thirteen seasoned puppies at Spartanburg. Again second to Duke's first. But the tide was swinging; on the scale of justice, reputations were beginning to balance. In the rain at the Mid-Carolina two weeks later, it was another second, Duke and Pat, but oh *so* close.

Before every trial now, Dub would grin and ask me, "When ya runnin' the good one?"

And I'd grin back and say, "They're all good."

For Beda was running well too, just unable to put quite enough power and reach with the class. By then we were fielding Thane also, and with a couple trials more, he would be a force. On a given day, he could most, but not quite, give Pat what-for.

"No," Dub would jest, "I mean *the good 'un.*"

Back at Elm Hill the following week, we avoided another calamity. Pat got out of hand again, managed the fence, and crossed Virginia 4, a perimeter highway. But I was right on her heels this time, warding off traffic and retrieving her safely. Good fortune was with me, thank God, riding double. It's a precarious trip, the long and haul, with a really powerful dog. Figuratively, over the years, I would die a dozen deaths.

But thirteen days later came Fort Mill, and all the anxiety siphoned to ascendancy. At Fort Mill, we were invincible.

Our littlest setter was a juggernaut. The genius flared and she claimed the course, searching and reaching—ever reaching. The throw of the grounds threaded a prelude of hardwoods, then broke dramatically into open, sprawling bottomland pasture, meandered by a creek run and interspersed with hedgerows. A dog could not hide there; its every notion, do or die, an exposé. Out of the hardwoods, Pat ricocheted off the first several hedgerows, then caught the grand edge of the pasture and reached away, leaving her bracemate to history. Stretching and stretching until she was a tiny white dot at the extremes, and we sat there spellbound—handler, judges, and gallery—watching every lick, while the power of her desire carried her farther and farther, to the distant berm of the highway, which was thought safely remote. Until she put my heart in my throat with the terror that she would go up and over into the busy traffic. You could see it on a Lilliputian scale, car after car, speeding heedlessly by, so far away you could barely hear the noise. You could feel the tension singing through the gallery, hear murmurs of trepidation, and with all my might I called on her.

"*Hheeeyeeah-now!*"

At the cliff of desperation, she whipped abruptly east, while I slumped in the saddle with relief. Catching the underrim of the roadway and the adjoining fenceline, she burned its edge like she was strung to it. Flying, driving, gathering up the ground, redefining the course to the dimensions of her determination. Now, at the limits of the property, you could barely see her, like a speck cast high in a clear blue sky that fades alternately in and out of vision. As whispers spilled anew through the gallery.

"She can run, but will she come back?" The bet was half and half.

"We were coming in to the grounds on the highway," Jim Gilmer told me afterward, "and below we could see this little white setter at the clip of the shoulder, at the last of the big bottom.

"She had a black rump patch and she was flying, a-lick-a-stroke. Lookin' good a-doin' it. We could barely see ya-all, just a knot of horses— we thought—way the other side of the pasture. I figured it must be the puppy stake, and I told the rest of 'em . . . if that dog's not lost, she's winning the trial."

She was flung as far as she could be now, into the last distant corner, and in the next few moments the story would be told.

Once again, I summoned the might of my lungs and questioned her.

"*Yeeeahoww, Paaattt! Yheaayyupp!*"

She had disappeared. Moments raced by, long anxious moments, and again I called. Long and loud.

And suddenly a tiny fleck of white emerged at the gray sketch of the bottom, ten o'clock ahead and closing, turning for the front. I glanced quickly at my watch. Twenty minutes were gone. Still the judges said nothing. I urged the mare, struck up a fast walk, moved forward to a newer vantage. Behind me, horses followed. Nobody wanted it to end, and still Pat pulled away, far to the front now, as powerfully as she had started. A hundred more yards now and she would fade into the trees.

"Pick 'im uppp."

At last. I slapped the mare to a gallop and made for my dog. When I caught up, she was happily at the trailer, in Loretta's arms. She had taken the bold expanse of the holding, and would I let her, could have done it again.

It was unequivocally Zip Zap, and she won the stake outright, dominating twenty-one of the best trial-hardened puppies on the Palmetto circuit. Including Saw Buck, who in the eleventh hour had edged Duke for points puppy of the year. So eloquent was the final stroke of her triumph that it sank as evocatively upon all who saw it as the conclusive line of a great sonnet. Even I had sat in the saddle near the end of her heat, stunned with the intensity of her brilliance. Struck with the same recurring enigma. *How* was it physiologically possible for organic energy to combust so powerfully and profoundly in nerves, flesh, and bones? Taken with the same answer. *It wasn't.* Incredibly, she was getting stronger and stronger, the melding of supreme athleticism with burgeoning trial savvy. I could see it every workout, every trial.

Before we left, Judge Bob Tate swung by. "Hang on to that little setter, Mr. Gaddis," he encouraged. "Barring misfortune, she's going a long, long way."

Please God, I prayed.

After Fort Mill, though, the climax of our puppy season was frenetic. At Alamance County, Pat outran the course, was too long out of ken. My fault. I had no business running her there. It was yet another lesson, the hard way. Joe Montana, however, found the tighter round quite to his suiting, wowed the judges, and garnered a win to match his ego. There'd be no living with him now. Beda didn't make the trip, and I missed her. Our little warrior maiden had become a woman. Indisposed with estrus, she waited unhappily at home in the kennel. At the Sandlapper Trial the next day, Thane excelled once more. Intrepidly he devoured the course, and I thought well for him.

But he was deprived, perhaps not properly, of a placement. The sixth pup took another grand tour, got off on birds, and was pointing when the scout found her. They'd all been getting a little more birdy the last few weeks. It was hard to be disappointed, for it was in most ways desirable, a good omen and rite of passage. A message to their handler.

Once more as a juvenile, the rump-spot setter would win superbly at Greenville, Tennessee, but puppy days were past.

It was hard to let them go—as if we had a choice—though thrice they had tempted us to the brink of death, and more times than that had inflicted dreadful risk. For, as regularly, they had gifted occasions of tremendous pride and incomparable joy. It was like exile from a fabled and enchanting land, one you had waited your life to reach, knowing as it faded to the past—no matter your heart's wish—you could never return.

For all that, life would lapse now to a thing of even greater sadness. On May 6, a day bittersweet, we celebrated a birthday. The one-year grace period we had established for the sovereignty of the litter had passed. It was time to part soon with those we would not keep.

Looking back, it was a thing we could not do again. A thing we have not done since. I fail drearily at culling puppies, for first there is the impossible task of placing a market value on a piece of my heart, and second and most dreadful, handing to fate unknown something that worships me. Suffering the shattering trust as I look for the last time into frightened, yet ever-adoring eyes.

Every occasion since, Loretta has said it best, cupping before her Buddha-like in a palm a six-week pup, looking into its chubby little face, and saying to me, "I cannot tell it 'I love you' and send it away."

So we have not, except to very dear and trusted friends, and I must tell you someday of the joys, and the sorrows, of siblings who are granted a lifetime together. Of the revelations that unfold with each little life beyond eight weeks that prove to you how ambiguous your assessment was at the seventh. Of the challenge in nurturing a half dozen budding personalities past addled essence to a peculiar facet of excellence. For only in the rarest of cases do you get a Patty. So nearly faultless. One dog that so completely possesses at birth all the many attributes for greatness. Mostly, they're like us, a little less than perfect and a lot more than flawed. Given the chance, some will flower most beautifully in a second spring.

But then, we had felt we must. So we set stoically about the task. Only a small percentage of youngsters are geared by disposition or ability for the rhyme and rigors of field trialing. Most will be cast upon fortune as gun dogs. Granted kind, patient, and well-reasoned training, ample opportunity on game, the majority can become very fine ones. So it would be, hopefully, with Joe, Suzy, Dax, Luke, Jake, and Storm. Jill and Ben would pursue the same purpose but remain with us, and Hank would aspire to grouse with his godfather, Bennie Yates, in the swell and pitch of the Blue Ridge. Since we would suffer the rest to leave, we wanted dearly to give them a boost, our best at ensuring their welfare and happiness.

In the minutes I could wrest from the stringent demands of a field-trial campaign, I had strained to make time for the gun pups. To take them out, encourage them further to hunt, let them chase and learn that things with wings, no matter how good they smell, must be stalked and held to wait a bit. Else they fly away. With that smattering of knowledge, most were beginning to point and ponder before a pounce. It was time now for school drills. Time to yank them away from fields and fowl for a semester, put them in the backyard, and further the patience in the ponder.

For all of June and July, we trained diligently on "Whoa," "Heel," and "Come," the fundamental triad of commands in a bird dog's orders. "Whoa" for the understanding to hold firmly in place, do not move. "Heel" for the willingness to walk regimentally by their master's side. "Come" to return, please, when called. We made serious fun of it. In Loretta's classroom were Ben, Hank, Joe, Jill, Luke, and Dax. To mine came Pat, Thane, Beda, Storm, Jake, and Suzy. Melanie, of course, tutored Patty as well. In homeroom every evening at suppertime, we traded the progress of our pupils, bragging on the precocity of the fast studies, searching the way forward with those who trailed the norm.

"Dax about jerks me down every time I whisper 'Heel,'" Retta fretted. "Whatda I do?"

"Throw a half hitch round his waist and jerk back," I advised. "Pinch his wuttle sing."

She laughed and threw a dish towel at me. "I might pinch yours."

"How's Pat doin'?" she wanted to know.

"Two gold stars and a demerit. She's not too good on 'Come.'"

"Imagine!" Retta teased.

"Melanie's workin' on it," I promised, pinching my daughter on the shoulder. She threatened me with a fork.

"Suzy-Q's a whiz," I said. "Right now she's valedictorian."

"Whoa now, I don't know," Retta defended. "Wait'll you see Ben. He's Mama's little man."

"Wouldn't have anything to do with him sittin' in your lap twenty minutes Sunday, would it?"

"Are you accusing me of favoritism?"

"Yes."

By the end of the quarter, we could agree, all were achieving admirably. The balance of the lesson plan would be composed of repetition and polish, third-quarter introduction of a blank pistol shot, and a practicum on pigeons, all in postulation for a simultaneous graduation the end of the term.

Two weeks out, the faculty suffered a setback. Melanie came down with a blistering case of chicken pox and had to miss several training days. Bedside, at its worst, I gazed down into her small face. It was flushed and swollen, the soft beauty of it blemished mercilessly by angry red welts. She was sobbing softly. How I wished I could cleanse the hurt away.

She looked up at me through weeping eyes. "Will Patty graduate?" she asked.

I could feel the burn at the bridge of my nose. Caressing her forehead lightly, I brushed back the wispy blond hair that glinted like corn silk in the glow of the table lamp.

"Of course she will, Sweetheart. You've done a good job. She's ahead of the class. I'll fill in while you're out, and you'll be back in jig time to finish up. She'll be right there with the rest of them."

She seemed to accept that. Had nothing more to say. Just lay there and looked up at me, meek and miserable, and I could do little more than look back. But that was wrong. There had to be something. Five minutes later, I was back with the sixth puppy.

Through the hurt, her eyes brightened. "Patty!" she exclaimed, and then the two of them were arm in arm. With love you can forget the pain.

Come the end of July, the entire class matriculated with honors, each receiving as a graduation gift a new latigo collar. Upon each brass plate was engraved name, honor, and date. But the celebration was less than jubilant. Behind it lay the parting.

We composed the ad shortly afterward. You never really know a hard place until you're pulled up against it. When we held it in our hand, finished on a piece of paper, we almost decided not to run it. To just let life wash on and sweep all of us with it, and bear it as we may. But the nagging voice of practicality pinged away, until finally we were hounded to relent. We hadn't lived long enough then to glean the wisdom of the years, to know that if you truly want something enough, time becomes a partner and somehow you'll find the way.

Sadly, on August 6, 1977, upon the cold and capricious marketplace of the world were presented six trusting setter pups:

> CLASS SETTER PUPS. Sire direct by 1970 National Champion Johnny Crockett. Dam, shooting dog extraordinary, linebred Sam L's Rebel. Strong, bold, started and stylish. All shots and wormed. $100. Caring buyers only.

When initially it appeared, the day it became reality, I felt as though I'd been stomach-punched. It was all the dread again, anviled into a living nightmare.

We tried to screen, but folks perform best on an anonymous stage. It was hard enough to interpret their sincerity, almost impracticable their commitment. Selling flesh and blood is the Devil's due, and I could imagine in good part how horribly painful and dehabilitating it must have been in olden days to sacrifice family to an auction block, to have a piece of yourself torn loose and borne away, never, no matter your wish, to be returned again. The more so when the guilt must be on your own conscious. People ask Loretta and me nowadays how it is that we've kept every pup in the last two litters. There's the answer.

For only one pup could we feel truly happy, honestly at ease. Jake, cocky little Number Five, went to live and hunt with Graham Dean, father of my old friend Jim. Graham Dean had grown up a bird hunter, much as his father and grandfather before him. In a life of love for woods and wonder, which spilled in pleasing degree to each of his three sons, birds before dogs were first water. His paradigm was a good setter, a vintage double gun, and grace before a covey rise. I never saw him shoot less gently than he dressed. Most fortunate for us and the fifth puppy was his decision for another dog. For he was in the winter of his years then, uncertain of his mettle for another rambunctious puppy. Jake would be his last.

Upon Jake he would dote, lavishing the greatest attention, and passion, of his shooting life. They would share it together, no more given than returned. The rapport between them was a lovely thing. Most wonderfully of all, I would tag along on many occasions, sharing a gentleman's side of a bevy rise over a crackin'-good shooting dog that came into the world through our backyard, a blind and squirming piece of puppydom no bigger than a wrung-out washcloth. I watched the precious years and seasons trail elegantly by for them, and thanked God again and again for the fate that saw them together.

Among the most poignant volumes of my sporting library is some movie footage from their declining days, illuminated by the mellow timbre of a November afternoon, the mellifluous voice of Andy Williams, and the haunting mood and melody of:

> *"Memories, pressed between the pages of my mind,*
> *Memories, sweetened through the ages just like wine . . ."*

In the closing scene, the two of them trickle away through a ragweed field, down the dirt path by an old tobacco barn, an old man bent slightly by the lessons of the years and a double gun, behind an aged white-and-ticked setter with a jaunty-still lick to his tail.

The others scattered with strangers here and yon—handsome Dax, James Bond–gorgeous Dax; Luke of the gentle soul; gentleman Joe; bouncy little Suzy-Q; chic little Storm. These we would never see again. Five little lives we'd watched into this world from the first whoosh and whimper. With them went our tears and our blessing, and many's the time I have wondered, ever afraid to ask, ever afraid to know.

With a heavy heart, we turned back to a training regimen for the ones that would remain as family, looking for a way past the melancholy. Twice a week, in the cool and dew of dawn, we worked them on birds, check-cording them crosswind into a scent stream, encouraging a crisp point, and building the beginnings of staunchness by recalling from their schooling the word "Whoa!" It was mesmerizing, the split-instant thrill of arrested motion, the moment rampant energy was slammed by instinct into motionless yearning and a puppy was transfixed into an art form by a whiff of molecules. A force so small yet powerful, it left them stricken and fearful to move, so tautened them they quivered, so bemused them they panted before it bug-eyed and drooling.

"Whoa, Pat. Whoa, Jill."

There was the privilege of the flush as well, the lurch, whirl, and whimper of hampered desire when we stepped before them, held fast the cord, and put wings to air. The fire in their eyes as they whined and watched the bird away, the bounce and hop at the pop of the pistol.

"Whoa, pup."

As the weeks turned by, the persistence of our efforts grew to progress. All were hunting freely out of hand now, dragging the cord within the confined space of the pasture fence, pointing and holding for the stint it took us to get there and claim the tag end of the rope. Pat, Beda, and Thane were scintillating, grabbing your breath with their style and intensity. It was still bolt and bounce at flush and shot. This we made only token efforts to curb, for it was much too early to demand steadiness. That was the grail, of course, in their finish, but it would be achieved in bits with tempered restraint, not wholly before their third year, until they would swell proudly before a flush, marking the birds away with just the movement of their head and eyes, the burn of their desire undiminished and banked only for the scant minutes it took to transact the flush and shot. Only until they were sent on, to race happily and boldly off to the next find. Desire, you discover, is the essence of canine brilliance, steadiness the resolution of discipline and desire. The greatest of young dogs can be reduced to ruin by careless exchange.

The desire in an exceptional pup is like a rare young wine, kegged from a proven vineyard. Nurture it slowly to perfection and it will pleasure the years, tap it prematurely and you will squander its bouquet in infancy.

Through August also, even against the sweat and swelter of dog days, we reinstituted a conditioning program. This was imperative, for many of the adolescents we would compete against in the upcoming derby stakes were being professionally hardened now under the cool mornings of the prairies, across the Dakotas, Saskatchewan, Alberta, and Manitoba. I dreamed of being there also, mostly for the advantage of the wild-bird work on the young chickens and sharptails. There was no substitute, of course, for the vast throw of the prairies upon which to cast and pattern a young dog, or the lessons of the endless wind in working and handling birds. I pined and worried over this. Our little pasture pen-bird sessions were a puny pretense. It was all we had.

But the conditioning of muscle, sinew, and lung I could do something about. In the evening, thrice a week, I would road the youngsters a half hour before the horse, purposely waiting for the build of temperature and humidity. For it was important to achieve not only superlative physical fitness, but a tolerance to heat as well. Where before they had been roaded individually, we paired them now into braces, so they might work one against the other. By September, you could see the fruit of it in the knotted, rock-hard definition of their haunches, each muscle bulging and cut apart like chiseled granite. In the comparative ease of their breathing. Dig, pull. Dig, pull. The courage of our chosen three, Pat, Beda, and Thane, was inspiring, and time and again I found it a touchstone of self-discipline, not to let up, to keep on working, to never lose sight of the dream. I see it now as clearly as then.

Sometimes I would harness the three of them in tandem, the male dog at center, females on either flank. They would fight each other for advantage, heaving and lunging to carry the momentum. Mostly it was between Pat and Thane, and neither would relent nor concede to the other any smattering of a compromise, while bravely Beda would battle back, clawing with her toenails to hold her own, sacrificing herself to manage now and then a moment of triumph. Until the contest turned gradually to an endurance fest, and once again she would have to concede to the greater physical prowess of her teammates, relaxing in the traces a moment before flinging herself again into the fray. But she never quit. Never.

When at the end of thirty or forty minutes, they were hot and tiring and deeply into themselves, I would suddenly hit the whistle. And sing to them. *"Yeeaapp!"* The effect was electrical, inciting them to reiterated energy and an explosive burst of power. Hindquarters pumped like pistons, dirt flew in the wake, and you could feel the catch of the mare as she sat back against them, steadying herself to the drag. I loved the snatch and surge of it. Midmonth, with the sweet gums beginning to color crimson at the hems, they were going forty-five minutes full tilt and, save a breather or two for the little warrior maiden, wilting not the least. Only a few weeks from the first of the derby trials, we were confident. Physically, at least.

On birds there remained a bit of conciliation. Off the check cord, all three would point them in a heartbeat, straight up and head-on. Holding them was another transaction, and we bargained stringently over it. The contention centered on respective interpretations of the word "Whoa." With typical adolescent reticence, it was the position of the pups that a degree of discretion might be exacted in practice, particularly in those moments when I might not be convenient enough to consider the difference. I, on the other hand, preferred and promoted a more definitive and less elastic understanding, translating to "Toss anchor and stay the hell in place until I can get there!"

"Well," they supposed, "that's okay, but why waste all that time for you and the horse to get here when we can put the bird out a heck of a lot quicker on our own?" They weren't old enough to cuss yet.

"Because if you do, we ain't gonna win any field trials," I said. Course, they pretended not to understand. As Harold Ray of Smith Setter fame says suspiciously, "They're just dogs."

Upon the previous position, Patty was most obdurate and persisted most stridently. In other words, after a pause that could be debated a flash point, she jumped in and busted hell out of every bird, chasing lustily, matching foot for foot every wingbeat. Given an open airfield, she was fast enough to sustain a ground position that equated with the airspeed of the flight, so that when the desperately flapping pen bird began to tire and drop altitude, she would be strategically handy to its landing. In this manner she caught several, God forbid, and was soon totally out of hand. On occasion she messed up; we got into wild birds, and they left her flat-footed. This she was disposed to think about, since it found her with less reward and greater consequence. Beda and Thane maintained similarly, but a hair less stubbornly, meeting me partway now and again. Still, something had to give.

Finally I resorted to a more colloquial argument. Each time they found cause for a unilateral flush, I proposed to the contrary and threw in an incentive. Went a lot like this:

"Whoa—Whoa—Hey!—Heeyy!—Waddid you dooo?" And then picked them up, shook hell out of them, and set them back where they started. "Whoa," I said again.

Somewhat indignantly, then, they agreed that, yes, this was a new basis for negotiation and conceded to further the contract. Subsequently, when the ad for our first derby conquest hit the pages of the *Field,* we had reached terms that actually appeared purposeful. At least 50 percent of the time, provided I was expedient about it, they would allow me a share of the flushing rights. At the pop of the gun, yet, all requisites were adjourned.

Twice a week for the trailing half of September as well, we returned to Elm Hill, and the dogs were loosed again to run and hunt at will. It was wonderfully thrilling, unsnapping for the first time in five months the restraints from a young dog shivering with excitement, cutting with one keen snip of a whistle the last invisible bond and inciting to awesome explosion the pent-up power of mind and muscle. All summer I had waited. Fires banked since April blew wildly into flame, blazing with reckless abandon. Fast and far they ran, class and cause. Now, with the increasing attention to birds, you could see each time the hunt grow in their race, and I encouraged this with planted quail on strategic corners and at the conclusion of far-flung edges, pressing them not only to hunt, but to reach ever forward.

Upon the first perfect day of October, chill and clear, hardened by summer roading sessions and honed by progressive sprints, all three went an hour without the blemish of a pause. So compulsively that I was scared all over again, especially for Pat. For always she dwelled at life's edge, and with light speed. Within the thump of a heartbeat, she could evaporate as if she were nothing more than air, reappear two hundred yards gone before I drew another ragged breath. Many days I wondered of our time together, how long could it last?

∼ CHAPTER 9 ∼

AT THE END OF THE WEEK, WE CHRISTENED OUR DERBY SEASON NEAR home—the Alamance County trial, over farmland at the outskirts of Graham, North Carolina. Beda and Thane shouldered family honors, the course much too restrictive for Patty. So, unfortunately, it proved for Thane. Though he was picture perfect doing it, he sold out to a tempting but tangent edge, AWOL too long for a placement. Beda, to the contrary, ran an almost perfect race, fast and pretty. It was the beauty of fielding three dogs, each with a proclivity to show best on a dissimilar venue. That would change gradually over the next two years, Beda running larger and larger. As many good dogs do once they are inspired by birds.

But then, she looked strongest on a course of modest dimensions. Alamance fit the bill, and she grabbed the first edge, reached ever stylishly for the next, hunted the way, and pointed beautifully at twenty minutes. Bold and intense, she waited until I put the bird out, then chased lustily at wing and shot. A nice fall derby find. From there, she gathered herself and flew on, to a rousing, hard-away finish. Only the other couple of dogs that finished—one, more ambitiously, and two, no more ambitiously but slightly steadier on birds—bettered her in the judges' eyes.

I did little more than ride the course and swing the horse. She handled herself, and impressed a lot of people with the way she did it.

I hugged her when I picked her up. Little warrior maiden. Tried so hard.

"Good girl, Beda." She was sky-high, radiantly happy. We both knew she had done well.

We left that evening with our first officially recorded Field Dog Stud Book win, third place and the yellow ribbon in a recognized amateur derby stake. Loretta was elated, overjoyed with the pup that had been her favorite from the day they were born. All the more when later she received the validating win certificate from the AFTCA, the Amateur Field Trial Clubs of America, and found her name as owner in the *Field,* along with the account of Beda's triumph.

Exuberant with success at the very first trial, we set in earnest preparations for the next, the following weekend at Fort Mill. Melanie was excited, for Patty would run this time. Roland Kane, many a good dog to his credit—amateur and open—and a veteran across the major trial circuit of the Northeast, told me one time, "Thirds have a way of turning into firsts, if you just keep on digging." That was our goal, and we kept on digging.

On the Wednesday between, we loaded up and went training again at Elm Hill. Loretta put together another picnic basket, and Melanie stole away from school. There was a much greater education outside four walls that gorgeous October morning. Dolly was full of herself, and the dogs seemed especially eager. Life was pretty complete that special day, for all of us. We left before dawn to the tune of "Here We Go Round the Mulberry Bush," never let up, and by the time we repeated for a third time the chorus for "Go Tell It on the Mountain," the morning was being born. Virginia loomed and we could glimpse from the Buggs Island Dam the old plantation. The tops of the trees were burning red and gold with the first light of the waking sun, and the cool breath of the Roanoke River ascended in gentle silver mists over waters touched by the shimmer of diamonds. Upon the grassy hillsides ahead, the dew glistened so vividly that at the distance it looked like frost.

When we turned onto the graveled road into the grounds and reached the entrance, we were surprised and disappointed to find the gate locked. It had never been before, and I wondered at the occasion. My first assumption was that Danny Johnson, the area manager, and his crew had for some reason secured it, but it was just past eight o'clock, and they should normally be inside by now starting to work. I could go somewhere and call Danny, except I didn't have his number. Nor any idea of where he lived or where else to look for him. There was no way to get through; the perimeter fence abutted the pilot posts on each side of the gate. So I did the only thing left. I got the mare off, threw a saddle on, left Loretta with the truck, and rode in to the barn to see if I could find someone there.

There was a delicious chill to the air, the feel of a good walking horse under me. The steam was wafting from the grassy fields now. I wished I had a dog down.

Three-quarters of the way, I met Danny, swinging his truck onto a side path, on his way to check a farm crew. I could hear the low-case grumble of a tractor and the clatter of a Bush Hog just over the hillside. He threw up a hand same time I did.

"Mornin'," he nodded.

"Same," I returned. "It's a fine one."

"Where's your dog?" he asked.

"That's just it," I said. "Gate's locked."

He looked surprised.

"I figured you were either late or somebody had a reason."

"Naw," he said, "we've been here since seven-thirty." He threw the gear lever into reverse. "Head on back. It'll be open time you get there."

"Thanks . . . sorry."

He waved a "no bother" with a flap of a hand, backed onto the main road, and scratched off for the gate. I fell in at a leisurely pace behind. As I reined, I could see the barn in the distance. There were two horse-and-dog rigs parked there, a pair of riders just leaving, loosing the same number of dogs. I wondered when they had arrived, how they had gotten in.

We drove in and pulled into our usual place under the big elm trees behind the old mansion. Trading in and away from the barn as we ran our dogs, our path intersected only casually with that of the other two handlers, for I was careful to anticipate the direction of their travel over the grounds and choose an alternate course that would in the main avoid overlap. Often I ran the mile-long river bottom, which was a good hour around. We threw up a cordial hand the first time, never closing below a good shooting-dog cast. I recognized them, of course, Parke Brinkley and Aubrey Morgan. Had seen them before. They trained there frequently then and were a regular fixture at Virginia-Carolina trials, running all-age pointers generally under the Arcanum prefix. Parke was on the downslope side of his middle years, a times-past commissioner of agriculture in Virginia, and a lifelong devotee of field trials. Nationally respected, he had, before his deference to all-age dogs, penned the acclaimed standard for the National Shooting Dog Championship. He was a director on the board of several major trials. Aubrey was his understudy. They usually brought a kennel-full of dogs and would train all day. They maintained then a schedule of "johnny house" recall pens for training quail, scattered strategically about the grounds.

Our dogs were inspired that day. All three lay down big, scorching ground races, Pat to the usual extremes, Thane and Beda pausing at least long enough to point and hold respectably the birds I set out. Patty, whom I normally ran first, had additionally the benefit of a wild covey, which she flash-pointed, put out joyfully, and chased kingdom-come. After she had already bumped two of three training birds. When finally I could run her down, get off, shake her until she rattled, and set her in place where she should have stayed, we had a talk about it. You know, "What part of 'whoa' don't you understand?"

She'd stand there with her tail clicking away, a cocked-to-go, let's-get-this-over-with notion on her face, burning to be released so she could fly off three hundred yards and do it again. So much fire. So hot the flames. It was a while to staunch, I could see. Derbies were at minimum expected to point. Were they to win consistently—as the season progressed, fall to spring—staying for the flush became equally obligatory. It'd be a trip this year with Patty. But God, what a thrill still she was on the ground.

Off to Fort Mill a couple days later, I was feeling pretty good really. *Nobody* would beat Pat on race. If the stake was shy of bird work, she might gain a place on ground and potential alone. It happened. Lord of lords, she might even surprise herself, get jammed up on instinct, and point something for a time. Beda and Thane, nothing shabby on the turf of their own, were jelling nicely on birds as well; a little luck and a find or two, and we might all go to the winner's circle. You got to have hope.

Turned out we didn't win anything. That's field trialing. Funny, though, as I walked Pat to the line, Dr. Billy McCathern was judging.

"Zip Zap," he read from his book. "Now that's the way to name a dog."

Another South Carolina stalwart watched her away, the blaze and beauty of her going. "If nothing happens, that little dog's gonna make the big time," he posed, echoing Bob Tate's prophesy the spring before. The rewards came in a lot of quiet, little packages.

But then I lost the handle on her three-quarters of the way around, she took a big loop out of turn, got herself off course, and didn't get back in time to quit properly. Bumped a brace of birds shamelessly while she was

about it. Thane came along strong and correctly enough, but went somehow birdless in a birdy stake—a surprise, for he was a good bird finder. And
Beda, who had a good derby find and knocked soundly on the door, was
deterred from a placement by a too-modest race, victim of the stifling heat
in an unseasonably warm day. She spent herself dangerously, to the final second, and was twice when I stopped her for water close to overheating. But
she wanted so badly to continue that I sent her on, wishing at time that I
had not as she wobbled on fading legs, hassled furiously, and finally sank to
the ground. Her eyes were red and frenzied, and she was close to trouble.
Quickly I emptied my water jug over her, borrowed another, rolled her and
drenched her belly. Then draped her over the pommel and rushed to
immerse her in a nearby creek. Presently, in the cool flowing water, she leveled and later seemed fine. It scared me, and I learned from that day her
limit and a lesson. A dog with that kind of heart and borderline tolerance
can quickly kill itself in the heat. The cardiorespiratory burden loads up so
rapidly that it can red-line before you know it. Nothing is more peculiarly
threatening, and I'd never wait so long again.

Loretta was particularly frightened.

"*Never* take that chance again," she said. "No trial's worth that."

No trial was.

$\backsim$ CHAPTER 10 $\backsim$

IN RECOMPENSE, THE WINDS BLEW FAIR FOR A TIME. JOE MONTANA PUT together a stem-winder of a trip at the Mid-Carolina the following weekend, standing until shot two birds and running away with the whole thing, first place and the blue. Turned right around and commanded second and a red at Spartanburg seven days later, beating for one of the few times his sister, who was close behind for third and the gold. Not Beda, but Zip Zap, who happened to be seen by an especially attentive judge for a fleeting few seconds pointing a bird and who put on such a spectacular ground show she would not be denied. Melanie stood beaming for a photo, her dog by the collar in one hand, a ribbon the color of her hair in the other. Now it would be Melanie's name in the *Field*. I was but the handler, you know.

Two weeks later, at Sumter County, Thane struck blue again, a silky exhibition of birds and heels, and Beda snuck tightly in for another third. Days hence, over a sprawling piece of eastern Carolina farmland near Ayden, our male dog started once more as brilliantly, but this time suffered a lengthy absence, misled by a deep and discouraging drainage ditch. By the time I could get him back, judicial grace had expired. So Zip Zap came along, and so spectacularly devoured the huge grounds she had the entire gallery abuzz. Her one find, seconds late, came just after pickup.

For a second time in less than a year, we were approached after she ran with a proposition, this occasion by a professional handler. The money would have paid three years of mortgage.

"I can give her opportunity you can't," he said, even before I spoke. As he read my inclination.

Considering the major, open stakes, maybe he could. She was that much dog. But the condescending tone of it rankled me. I don't think he really meant it that way. It was a thing of the moment.

"No, thank you," I said. "I'll carry her on and we'll do the best we can."

"Well, if you change your mind, call me," came the customary reply.

Retta walked to my side as he trod away, and spoke what I hadn't. "He might give her the opportunity," she said, "not the love."

I leaned over and kissed her. Happily we loaded the mare, Mr. Montana, our sixth pup, and left for home.

Spring was a trying time for fiery young derbies, I would find. The more so for dogs trained and handled by amateurs in quality amateur stakes. By March, many of the youngsters fielded by amateurs from professionally trained strings had been brought or pushed to steadiness on game—immobility through flush, flight, and shot. Of these, a few were those remarkably rare individuals with flair that naturally develop and finish early, with no loss of genius. By the odds of sheer numbers, a greater percentage of these occur among professional ranks. Most, though, were tough young dogs that could take an extreme dose of discipline and keep on ticking. By either measure, the competition had stiffened. To win, finished manners became increasingly imperative, and there was, particularly for an amateur trainer, a great temptation to achieve them at the expense of squandering a treasure. An amateur breeder, trainer, and handler is very, *very* lucky to get a young dog that has the potential for winning major field trial stakes. It's a trust gifted only to the few. It had been gifted to me. It would have to be carefully nurtured. There would not, as with most leading professionals, be another half dozen youngsters in the wings to sort through and venture next month or as many more another few months after that. Pat, Beda, and Thane would pass their derby eligibility at less than two years of age. Afterward, they would compete in all-age stakes for the rest of their lives. To be eminently successful through the six to eight years of intense competition, with any idea toward major regional and national events, they would need to carry every possible ounce of youthful desire and brilliance to maturity.

Thankfully, along then, Mister Howell Cockfield pressed that upon me. "Mister" in the finest Southern tradition, for he was a Palmetto State pointing-dog veteran of nineteenth-century grace, great wisdom, and many capacities—the most distinguished as a judge of fine field trial dogs. I ran under him several times, then and later, won a time or two, and as with Ernie Newman, his contemporary, never was it less than a privilege and a pleasure. Cockfield was a large, imposing man. There was a sternness in him, the confidence of familiarity, that backed you against the wall and bled the truth into his every word.

"Steadiness is a hard order for a great young dog," he said, "and many a fine one has been ruined gittin' there. You go tamperin' with the very things that make 'em great. The thing that sends 'em a-huntin' far and wide, the blood-hot need for game, the urge to knock down and catch a bird . . . natural-as-the-day's-long," he said, with the flip of his hand, ". . . the happiness in 'em, even, that says 'look at me' in everything they do.

"Push 'em on too soon, jerk 'em around once too often, you kill the spark, and it's never the same again. You don't put it back. Take it out, it's gone. A lot of it's mystery. You got to treat it that-a-way.

"You want a dog that reaches out yonder with a fire on his heels," he told me, "one that does it like he'uz born to do it, scratches up birds and stands 'em like Joshua's blowin' the horn . . . you bring 'em on slow. You take these good young dogs of yours, especially the one, and remember that.

"They'll come," he said, "they'll come."

I was trying, mightily, to remember that as January hurried past. As the dogs bumped bird after bird . . . in trials and workouts. Particularly Pat. Trying to be patient, trying to remember with each infraction that you drove up a barn one nail at a time. Pick them up, put them back, "Whoa, Pat, whoa." Again and again, with but a light shaking, to gain the impression but hedge the humility.

The more I tried, the further I was behind. Or so it seemed. With Thane and Beda, maybe, the care and regimen were showing a profit. They were miles from steady, but more and more they would point and hold intensely until I flushed the bird. Pat was a deeper worry. No matter my persistence, she wanted on her own to see them fly. This she continued to accomplish incorrigibly, a flash point, if at all, the only warning. When she did stand, it was loosely, flagging with the desire to bump and chase. A dog must point certainly to win a field trial, taut and tall. If, on that account, I hurried in to flush, she would comply—tightening, swelling onto her toes, her eyes livid with anticipation. Leaning against the scent, she was breath-taking. There lay the goal. That was what I wanted, point-to-shot, and more. That kind of eloquence would win field trials. But ever, as I reached her side, she would jump in, beating me again to the bird. There was noth-ing left to do then but *pick her up, bring her back. "Whoa, Pat, whoa!"* Over and over, as gainlessly as pitching pennies in a posthole.

Night after night I'd lie in bed, looking for the answer, frustrated upon occasion almost to tears. Time and again, Loretta would give it to me.

"Good things you must wait for."

But that was hard. I wanted so to bring her back to winning form. It was my job to help her. Yet the entire fall had been rutted with mishap. She was making a name for herself everywhere she went, with stunning ground coverage, the grace of her going, and her electricity on game, but the wins came hard. It was disturbing, and I felt much to blame, since in good part it was handling error. I had lost her almost every trial. I was learning—learn-ing to have faith in my dog, learning to trust my scout—but it was costly. Sumter County had been a good example. Three-quarters of the way through the heat, Pat was winning the trial. She had one exciting derby find to her credit and was setting the ground afire, far and forward. Then, inexplicably, she disappeared into a distant corner, the course took a turn, and she was awhile too gone. I rode on, singing, without a dog, prickled by fear as the moments grew. She was a handful, so fast. You never had more than a minute or two to react. I glanced for Dub, who was scouting. He was nowhere in sight. My instincts screamed that she had gone deeply into the corner, gotten behind. Then I made a foolish, fatal mistake. I wheeled the mare and galloped back to look for her.

Two hundred yards to the rear, my attention riveted to the timber, I rounded a blind curve and almost ran slap and saddle into Dub, riding drag and flank and coming up hard for the front. Both horses shied wildly, and it took some scrubbing to gather them up. They stood crow-hopping under the reins.

"What the hell are you doin' back here?" Dub hollered.

"Trying hell to find my dog!" I yelled back.

"I been all back in that corner," he said impatiently. "That's my job. She's already through. Probably up front. That's your job. Probably up there now where you still ought to be."

In a rush, I knew he was right. A hundred percent right. It's the oldest adage in dog handling: You got a good scout, trust him. Stay up front, keep singing, wait for your dog. Most times, they show. I frowned, and we both tore hard away for the front. She had been there, flashed in fore of the gallery, then flown off again on a tangent. When we caught up, she was two fields away.

I apologized openly to Dub, grabbed myself up and shook myself good and hard. Mostly I apologized to my dog. We could have had all three places in that trial. She had done everything she needed to win but win. That was my fault, and it had to change.

Now, coming into spring, there was the steadiness problem as well. But I'd not mend one mistake with another. I'd not push it. I'd wish and wait, keep prodding gently along. Somewhere, *somehow,* we must be making progress. Then, in March, came the Swamp Fox Derby Classic on Medway Plantation, and afterward I knew. Every word Howell Cockfield had said was religion.

The Swamp Fox Classic, flagship event of the Swamp Fox Sportsmen's Club of Charleston, was that year a class stake of fifteen trial-seasoned youngsters, mostly multiple winners, over a low-country shooting-dog course that demanded nothing less than their best. Medway was the Old South, a gift to gentlemen at the grant of a king. An aura of big house and boxwoods, mists and magnolias, grace and three centuries. A place of mood and magic, a pause of wish and wonder. The call of a cock bird at the rim of day. The challenge of another . . . how Someone had written, in just two notes, no less than a symphony. It was the rhythm and stroll of a good walking horse, over an avenue two hundred years to dust under the hooves of a thousand others. It was boots and chaps. Stirrups and straps. Gents and hats. Shotguns and spats. It was dog folks—gentle and gay. The stiff, sharp scent of newly crushed bay. It was dignified old live oaks, bearded, grizzled, and gray. A lazy old mule wagon, creak, rattle, and sway. It was the shiver in the silver of dawn, the sparkle of frost in a fresh Dixie morn. That was Medway, much as it was and much as I wanted it to be. A storybook trip through a time warp of piney woods and short grass behind one more generation of fierce, young pointing dogs, and completing it all was the reality that three of them were mine.

They must have known, for all excelled that day.

Beda broke boldly, layed in and out of the shinnery, popping forward, evening into a busy, searching ground heat that was at times moderate, but fluent and evocative, and wholly adequate for the stake. Five minutes to go, she slid sideways, feathered a few feet, and stiffened, about the time a bird went up, then the balance of the bevy. It was a close call, but technically a bump. She chased, and I watched like a stob in a bog, disheartened, when I should have remembered it was a derby stake, whoaed, and shot over her. She would have stopped and stood—she had in workouts—and, looking back, would probably have gained a placement. I flogged myself over it for a week. It was the very kind of thing I'd told myself over and over we couldn't afford. Once again, the blame was mine, and once again, it had to stop.

Thane, conversely, breaking a bit slowly, took a full minute or two getting uncorked. When he did, he surged stronger and stronger, with his typical swashbuckling style, until he was knocking the front door down. Where I wanted him, except that this was a continuous-course trial, and the portion of the course he had drawn was the thickest on the venue. Heavy with bay heads and blackjack. He was too much dog for that. He had a keen and honest stop-to-flush on a whale of a covey along the railroad track, let me get off the horse, and stayed nicely for the shot, took only token steps as two lay birds whirred away. But then he really ran out of ken, hung the thick stuff too much to show well, and lost the advantage of the find.

At the end of the heat, while I was picking him up, Jim Gilmer rode up. Looked at my dog. Gilmer had a way of making meat out of matter. *"Thing,"* he said to the setter, "it warn't all your fault, but be damned if I'll give you the difference."

And then there was Pat. How I'd love that day back again. She broke to a friendly course, stately live oaks, fern and short grass, scattered bays, opening occasionally to brief green-golden vistas of longleaf and wire grass. I remember vividly her break. She was gone so fast at the whistle, it was hardly more than a blur and an illusion. We didn't see her for three hundred yards, then she flashed out of the shadow of the pines far right and front, emerging brilliantly into a patch of sunlight, and snappily burning a long diagonal across the front before fading again into the left corner. She was hunting and she was handling, in all the right places, and soon she had sewn together a ground race that was consistently big, strong, and showy, the kind you hallucinate about in the small hours you can't sleep, the night before a trial. The kind you visualize when you're searching for a synonym for *perfect*. Twenty minutes through, she had a short, scary absence. Better put, I and the scout did. Pat knew exactly where she was, showing again to the front and scoring the first of two good covey finds. Shortly afterward, when I regained the front, the gallery was abuzz. She had been zipping full tilt when she ran into her nose, slid to a stop, and jacked up supremely on those birds, stood to watch as they erupted, then burst loose and took them away.

Now she was reaching again, tearing to the front, looking anew.

"Whup, whup, *whuup! Yeaah-now!*" I called on her as she veered laterally, nervously jerking my eyes rearward for my scout. A tip of a finger and he was off, spurring his big dun gelding into a canter, hanging drag and circling deeper. The last thing we needed now was for her to dig in after the singles. Seconds later, she whipped out again, swinging ecstatically to the front. Hallelujah! I felt like whooping.

With five minutes to go, she iced the cake. Pulled up hard, threw her head into the wind, weaved and roaded thirty yards, and stacked up sharp as a salute in a cemetery. Then took two steps and the birds boiled up.

"Whoa, Pat! Whoa!"

And God knows how, but the training took hold. Wonder of wonders, she stayed, swelling up and watching the covey away. Higher and higher, with the sparks flying, and her flag stiff as a poker. Waited the length it took me to stumble off the saddle, jerk the shotgun out, get up there and fire the shot.

I glanced doubtfully at the judges. One of them smiled.

I don't remember climbing back on the horse atall. Maybe I floated up there. But I hit the whistle and sent her on, and she faded swiftly away. Knocked the far front door out of the course. Under those tall Dixie pines.

Thelmer Page rode quietly up beside me. Thelmer was another Palmetto State pro, and a good one, who trained and handled then the Grouse Ridge string of setters for Dr. Tom Flannagan. He was judging, along with Stewart Heath from the East Carolina Club at Lake City.

"Hate to, but pick her up." I tipped my hat and heeled the mare.

When the smoke lifted, and the trial party gathered on the grounds of the old mansion for the announcement, I was tingly to the toe-tips. Nothing's ever sure, but I thought we might be close. Dr. Gibson, the stake chairman, read them off:

"Swamp Fox Derby Classic, third place . . . Knight's Rambling Bo, Mr. P. E. Knight." There ensued a solid chorus of clapping.

"Second . . . Rick's Nick, Roy Rickman." Applause, while well-wishers extended a round of hands.

"And the winner" . . . the standard pause, while my heart drummed between dread and delirium . . . "Zip Zap, Mr. Gaddis."

Now the clapping was for my dog, and the hands were given to me, and it hurt so good I bit my lip until it bled. My wife was crying, and my daughter had twisted her curls into a knot. It was a happy day.

I walked over to thank the judges.

"Thanks for looking at my dogs," I told Thelmer. "I wished she had held that last bunch of birds," I added.

"She had birds, flash, and fire," Thelmer replied, "and she stopped when you asked her to, showed she could take training. That's what we were look-ing for."

I've never forgotten that, and it's what I've looked for in derby dogs also, all the years since, over many a judging assignment, and always will. Derby stakes are about promise. As Howell Cockfield said, "a promise that's about to come true, if you'll let it." They're about the one young dog in a hundred blue-breds that has the blazing desire to find birds, the athletic agility to go with it, the heart and spirit *never* to quit. A dog that possesses the intelligence and ambition to lay always forward, always to the right places. With a way of going that unwinds like poetry, style and class that jams a lump in your throat. A willingness to listen, a willingness to accept training. It's a lot to ask. Exactly why the dogs that win them are such a privilege. Ask any man who's ever owned one. Because eloquent young derbies, with careful and patient training, finish out into thrilling all-age dogs that can win the best of all-age and shooting-dog championships, and hold their polish over the grinding six or seven years of a field trial career.

Trainers, professional and amateur, judges alike, have pushed the impa-tience envelope on derbies in the past two decades, demanding finished manners on game by the spring trial season, when many derbies are yet less than two years old. For every young dog that can accommodate that kind of pressure, there are nine more with promise that can't. With that, I'll quit meddling and go to preaching. Fall, spring, makes no difference. If you're hung up on finished manners in a derby stake, above the hunt, flash, and fire that, from inception, have been the inspirational cornerstone of field trial-ing, you're hurting the dogs and you're hurting the sport. And you'd as well be running an all-age or shooting-dog stake.

There was a thing more about the Swamp Fox trial that left me proud. It was a wild-bird trial, and there are days when wild birds can spin a mys-tery, become so much a riddle in an enigma you must wonder if even they are there. Days that confound even the most seasoned dogs, moreover those still putting the numbers together. Such was the test that early March day at Medway, in 1978. Birds were uncommonly scarce. Of the fifteen-dog entry, only three dogs had bird contacts. Our three. Not all clean, but finds, and I was never happier with them.

∾ CHAPTER 11 ∾

DESPITE THE DOUBT, I REALIZED AFTER MEDWAY WE WERE MAKING progress. Above all, I recognized we'd been finding wild birds, virtually every workout, and the indispensable value of that in putting the topspin on a class dog. I had three bird finders, and that went a long ways. They weren't always Molly Manners when they found them. But every time out, they were learning.

Be damned then, even on the heels of Medway, if Pat didn't come completely unglued at the Fort Mill trial, rattling up four corking good finds and jumping right in every time, didn't even point, chased like a puppy. Not to be outdone, Beda and Thane did the same. Fort Mill left me scratching my head all over again. Thinking I simply wasn't going to run them competitively anymore until I had them more reliably finished on wild birds. But most fools are stubborn fools, and I decided to take Pat alone, one last time as a derby, to the Tidewater Trial at Amelia, Virginia, a month later.

Twixt time, seems like everything came loose. Beda was sidelined with a persistent abscess, and Joe Montana was giving me night sweats, trying to figure how to polish the squirreliness out of him at the scrimmage line. When he got birds pinned, he'd stand like a million on point, mark flight beautifully, and honor the shot, but immediately afterward he'd go whang-clang nitsy—whining feverishly, teeth clicking like a knitting machine, crouching and creeping toward me—begging to be released, so he could fly off again and find another bird. Time and again I'd set him back, talk him down, stroke him up, and tell him he would be God's gift to dogdom if he'd only stand like somebody a half minute longer. The desire was as laudable as the dilemma seemed invincible. And I tinkered gingerly with the balance, working and working to help him through it, though it became the bane of our existence.

So Pat and I went it alone to Amelia, with the family banner. She had the ground race of the stake, and two nice finds, the last a far-flung, limb-hung beauty. Was staunch both times until I got there. But my sharp "Whoa!" caught her midair when she jumped in on the first, and the arrested momentum dropped her virtually on top of the bird. She landed pointing, but crouching also, jammed so firmly against hot scent that it whipped her double. The compromise in style was circumstantial, of course, but you don't win trials that way. On the second, she let me flush, then chased lustily, stopping after a few yards to a "Whoa!" giving me a quick what-for over her shoulder, and jacking up tighter to watch the bird away. We didn't place, and I didn't expect to, but I came away pleased nonetheless. It was the first time she had been honest-to-God staunch in a trial, held the birds until I could get there, and allowed me out front to flush. Progress. I'd take that, put it in the bank. Nest it for fall.

We'd need it. Derby days were done. A lot of fun, a lot of frustration. Come fall, it'd be whole hog or die. Shooting-dog or all-age stakes and finished manners. It was a tough row for first-year dogs, still settling in, competing against the whit-leather wisdom of the seasoned campaigners. It was hard to win.

We'd been working a regular schedule at Elm Hill. Loretta and Melanie were still going with me routinely, but regrettably I could see that changing as Melanie became more involved with friends and school. She was coming nine now. We were looking for a second horse.

Several times when we got to the main gate, it would be strangely locked again, and I'd have to saddle up and go looking for Danny, and he'd know nothing about it. It was wholly coincidence, I'm sure, that once we were in each time, we'd find Parke and Aubrey there running dogs already. Turned into quite a mystery. Finally I figured I must be a real threat to somebody . . . me, a green-banana amateur with his wife and daughter, one horse, and three dogs. It was kind of flattering, actually. But aggravating, and finally I told Retta "to blazes with it," quit bothering Danny, just parked the rig and ran from the gate. Kinda quit worrying so much about whatever, too, and Pat and Thane lapped them twice one morning, Parke, Aubrey, and their dogs, on the milk route to three of their johnny houses. Before I sent Beda around them once more for good measure.

Then to really compensate for it all, I met Verle Farrow there one day. Verle Farrow was the South when the South was still Southern. A gentleman's gentleman, a Virginia aristocrat threaded without pretense in everyday clothes and a smile. And that never changed, no matter the weather or the whether. Moreover, Verle was a dog man, setter man, to the fingertips, and he always ran a good one. His all-age champion, Long Gone Sam, was a legend. Almost the equal of the man. Farrow had already been enshrined in the Field Trial Hall of Fame when first we came to know him. He had contributed much, nationally, to the field trial game. I would, over years to come, grow to know a number of Hall of Famers. But never another that elevated the honor and the standard like Verle. We ran dogs together some, along then, when we'd cross paths at Elm Hill. At his invitation. Always I hoped for it, and always it came. I, Pat, Thane, and Beda learned a lot from him and his dogs, and he wanted us to. We'd run into him at trials, down the line, and ever he had a word of encouragement, and a genuine interest and desire for our success. In the afteryears, we would even team to judge a trial or two. Meeting Verle that day would be a measure of considerable fortune, I would find, not the least of which was the inspiration. Verle furthered many a young man into dogs and field trialing. Did it simply by quiet words and an example, and I was one of them.

"I never figured field trials much different from life at large," Verle told me one time. "We strive and we fail. Sometimes we win.

"It's how you go about it that counts."

By the end of April, it was coming time to pull off the fieldwork. The birds were pairing, the land was greening, and the fields had been planted. The sun had grown unneighborly, beating down more mercilessly day by day. Before long, it would be a brassy ogre in a hazy, hellish sky. It was time to hunker in and suffer a long, hot summer, brush up on yard manners, stay as close to peak condition as we could, and most of all, pray for September. I hated the sweat and smother of the scorching heat and the sopping humidity. When both lay so thickly in the air, it was like living and breathing beneath a wet wool blanket. It was a special kind of misery for the dogs, who sought to escape the worst of it by scratching out deep, dark cellars under their houses and harboring there against the scorching heat in the relative comfort of the cool, damp earth. It brought ticks and fleas, and snakes, and ants that got in your food pan and stinging bugs that fell in your water, and red, itchy skin rashes that sored up about as painfully sometimes as the mange.

About the only thing good it brought was butterflies. Big, flitty, yellow, tiger-striped swallowtails that danced enticingly about the kennel and made for great fun, when all else of life was dust and doldrums. Especially when they lit and you could point them.

We'd have some great chases. We adopted an early-alert system, Loretta, Melanie, and I, much like the present-day hurricane advisories by the National Weather Service. "Butterfly watch!" meant the distinct possibly of a sighting, that flowers were about and conditions were right, and there had been reports of them around the yard and premises. "Butterfly warning!" on the other hand, was used only with an actual sighting, particularly when we spotted one of the colorful creatures before the dogs did.

Then we'd holler dramatically, *"Butterfly watch!"* which meant stand ready and keep your eyes peeled, 'cause he's about to light on your nose. The dogs picked it up quickly, and would come running, and if you can imagine nine or ten dogs instantly milling into a frenzy, whirling and bumping, tails popping, eyes hiked and livid with anticipation, you have some idea of the picture. Pat would be forever at the center of it, like a cap over powder, clamoring for first sight. And when the flitting wings got close enough that we knew a canine sighting was imminent, we'd all yell "BUTTERFLY WARNING!" to the top of our lungs. Then it would really be on. The dogs would leap and snap, as high in the air as they could, trying to catch it, pirouetting in midair, while bodies thumped and jaws clicked. They'd fall back hard, get right up and do it over again, following the bright and erratic insect for as long as it was available. When often several of them would lose sight of it among the limbs and leaves, another of them would find it once more, and all would race at the summons to cluster under it again in a hysterical knot.

Always the best part was when one caught them by surprise and lit close by, fanning its wings gently and turning slowly about. The first pup to notice would road into a point, and within a few seconds five more would be stacked up behind, honoring the find. They'd stand until they quivered and drooled, as long as the creature would tarry, shifting their weight uneasily paw to paw to accommodate their patience. It was good training of sorts. But mainly just grand fun.

There was ever the more serious matter of staying fit. I was up before day three times a week, on a religious rhythm, right on through the oppressive dog days of July and August. Loading the dogs in the dark, driving the thirty minutes to the boarding stable, haying, graining, and grooming the mare. There were the regular leather chores while she ate—saddle, tack, and roading harnesses to brush; soap and oil so they didn't dry, stiffen, and crack. Ropes and knots, swivels and snaps to check. By dawn, I'd be saddling in the hallway of the barn, to the company of Merle Haggard from the radio, and outside the dogs would be whining anxiously from the truck with the growing light. There was hard work ahead, but they craved it.

Which was good, because it was absolute necessity. All across the prairies, up through Nebraska, the Dakotas, and on to the Canadian provinces of Saskatchewan, Ontario, and Manitoba, there were pros and strings of pointing dogs going through the same regime, except when daylight broke, they'd be turning loose into the cool of the morning on a vast expanse of grassy plain, into a treasure trove of wild birds. Where a combination of the wind, land, and juvenile broods of prairie chicken, sharptail grouse, and pheasant would spark the ambition and put the education in a dog's head like nothing else could. A lot of those same dogs would be back come October, and we'd be running against them no holds barred.

I pined for us to be there too, but that was beyond even hope then, for I had neither the freedom nor the wherewithal. So our lot was to abhor the misfortune, buckle stiffly into a conditioning program, and wish for the first of the Canadian fronts. Which brought the clear, cool mornings that would kick the summer heat in the teeth and off to Florida, liberating us to run free once more. And after that, for October and an early frost to put the high green cover to wither. The rains had been friendly. By mid-August, we were seeing occasional caravans of bumblebee-sized chicks behind the mama hens, which meant the local bird hatch was proceeding profitably. Something to keep us going.

We'd upped the ante on our roading program, now that the dogs had reached maturity, going a tough hour each time. While to the D-rings either side of each roading harness, I'd attached a couple pounds of steel chain. It was the equivalent of adding another forty-five-pound plate each side of the leg press sled in the gym. Increasing the resistance stress on the body and demanding a corresponding advancement of wind and muscle. I'd yoked the three dogs into a trinity, so that they pulled abreast, not just against the weight of the chains, but against themselves as well. So that it maximized the strength and cardio gain, and augmented agility and balance together. Periodically during the pull, not enough to make it stale, I'd hit the whistle, *"Stweeettt!"* and it had the kick-in-the-butt effect of the turbo cutting into a combustion engine. The quadriceps muscles in rippling hindquarters would knot hard and pump explosively for several yards before gearing back into the grind, like they would do off the line at breakaway, except then there would be no chains to drag them back, and the effect would be the breathtaking burst of speed that I loved.

We'd start at gray day, and once in harness, the dogs would be eagerly bucking at the end of the rope, causing even the mare a stumble step to maintain a ballast. The first flocks of crows would be on the wing, barking raucous warnings to the owls that ought still to be in bed, and the doves would be softly cooing from the pines. Our course wound across farmland hills and beside shadowy creekside bottoms, edged green pastures and golden grainfields, and twisted through cathedral stands of forest that would be cut by long, slanting shafts of pale yellow sunlight once the sun woke up. We had a schedule of ponds along the route, where the dogs could dip and cool a minute or so, before leaning again into the harness.

The endurance of dogs under such trying conditions is no less than amazing. More than amazing . . . *incredible.* Saddle a human with a proportional load under similar circumstances, and he'd do good to make fifteen minutes and live, much less an hour. But the dogs . . . my God . . . the dogs. Tongues would loll until mouths were cotton white with foam, breathing would be grated to a rasp; it was killing hot down that close to the ground—yet every ounce and fiber of them would be thrown into a relentless load against the harness. Most incredible of all was Zip Zap. Thane was almost twice again her size, Beda a good half. All three were honest as the hour was long. They'd struggle against the horse and the chains and each other in a competitive fight for dominance, and you could see the psychological exertion of it no less surely than the physical. Ever, the least female would prevail. I'd put her in the middle, ask her to maintain the point. She'd never falter. She had matured into an ultracompact corundum of power, and where it came from in such force, as always, was a matter of wonder. It defied muscle, bone, lever, and logic. It was pure grit.

She'd stand at the end of the haul, leaning against the harness, panting deeply but steadily. Eager to do it over again should I ask. While Beda and Thane, though willing if ordered, hassled laboriously and looked up at me with the hope it was over.

In the cool of early morning another two days of the week, we worked at bird drills. Building steadiness to wing and shot. Training diligently, but never enough to grow sour on the tame birds. I'd been working the gun-dog pups along too, Jill and Ben, though never quite fairly, for we were so into trialing. But now we could consolidate again, all into the same class-room. An alfalfa hayfield of about five acres, behind the barn, constituted the schooling grounds. Tri-Tronics had the first radio-remote bird traps out about then, on the Jack Stuart design, that'd kick a bird up from a distance at the flick of a transmitter button—quite a revolution. I peddled an out-door story and Loretta pilfered the cookie jar once again, and we mustered the couple hundred dollars it took to acquisition a pair.

Coincidentally, I finagled an agreement with Tom Jones—not the British pop singer, but the local friend of my barber, who was a homing pigeon fancier—for the surreptitious use of his birds. I'd pick up a dozen the evening before a training outing. It was symbiotic, really, our arrangement. The dogs got the training benefit, and the birds a homing opportunity that would better them for the races. Between the automatic traps and the flighty pigeons, we could more closely simulate the unpredictability of wild birds, the spontaneity of a flush. Thereby encouraging intensity on point.

We'd put out the traps, hide them in the grass and load them with birds, work one dog at a time. Off the rope and into the wind. While the rest of the class watched, reared, and barked from the stake-out chain. On the Er Shelley *Twentieth Century Dog Training* principle that all were learning contiguously. If a solid point was established, all and well, I'd walk in front and rote through the steadiness routine: flush, caution, and shot. Correction if necessary. By now it was mostly a matter of a few stutter steps, when the bird went up and the gun went off. A mild shaking and admonition, setting the offender back in place and planting it firmly again with a "Whoa!" If, instead of a point, there was the slightest liberty in nose, crowding scent or racing in hell-bound with the obvious mischief of catching the bird, the pigeon was thrown out and gone, and the miscreant apprehended flat-footed and without appeal, short even the satisfaction of a feather. Picked up, it was shaken sternly and dropped back to stand where it should have in the first place. The dogs learned quickly they couldn't catch the Birming-ham rollers like they could the piddly flying, pen-bred quail. Sometimes I'd kick the bird out first notice a dog caught scent, or even before, demanding

the unexpected stop-to-flush—the halt, mark the bird, and stand for shot—
that was part and parcel of polished manners. It kept all off guard, sharpening performance. Progress was pleasing.

Less frequently, because it could so easily go stale, we worked on backing. In a shooting-dog or all-age stake, it is mandatory that a dog back, or
honor, the established point of its bracemate. Voluntarily, preferably, without
command. Back and stand as on point itself through flush and shot. No
exceptions. A dog that refused to back was a ticket to home in a hurry.

Training a dog to back has its nuances. Foremost, it requires a rock-
steady, finished dog that will stand intensely on point through the distrac-
tion of leading a young pupil in and establishing a back, and subsequent
reinforcement of steadiness with flush and shot. Occasionally young dogs do
it so instinctively it's almost ordained; more often it requires degrees of verbal caution—a sharp "Whoa" or three—disturbing and confusing to the
older dog doing perfectly what it's supposed to. Particularly true if you have
a classroom full of students and only one staunch tutor. It's a considerable
imposition on polished manners, and one that, impressed too frequently, can
at least foster lackadaisical style in the finished dog, and at worst chip away
at the hard-earned steadiness you've labored for when a green youngster
violates general orders and goes charging past the standing dog to steal
point or rout the bird. Anything in the early stages that can alleviate pressure on the older dog is a boon to benevolence.

That in mind, we borrowed a trick, long since commonplace, from Paul
Long. Long was legendary, another crafty, old-school professional trainer,
not far removed from us in the Tar Heel town of Maiden. Forty-five years
of dog sense under his hat, he had apprenticed under the likes of Hall of
Famer Mike Seminatore, the acclaimed "dean of New England bird-dog
trainers," and renowned gun-dog trainer Elias Veil, before aspiring to a stellar career of his own. He was associated with the development of a number
of all-breed pointing-dog greats, of particular note the Irish setters Rufus
McTybe of Cloister and Ike Jack Kendrick; Britt of Bellows Falls, the first
Brittany field champion; and the English pointer Colonial Lady, depicted in
the vintage Coca-Cola Company series of commissioned paintings of the
then ten greatest pointing dogs of all time. Paul had published a book a few
years before called *Training Pointing Dogs: All the Answers to All Your Questions,* to this day one of the most practical to shoestring training.

Long's proposition for backing, as frugal and pragmatic as one came, was Judas Priest. Judas was a lifesize dummy dog in a pointing pose, cut out of plywood and painted as the real thing. In the book, Long described how to make one. "Lay your dog down on its side on a half-inch sheet of plywood, and trace it off."

It was the only ragged piece of advice in the works. Pat utterly refused to lie still that long; Thane got his nose out of joint—"You expect me to do *what?*"—and peed on the whole deal; and Beda, surmising some kind of subterfuge for a rabies shot, burrowed under the kennel house for an hour.

"To hell with this," I told Loretta. "I'll draw one off."

Roy Burdeshaw of Alabama had a winning setter I liked called Chief Burdeshaw. We found the dog's facsimile in a recent copy of the *Field,* and I copied him onto the plywood best I could.

"He looks like a dachshund," Loretta observed. Abbreviating him six inches, deepening his muzzle, and painting him white with a black ear and some ticking was an improvement. Retta added an eye patch, and Melanie dabbed on a rump spot. "That's for Patty," she said. Some feathering on his tail, a wet black nose as the finishing touch, and we were credibly in business. Despite some skepticism over the portended effect, he did look like a pointing dog. One thing for sure, he was steady.

I kept him in a feed sack, carefully hidden from the real ones, so they couldn't see him ahead of time. The most advantageous element to backing is surprise, the sudden happening of one dog upon another that's pointed, so that the desired reaction is compelled virtually by instinct. It's then the honoring dog looks proudest.

In training sessions, we always set Chief Burdeshaw up in a hidden pocket behind a turn of the field, beyond view of the student body on the chain. That way, when we led them in, they'd not see the dummy dog until the critical moment. Usually we brought them in two-by-the-time, Loretta with one, me with another, while Mely "handled" Burdeshaw, going through the flushing ruse once we had the apprentices suitably planted, kicking the bird out of the trap, firing the shot, then returning to her "dog," rubbing him up and praising him before folding him to the ground and hiding him under the sack. All as we held the youngsters to anchor, styling them to grandeur, tendering words of praise, releasing them with a tap on the ear, and leading them quickly away.

Beda was a natural, Jill as well, slamming to a stop and caving at the backbone the instant they spied the pointing dog, then swelling slowly again into a proud, high pose. I'm sure they realized after a time or two that Burdeshaw was a hoax, though as quickly that the birds that always accompanied him were not, and their instinct to honor and desire for birds were so strong it trounced their skepticism. That was what you hoped for, of course. For once they imprinted so on the image of the pointing "dog" in the company of flushing birds, they would as surely stop for a similar image with a bona fide bracemate. The power of suggestion.

Pat, Thane, and Ben were matters of a differing magnitude. First time up, Pat stuttered to a halt, studying the wooden dog stiffly and veering into a cautious semicircle of inquiry. I stopped her with a "Whoa," propped her up, her tail arrested half-mast by uncertainty. When the bird went out, the voltage surged. Breaking, she stabbed forward, rearing against the cord, tail popping. I picked her up and set her back.

"Whoa, Pat."

Once she ascertained birds as part of the equation, she rapidly suffered herself to back, and proudly, but she was so strongly competitive that soon followed the fault of creeping—cat-walking in to steal the point. More whoas. Pick up and put back. Toward its resolution, our wills would clash for a long time.

Thane and Ben would back, not naturally but on command, and neither with proper enthusiasm. It would take repetitions . . . and birds. We started using both traps and loading two birds each, tripping them with a delay between. It kept the dogs off guard, expecting another, and they learned to stand taller and tighter.

Back training's a lot like castor oil; you smell and taste it long after it's gone. Soon every dog in class so anticipated Burdeshaw from the moment we led it off the chain, he'd start pussyfooting into a series of creeps and whoas, bracing for the encounter. Time then to move on, pull off and return less frequently, introduce a live dog in an actual field situation. The baby lesson had taken.

∽ CHAPTER 12 ∽

ALL THE WHILE, OUR LITTLE ACRE-AND-A-QUARTER LOT AT 1209 Chaney Road in Raleigh, which had before seemed plenteous, was shrinking. We had been happy there. But the thirty-minute trips to the barn for training, to gather up horse and trailer every time before a trial, and the two-hour-long stint to Elm Hill, was growing more onerous. Not to mention the proximity of the neighbors. At one time, we had twenty-six dogs on the premises, puppies and grown-ups. Setters, pointers, a Lab or two. In the days when Raleigh still had a little dirt under its toes, and you could evade town in ten minutes. Before urban ordinances decided for a body how many dogs were cordial. We kept kennels immaculate and the barking at bay, and avoided generally the conflict with society. But there were two exceptions, which broke upon the peace as pestilence upon Paradise, one as regularly as every Saturday midnight, and the other as unpredictably as madness under moonlight.

These were the seventies, dizzy with dance and disco. The Douglas family, which had for years lived traditionally and compatibly next door, had dissolved and departed. She had died, and he had sold out and moved away, taking Bobby with him, the boy I had enjoyed so deeply. Bobby loved the dogs, the hunting, and the fishing, and I had taken him along on many occasions, encouraging his affinity for wildness. But now that was done, and in its place was the younger, urbanesque couple newly in residence, hot with Saturday Night Fever, into ducktails, chains, and bell-bottoms. Every sixth evening, like Adventist religion, they threw a party, and the street was choked with cars, and noise, and beer cans the morning after. Revelry reached an apogee about midnight, spinning bright lights and gyrating silhouettes on the shades, driving the dogs into an utter frenzy. We did what we could, but our attempts at quelling the din were futile as Catholicism in Jerusalem. Portions of the music were particularly incendiary. John Travolta had absolutely nothing on us when the Bee Gees hit the top end of "Stayin' Alive." The whole kennel was strutting.

The pot calling the kettle black, the party pushers actually had the gall to call the Animal Control folks out on us. Two officers showed up on a Monday morning, while I was away. Loretta showed them the dogs and the kennels, explained the dilemma.

"Cleanest kennels we ever saw," they vowed before they left. All we ever heard from them.

But the sirens, from the emergency vehicles racing down Western Boulevard earshot close, were endless. Suddenly in the small obsidian hours of morning, into the black vacuum of semiconsciousness, Loretta would be punching me out of sleep again. The sirens would be wailing, first the cops and then the fire engines, and every dog on the place would be wailing. Sopranos, baritones, falsettos, and basses. We had a three-stage emergency management plan.

"Hit the lights," I would order, even as Loretta was up and rushing to comply, and I was stumbling out of bed, groping to find my second boot in the dark. The outside floodlamps would blink on about the time I made the back door in my underwear, bathing the kennels with light. Sometimes, if it was a one-car alarm, the crescendo was dampened by illumination. With an out-and-out catastrophe, it was hopeless. Then there was nothing to do but throw open the door and yell to the top of my lungs.

"*Hey! Hheyee!* Quit that fuss." Clap my hands. Which was usually greeted by a temporary lull, then the *"wheeeow, whheeow, wheeeow"* of the sirens again, and an instantaneous reincarnation of bedlam.

"*Hheyyee!* I'm comin' out there!"

Sometimes I had to, with the garden hose, to drench the din with water. They hated that, retreating to their house and shaking disdainfully. After a time, they became conditioned to the threat, dreading it enough, barring an out-and-out five-alarm catastrophe, to hush with the lights or a verbal assault or two. Nevertheless, it was aggravating to have to forever worry over an impulsive clash between instinct and civility. For our part, they could bark to heart's content. It was better than ADT.

But there was more. I craved the country. I had grown up in the country. I wanted it back. I wanted gray lizards on rail fence posts, whippoorwills to announce twilight, a bobwhite to herald dawn. The horse and dogs altogether, with a barn of our own, and a pasture, our own trees, a pond or two, and a log cabin I would build from scratch on a hill overlooking one of them. A place to homestead a few training quail, and to headquarter a pigeon loft. We had been looking, in Granville County about thirty minutes north, ever more seriously. Country we passed through on our way to Elm Hill every week or so during the training season. Thinking maybe to find an old, rambling clapboard farmhouse to restore, one with a porch that would collect a rocking chair or two, and be shady and inviting behind a trellis of summer roses. It was a swelling dream, which drummed on our souls like the song of a grouse, on his courting log, in the yearning of spring.

We found it that summer, after we were threadbare with looking, and it took all our wherewithal and a bit of fate, but we made it come true. I guess only rarely does it happen as precisely as you imagine it will, but scarcely either, if your heart says it's right, is the difference between the two. It was a small farm on a then dirt road, Route 1, Box 42, just northeast of the little erstwhile mule-market town of Creedmoor. Twenty acres, no mule, and nary an outbuilding, just the house. But all the makings. Three acres of green pasture, a secluded setting unseen from the byway, a pond site or two, mature hardwoods and pines, a clear gurgling creek along its western limit, a northern exposure for an heirloom orchard. Most important, a beautifully wooded and level two acres for a kennel.

Melanie ran down to explore the woods and the creek, while Loretta and I surveyed the house. Though not that of our dreams, it seemed almost equally to be. It was new but not modern, built in the fashion of a vintage gambrel-roofed barn, of cedar. With porches front and rear. As though that were not enough, the foyer past the front door, at the threshold of the great room, which reeked with the richly satiating scent of cedar, was blue flagstone, and at the center of the house, from the pine floor to the peak of the roof, stood an immense thirty-foot chimney of native fieldstone. The fireplace was big enough for half a log, and the whole of the front wall was picture window. I could fantasize snowfall, fine white flakes sifting past the windowpanes on a blizzardy January night, the soft circle of lamplight that feebly illuminated the icy mantle accumulating on the ground underneath, a cup of spiced cider in the darkened room, and the flicker of the fire on the orange walls. Loretta in my arms on the sofa, a quilt pulled up around, my daughter asleep in a great leather chair, and a setter or two dozing by the hearth.

Two steps onto the foyer, our eyes met, my wife's and my own, and there was not to be a question further, though there was more of the house to see—antique pine doors, dining room and a pewter chandelier, old porcelain faucet knobs, pie-safe cabinets, and claw-foot tubs.

"I want to live here," Retta said, "with you . . . for the rest of my life."

And so it has been now for twenty-six years. Every time we enter anew. And so it will likely be.

Tickled to my toenails, we told the dogs and started the kennels the day the closing was certain. First order was fencing in two acres of exercise ground, into which we would move and erect the kennel runs proper. Later, when we might manage it, a small kennel house. A friend, Karl Munson, volunteered to help, and with a rented two-man posthole auger, we shook, rattled, and rolled through a hundred or two holes. For weeks, we apportioned dogs between crates, the house in Raleigh, the horse trailer, and the backyard, while I worked night and day tearing down and reassembling the existing kennels onto their new home. Hauling rolls of two-by-four wire, fence posts, and the wooden Seagram's whiskey barrels we used then for dog housing behind a piled-high pickup on a borrowed flatbed trailer. For we had to make do with what was. There could be nothing new and fancy. Just the woodlot, dirt-and-gravel runs we'd always had.

Loretta planned flowers, and Melanie got promises for a treehouse and a playground. How very rich and happy we were.

More so when we sold the house in Raleigh for a larger sum than we'd supposed. The margin to buy Maggi, the second walking horse we'd wanted so long, and a new Gore horse-and-dog trailer to boot. Two stalls, eight built-in dog boxes, and a small tack room. Enough to squirrel away, even, the amount it would take to raise a barn.

On through the excitement of it all, August to mid-September, I religiously roaded and drilled the dogs. Longing for the field, to turn them loose again and run free. They were summer-stale. Beleaguered between Raleigh and Granville County, with the added anxiety of the move, I

wished for the time it could all be settled again. When I could plant both
boots on the same porch. Finally, on September 17, unable to wait one day
longer, we loaded up in the new trailer and set out for Elm Hill. Stopped by
Route 1, Box 42, going and coming. Wanting to stay. Soon, not soon
enough, we could call it home. And halve the distance.

The first field workout of the year was like a date with an old flame.
Not exactly what you hoped, but so good to see her again. The cover at
Elm Hill was head-high and green. The air was sticky hot, close and stifling.
Danny had bush-hogged lanes through the rampant weeds, but outside the
field edges, it was hard to keep up with a dog, even horseback. Scenting
conditions were atrocious. Still, it was thrilling to be back on a horse again
for real, to hit a whistle and send a hard-driving dog away. To see it pop
again somewhere way out yonder, through a break in the cover, and sail on.
Pat went a strong fifty minutes, mindless of the heat. Reaching and searching. Thane and Beda went less crisply, but gamely, tiring at thirty. For all the
hours of roading, conditioning for the circumstances was marginal. None of
the three could come up with a bird.

The following week was better. It was still asininely hot; as I rode, I
pleaded with the Man Upstairs for the first Canadian front and an early
frost. It was premature to provoke an answer, but at least I would be on
record with an order. Pat laid down a stirring ground race for most of an
hour, digging up a covey of birds before the Bear Trap crossing. They ran
ahead of her, confusing their scent with the fragrant green cover, and went
out as she was trying to establish point. She stopped on her own to honor
the flush, her tail flagging over her back self-consciously, knowing she was
victim to their ploy.

Beda, too, found birds, in a race that was pretty but more restricted than
her normal. Again, it was hard to beat through the matted sedge, dog fen-
nel, and trumpet vine. Her strength waned rapidly in the heat. She winded
the covey at a distance, throwing her head high and wafting back and forth
along the woven fence that prevented her from the hedgerow. Climbing
down, I hoisted her over, as the bulk of the bevy lifted. Efficiently she
pressed a lay-back, running single through the olive until it was coaxed to
hold, bringing the setter to pledge herself to point. She could be breathtak-
ingly intense and stylish, often the most fluent of the three. Then I walked
in to flush, and the picture evaporated as quickly as it was painted. The bird

blew out premature and Beda went, and with my flogging volley of "Whoas" Maggi went, and I was left to cuss my toes. It took fifteen minutes to gather what and wherewithal, before I could send Thane for what amounted, evenly, to a ragged thirty minutes.

On a hallmark day late in October, with the hickory leaves tobacco gold and Raleigh laid to the past, we moved lock, stock, and bedstead to Granville County, deliriously happy to be in the country. For us all, it was truly a homecoming. With Squaw the Lab, Melanie wandered the babbling little creek until dusk, catching little brown newts, with skins so translucent you could see their heartbeat, and large black salamanders with red polka dots. Loretta hung baskets of strawflowers under the eaves, and a welcome on the wall by the door. Buck naked, in full daylight and a proclamation of freedom, I peed on a tree in the front yard, and later fired a shotgun out the back door in sheer exorcism. The horses cavorted in the pasture, the setters in their new surroundings, barking at strangeness until they were hoarse. And there was not a soul in the world to be troubled about it.

~ CHAPTER 13 ~

THROUGH OCTOBER AND NOVEMBER, WE WORKED AT ELM HILL TO promote the dogs to steadiness, for that was requisite now with any hopes of winning, and they did not challenge the first shooting-dog trial of their maturing careers until the Christmas month. I knew they were not solidly ready to win. There was a chance. The odds were about even then that they would stay or break. But thanks to Howell Cockfield, Harold Ray, Thelmer Page, and others, I had a perspective on that now. I was beginning to understand that many of the most thrilling dogs in field trial history were never completely broke. You don't want them to be. You want them on that very fine edge between stay and go, so that stardust jumps off them when they point, and they lean into scent like it's the very spark of life, and swell like soldiers snapping to salute when the birds go off. You win good trials that way, and lose them too, much the same. When they break over, bump and chase like puppies, it's just the IOU—overdue—for pent-up perfection. For the life of our career, come what may, I would train that way.

They don't win in the kennel. You have to take the risks, suffer the breaks. At their best, field trials were never meant to be ordained or mechanical, but electrifying. That's why we loaded up the first of December and went to the Sandlapper Trial. Thane didn't go. Realistically, he was still too far off the pace to squander money we didn't have, so we took the closest two, Pat and Beda.

At best, our shooting-dog debut was inauspicious. Pat was due in season soon, and I could tell. She was unduly headstrong. I lost the handle on her shortly after breakaway, certain she was off somewhere playing with birds, unsewing the few stitches we had managed to steadiness. Hoping, on the other hand, that we hadn't ridden by and left her behind somewhere on point. Which wouldn't last long, and sum to the same thing. Warrior Maiden did a grand job on the ground, until about twenty, when she had an honest stop-to-flush, then came unbroke as I was climbing down to fire the shot, and went after the birds. All that was left was to pick up, hang our heads, and face the long drive home. Moments and miles. Win or lose. Moments and miles.

"Maybe we should wait till they're closer," Loretta said on the way back.

"Closer to what?"

"Closer to winning. Christmas is coming. I guess you know any money we get we'll have to turn back to the kitty, to pay for what we give."

"Yes, I know."

She was silent for a time.

"When does Sumter County run?" she asked at the end of it.

I turned to look at her. She smiled at me. I leaned across our sleeping daughter and kissed her. It's that kind of glue that's kept us together these forty-two years.

Disregarding the altruism, Sumter County waxed about the same. A combination of handling mistakes, broken manners. I failed to flush a bird, Pat didn't. Beda had a wreck at ten. Afterwards, I roaded Thane behind the gallery, we loaded up and turned once more for home. Six hours more of miles.

I asked myself again the following week if we were still making progress. Yes, I supposed. We were finding a few wild birds yet at Elm Hill, gradually whittling the steadiness thing down, from chase to steps, and oftentimes hold. Though increasingly it was being frustrated, it seemed, by collisions toward the same purpose with Parke and Aubrey and others who were coming newly there to train. What shaped a problem turned out a gift. Frank Gattis showed up among them.

We weren't related, we decided—by blood, anyway. He wore his name differently, with two t's instead of d's. But we were close kin. Frank loved a bird dog, especially puppies, lay-it-way-out-yonder, big-going ones. Shades of Bob Lindler. Frank had access to a couple of big fescue pastures in upper Carolina, where you could play a puppy out until he looked like an aspirin tablet. He had a part-time girlfriend, too, who rode and worked dogs with him. He'd had a wife, but she'd never managed much more than a hack-

amore over his head, and they had parted company along the way. The love
of his life was his horse, Hombre. Hombre was a big, red sweet-shanked,
four-lick gelding, with a running walk that could deliver a tray full of cock-
tails to a dinner party, spill nary a drop, and let you pour them on the way.

I had finished running our dogs, and Frank had a hot puppy to uncork
and nobody to hold the bottle, so I went along as scout. The pup was scour-
ing the countryside, but mostly out front, so there wasn't a lot of riding to
do. Just tag along and keep vigil.

"First-year dogs. Setters," Frank repeated for himself.

"Yep."

"Crockett dogs."

"Yep."

"Broke?"

"Uunhhh . . . ," I shrugged.

"Comin'," Frank surmised.

"We keep whackin' at it," I said.

The pup was out on the limb now, hitting a bigger lick.

"Yeeeahh-boyyy!" Frank sang to him, let him know he wasn't lost. The
pup made a huge swing left.

"A few more birds and we might get there," I added.

"You don't work the Low Ground?"

"The Low Ground?"

"Lot of birds on the Low Ground. Good place to run a dog. Don't tell
Charlie I told you," he said.

"Charlie?"

"Charlie Barker."

Charlie Barker was a respected amateur a county over, who also farmed
some dogs with the pros.

"He'd be ill with me," Frank said.

"Yea-a-hhhup-yoah!" He lapsed back to business. The pup had the bit in
his teeth, selling out now, down a big edge. Looking sharp, doing good. We
whooped a simultaneous approval.

"You're from Creedmoor?" he asked, watching his dog fade on.

"Three miles northeast."

Frank turned to me.

"You must be living on it," he said emphatically.

Almost. First I knew of it. Been a snake, it'd a bit us in the asp. Two thousand acres of unfenced cropland along the bottom ground of the Tar River, stretching away until it paled into the blue haze of the far woods lines. Big fields of corn, peas, vegetable crops, and soybeans broken by diverse woodland, ragged hedgerows, briery heads, weedy thickets, fallow corners, beggar-lice, and pockets of patch crops. Sewn together by woods trails and farming paths. Long, unchallenged edges that begged a dog to run them. Tawny thicketed aprons beautifully bespoken of quail, old homeplaces moldering to fern, sedge, and creeper under a trinity of heritage oaks, snaking stands of maple, gum, poplar, and pine. The sum of it rambling about so irresistibly as to construe an almost perfect three hours of running time, never touching the same ground twice. It would furnish a thrilling hour course for each dog, a safe haul from a major road, and only an occasional lazy freight train to worry about on the western fringe. It wasn't just a revelation, but a godsend, and would be for the next fifteen years. With it we would become a force.

Thereafter we would call it Corinth, Loretta and I—the total of the Low Grounds—for it was situated only a Sunday prayer from the white-washed, clapboard steeple of the Corinth Baptist Church, and because of it, in the Grecian sense of the Corinthian parable, we were indeed the wealthiest of amateur sportsmen.

The acreage was designated as state game land, under the auspices of the North Carolina Wildlife Commission, when we found it. Open to the public for hunting and training, but sparsely used beyond the families of the owners. It would revert, eventually, back to private privilege, but by then I would know the property keepers well. There were three of them, the best of rural America. Deedholders down through the generations, all living at various corners of the property—L. B. Averett, Madison Pitts, and Bill Crews. L. B. fought in the Big War, had the stories to tell. Madison could be as gruff and crusty as his looks and, treated squarely, kind as the summer wind. He was into tobacco research at the Oxford Station. Bill Crews, homespun and gentle in his bib overalls, at-leisure attire, was town postmaster at his day job. All farmed, as their fathers before them. By their grace, we were given the run of the land. Each accepted us in kind, even after I forgot myself in the heat of handling in the early going and allowed Dolly to plod across Madison's wet garden plot, and suffered a similar calamity on Crews's end of the holding, when once the mare went rampant with estrus, bolting and breaking down a pasture fence for the ineffectual attention of his quarter-horse gelding. I would come to know them and theirs across the years, would watch their young-uns, Frank and Ernie and Catherine and Neil, ascend, and the rest of us grow gray. Ever thankful for their tolerance and charity.

A week later, we ran there for the first time. We found five coveys of birds, and enough legroom to prepare for any quality shooting-dog stake in the country.

On through December into Christmas, we disregarded field trials and worked diligently at steadiness, mostly at Corinth. Unimpeded by outside intrusion, finding the numbers of wild birds we needed to prompt the polish. I made some mistakes and the dogs made some mistakes, but gradually the train was moving down the track. We were learning together, to read and trust each other, and more and more, Pat and Beda were standing their game and holding longer for me to get there. Haughty, taut, and bug-eyed, they'd totter on their toes like they'd been pinpricked, anticipating the flush as I beat the cover, watching the birds away, marking flight, staying proudly in their tracks for the shot. I cautioned myself constantly at keeping admonition and correction consistent and minimal. Increasingly, it became less necessary. Always I allowed them the benefit of doubt and erred to the flair of independence. Nearer and nearer they drew to our blueprinted standard of excellence: a high, tight edge.

I've seen it several times since with brilliant young dogs coming into their own. It's nothing short of amazing. You train and train, keep beating at the thing and beating at the thing, day after day, week on week, and you think you're getting nothing done. At its sag point, you lie in bed at night frustrated almost to tears, searching for some way to make them understand. To persuade them to accession. To find some means of laminating ingenuity upon instinct. Until you wonder if ever it will happen. And then one day that seems not a lot different from the rest, almost in a moment, they steady in. Stand as honorably as a flag snapping in the breeze, and rarely break back, and you've got *just* enough of a finished dog on your hands.

Only Thane lagged. He'd hunt and find birds beautifully, point and hold fifty percent, throw the difference to the winds. Lapse into flings of immaturity, take the birds away like a puppy, and resist my best efforts to dissuade him. I got as stiff with him as I dared, grabbing him up and shaking him until our jaws chattered, hauling him back to the scene of the crime, and propping him up with a "Whoa" and a warning. Praising him then, stroking him, restoring his dignity. Explaining what a convenient thing it could be to go on call as a stud dog once he'd won a bit more in the all-age wars. Then, with the very next bevy, he'd break like he knew no better. Bump and chase all over again. He was such a nice young dog, with thrilling potential, that I grew ever more vexed at my inability to bring him to completion.

At the end of my rope, I was driven to last measure. I had an early shock collar. Best on the market, but rudimentary by today's technology, it had a single, harsh and continuous level of "stimulation," limited by logic to negative reinforcement. Discouraging a behavior. I'd never used it before. Frankly, I was scared to death of e-training then. It hadn't been around long; there were a lot of horror stories. But the constant demand for discipline was beginning to erode my tediously built rapport with Thane, and I turned to it with the hope of instilling correction without the need of interjecting myself personally into the middle of it. The remote transmitter would afford the anonymity, timing the correction more instantly to the indiscretion as well. Still, I was wary.

I tried it on myself the night before the workout, holding the contact prongs of the collar to my palm.

"Hit it," I ordered, gritting my teeth as Loretta stabbed the transmitter button. I was ready, but even so, at the shock I slung the collar bang across the room into the refrigerator. Melanie's eyes were bright with awe.

The charge itself wasn't so very bad; it was just the trick and tingle of the thing. The same phenomenon I was counting on to reform Thing.

"Put it around your neck," Loretta said.

"Uuh-uh," I replied doubtfully.

I wondered whether all night long, then decided to proceed. Almost in retribution, it appeared, I was rewarded with disaster. Fifteen minutes into an hour session, Thane swapped ends on an edge, weaved ten feet into the cover, and stacked up on birds. I had the transmitter in hand, but for moments he stood, his pose spellbinding, no sign of breaking. I jammed the transmitter back into the saddle holster, swung off the horse, jerked the gun out of the scabbard, and started in to flush. Suddenly the setter yelped, jumped sideways, then dropped his tail and retreated skittishly in a circle to me. Asking what he'd done wrong. About the same time, the birds blew out. I stood dumbfounded, lost with what had happened, until I was poleaxed with the only explanation. Somehow, by radio or powerline inter-ference, or whatever, the damned collar had tripped and shocked him at the worst imaginable moment.

I just couldn't believe it. How fortune could go so foul. Thane was still looking up at me, perplexed. Goddammit. We'd be forever working past this. And then I got mad. I tore the collar off and flung it as far as I could into the brush. For all I know, it's still there. Seventeen years would pass before I would pick up another e-collar, and not until the perfection of momentary impulse, multilevel circuitry.

Thane seemed undamaged by the incident. He was a man. Sent on, he rebounded, exploding powerfully away with the whistle, tail cracking hap-pily over his back. Twenty minutes ahead, he pointed again, as arrogantly as his nature, then jumped squarely in the midst of the bevy as I got there. Birds splattered everywhere, away in a bluster. The dog took about five hops, then halted, looking acquiescently over his shoulder:

"Well, come on."

I did, but not without a chuckle. And a good bit of respect. Thing and I would suffer on, whatever happened. He and me, and a check cord. Pull and haul, but honest.

Meanwhile, his sisters were showing him what-for. Both were going stronger and stronger on the ground, lacing together wonderfully forward hunting patterns, doing it with dash and style. More confident with every find, their charisma around game was captivating. It was time to test another trial.

∾ CHAPTER 14 ∾

IN THOSE DAYS, OVER THE HOFFMAN GROUNDS, THE NORTH CAROLINA Field Trial Association presented an amateur endurance shooting-dog stake titled the NC Shooting Dog Celebration. It was a highly contested, prestige stake, a must on the schedule of serious amateur handlers the whole of the East Coast. To win required savoir faire, both human and canine, aside from the superior conditioning and physical courage it took for a dog to power without letup the grueling ninety-minute heats. A trial of fortitude, many claimed, that could often be brutal in the arid, hot sand and scrub oaks of the sandhills. People tried to win it with all-age dogs, "lean breed" canines with superior staying qualities and maximum run and range. Occasionally they did. But if the judges were honest, it was an elite shooting-dog stake, and excessive range in the absence of a demonstrable show of hunt went unrewarded. What it took was a horseback hunting dog of exceptional class and courage, one that owned the physical stamina to lay out fast and furious at an ambitious distance, that relentlessly sought and pointed birds.

To a shank's-mare bird hunter used to a meandering morning hunt through fallow field and wooded bottom, where the dogs gear themselves for three hours, ninety minutes seems undaunting. In a top-flight field trial at horseback pace and range, it's brutal. A warrior's quest.

It was a bit beyond Beda. Oh, she would go, with the dare-to-die mettle that endeared her so. Until she dropped. But much beyond an hour, particularly in the heat, she would begin to falter. Contrarily, I had sent Pat an hour and a quarter on the Corinth grounds a number of times. She did it big and breathlessly. I knew she could do more if I asked. A week before the trial, I sent her an hour and forty-five. She rolled through it with authority,

136

jammed my throat with the power of her finish, and handled two coveys of birds perfectly between. The chain-hauling grind of the summer's roading and four months of running had honed her natural athleticism to sculpture. I knew she was ready.

I hoped I was. Dogs with Pat's brand of courage know nothing of intimidation. Men are more fragile. I would be up against some of the toughest, winningest handlers in the game. On the amateur circuit, this was the big time. A classic of classics. With a little luck, I knew what Zip Zap could do. The worry of always was mine, that I would do something of my own to hamper her luster.

On New Year's Eve, Pat pulled Loretta to the line at Hoffman, and I brought the mare up behind, the same dozen butterflies in my stomach I'd had the first puppy trial. There were eighteen seasoned shooting dogs in the stake—sixteen English pointers, Pat, and a Brittany.

The Trial Chairman formally announced the brace, as is the ritual of major stakes, first one dog and then the next, before acceding the running to the judges.

"Gentlemen, when you're ready . . ."

Both whistles screamed, and we were off. Together and hard away, both dogs dug for the front, splitting off right and left to respective edges a hundred yards out, scrambling for the forward advantage. Two hundred yards more they carried the opposing edges, tit for tat, then the course took a dip through a drainage and they were temporarily jerked from sight. Ten seconds later the pointer emerged, traveling the same side of the forward hill. On to the top of the hill we watched it go, hunting nicely the territory, then doubling back, almost to its handler, before being blown on and away again.

We made the dip, reached the crest of the knoll. Pat was yet to show.

My scout was a stranger. Virtually so. Pleasant fellow, name of Norman Melton, from Burlington. Different in the right kind of way, I thought. A dry wit and a gentle manner, a look of honest caring about his dogs and horses, the steely glint in his eye of a man who means to win. But fairly. We had met Norman and his wife, Gloria, only an hour before, on the grounds, while we waited reins-in-hand for the opening brace. They ran Brits strongly then, take them as they come, no deference to the all-breed trials. The one Brittany in the stake was theirs.

I thought of Norman now, knew he was back there. But this was broad country, Pat's kind of country, and I thought I knew where we would see her next.

"*Yeeeahh-up, yoahh!*" I sang to her, giving her the fix.

On cue, two hundred yards on and three ahead, she zipped left to right across the front, bouncing and popping. Flashing like intermittent points of light from the pine, oak, and sedge. It was beautiful. Well ahead of the pointer now, which was lined out and posting a respectable showing of its own, she was reaching on, carrying away. Hunting with a vengeance. Doing what needed to be done.

Fading from view again, she showed next in all the right places, at ten, fifteen, twenty-five. Pulling together a lovely shooting-dog pattern. Ever forward, ever stronger. The course swept left; to the right was a side path. I tipped Norman out to drag, knowing he would check it quickly. God save us if we lost her.

Thirty-five. She was gone again.

"Dog's on the far rise, straight ahead," came the welcome herald from a voice in the gallery. People were getting into her race now, thrilling with the excitement of a mounting challenge.

"Yes, Pat. Yes," I was chanting under my breath. I hit the whistle three long blasts, to call Norman back to post, let him know we had our dog.

Riding on, we reached the spot we'd seen her last, but didn't see her again for a time. I flared right, Norman drug the left, checking the edges. And then I saw her, a piece of her, standing high and stiff at a tuck of the course eighty yards ahead. She was gorgeously pledged to quail, and as my heart thumped and my head went light with the adrenaline rush, I lifted my hat off and high overhead.

"*Po-in-n-nt!*"

Spurring the mare to life, I raced to the find. The little setter stood solidly as I pulled the horse to sliding halt and piled off, snatching the shotgun from the scabbard in the same motion.

"Whoa, Pat." I cautioned her. She was cocked as precariously as the hammer over a percussion cap. Tail twelve straight and rigid as a rock, but wanting to go. "Whoa, Pat."

I waited beside her as Norman came pounding up, slid to the ground, caught up the reins of my mare, and held things in order on the sidelines.

Presently the judge came loping up, in a measured easy canter, a major part
of the gallery hard behind. An enveloping cloud of dust billowed and
passed. On our sixth pup stood, evocatively, just as she had in workouts
recently. I was proud enough to burst.

Slipping a blank into the gun, I snapped the breech closed and started
in to flush. I'd taken no more than a dozen steps in front of my dog, into
the sedge and scrub, when the birds started blowing out. The majority of
the covey almost as one, with a thunderous flutter like a scrap of cardboard
slapping the whirling spokes of a bicycle wheel, then one—two—three lay
birds in staggered seconds behind the report of the gun. Blasting away on
sputtering wings behind the covey, lapsing to a long, dipping glide as they
neared the safety of a far weedy head. Pat was swollen with desire, leaning
over her toes, watching them away. Took not a step. I was numb with
excitement.

I walked carefully to her. "Whoa, Pat, good girrl." I glanced at the judge,
sitting his horse sideways, a knee hung across the pommel, scribbling details
into his notebook. Kneeling, I stroked the setter's flanks. "Good girl, Pat."
Then collared her, released her with a tap on the ear, and led her back out on
the course. Leaned and grabbed with my off hand as Norman passed me the
reins of the mare and carefully slipped his fingers under the setter's collar.

"Good job, man," he said. I smiled, tense with adrenaline.

Norman guided her a safe distance from the stand, to remove the
temptation of a loop back to the site of the find, which can sometimes be
disaster when an excited dog bounces atop a laggard bird. Pat was afire,
straining to go. Would only lap a terse time or two at the water I offered.

Meanwhile, the pointer gained the front. Mounting quickly, I hit the
whistle. It cut the air like a cleaver, sending Pat sharp away. For several seconds the two dogs ran together. Then I hit the whistle again, like the stab of
a knife, and Pat drew fast and far away, not to show again until the passing
minutes said it was just time for her to. Popping out distantly forward, she
bounced and hunted the tawny trace of a long, rambling edge. Fading on.
Sewing together a hell of a ground heat, a big shooting-dog race. At the
hour, the pointer was standing prettily, at the right fringe of the course. Its
handler was up and dismounting. We rode on, I, our judge, Norman, and
most of the gallery, glued to the gallantry of the setter. When the majority
of a gallery forsakes a point to ride on to your dog, you know you're get-

ting something done. Shortly the balance of the judiciary came up. Evidently, there was calamity.

Now Pat had the course to herself, and she was making the best of it. Driving on with a quick and thrilling lick. Twenty to go and she was strong as she started. We needed another find, if possible; just one.

And then, with fifteen minutes to go, we lost her. The judge and gallery waited, all eyes searching, while Norman and I rode madly back, right and left.

"*Po-innt!*" Norman, somewhere from the near left rear. I spurred the mare, had no time to avoid a fallen log that loomed from the brush and sand like an ogre. I gave the mare her head and we went up and over it.

Pat was pointed as beautifully as before. Norman was standing guard close by, deferring to me as I walked in. I looked at my dog. She was certain, her head and eyes shoulder-level, locked left. The breeze was at her nose.

"*Wsshhheeh, wsshhheeh.*" I blew through my teeth, kicked at the dry brush, starting close in where the body language said they would be, then widening out to some distance. Flushed desperately, for we needed these birds. Flushed for as long as we could afford on the clock. Nothing. I walked back to her, praying I hadn't messed up. I studied her closely again. She had relaxed little. I had to take the chance. I tapped her on the ear, asked her to relocate. Stabbing forward, she locked again, then broke off and whipped to and fro, screening the air for hot scent. Couldn't dig up a bird. I had no doubt the birds had been there; it was a known covey haunt. Likely they had left, just ahead of her stand. With Pat, the fires blazed too high for false points.

Enough time wasted. I had to send her on. We accepted the tarnish of an unproductive and drove on.

At time she was fogging again to the far front, every fiber and sinew in the thirty-four pounds of her, bottom to spare. Every man jack there knew she was a threat.

The judges were carrying her as top dog at the end of the day, with three braces to go on the morrow. I didn't sleep a wink the whole of twelve hours.

Norman ran Clyde the first brace after daylight. Nor-Mel's Clyde was the Brit. A hell of a good one. Norm and Gloria had several good Brits over the years. Dogs that could go toe-to-toe with the cream of pointers and setters, and handicap nothing in the bargain. I came to know most of them. Clyde was the best. The best I've ever seen. As pretty goes, Clyde could string out about as pretty a shooting-dog race over the rolling, winding venue of Hoffman as you'd ever see. He'd lay out about a hundred-fifty, two hundred yards, and just hang there, sweeping the course as smoothly as a windshield wiper. Norman'd lay back as well, pulling on a cigar, letting his dog do his stuff.

Smooth that particular day they were, man and dog. Smooth, when smooth enough wins field trials, and Clyde came close. Gloria scouted. Turnabout being fair play, I would have done my best for Norman as he did for me. That's the code. But Gloria was family, had the great advantage of living with and knowing those dogs, and was a fast and fearless rider. I wasn't needed.

Clyde's contention was similar to Pat's in that he had one nice find at forty-five, then a circumstance near time, when he established point again on an edge near McGee's Castle. Clyde was standing tightly, but his pointer bracemate failed to honor the stand, fussed by, jumped into the cover, and took the birds out. Clyde stood unmussed through most of it, but was flustered into a slight loss of composure. All before the judges got up. They suspected what had happened, were told as much. But they couldn't sort out what they didn't see, and with Clyde standing loosely now and the birds gone, it waxed the kind of thing that spoils a spectacle, like mouse shit on a wedding cake.

The owner of the pointer stood slack-jawed, blubbering the lamest excuse in the book. "My dog didn't see no tail. Can't expect him to back."

"Tail, hell," Norman said. "He never took time to look."

They clabbered around until there could have been a fight, handlers and dogs, because by then the Brittany and the pointer were squared off too, hackled and snarling. Except Norman was too much the gentleman.

Then the two dogs in the final brace of the stake came along pretty neatly, with good, consistent races and two finished finds apiece. One was a little moderate in range, no paragon of style, just adequate. The other about what you wanted.

As I could see it, it boiled down to the better of those two, and Pat and Clyde. But when the announcement was made, neither Pat nor Clyde was in it. The judges had named one the Winner and the other Runner-Up.

Wrongly, I still believe. It could as easily have been Pat and Clyde. Pat was in there, or should have been. For that's where the excitement was. A year later, after she'd won a good bit more, she likely would have been. But the two pointers were "clean," free of any blemish—like an unproductive—which is always a convenient way to judge.

What do you do but load up and go home? But, Lord in heaven, I was proud of my dog. She'd given fair notice, in no uncertain terms. She might have a sandlot handler, but she herself was the big time. From that day forward and the rest of her career, when the judging was square, she was never beaten by another dog. Not on birds, and definitely not on the ground. There would be times we didn't win. When I failed someway on my end—bumbled a flushing attempt or didn't send a scout out in time—and ruined the day, or when Pat, who lived the edge, simply took herself out of it by touring an excess of country or breaking over on a bird. But the premise was posted. When she would be beaten, she would beat herself.

~ CHAPTER 15 ~

TWO WEEKS LATER, I JOINED BOB TATE FOR THE FIRST MAJOR JUDGING assignment of my own. The South Carolina Shooting Dog Celebration, comparable event for the Palmetto State, was an hourlong plantation trial. I had anticipated it eagerly, but I was nervous.

It's a different load you shoulder when you swap your whistle for a stopwatch and gavel. An invitation to judge a field trial is an honor, one no man should accept for less nor underestimate the more. The requisites are stringent: to set and maintain a ground pace consistent with the stake, to give every dog your full attention for every second of its heat, to arbitrate faithfully upon canine performance and not upon tangents of social persuasion or status, and to comport yourself with the dignity deserving of the station.

With every performance, there are issues of discretion, I would come to find over the ensuing years, from the smallest stake to the largest, that must be discussed and resolved. Issues of weather, nature, and whether that wend themselves into confounding puzzles of logic, which must be unwound as objectively as they entwine. Their equitable resolution calls for all you can possibly know about dogs and birds and horses and frost and wind and sun and rain . . . and integrity . . . and more. The bigger the stake, the harder it becomes, and there are occasions when the separation of ten dogs to two will be so finite as to question the reality or fairness of what has been decided. But it must be done. Done as fairly as is humanly possible, so that it is not afterwards beleaguered by conscience. With the task, decisions of the past, which as a handler or member of a gallery may have seemed blatantly flawed, come to be understood in hindsight as not so injudicious as indefinite. Reflections of infinite judgment, as the job implies, the arbitration of which is rightfully achievable only by the two people who by charge have witnessed and considered every incident.

These are only the cognitive requirements.

By temperament, you must be willing to work in concert with the man riding beside you, to accord him the same respect you grant yourself, to debate cordially with him all items of reason, to discuss, persuade, and listen. To work toward a final consensus, but remain undaunted at reasonable dissension. When, nearing the end of the haul, you are understandably tired and irritable, you must guard yourself at remaining congenial and wholehearted. Right yourself with dignity. For you and your peer, for the extent of that trial, are trusted with a tradition of gentility that's a quarter into its second century. Should you be amicably asked, you should welcome an explanation of your decision. Sometimes with the additional burden of remaining unruffled in the face of belligerence. For as much as consensus is an attainable goal with your peer, it is an unreasonable expectation with the totality of handlers and gallery.

Physically, you must be a better than average horseman, confident and comfortable on a thousand-pound animal whose first concern by instinct is its own welfare, not yours. Know enough about horses to anticipate their behavior, be able to remain calm and collected in harrowing moments, and accept the ever-present risks that go with the unexpected. In championships and classics, you will confront the necessity of riding eight-hour days, rain, sleet, snow, or hail—days on end—affording every contender full, fair, and undiminished opportunity to excel, until a stake can be carried to its reasonable conclusion. In other words, you don't come to trim minutes, to abbreviate heats, to see how fast you can return home. If so, you should have stayed there in the first place.

It will be of great advantage if you have trained and hunted your own dogs, for the experience will be invaluable in helping you interpret the behavior of others. At the very least, you should have hunted upland birds behind pointing dogs, and participated as spectator to sanctioned field trials. Most practically, you should have handled dogs competitively in a number of them, at the level you are being asked to judge.

Judging is an honor, but a painfully demanding and accountable one.

I was green as a gourd that first engagement, and more than a little scared. Scared of making a mistake, sober with the responsibility of making any number of momentary decisions that would determine the competitive fate of good dogs and the people who had brought them there, at a considerable expense of time, hope, money, and effort. Pat had gotten me there, of course, opened another door as she has so many times. I'd take my example from her, buckle in, and do it with all the class I could manage.

One of the more difficult calls in judging pointing dogs can be a backing dilemma, whether a dog in the proximity and presence of a rigidly pointing bracemate was presented a clear opportunity to honor and purposely didn't. Not the condition where it is blatantly obvious, but the occasions when the question is cloaked in doubt and circumstance—horses, cover, or people between the two dogs, or where a bracemate is working to establish a point but has not yet firmly done so and still exhibits some movement. I recall such a situation from that first turn at the bench that illustrates the predicament quite dramatically. The second day of the trial, a handler of repute, both for winning and an aggressive personality, was running an acclaimed pointer bitch. Since two dogs hunting at will are not within the practical purview of both judges throughout their heat, one judge normally "takes" or assumes the principal liability for following one dog of a brace, and his partner the other. I was following this one.

The handler was a showman, piloting his dog to advantage, and the sprightly pointer female was doing an equally flamboyant job in her own right. Thirty-five minutes into the hour, she had an inspiring ground race going, and had charted two poetic and letter-perfect finds, the second including a snappy and intelligent relocation of the running birds. If she stayed at her fine deeds, in my mind she was going to displace the two good dogs we were carrying for winners at that stage. It is also wise practice in judging a major stake with hour heats, should you have a challenge of this magnitude in progress, to switch with your partner at the halfway mark, so that both judges will have seen the dog and strengthen the credibility of the decision should it, in fact, emerge a winner. I was about to do just that, cantering back to the front with the handler to rejoin Bob after the ten-minute hiatus it had taken to cover an on-the-limb point, when *bang,* I could see Bob's dog whip into an expressive U along the opposite edge of the wild-plum strip ahead. The cover veiled the find to a degree, but from my vantage, the solidly standing dog was almost wholly white and reasonably discernible. The thing you have to consider is whether it is similarly so from the ground level and approach of its bracemate.

My pointer female was coming up hard on the off side of the plum strip, her handler in a predicament he wished to avoid, but couldn't. The gallery had crowded around the pointing dog, scattered but confusing the view. Just as my dog reached the proximity of the find, the scene shifted slightly and presented what appeared to be a brief open window to the standing dog. I jerked my horse sideways for an unobscured view and strained to see what the female would do. Her handler said nothing. She didn't stop, might have stuttered almost imperceptibly, before sidling around the whole of the scene and racing on ahead up the course.

"You know there were people in the way," the handler said to me, turning in the saddle. "She didn't see that dog."

I didn't reply, my mind locked into a wrestling match with reason. Some old dogs are as slick at dodging a back as they are hiding a blink—a failure to point scented birds. Had it happened? If so, the old gal had masqueraded it as anonymously as the meat in a mulligan stew.

It's important in a trial to make a decision as close to an incident as you can, and I was trying. It's just that my gut was telling me one thing and my head another. At heart, I felt the dog had observed its bracemate sufficiently to create the obligation, and should have honored. Old, seasoned dogs that know the game can sense a pointing situation like you can sense your toes. Most learn to be automatically cautious for a back. Still, there was a modicum of doubt, and faced with the trepidation of being decisive, I let myself be intimidated and deferred to the dog.

I wouldn't make the same mistake today. I've been in the same circumstance any number of times since, and wouldn't be as easily fooled nor as smoothly intimidated, by handler or dog. But that day, my inexperience almost cost an honest dog. Not the dog I was looking at; the other. Bob's charge pointed again ten minutes later, and this time my dog was without an excuse, failing to stop again even with a blister of whoas and stealing the point. This time, of course, she was promptly ordered up. But her flagrant indiscretion was almost the undoing of her bracemate's composure, which would have unfairly ended another fine challenge that was unwinding on its own, an injustice I could have avoided.

I made a couple other, more minor blunders that trial, for which I apologize to the folks who were there. But I guess you have to start somewhere. What has lasted is the lesson I got on judging decisions, good and bad.

~ CHAPTER 16 ~

CLOSE AGAIN TWO WEEKS LATER, BOTH PAT AND BEDA PUT TOGETHER enough to win in respective heats at the Port City Trial near Wilmington, then sinfully undid it all like defiant teenagers in the gasping minutes of the clock. Pat was down with a heralded pointer of the day called Long Time Coming, beat him like a drum on the ground and rang up three star-cast, immaculate finds, before bumping and chasing on a fourth, temple over teakettle. She went twenty yards on sheer momentum before I could get her whoaed, hopes evaporating as swiftly as a breath on dry glass, and the only thing left to say was she looked good doing it.

Beda hunted the big, long edges with speed and style, like you'd sewn her to them, had one bang-up find on a tangled hedgerow—standing proudly for the long time it took to poke the bird out of the briers—then absolutely blew the farm on a second limb find, w-a-y out there, that would have put the nail in the coffin. By taking stutter steps at shot.

It was a four-wagon effort at a five-wagon trial, but despite it all, I was proud of the progress. Nevertheless, it was time to talk. I pulled Thane off the bench for good measure, lined the three of them up on the stake-out chain like ballplayers in a halftime locker room, and while Loretta and Melanie snickered from the sidelines, read them the riot act.

"Hey, you dogs, I've done all the hell I can. From here on, all I can do is haul you to the game and call the plays—you want to win, you got to git your mind outter yer butt and do it on your own.

"Now git out there and quit playing fumbly ass with the birds; let's put together something that works."

Thane allowed how alls he did was get roaded, and I said it didn't matter, he needed to hear it on principle alone.

First they listened, then looked at each other, and first one and then another shook vigorously. Hides rolling and shaking the words off, I could imagine, like shedding water.

Loretta clapped a hand over her mouth trying to stifle, then laughed out loud.

"And I could use a little more help from the owners," I said, "than bleacher kibble and criticism."

Melanie stuck her tongue out at me.

The next day was Sunday, and I drug the lot of them out at dawn for a backing session with Chief Burdeshaw. Which went reasonably well, but I'll still have to say the Chief was the steadiest of the bunch. Even the dogs looked sleepy.

"It's Sunday," Loretta protested.

"Who'd-a thought?" I said. I forgot she had the shotgun.

Somebody listened. Early in February of '79, the Gamecock Association ran an influential Shooting Dog Classic at Sumter, South Carolina, that featured one-hour heats over a plantation course and drew a strong slate of dogs, not only from the palmettos, but upper Carolina, Florida, Alabama, and Georgia as well. There were several champions in the field, and it shaped up a hoo-rah. I threw Pat and Beda right square in the middle of it.

In a clash of canine titans where nobody meant to follow, Pat fronted the trial as a bellwether. Lacing together one of the most scintillating, picture-perfect ground races I've ever witnessed, she took the course apart. On her own. I did nothing more than lay back and sing a reckoning song. At forty-eight, she was hanging far afront, at the logical extreme of a determined cast. At fifty, she was missing. John Little and I went scrambling. Prickling minutes later, we found her, tacked twelve-up to a bevy in a bay head, standing so stiffly you could have struck a match on her back. The birds, twenty strong, boiled out and back over the gallery as the shotgun boomed, and the little setter whirled in her tracks to mark, jacking all the higher. Sent on, she hammered heaven to the ground, finishing as forcibly as she started. Far to the piney front, tail cracking and tiny spurts of dust from her heels rising faintly behind into the yellow sunlight.

Sim Wright, who had good setters of his own, rode by as I was gathering her up. Lifted an index finger to his hat brim.

"That dog could raise the hair on a dead man," he said.

Beda came boldly behind, but left big and got out of ken on the break-away, then muddled for ten minutes with the course. Rare for her, and it marred an otherwise distinguished ground gamut. She hunted her heart out, but try as she might, couldn't turn a bird. Rare as well, for she was the equal of her sister as a bird finder. When I called her in at pickup, she seemed embarrassed. Disappointed with herself.

"It's all right, girl," I said. "It's just a thing. You tried."

Suspense grew as we waited the trial through. I rode several key braces, watching dog after dog challenge and plateau, all but one, beneath the high plain to which Pat had ascended. Until finally it was over, and the whistle shrieked, and with my stomach doing pirouettes, the Trial Chairman announced to the world that Pat had her first shooting-dog win. She was the class act in a class stake, and it was a big win for us.

Back at the trailer, Melanie and I got down on our knees beside her, told her so. She was totally enamored with a big, fuzzy brown caterpillar she'd scratched out of a leaf pile, and allowed it was just an ordinary thing. Oh yes, as ordinary, I agreed, as a rainbow behind a snow shower, and she had my welcome to do it again any next time she felt like it.

"You don't think she's getting the big head, do you?" Loretta asked.

"You can't acquire somethin' you's born with," I thought.

It snowed, in fact, for two days the trailing week. Powdering the face of the world a wonderland, and we turned loose the kennel and went playing out back like we had when they were all puppies. Red holly berries again, standing as brightly as blood drops on a wedding veil. And we wondered if Dax and Joe and Storm and Jake were gamboling in it also. I hoped so. A week more to the day, it snowed, moreover an honest foot this time, deeper in the drifts, enough to bury Dolly up to her shoulders in places. It stayed icy cold, defying the sun. We hooked up and roaded, shards of dry snow spattering up withers-high from the vigor of our going, into the sunlight against the laundered blue sky, powdering and scudding away behind us in small clouds on a stiff north wind. The punch of our breath fogging rhyth-mically onto the burdened air. The dogs loved it, digging and huffing with excitement, grabbing up mouthfuls of snow. Always there was the sixth pup, who loved it more than all, who met it to a moment, who bored stolidly into the bitter wind and ignored the ice balls in her paws, while the others begged time to chew them free. And every hundred yards, I had to pull up and get off to pick loose the pods that had frozen to the mare's hooves.

When the snow was spent, it rained, and rained. The ground grew rotten, and the mare's hooves mucked and sucked air with each stride, throwing stringy ropes of mud onto my back as we slogged through bottom and bog. The coats of the dogs parted along their backs, waterlogged, and the water streamed down their flanks and haunches to freeze into dirty balls on the feathery hair of their legs and bellies. Still we ran and roaded, hanging on to our conditioning edge. At Corinth, we ran and hunted until pads wore raw and bloody on the ice, but found little, the birds stressed with survival, holed up and moving scantly. From horseback, I scattered shelled corn at known covey sites, hoping to help them through.

And then, unbelievably, on the first day of March, the sun fought through, established a beachhead, and a southwest breeze lofted in all the way from the tropics—the harbinger of spring. The daily highs ran mid-seventies for two weeks, and the willows by the waters drooped in umbrellas of mint green, and the tops of redbuds and maples at the woods lines blushed ruddy with buds. We cast our lot into the Swamp Fox Shooting Dog Classic midmonth, Thane and Pat, happily reunited with the mesmerizing mood of old Medway. Where Pat had won so ebulliently as a derby, but this time was burdened with the accountabilities of maturity. She rose to the occasion as always, with a gripping ground heat, hunting far and hard for the hour. Doing everything she needed to win but come up with birds. Thane was undone by the road gallery, a noisy caravan of trucks and spectators winding along the fringes of the course, the first time he had encountered such. Listing to his nitsy side, he came unstrung and failed to fire, running less than his usual inspired race. At fifty, no birds to boast either, I picked him up.

In a shooting-dog stake, it's paramount; you have to find birds. Of the sixteen dogs in the stake, only five had bird work. Billy McCathern's Judy, most notably, with two finds. Judy was a consistent and alluring little gyp, liver and white as I remember, hard to beat on her home turf. The second-place dog had birds, but took the liberty of steps after them, and third place was awarded on a back of sorts. It was a ragged stake, the best dogs, other than Judy, going birdless. But it happens that way now and again. One of the loose fortunes of field trialing, along with the luck of the draw, which might have you running the only foul day in five. One more way of spelling disaster, another way of holding the best dog in the stake doesn't sometimes win.

The mistake I made was not running Beda. We carried her and roaded her behind the gallery, and she wanted so badly to run. But it had been downright hot right up to the trial, pushing the mid–eighties at home, worse south. So we had opted not to run her, recalling the occasion she had overheated before I knew it at Fort Mill. Then, the very day of the trial, a Canadian front had built in, and it was pleasantly in the fifties again. It was a shame, because she had been looking great and finding birds in workouts, in honesty the most consistent of the three. I believe yet she could have won that day. But you toss the dice on such things the best way you can, and only scarcely do they come up sevens.

Pat and I alone made the journey to the Region 2 Shooting Dog Championship over the Assunpink grounds in New Jersey the next week. It was our first titular event, and we came so close. I carried both horses and rode virtually every brace of the trial. There were maybe seven dogs that had championship-caliber performances, and Pat was solidly one of them. Her ground coverage was powerful and eloquent, the animation of her going compelling. At ten, she had an elegant, steady find. At twenty-five, another its match. The space was about perfect. One more of equal dimension at about forty-five, and coupled with the ground fire we had going, we'd scorch somebody's boots.

At forty-seven, she was absent, rolling off a long forward cast into a swale of cover and not yet showing on the far end. I was getting nervous, and asked the Union cavalry to take a look. We had kidded each other since I got there, my scout and I. I was J.E.B. Stuart and he was John Buford, and we were fighting Gettysburg all over again. I had ridden for him the first day, and now on the second, he was returning the deed. For a Yankee, he was proving unusually reliable.

"Hey Buford, how 'bout checking the course of that bottom?" I hollered over my shoulder.

"Well, that's the low ground, so she's probably down there," he threw back as he spurred his horse and tore off. A minute or two later, a muted summons came floating up out of the hollow.

"Po-i-nn-t!" A few seconds afterward came another, more distinctly. *"PO-I-N-N-T!"* He had backtracked to the crest of the declivity, was up in the stirrups with his hat hoisted high above his head, but looking down below. It was a pretty thing.

I gave the mare the reins and clucked, and felt the power of her bunch under me, exploding into a gallop. Judge and gallery closed hard behind, in a dash to question destiny. I pulled up hard at the top of the hill, the mare fretting under me. Buford had peeled back down off the hill. I could see that he had dismounted, was standing beside his horse a quarter of the way up the bottom, the buttermilk gray gelding a sketch of alabaster against the mute silver tones of the trees. I searched hastily, but couldn't see my setter. Sending the mare over the edge, we slid and tacked our way down the greasy bank, to the foot of the hill. A few lopes more and we made Buford's position. Glancing back, I could see judge and gallery above, a single-file parade of horses and riders, guardedly crosscutting the slope.

I questioned Buford with anxious eyes. "Where?"

He had in a chaw of tobacco. He cocked his head sideways, discharged a copious gush of amber. Wiped his mouth with a sleeve. Not bad for a Blue-belly. Raising his arm, he extended the finger at the end of it deeper into the bottom. I still couldn't find her. I shifted a few feet, searched more intently. Got down off the horse to peer under the cover. Suddenly she loomed, like an image from a picture puzzle. She was planted along the meander of a small, glassy stream, amid alder and a copse of green fern. Hiked beautifully onto her toes, she stood sky-proud, winding the bird from some distance. The incoming breeze faintly teased the plume of her up-tight tail.

"Didn't know a Confederate dog could stand 'at proper," Buford clipped. I cut him a grin.

About then the judge rode up, the mounted entourage fanning around him. I slipped the shotgun from the scabbard, and pointed to my dog. He got down off his horse, stepped beside me, and followed my finger. Looking intently, he bent, twisted, and peered. "I got her," he said after endless moments.

"Wait," he requested, "I'll go in with you."

"Whoa, Pat," I cautioned as we neared her. She cut her gaze stiffly to me, then back, her nostrils working the fragrant slip of air. From the height of her stand, I judged the bird to be across the branch. Breaking the gun, I shoved a blank into the breech, then circled a safe distance and jumped across. I checked my dog, started in to flush. Only a few steps and a wood-cock whistled up, lifting through the alder. I triggered the shot as it topped and stalled in a flurry of wingbeats, then watched it flitter away.

The little setter was ballooned and bug-eyed, twitching at the report. Had the bird flown on, she would have stayed, I've no doubt, but it was at that moment, after only a modest few yards, that it fluttered attractively to earth again. It was maybe the third woodcock she'd pointed in her life, and inebriated with the power of its scent and the tease of its travel, Gettysburg fell to Waterloo. Sensing it happening, I yelled, too late. She broke like a puppy, fussed, bumped, and chased.

"Uhgh. I hate that," the judge said, shaking his head, and walked away to his horse.

I collected my dog, stopped and standing after the second flush, shook her in token, and returned her to the spot of disaster. Just let her stand there a while, and think about it.

Buford came up. "Sorry, J.E.B. Truly. That find, clean, woulda prob'ly put the prize in your pocket. She's a hell of a nice dog."

My spirits were dropping into my boots, and I didn't say anything.

"You need me?" he asked differently. He knew I wanted privacy. "If not, think I'll mosey on."

"You're alright, Buford," I said.

"Whereuz you born, anyway?" I asked.

"Mississippi," he said.

I stood there for a while with my dog. She waited compliantly in place, tail beating softly over her back. After a minute or so, I could hear the handling songs from the beginning of the next brace. Hard it was, given the fate and fortitude it took to ascend so close, knowing as abruptly you were out of it. Particularly a championship. Our first. I felt hollow. Tingly. Like my insides had been jerked out, or someone had just shoved a saber through my gut. I looked down at Pat again. She had beaten herself, she alone. Yet there she stood, happiness in her eyes. Losing was a human invention. She knew nothing of it, I thought. Nor should she. And I reminded myself, it was about her, not me. If I harbored any sadness, it should be only that an extraordinary forty-five minutes of her life would go unrecorded through time. But that was not really true, either. You didn't need a field trial scroll or a stud book for that. This evening, we'd sit down by the fire, inscribe kit and kettle of it into our training log. And once we'd committed this aspiration to history, tomorrow we'd toss our hat into the next one.

I got down on a knee, stroked her gently.

"C'mon, girl, we're turnin' for home."

∾ CHAPTER 17 ∾

OUR FIRST SHOOTING-DOG SEASON CLOSED IN APRIL, BALANCING well into the red. Encumbered with debits of youth and exuberance, handling hesitancy, and plain hard luck. We had been to only a few trials, just enough to stay close to the game. Mostly we had trained, honing ourselves to the keen edge it took to win against the circuit veterans. Strop by strop, we were getting there.

The last two outings, the Sandlapper and Richburg Junction, were cases of point. We didn't win, but each brought small tokens of triumph, omens for faith. In the Sandlapper, I lost Pat slap off the breakaway, listening to the gallery when I should have been listening to me. She was out front where she belonged, and I was sent searching a tangent, and you didn't have that kind of time with Pat. When as swiftly as possible I cut a loop and remade the front, she was hell and gone again. Too long out of judgment. Thane had one nice find and the gallery murmuring, going big and beautiful on the ground, then suffering the rank misfortune of a weak bird that fluttered a foot up and back. No fault yet, and had the quail flown on, it could have eventuated a clean stop-to-flush. As it was, the big setter slid to his haunches in a boil of dust, gathering and reversing, as the bird hopped again and the dog simply flipped back and scooped it up. Brought it happily to me. He was doing what his instincts expected, for I had been shooting birds for him that sometimes did the same, and you couldn't hang him for that. It jerked us out of the trial no less.

But then along came little Beda, and she pulled us up by the bootstraps. John Temples had a veteran pointer male along then called Selpmet's Big Sam. I want to say orange and white, a handsome and boldly going dog that had made a mark for himself in southeastern stakes. Beda gave him why-

and-what-for that day on the ground, beating him twice to birds, and nailing a running single precisely while the pointer fussed around. It was a coup, and I was bursting with pride for her. But then the bird jumped up wild, and the pot boiled over, and she broke and chased. I'll share the blame, because I should have gone in more positively to flush. Maybe she would have stayed.

She stopped again about the second "Whoa," looked back at me. "Damn, and I almost had him," she as much as said.

Beda was ever impish. For every stake she drove in my heart, she threw me a Hershey kiss.

Thane was the one to shine at Richburg, after I lost Pat again for an hour, while Beda chaffed at home in season. Glory on the ground and what a nose, he chalked up two sparkling finds, standing head high and winding at walking distance on both. Exclamations went up like flighted doves. Then, for lack of a better reason, the self-satisfying rascal decided to donate it all to Denmark on a third. There were extenuating circumstances, liberated birds running in open view about him, and he made the best of them. Dog and birds exploded as one. Five minutes from a finish. I let my chin drop glumly to my chest. Shot down again, a fret short of fame.

Still and all, it was progress. Through the year, success had glimmered near then far, much as the wick and wane of a distant star. But the difference overall was diminishing.

The pieces were blending: the savvy on birds, the stick and stay on finds, the loft and style on point, the steadiness and charisma at wing and shot. I was proudest of all of our ground flair. For not once had any one of the three been beaten on the ground. They were fast and flamboyant, wide and wise. They went to the right places, they got there first, and they looked great doing it. Particularly Pat. We had worked hard for that, built on something already natural, and in the end it would be the difference. To win, you had to have it all. The majority of dogs running finished stakes were steady; some were stylish, the best supremely. Most would run and most would handle. But at the top of a stake, when among several dogs most else was equal, and you were down to fine points—looking for the separating distinction between greatness and its approximation—it would be hunt, dash, and style over the ground that would carry the day. It would be the dog that kept your toes in the stirrups and your heart in your throat, whether you were judging, riding, or handling, whether it was your dog or another's.

It would be the dog that could incite chill bumps in a heat wave, raise a brow sweat in a snowstorm. The bigger the stake, the more it would count.

I knew we could create that kind of excitement on the ground. Every time. Nobody won perpetually. But I knew, believed with my heart, could we get the rest together here and there, we would win. Win enough, and win well. When we didn't . . . whatever the case . . . they'd know we were there.

It was that faith and determination that carried us through another hot, grueling summer of roading and conditioning—that kind of stubborn, amateur, homebred fly-in-face-of-the-odds resolve—that brought us through to the next September at the pinnacle of our powers.

There were some strangers yet, out and about, who didn't take us seriously. But only once. Pat saw to that. Beda close behind. Thane was still deciding. Me, I just hung on for the ride, while folks gave me more credit than I deserved.

We ran close in every trial through early fall, still beating ourselves with bird bobbles. But the dogs were getting sharper each workout. Pat with the power, Beda with the finesse. I was especially thrilled with our warrior maiden. She had chased the shadow of her mesmeric sister from the time she was born, had less to do it with, but now, increasingly, she was exuding a magnetism of her own. Her ground race, already good, was becoming more and more mature, magic in motion. So smooth, so consistent. Her bird work, every stand, a stanza of poetry. Until mid-November, when adversity arrived, and we almost lost her.

She showed some stiffness in the haunches one training outing, worked on through it with trademark determination, came back reasonably well four days later for the next. But she ran without the usual zest, and at thirty minutes into an hour, was tiring strangely. At fifty, her hindquarters gave, and she sank to the ground. It scared me. I piled off the mare, my stomach queasy, and ran to her. She tried to get up, but floundered. She lay there, something she would only do with distress, looking to me for help.

"Okay, girl, I'm here . . . legs don't work?"

The age-old problem. They can't talk to you, in words anyhow, so you're left with the mystery.

My heart was thumping. I was really worried now. Quickly I checked her signs. They seemed normal, her breathing unhampered, her eyes level and aware. Her gums maybe a hair pale. I looked for blood, a puncture, an injury of any sort, could see nothing. She suffered me to test her rear legs one after the other without a whimper, but I could see the pain in her gaze. The only thing I could think of was getting her to Danny Allen. Lifting her into my arms, I put us in the saddle, and rode in a canter back to the truck. Loretta's face ran bloodless as I drew up.

"What's happened?" she cried. Beda was very special to her. Melanie climbed off Maggi, closed to her mother's side, her face tight with fright.

"I wish I knew," I said as I passed the listless setter down to Loretta. "Something with her rear legs. We've got to go, get her to Danny."

I jerked the tack off the horses, threw it loosely into the trailer. Loading all else, we left for home. I drove unreasonably, my mind reeling for a reason. There was just nothing of immediate memory to suggest the condition. Maladies without explanations are the scariest. The more elusive the answer, the more frightened I became. Beda lay loosely across Loretta's lap, her head draped over Melanie's knee. I don't think we exchanged six words in forty miles.

It was after hours when we reached the clinic. By grace, Danny had stopped back in to check on an ICU patient, a Scottie that had been hit that afternoon by a car. He answered my bang on the door. I stood there with Beda in my arms, Loretta and Melanie either side of me.

"Another something strange," I told him. "She needs your help."

We moved to an examining room, and I propped her on the stainless steel table. Her legs were so weak she wobbled in my hands, near collapse, until finally I eased her to prone. Danny examined her, took a temperature, asked me a host of questions. The answers were all no. Her temperature was elevated.

"You need to leave her with me, where we can watch her," he said. He motioned to the intern, an Auburn postgrad, who was standing by the inquest. "David will be here all night, can call me were things to worsen.

"Frankly, I'm not sure at the moment what we've got. I suspect some kind of deep-seated infection—from what, I don't know. I'm gonna give her a shot of antibiotic on speculation.

"We need the bloodwork. I'll call as soon as we have it, probably noon or after. Till then, we'll just have to wait and hope."

How many times have I been through it now? The vacuum at your gut that's a piecemeal stage of death, when you're racked with helplessness and expected to walk away from something you love as your next breath, something that lies hurting and only with wounded eyes can ask you why. It's hard with any dog. I think maybe the deeper with a sporting dog. You ask them for so much, and they give you even more. You thrill with the limits of their courage, and suddenly one dark hour they are asking for yours.

Loretta was crying, Melanie quiet and uncertain. My throat was constricted and dry. It was so hard to turn and go.

Loretta didn't. "I can't," she told me. "You and Melanie go on home. There's a couch in the waiting room . . ." She paused, her face contorting. "I just can't leave."

Even in the face of helplessness, hope floats best with a presence.

I wiped a tear away from her cheek with the backside of one finger. Looked at Danny for an okay. He nodded.

"Go on along. You've got to feed. Take care of the rest."

"See you in the mornin'," I said. I've never loved Loretta more.

I was there by seven. She let me in. Her eyes were red and swollen, her hair undone. I handed her a cup of hot tea and questioned her with a look.

"The same," she replied. "No change, either way."

"Now you go home," I said. "The chores are done. Mely's off to school. Just go and rest. I've called in. I'll be here."

She was still reluctant.

"I'll call. When we know, I'll call."

"Please God, let her be all right," she said, then looked in at Beda one last time and left. Was back before twelve.

It was well into the afternoon before Danny received and read the blood analysis.

"Well, we have got some infection," he told us in his usual thoughtful drawl. "Her white count is up to twenty-nine thousand. It'll probably go worse before it gets better. As to why, my feeling is an injury of some sort, a hard, sharp blow of some kind, maybe to her lower back and spine.

"Everything else looks tolerable at the moment. If it is a spinal thing, the big question, of course, is how much damage has been done."

"You mean it could be permanent?" I said. Loretta was clutching my forearm.

"Well, yes, but there's as much chance it won't. Our main concern now is reducing the trauma; the rest is pretty much in Other hands."

There was nothing to say.

"We'll let the antibiotics do their thing, and see where we go. I'd like to keep her a couple of days."

We nodded.

The evening was glum and lonely. As the next. And the next. The plight did indeed worsen, and for the period of three days, our little warrior maiden hovered near twilight, racked and reduced by fever. Inside her body, the battle raged. For life or death. Only three years past the time she was born.

Loretta spent the long nights at the clinic praying to sway the balance, and I'm not sure Danny went home either. I lay sleepless. I brought Pat in for company, that I might draw from her strength. But over and over, as so many times for real, I could see Beda carrying the fields of my mind, going faster and farther and merrier than ever she had before, as if to portray the great potential that lay unrequited but yet could be . . . the soaring joy that lay hidden there waiting for wing. If only Providence would permit. While my voice, pleading with all my might, seemed cast so punily against the force of the doubt. Like the final naked struggle with a nightmare, just before you awake. To find whether you had prevailed or failed.

I think finally Loretta and I both went numb.

"Honestly," Danny said at its worst, "I don't know how she's holding on."

But she did. Fought it and fought it, the demon at her insides, and with God's will and the resiliency of youth, beat it away. So that on the morning of the fourth day, we found her standing in the cage, standing and brightened, her tail clicking feebly, but positively, away.

We got down on our knees and hugged her, whispered the thanks of relief and desperation you attempt when really you don't know how, and took her home the next morning. For three weeks we rested her, and she improved with every meal, and two weeks before Christmas, she was demolishing a present a day. The mischief was back, and so was she, and she resumed kennel residence then with Pat, who had noticeably missed her. It was the greatest gift of the season.

$\sim$ CHAPTER 18 $\sim$

I HAD NOT BEEN IN THE SADDLE, HAD NOT TRAINED TRIAL OR GUN dogs for three weeks. Hadn't the heart really, but now it was past time to catch up, and I fell to it with a vengeance. We took to the field, Hank, Jill, Cindy, Gabe, Pat, Thane, Beda, Dolly, and I. Left before day and drug in after dark, and soon Loretta was complaining so of our absence that she shamed me into domestication not only on Christmas Day as planned, but its eve as well. It was a welcome respite, I would admit, and there was the affecting radiance and romance of Christmas, but I was excited too about the work of the dogs. It was as if the hiatus had only sharpened them, heated their desire to a boiling point. They had lost surprisingly little of conditioning; even Beda, after the physical depreciation of her ordeal, came back with bounce and verve. Zip Zap was running out of the world, though handling handsomely, and Joe Montana had actually stood twice to shot without gnashing his teeth.

The bird work had reeked of genius. Tack sharp. Transfixing stands on perfectly located coveys, talented countermaneuvers of nose and strategy that intimidated runners to a halt, stabbing pledges to singles that flashed together with the shock of a lightning bolt. I was shooting birds regularly over the gun dogs, effectively enough that a dozen "pottiges," golden-brown, adorned our holiday table. On a floral platter, in a roosting circle around a bed of rice and ensembled colorfully amid sprigs of holly. But the pinnacle of my exhilaration stood over the keenness of the trial dogs. Their work had been superb, find after find. Steady, articulate, and complete, with an energy that wired them so tautly the intensity flashed like a strobe.

Of curiosity, I polled the training log and, by dog, totaled finds for the spring and fall seasons. I think I already knew. Pat, by almost double. Beda and Thane were better than average, but Pat could find a bird at a bench show.

After Mely was off to bed Christmas Eve, and we had properly assisted Santa Claus, Loretta and I sat tightly together by the glow of the tree, listening to the gentle message of the carols, and waiting for midnight. We counted our years that way. Contrary to the calendar, the old year folded best on this most wonderful of eves, among quiet moments of warmly painted melancholy. The sum of both blessings and fears came better to rest that way, and what regrets and losses lay harbored in the twelve months past could be considered and then left there, more easily cleansed by the hope of Christmas morning than the vast, bleak landscape of another January.

At the height and stroke of the clock, we touched and tipped glasses of wine, and then, with a Christmas and New Year's wish as one, I kissed her. Afterwards, as an equal part of the tradition, we strolled out to the kennel to see the dogs. We had left a radio on there too, so they could enjoy the soothing strains of the season. They do, you know, horses and dogs alike.

We paused by each nose, offering a fingertip and a soft voice. It was our gift to them, the greatest we knew to give, for should you truly wish to confirm the joy of giving and receiving, extend the faintest touch and word to a dog.

We lingered with Beda, saying thanks anew. And with Pat, grateful ever for the blessing of her.

"It'll be a good year coming," I said.

"They've all been good the last several," Loretta returned. "It scares me."

"We'll win a bit this year," I ventured, considering the promise of the dogs.

"Just get us all safely through it," she said prayerfully. "That'll be enough."

Leave it to a woman to put matter adequately to emotion. A man forgets, too easily, what's important. It took the one, I supposed, to leaven the other.

We walked back to the house, arm in arm.

"Two big ones coming up, the Region 3 and Belmont?"

"Just a few days," I replied.

"You're jumpin' hard in the middle of it?" she replied.

"It's time," I said. "From now on, it's a thing of brass and breaks."

"A championship and a celebration. Both hour stakes?"

"Yep."

"Are we ready?"

"They're gonna break over, beat themselves some," I hedged. "They've been doin' that for a while. Less and less.

"I don't want 'em too broke, ever. That fine, high edge is the only chance we've got at the big trials. They'll break over some, and when it happens, it'll hurt. But when they're together, they can run with the best, and they can win; I know they can, and that's what we're gonna do."

"Even if we don't, I'll be proud," Retta vowed.

"You got to want to win," I declared. "If you can go and show well, it's somethin' close."

I challenged myself the moment I said it. I aimed to win. But it's a hell of a class thing, always will be, when a dog goes out and redefines the concept of excellence in a stake. Lifts it right on up and knocks the top out of thrilling. I'd seen enough now to know. My dog, your dog . . . don't matter. It's a gift to everybody in the trial community, win or no, and the man who can't appreciate it, no matter whose collar is in the mix, need not be there. I was beginning to forge some misgivings anyhow. It's a trite difference so many times, you come to believe. Is the one dog who ascribes a ground race to fluent, incendiary artistry, who stands game as if the next moment the world will detonate, and graces two finds so compellingly your throat goes dry—then of fire and desire, breaks on a third and takes two exuberant hops—truly eclipsed by another that canvasses the course with workmanship, tentatively tapping at the threshold of exciting, and cards three rigid but undistinguished finds? By judgment, it happens quite frequently in trialing. The clean dog wins. It's inviolable. Not out hunting. And not for years at the genesis of trialing itself, in so exalted a stake as the National Championship in Grand Junction.

The dog that placed would have given you more opportunities to shoot, it's contended. More and more, ironically, by people who are judging and have never even hunted a wild bird. Is that what we're after in a field trial? Then's when you realize all over again it's a game. I did then. As long as you do, you keep your feet on the ground. But one of these days when asked to judge again, probably for the last time, I'm going to use the showman over the journeyman, ride off contented into the sunset, and let the pieces fall where they may.

"We need to run them," I said finally. "They've got to learn how to handle the pressure. They're closer. They'll put it together."

But not at the Region 3 or Belmont, or even the Mid-Carolina Trial afterwards. In spite of my mounting confidence, we fared poorly. The Region 3 was held over the Hoffman sandhills, a total of fifty-four dogs contending. We took Pat and Beda, and Pat got off on deer for fifteen, and subsequently took a covey out after I got her back. Beda was apparently battling a relapse of sorts, running as if she didn't feel well, and I relieved her of the struggle after twenty minutes. It's hard to win a championship, amateur or open. You have to be near perfect. Have the breaks. That's what makes winning one so rewarding. Only rarely it happens, as then, that fifty-some of the best dogs on the circuit can run, and none, somehow, emerges with greatness. That trip, birds were at a premium, and for this and other reasons, neither champion nor runner-up achieved true class. In other words, they could have been beaten readily with a solid, inspired perform-ance. Which rendered losing all the more perplexing.

The Belmont Celebration near Augusta was similarly discouraging, except that waiting under brooding, leaden skies for the third brace, we noticed a young man and his wife lead two paint horses and a pointer, obviously Elhew, to the line. There was a thing about the man, not just the square, solid size of him, or that he was about my age, or even that he was wearing the Dunn's western-style down vest I had promised myself to order the next week. It was that this young man had style, and the more you looked, the more it showed. He had that Deep South, grub-and-grits set to his face that said he was likely from Georgia, that he wrapped his breakfast biscuit around a dollop of mayhaw jelly, and knew what a bird dog was about. That if you said, "Howdy," you'd likely get one back. I knew before we ever traded a word I'd like him.

He ran a good dog, too, and his wife, tall, willowy, and fine, scouted. On that paint horse that hit a fancy lick. Though the bottom dropped, and it poured buckets-full—and it was hard getting anything done.

I forget who spoke first. I think it simply opened with a nod. But one point we rode side by side, horseback in the gallery. Along in the drip. And he pulled his leather glove off his right hand, which was the custom, as I did mine, and we shook hands across the cantles.

"Tommy Mock," he garbled, before he leaned and spit off-side the excess of tobacco juice that was clabbering his speech.

"Like your horse," I said.

"Name's Buck," he drawled.

"Your dog's name, too," I had noticed.

"The horse, the help, the mules, the dogs," he allowed. "That way, when I git ready to load, I ain't got to call but once." He said it with a twinkle.

"Your wife?" I included whimsically.

"Wal', uh, most times to get her to come," he stammered, "I have to whisper 'Nancy.'"

We busted out laughing, the both of us, and for the rest of the hour rode along gabbing and yarning.

"You got to be from Georgia," I said.

He raised an eyebrow. "South Georgia, you'll please."

"Pardon," I said. The difference between north Georgia and south Georgia was the difference between the sitting room and the back porch.

"Early County," he finished.

"Colquitt?"

"Blakely."

I nodded.

Bobwhite quail and pointing dogs were the measure of his next breath, I wasn't surprised to find. In winter. Second only to wing-bone calls and strutting tom turkeys in spring. Born at the door stoop of the old-line plantation country—the great bird-hunting estates of the Albany-Thomasville-Bainbridge triangle—he was cradled in their lore. Stories of horses, dogs, birds, and men, as fabled as their bird-hunting empires. Places like Ichaway and Pinebloom and Blue Springs, which glided off your tongue as lines of poetry, appending romance and distinction to vast holdings of whiskered live oaks and lush savannas, dense gray heads of bay, silver-green footings of resurrection fern and wire grass that rolled amicably along under the pines. Raised up among many of the old-time keepers, the colorful and successful trainers of the day, he had learned from them what a plantation shooting dog was meant to be, and the class you had to have on top of that to make a formidable field trial contender. Bob Wehle was a friend and mentor, hence the Elhew pointers. And now a man grown, a dog man of growing repute with stables and a kennel of his own, Tommy was handling in major amateur stakes for Bob some too. In the small time between, Mock taught the hometown kids football, and folks there called him Coach.

We were easy, Tommy Mock and me, from the breakaway. We would compete intensely at leading amateur events for years to come. No quarter given, nary a bit asked. I would help him, he would help me. May the best dog win.

Years on, we would hunt, run puppies together, just call and trade dogdoms over the phone. Every reunion, a brotherhood. It started there at Belmont, and it's never ended.

Tommy rode for Zap that day—he always called her Zap—and for Maiden, and together we threw our best against the worst to smooth them through.

Pat ran impressively, damn the high winds and rain, with a great finish that lacked a find. Beda, under the same conditions, finished strong away as well, but ditto on the birds. Next day, the front blew out and the sky blued, and dogs found game. So goes the fortune of the draw. The most notable calamity of the occasion was a bad fall. Beda appeared birdy to the front at one venture, and Dolly and I were hurrying up to cover, when the mare was tripped by a vagrant strand of barbwire. We were hurtled several yards through the air, it seemed, and deposited in a pile, the mare on her side and atop my leg, kicking and struggling to rise. Luckily, neither of us was more than bruised, and I clambered aboard again and we were off. But the omens ran evil.

So persistently that at the Mid-Carolina Jubilee, we ran under the same black cloud. The day darkened. The sky, soiled and sullen, bellied like a burdened bedsheet, split asunder as the rain gushed through. It spilled in a drenching deluge through the morning, then fell to wind-driven sheets for the afternoon, arising in the distance like wraithful waves of militia. You could see them coming, advancing menacingly across the post oaks and gray sand and through the dusky shadows under the pines. Pat ran at the pelting onslaught, undaunted as usual, but failed to hinge around a corner cast at the gape of a deep, dark bottom. And we lost her for thirty minutes. Too long, only to have her reappear and blunder over a sopping-wet, liberated bird. Which she wasted no time in catching. I winced and closed my eyes, lifting my face to the rain, letting it cool away the heat of the disappointment.

Two braces later, I loosed Beda into the fracas, and halfway through a gust-and-gutsy ground race in sloppy going, she blew out of a woods head into the pocket of calamity. Just ahead, the considerable gallery had tightened like a granny knot around her bracemate's find, and her momentum threw her against the impression like a spatter of paint. I do not yet believe she could see immediately the pointing dog beneath the horses, for when seconds later she recognized what was happening, she whirled and stopped, standing proudly through flush and shot. I said as much, from an even better vantage, beside her on the ground. But the judges felt otherwise, and asked her up. Just misfortune number twenty-six in a list of three dozen.

Five trials and as many frustrations, and I was pressed against the same gnawing interrogative I had suffered during our derby season. In our second shooting-dog year now, the more so. Would we ever win again?

Four times more—the Region 3 All-Age Championship, Tidewater, Gamecock, and Blackstone—we tried and, one reason or another, failed. Then the answer arrived with the stroke of a thunderclap. Over the rolling green hills and gray stone walls of Winchester County, Virginia, Beda won at Rappahannock with aplomb, lacing together two sparkling finds and a symphony of determined casts as grandly as the stitching in a fine silk purse. Upending her sister, who had three good finds of her own and a ground race that would scorch asphalt, by only the slimmest uncertainty about a flighted bird. Two weeks later, there would be no uncertainty. On an unseasonable, boiling day in April, with no concern for the heat, Pat prevailed so charismatically in the All-Age Stake of the Central Virginia Club near Amelia Courthouse that there was barely the contest. Morgan's dogs and Virginia Kennels went down in the flames, and it was payback, my friends, for the Blackstone Puppy Stake. The drought was broken. Destiny was not to be denied.

I was overjoyed with our dogs. Astounded, really, all over again, at how dogs come to settle in. Remember themselves almost overnight. You beat along and beat along at the training game, especially with the most promising, trying tediously with each one to control the flames but not extinguish the fire. Trying to bank the break, but boost the brilliance. Working for the polish that will bring it all to head, the finish that stands them up, stiff, styl-

ish, and steady, against the very best. While you think, time and again, it
seems never to happen. It may take three years, but then one day . . . one
day . . . like something you have wanted for, oh, so long, upon which you
have exhausted every hope and means, then given virtually to lost. Almost
abruptly, one midnight it happens, and you wake the next morning and
find yourself wonderfully in its lap. Know that it has arrived, and that for
the wonder of its season, it will stand true.

For Beda, it was simple justice. Ever she was against the force of her sister, and ever she tried so hard. For months, she had spent herself relentlessly
against workouts—in truth, the most consistent and effective of the three.
With Pat, I knew it was happening before I ever loosed her at Central Virginia. After several near losses, it was as if she reached into herself and said,
"Not again. Not today." She was always that way. If you threw water on the
fire, it blazed the hotter. When she decided to win, she would.

Joy prevailed. Loretta made flapjacks Sunday morning, and Melanie
served, and every dog in the kennel had a stack. Pat and Beda had two.

"On the house," Loretta told them, stopping before Beda's kennel.
"Compliments of the court . . . and hail to the queen."

"If we keep her . . . ," she mimicked, singsonging a reminder of my pup-
pyhood indiscretions.

"Little warrior maiden," she cooed to her dog. "If Grandpa's good, we
might let him take you to another trial."

"I'll take Pat, then," I countered.

"Mine's," Melanie said.

"When's your dog gonna win?" Loretta said smugly.

I cast a doubtful look at Thane. He had his leg cocked, pissing on a
post.

It's hell when you're only the handler.

～ CHAPTER 19 ～

GOOD TIMES, AND WE REVELED IN THEM. INOPPORTUNELY PERHAPS. For just with our luck swinging south, the trial season was ending. All we could do was yearn for fall.

In May, we renewed the summer's long roading drills, saddle, sweat, and harness. Every week I'd get the *Field,* and long for Saskatchewan.

But that was before CPV. I could not know that around the corner lurked the most precipitous peril we have known in a half century with sporting dogs. Could not know that before it submitted to a semblance of attrition a year later, it would bring one of the most nightmarish times of our lives.

Canine parvovirus ran through dogdom that summer like beets through a hog. By fall, it was epidemic, as menacing as the skull and cross-bones on a lye bottle. And for months there was nothing, absolutely nothing, to stop it. Not a moment, not a miracle, no act of God. Not the merciful revelation, to come much later, that while it was among the most environmentally persistent of viruses, it could be killed by common household bleach. Medicine was stymied. Vets were distraught. Dog owners, us among them, were terrified.

First wind of it reached our vicinity in June 1979, and by July, blew brutally ill. Horrible and strange, as symptomatically it imitated other malevolent viruses like distemper and hepatitis, but resisted the usual treatments. Puppies were dying by the score. Whole litters—years of selective breeding—wasting away in hideous and pitiful bouts of diarrhea, vomiting, dehydration, and depression. Then, the etiology yet to be defined, there came word it was bridging to mature dogs. Entire kennels were being devastated. Particularly hounds, which were often kept in packs and thus immediate proximity to one another. But every breed was at risk, and no dog was immune. Rumors were escalating. The scare was nationwide.

Within the field-trialing community, the threat was especially ominous. With the approach of the fall season, and the association of large numbers of dogs from diverse locales, the prospects of contracting the deadly disease seemed inevitable. Already there were reports of devastation in kennels that fielded dogs we had been braced against. As September neared, anxiety reached a fever pitch. Everyone was clamoring for a deterrent, something—anything—that would afford protection.

"It's a totally new virus, as far as we can tell," Danny Allen told me. "There's some suggestion it mutated from a cat virus, the feline equivalent of distemper."

"What do we do?" I asked desperately.

"Like always, keep the kennel clean," he said. "Avoid outside association. Other than that, I don't know."

Avoid outside association. He'd as well as said, "Don't go to field trials."

Pharmaceutical labs scrambled. Bleary-eyed scientists burned the midnight oil. Veterinarians, caught between fearful owners and a research community that was, so far, vacuum-sealed into a stalemate, pleaded for help.

Finally, from Cornell University, an early and crucial leader in the research, came a modicum of hope. At least a stopgap. Since, by derivation, the malady appeared closely related to feline distemper, there followed a logical supposition that inoculation utilizing the existing modified live virus (MLV) feline vaccine might offer a degree of immunity in canines. The word was "might." It was a half-mast solution to a full-staff problem. But it was all science had. The feline vaccine was rushed through a test and validation process, and cautiously approved for use with dogs.

It did little to relieve the concern. On a personal level, the dilemma remained agonizing. There was uncertainty as to side effects, and no reasonable comfort of security. Dogs exposed to the hot parvovirus continued being susceptible at odds that were alarming. What was needed, quickly, was an accepted MLV vaccine of canine parvo derivation. When it would be available was wholly unknown.

Loretta and I would walk to the kennels in the evening and sit at length with the dogs, fraught with the absence of a clear and prudent path. It's agonized hell to look into the eyes of a living thing you love implicitly, that trusts you beyond the shadow of life itself—a living thing that adores you beyond devotion, that knows no threat in the world because you *are* the world, that assumes unequivocally you will keep it that way—and know in your heart there is no clear path to assurance. Two months before, we were jubilant with our first shooting-dog and all-age wins, and the promise of fall; now we were burdened by depression and the acid taste of jeopardy. It was just one more lesson in living. Just when you make the straightaway, something comes along to force you into a curve.

In mid-August, we suspended our roading program, resolving to abstain until the parvo problem was reconciled. It hurt awfully, to watch the physical peak for we had toiled so hard flatten away. With it, our competitive edge. Taking the only clinical precaution we could, we vaccinated Pat, Beda, and Thane with the feline MLV serum. The first dose of three. We would wait on the balance of the kennel, at least until October, pending the return of the gun dogs to the field, hoping for a break on the canine vaccine. With the fall trials a heartbeat around the corner, we now debated whether to go at all, before this insidious horror could be resolved.

Loretta was against it. "I'll say what I've always said," she vowed. "No field trial is worth the death of a dog."

Dearly, I wanted it otherwise, but there was no bucking the truth.

I had Danny searching, was calling the country over, for a canine-derived vaccine. By late August, you could find the killed-virus version. But that was insufficient. Only the live strain would provide acceptable immunity and the peace of mind to bring life back to center. Purportedly, Norden Labs was working on one, very close to its release. There I concentrated my efforts. Beleaguered as they were, considering that ours was only one of an avalanche of requests from worried and persistent dog owners, the people there were empathetic and cooperative. Particularly the gal who had and loved setters. They couldn't send it to me directly, but they would ship it to Danny. By mid-September, the November Setters were among the very first dogs in the nation to be inoculated with a modified live parvovirus vaccine, and I could look levelly into their eyes once more, comfortable that I had not betrayed their faith. Life resurrected, we resumed our roading and field-training program, and were soon looking forward to October trials again. Happy to lay behind us a terror that, for a time, seemed determined to become a truth.

We were very fortunate. Thousands were not.

The untoward hiatus had thrown us behind. It took the balance of September, roading and running—a lot of hamburger and honey—to climb back to a physical peak. The end of the month, I was honored to judge the Central Virginia Trial at Amelia, and dues paid, we settled hard into the saddle for October.

Beda won at Tidewater. Pat at Virginia Capital. Beda at the Mid-Carolina. Beda was running smoothly as butter covers toast; Pat was pure, patented power. Big-time power. Irrepressible occasionally, but big-time. Only Joe Montana lagged, unabashedly hauling up the rear, embarrassing his namesake, and still breaking over on his birds. Most noticeably at field trials. I kept brushing him down and propping him up, stroking him back to happy, and advising him he was making snail progress as a stud dog. Otherwise we suffered the usual mishaps of fortune, but less and less were we to blame. Everywhere we went, folks knew we were there.

Our dogs had arrived. We didn't win every time; nobody does. But we were winning a share, all good trials, and very regularly now, we were up there knocking on the door. Here on, it would be fate, finish, polish, and power, and we pushed ourselves relentlessly, and set our sights for the stars.

∼ CHAPTER 20 ∼

THE REGION 4 SHOOTING DOG CHAMPIONSHIP WAS HELD THAT YEAR at the Central Kentucky Wildlife Management Area near Berea.

Tommy Mock called. "You goin' to the Region 4?"

"Yep. You?"

"Yep . . . We'll help each other."

The number-one apprehension attended, a good scout, we fell hard into preparing.

Loretta and Melanie didn't make that trip. Something intervened that had to do with mamas and daughters, and the something special men can't share. The rest of us loaded up on a Thursday and headed west. All in all, it would be a miserable venture. One of those times there ain't an angel in heaven. For three days of four, it rained brazenly, almost from the moment we arrived until the minute we left. It was raw, blustery, and cold, bordering ice, and fog settled in over the grounds as thick as the murk over a Low Country graveyard. The ground went rotten and grubby, and at every crossing, great frigid splatters of muddy water were hurled hat-high from churning and sucking hooves. The end of the first day, the gallery looked like something drug out of a mucky trench. It took a lot of cussing.

Joe Montana was drawn Saturday in fog and a worsening downpour. He never ate well on trips, hadn't taken a bite in thirty-six hours, but ran gallantly, laying down a big championship-quality race, easily the equal of his bracemate, Dr. Gattuso's good dog Short Circuit. He traveled, fast and fine, to the right places, with one unproductive—but both dogs went the hour without a find. Conditions were horrendous, and rapidly deteriorating.

Sunday was the only decent day of the trial. And that was relative. Overcast and cold, dismal and gray, the major concession was the rain, which had retreated temporarily during the night. The respite was short-lived, while some good dogs, lucky enough to be called, made the best of it. By evening, the soggy low-pressure area had backtracked and hunkered over middle Kentucky anew, and the rains marched in again.

Tommy had a big male dog then called Elhew Knickermock. Old Nick was a stand-up liver-and-white pointer with a lot of leg, and a time later, his son Elhew Sputnik would win the Runner-Up title in a National Amateur Shooting Dog Championship. Sputnik's pop should have been titled earlier, for he did a heck of a job that Sunday.

We put him down in the slop, and he proceeded to meter out a smooth and consistent shooting-dog race of the right proportions the better of the way. I rode easy, for there was little scouting to be done, just a bit of checking here and there where the course swung hard or he was a short while gone. The apogee of his effort came about forty. He carried a far-flung cast deep into a forward left corner, across a plunging bottom, and onto a bench of high ground on its other side. On his own, for we all—handler, judge, and scout—sat on an opposite knoll, watching it unfold.

"*Yuuuuppp! Yeahh, boy!*" Tommy was singing him around, and he was swinging to the front like a ball on a string when suddenly he slapped sideways and never moved again. And you could see him, standing tight, way across there into the flat-woods. He waited perfectly for us while we rode over, and Tommy got down and put his birds out, a bluster of about eighteen wild quail. Nick never wiggled a whisker, marking them away.

"A nice piece of doin's," I told my friend as I collared his dog while he climbed onto his paint horse. Tommy, exhilarated, could barely speak, just nodded, "Turn 'im aloose." I did, and Tommy heeled him back to the course. Nick stopped once for an unproductive we could have avoided, then finished nicely away.

"That might stand a chance," we thought that evening upon summation. There were other dogs, too, that toed a good mark that day. Questionably as deserving as Nick.

Then the weather soured up again before dawn, and we were against its ugliest as I led Pat to the line Monday morning.

"We need something big here," Tommy said.

"Like a miracle," I vowed.

Tommy stacked her up at the line, the judges tipped a finger, and I hit the whistle, loosing her into a cold, driving, windblown rain. Water was falling so stiffly it stung your face, and you could do little more than hunker under your hat and try to keep enough of it out of your eyes that you could see. Pat left big and unaffected for the first thirty, a handful for Tommy and me in the soup. Time and again she faded from sight, and all you could hope was she came around. Like a beacon she did. Tommy found her on point at thirty-five, a nice, high stand on a wild bevy in a forward hedgerow. The rain was beating down so hard it hurt, but I put the birds up and they sputtered away, wet and black, and she swelled on her toes to watch them go. We had something going, and despite the elements, I could feel the voltage rising. Pat was fired sky-high, kicked mud waist-level getting away. But by forty-five, the muck was dragging hard at her, and the rain was pounding, and you couldn't see her enough to really follow her race. It was pouring the hardest it did for the four days, and getting colder by the minute. A mince of a mess.

I looked back several times at our judge, and he was bowed against the blow, and I didn't know how much he could see.

Pat was still going well at fifty, but had shortened a bit, and I whoaed her. She was caked with ice and shivering, but fighting me, wanting to go. Tommy held her while I dug a dry burlap sack out of a saddlebag and briskly rubbed her down. All of us were cold, drenched to the skin. The icy water had snuck down our backs, under the oilskins, and wicked up our pants from the cuffs.

"She's done a hell of a job," Tommy said. "It's tough, boy. Tough."

I climbed back in the saddle, and Pat looked up at me, and tough or no, I saw that hell-and-do-it desire in her eyes. And I knew what was about to happen. My hands were so numb I could hardly hold the whistle, but I fumbled it to my mouth and blew her away, and she gathered up and flung herself to the extreme of the course. We found her at time, on birds, and she had them where she said, was standing tight, but drooping some from the spattering rain. I kicked out the covey, and we finished clean. It was a strong effort, whether enough under the conditions, I couldn't begin to say. It was a damn far cry from running in the sunshine.

I honestly wasn't concentrating on it just then. I was more concerned about my dog. She was ice-bound nose to toenail, and I rubbed her down again and hurried her to the dog box.

Beda also left in the driving rain. The temperature had leavened a little, but only a little. She ran her usual even and searching race for a brave half hour. She kept reaching into herself, and digging, but gradually her range suffered the elements. To make matters worse, we rode by her at forty, and went back to find her on point. She was standing loosely in the maddening rain, flagging, and her birds were gone.

"I'm sorry, girl," I said, and I truly was. She had another find, quite nice under the circumstances, about six minutes to go. But she had closed more handily than she needed to in the preceding minutes, was cold, shaking, and wet, and I picked her up. She looked into my eyes and whined, still wanting to go.

Tommy ran another dog, but we got no more done, and by the time it was all dreaded and run Tuesday afternoon, I was ready to see North Carolina and blue skies again. Everybody gathered in the clubhouse for the decision, the rain still roaring on the roof and the wind whipping the eaves. Skip Brown, another avid setter man, was there. I knew him from the South Carolina circuit. We had been braced together in several trials. Skip had Molly then, and a couple of other nice shooting dogs. He'd suffered the same drowning as the rest of us.

"You boys got a dog in this fight?" he asked.

"Hard to tell," I allowed. Tommy grinned and proposed next time we run water spaniels.

Quietly, my Georgia compadre was confident Nick was in the thick of it. I thought Pat *might* be. When the decision was announced, neither was. Rain or shine, championships come tough. Two other dogs were named from Sunday's running, and that was the sum of it. I was disappointed. Tommy was utterly disheartened. So much so that he asked the judge. You do that as a last resort.

"What else did my dog need to do?"

The judge, hardly helping matters, made liver pudding out of an answer, and concluded with a meaningless promise: "I'll catch you down the line."

Judges say some dumb things sometimes; that one bungs the barrel. If Nick won, he should have been named then and there, not inscripted an IOU for some hypothetical juncture in the future that, everybody knew, wouldn't pass. If a dog didn't win, then a judge owes a man to tell him so, and why.

Tommy got mad, then sad, faced with the futility of a thing said but undone.

"You saw those two dogs from Sunday. Do *you* think they beat Nick?"

"No," I said honestly.

"Then why?"

"Uuhmm. I think I've ask myself that about a dozen other places. Right or not, you won't change it. You know that. It's hard, but we'd as well load up and go home. I got clothes to wring for a week."

"It ain't about me," Tommy said, not wanting to leave it. "It just bites my ass an honest dog gets cheated."

Sometimes they do. In field trialing, it's the bitterest pill of all.

I shook my head, at a loss for else to say.

"Regrets, old friend," I offered over a handshake, and walked out the door. It took five minutes to throw the rest of our waterlogged, mud-caked gear into the trailer, and me and the November Setters got the hell out of Berea.

Kentucky and the Region 4 that November became the benchmark for meteorological hades. Years afterward, Tommy and I or Skip would be running this place or another in some sort of atmospheric annoyance, and one of us would say, "Well, hell, it could be Kentucky."

Back home, our workouts glistened. We were finding wild birds, and doing it right. Zap and Maiden were all Miss Manners, and Thane was finally turning the corner, coming to steady. I started shooting a few birds for them, to jack them even higher at flush and shot. They loved it. All were ready, I thought, for the Region 3 Championship at Hoffman.

But Pat, after breaking away in falling snow and wowing the judges for a quarter hour with a shining ground heat, simply vanished. Norman wasn't there to scout, and I had poor help, and she was too big and too gone. I saw no more of her until two hours later, at the lunch break, when she checked back at the barn. Beda ran short, and I never knew why. Next time down, she was her considerable self again. Thane had something going, the cocky rascal, stopping beautifully at fifty in front of a glamorous ground race to announce a wild covey. Birds were at a premium, and he was standing in the very middle of a bunch, and when I got down to flush, they blew up all around him. It was too terribly much. He held for a nefarious moment, glanced to see if I could reach him, and then sailed off with them.

Once again, we left our ashes at a major trial. Ruckus was, I knew Pat, and Beda yet, could win any one of them. Thane, too, if I could ever get him together. You got to believe, and we did.

Things weren't exactly slack. We were winning some good trials, against some good dogs. Beda and her consistency were holding us in there. At the Ingleside Trial at Iron Station, she was down with Bob and Helene Abric's Rosemary dog. The temperature was in the teens, and the howling wind cut like a knife. Leaves were chasing across the grounds in small brown cyclones. Two fine setter bitches—you'd think a dog couldn't point a bird, and they royally put on a show. Running Pat along then was like lighting the trigger to a dynamite keg, then lagging around to watch the fuse burn short. She would soar higher and higher during the heat, finding and pointing birds, hustling and hunting, going bigger and bigger, and maybe she'd keep the manners together until the clock expired, and maybe she wouldn't. Any time she did, whatever the stake, she won. I figured when she settled to Beda's constancy, maybe about six, somebody'd better really look out.

For all of that, things kept going sour at the big ones. We drove twenty hours to the National Amateur Shooting Dog Championship the first time it was held over the open, piney woods understory of the Blackwater Forest near Munson, Florida. Running the initial brace after lunch the first day of the trial, Pat was going great and getting better, one sterling stand already under her belt and a ground race that would toast your toes, when she swapped ends and stood again at twenty-five. She was far ahead across the woods, sketched in a flourish of white against the gray-green flank of the hill, above a gentle, winding swale. It was a stylish, laid-out find, just the kind you want in a stake of that caliber, and my heart was choking my throat as I pushed the mare to a smart running walk and threaded my way through the trees. Behind surged judge and gallery, and as I pulled up to dismount, through the sun shafts small clouds of golden dust filtered past.

I knew from her stance she was close to the covey. She had hit those birds hard, and they had to be right under her nose. I studied the lay several moments, wanting above all to avoid a bad flush. When I had it figured, I thought, I walked gingerly in. Before I could be a factor, the whole covey blew up and blustered back right into her face. Pat whirled with them, took just three steps in their direction, and stopped to mark flight. Just three steps. She didn't chase, was under control. It was only fire and desire. You can't hope to win a field trial without it. But it was then, as now, sudden death in a stake that size. There's just no margin. You have to be perfect.

As so many times before, we had it going and it fell apart. That suddenly. There was not a thing left in God's world we could do about it. I felt a queasy weightlessness inside, as hope slammed against heartbreak. More so a day later, when Beda came along. Starting well, she was crosscutting the course at fifteen, tearing toward a distant corner, when she ran squarely from upwind over a single bird. Stopping properly, she styled and stood for the shot. About three seconds. Then tore loose and chased like a puppy. First time in months. I thundered "Whoa!" and she halted after three bounces. But the blister was on the bunion. I put my dog in the harness, roaded her back to the truck, and we drove the twenty hours back.

Moments and miles—win or lose—moments and miles.

I forgot myself twixt there and home. Suffered a lot of useless worrying. Allowing my hurt to second-guess my headwind. Wondering again if we really had the wild birds or grounds to train well for the big ones. Against all the big-time dogs, and all the big-time trainers, and all the money that bought them grouse-and-chicken summers on the prairies and quail-privileged winters on the plantations. Where we had one opportunity, they had a dozen. Wild birds had been strangely scarce the last few weeks at Corinth, and the slack in training occurrences had hurt. I could see it in the dogs. Course they get excited, too, in the big ones, just like we do. Spillover. If we all didn't, there'd be no reason to go.

Hell and Georgia. You can't always be flawless. You can only try. That way you stay close. It had been our creed.

By the South Carolina line, I'd shucked the doubt aside. Again, in mind's eye, I had us at our best. Especially Pat. They could come. Come one and all. It didn't matter a hoot in a haymow. I was back on the sheet music, maverick as Hank Williams.

"Move over Beethoven, the setters gonna rise again."

The next month, we entered four good trials and won or placed in them all.

∼ CHAPTER 21 ∼

MEANWHILE, OUT OF THE EASTERN CAROLINA TOBACCO FIELDS NEAR Goldsboro sprang an amicable, good-timing country boy named Lewis Clements. Lewis chewed a little and laughed a lot, generally kept the company of a bird dog, and wasn't no particular trouble to nobody. Folks usually took a cotton to him. Unbeknownst to all, but not for long, Lewis had married up a Tennessee stud dog and a back-porch bitch a spell before, and from scratch, come up with the pointing-dog equivalent of the Hope Diamond. Sometime around spring of 1980, he arrived as dramatically upon the Virginia field trial universe as Halley's Comet. To disappear a season or two later almost as permanently. He had a pickup truck with tobacco stains down the side, a Styrofoam cup on the dash for when he couldn't let the window down, a portable airline crate he hauled behind the cab in an open cargo bed, no horse that I remember—just a few dollars to rent one from Billy Kuser—and one dog. But Nellie knot her knickers, *what a dog!*

From the trialing seasons of '80–'82, I have good reason to remember most the miniseries *Roots,* which had debuted in 1979 to garner the greatest viewing audience in television history, and Lewis Clements's pointer bitch Kizzy, who wore the name of its most revered female character. Roll On Kizzy would descend on the Virginia shooting-dog circuit like the wind before a storm. And it was batten the hatches, pros and amateurs alike.

Kizzy was a striking, black, white, and ticked, straight-up Evolution bitch of medium stature, lean and lithe, with the speed of a gazelle and the mien of nobility. Indeed, the contrast between the lady and her master was no less than remarkable. It was the story of Beauty and the Beast, long before Disney ever told it. Together a most disarming pair, the deception was a great part of their charm. And considerable effectiveness.

For three seasons, Kizzy was as complete a horseback shooting dog as the good Lord ever minted, and Lewis Clements was as astute and crafty a handler as ever split a saddle. Together, for that time, they were almost unconquerable. The hallmark of a great shooting dog is consistency, and week after week, Kizzy ran with impervious alacrity to the plethora of distractions that work regularly to undermine it. Clements, as truly, was haut and bold. Typically, the open and amateur stakes of a given trial were conducted consecutively, a day between, and Lewis and Kizzy would run them fearlessly, back-to-back. More than not, they'd win, take all. It was the combination of a super-smooth shooting dog of radiant style and talent, and a Br'er Rabbit handler that stayed one bounce ahead of the fox. That and a shotgun that would rattle Satan's eyeteeth.

But for the shotgun, Lewis Clements's pragmatic country philosophy was less is more. But there he made the one cunning dissension. It was daunting enough you had to beat them on the usual terms, a great ground race and king's-ransom bird work. You also had to pray, were you drawn with them, it didn't come to a backing situation. For most dogs braced with Kizzy, backing was only a hair less likely than breathing. When the dreaded moment arose, it required not only articulate style to match the superbly postured pointer female, but also survival of the flushing salvo. Where most handlers packed a .32 side arm, or in a long arm at best a light 20-gauge, Lewis scabbarded a full-grown 12. While the running rules were explicit concerning ammunition, stipulating nothing live nor less than a .32-caliber blank, they understandably disregarded the probability of a cannon. If you wanted to use the decibel equivalent of twelve balls to the pound, you could have at it. Lewis did. For this thunderbuss, much to the disdain of the opposition, he rolled his own, stuffing fat, red shells full of black powder until the crimp groaned. The net effect was that the muzzle blast alone undid all but the steadiest of contenders, who were still left to survive the defoliation from the concussion.

Lewis and Kizzy were already beating the socks off Bill Kuser and one of his Adios dogs in an open stake one morning at Amelia when, twenty minutes into the heat, Bill's charge, forced to honor, was further reduced to doom by the *"Wha-ooom!"* of the flushing report. Sent off the blocks like a sprinter to a starting gun, the startled beast broke past the statuary Kizzy and chased out of sight.

"Whoa! Whoa! *Whooaa!*" Bill sputtered, too late. "Goddammit, Clements!" he thundered, jerking off his hat and slapping it to the ground. "Why in hell do you have to use such a cannon?"

"Can't hear an elephant fart," Lewis said, as a grin grew from the corner of his jaw, and he stroked Kizzy up all the higher for the judges to see, and ejected between the fork of two fingers a copious brown swatch of tobacco spittle. While Kuser's dog, jack-wild, still chased birds lustily in the distance.

He wiped his mouth and redid the grin, likely calculating 50 percent of the purse. "Need to know I've shot."

Kuser fumed to the barn.

Back from the National Amateur, we first encountered Lewis and Kizzy at the Blackstone Trial, decided over the old Camp Pickett grounds. We were attending Virginia trials pretty regularly then. The Old Dominion hosted a distinguished schedule of all-age and shooting-dog events, each hotly and honorably contended. There continued there an appreciable degree of tradition and decorum, from the earliest of the plantation stakes. Not the least of which were the people, vividly interesting, warm and welcoming. We enjoyed them all: the ever chivalrous Verle Farrow, epitome of colonial Virginia; stolid Art Hillhouse and rakish Roland Kane of the Old Guard; the perennially irascible Billy Kuser, an adept incarnation of Billy Goat Gruff; dapper Walker Smith; happy-gone-lucky Jack Warren; the trench-coated Tidewater trio of Bob Smith, Larry White, and Gene Hogge. Frank Slaw and Tommy Liesfield, the Waylon Jennings and Willie Nelson outlaws of Virginia Kennels, who were sideways nice and always fun to beat. That redoubtable alliance of smoothies, Paul Cameron and Ed Emerson. Not to forget, either, Bobby, Joyce, and Robin Clay, impresarios of Saturday night handlers' parties, grub-and-glory table fixings midday. Or Til Hankley, Gary Winall, Andy Crowell, and Tommy Stargell, young fellers then afore their chaps got stiff, starting out. An up-and-coming black man, Mike Hester, daring a foothold to the horseback game. The staunch setter sidekicks Jim Jones and Scotty Morrel. All would blaze a bright path along the field trial trail.

One of the first folks I ever lapsed words with at a Virginia trial was Scotty Morrel. He noticed at once my old Stetson, veteran and victim by then of many trialing wars. Dented and dirty. "Your trademark," Helene

Abric always said of it, when each time we met down south. Scotty had a fresher view.

"Were you under that hat when the horse fell on it?" he wanted to know, sticking out a hand. He had one on his head about the difference. Easy to like, Scotty, and I always did.

And venerable old Jake Vaughn, who, I guess—for the time he lived—watched away about every brace that ever ran, from the Amelia clubhouse. He was a gentle and amicable soul, genuinely loved a good pointing dog, and was more than a fair hand at putting the pride-and-polish on one. He was retained by Leonard Wilson periodically, and it was Jake's kind and knowing start that enabled latter-day champion Tiger Woods to fame.

He always said of Pat, "she lef' so fas' you'd do good to see 'er." Jake would know.

But of all the cast and characters of the Virginia stage, each with dogs the mirror of them, the one we loved most was Billy Blankenship. Aside from Verle Farrow, he was the first trialer, really, we met and came to know from the Virginia circuit, and that was long before March of '81, back in our puppy days. We met him first because he cared first, about a visiting and eager young couple and three fiery setter pups. Cared because of the man he was. Which wasn't obvious. You'd not have known. That here was a man as inwardly kind as he was outwardly gruff.

It was at Camp Pickett, in fact, when first we saw him. We arrived near the conclusion of the shooting-dog stake. I rode the last brace, and we gathered with the party for the announcement of winners. When it came time for first place, the Trial Chairman sang out two names: "Hi-Crest Sport, Billy Blankenship." I'd hear that a lot over years to come: first place, a Hi-Crest dog, and Billy Blankenship. Later, on the day we finally managed to best him, I'd know we'd come far. He wanted it that way; gave me a leg up onto a scary horse. Taught me how to ride. When you stand upon the height of your accomplishments in any endeavor, and look below to where you started, the distance between is often the measure of the men who helped you there. Who, upon occasion, bowed honorably to defeat to have you win. Billy Blankenship measures among the greatest men of my life.

But that first day, we knew nothing of him. He stepped up to receive the blue, a short, solid man, his face furrowed and bronzed by wind and sun, the underspoken glint of flint in his eyes. He shook hands with the Stake

Manager, accepted the ribbon wryly, and retreated. In his demeanor was neither elation nor arrogance, just the gratification of a man who had known he had a difficult job to do, and had gone out and done it. I watched him back to his old truck and horse trailer, outfitted only as far as necessity, watched him speak something to the two big, hard, and callused pointers tethered there on a chain. Almost as emotionlessly as he, they arose, and the stoutest, with a liver head, reared to place his paws on the man's chest.

Through the seasons, it was always that way. When he won, he did it without pretense, and when he lost, as long as he believed fairly, he conceded as graciously as Lee at Appomattox.

Between times, truth be known, he was a hard man, not mean, but stubborn and sot in his ways, as crusty and starchy as week-old wheat bread. Hard on men and harder on dogs. It took a good one to weather him. Swift to ire, he wasted no time retaliating, with sharpened words that sliced to the quick. Or worse. But never, in all the years, did I ever think, wrongly. A crotchety rascal he could recurrently be, a little like a sleeping dog you walked a circle around for fear of waking it and getting bitten. Tough as whit-leather, he expected to be accepted for no more, or less, than he was. And that was a lot.

His pointer dogs were the equal of him. They had to be. Hard and strong, tireless and tough. Workmen all, with the clip and class to get things done. As uncompromising as their handler, they allowed themselves nothing short their best, and were stubborn about doing it. They could be jerked up and set back, stand there and take it like a man. Stand there hide and hackles, glower and growl right back. Find birds on a baseball diamond. Tough they were, tough to beat. Could have expected, the old man always named the best of them Bull.

A stalwart of the Virginia trials, Billy Blankenship did as much as any man ever did to see them true. Were there an indiscretion, he would seek with might to set it right. Were there a need, he would find a way. Many were the raw, cold, wet, and nasty mornings we would arrive upon the grounds before the peep of day to see, as we approached, a wraith in blackened oilskins cross the headlights and the road ahead. Straight in the saddle, unbending to the blow. It would be Billy, off to plant birds, well in time for the opening brace, while lesser men only turned the second time in a warm, dry bed.

Billy's life was a series of incidents, good, bad, and indifferent, and he could relate the least of them as gospel, getting close up in your face and gilding every twist with expression. While in a gravelly voice he unwound the words round by round, like raw twine turn after turn from a ball, until they were finished into a story. With a nickering little laugh, to punctuate the highlights. He wasn't all grump and growl. He had some mischief in him, too. There was a period of three consecutive trials when me and the dogs had a wreck on the first corner of the course. Had to pick up, tuck tail, and draggle back to the clubhouse. Driving in one dawning morning, I caught the old rascal there, down under the hill where he thought I couldn't, tacking something on a tree. I didn't say stop or say anything—until later, when we rode through with the first brace, and there on an oak for all to see was a big, stark sign labeled, "Gaddis' Folly." I had to suffer it for another three weeks—actually thirty more years, for he has never let me forget it.

Times later, he took to wearing a set of bib overalls, and grew a set of stiff, silver whiskers to go with them. Handled his dogs that way. Suited him.

All of these things I'll ever remember about Billy Blankenship, but the thing I'll remember most was later that first day, when I was about to loose Pat in the puppy stake, and knew nobody and had nobody, he was the only one who rode up and said, "Do you need a hand?"

And with relief, I shook his, and said, "Yes, thank you."

He scouted Pat that day, and many others to come, and he was one of the few who ever really could. We've been staunch friends since.

Of him overall, Loretta would say most accurately: "He'd have made the very best of Confederate generals."

Upon this garrison of color and character, by March 1980, Lewis Clements and Roll On Kizzy had descended, bringing an era of shooting-dog contention few could wish to forget. The battle lines were drawn. Up from the land of the pines, we found ourselves on the short end of a war. It was Virginia and Carolina, and every man of honor had a dog in the fight. For a while, the division between North and South was the boundary between Tarheelia and Old Dominion. For a while, we forgot all had worn gray.

For two seasons, Kizzy would contest with Pat, the most inspiring rivalry of our career, eclipsing only Duke from her puppy days. Though many would wish it, given the sensation they would create, they were never drawn together. But week after week, it was head-to-head.

It was Beda, actually, drawn with Kizzy in that first skirmish at Blackstone. We stood the two dogs up at the line, and both would pose with the best, and they stood there stiffly, throwing sparks until the signal went off.

"*Yeeeahiiahh!*" Lewis let out this ungodly screech on the shrill heels of the whistles, and not allowing my dog to be handicapped, I threw one in too. And Kizzy and Beda went away like beasts out of hell. The breakaway vista canvassed a quarter of a mile of hilly upcountry, and when the dogs reached the dip and swallow at the halfway point, they were neck and neck. Both cut behind the edge cover out of the draw, and the next time we saw them was at the extremes, giving little either way and racing out of sight left and right into the "bowling alley," a long, straight chute that broke at the top into rambling farmland meadows and hedgerows. You could usually count on birds at the cap of the hill, before the country opened. It was there we found Kizzy, straight ahead on the course, pointed beautifully into the autumn olive contiguous to a tremendous red oak.

I looked quickly around for Beda, just as she popped from the far side, the cover impeding the view of the other dog, and slid into an eloquent stand of her own. There they stood, divided over the find, and Lewis and I both climbed off, pulling guns. Two birds went out, and the air thundered, and the leaves rained down, and I could see Lewis sneak a glance to see if Beda had stayed. She had, solidly, and round one was in the books.

We led the dogs out, and watered them, and the scouts walked them by the collar out front, while we saw who could slap his gun back in the scabbard, get on his horse the fastest, and send his dog away. We hit leather about the same moment, two whistles sliced the tension almost to the instant, and the dogs were plumb gone. Or so I thought, until I noticed Beda on the far side of the course, doubling back. She had a problem with that sometimes, wanting the liberty to go back to where she last found birds.

Billy was riding scout, and he hollered at me, "Watch yer dog!"

"*Heyyee!*" I squalled at her like the clap of doom, and she stubbornly disregarded me the first summons, before jerking about-face on the second, and tearing on. The bobble was slight, but one we could have done without. Beda quickly sewed back the difference, but signed over a minor deficit to the patently smooth Kizzy, who was laying down a near-perfect race. Otherwise, at the three-quarter mark, neither had earned a clear advantage on the ground. Both were fast and forward through the middle of the course, and each had found again cleanly. Beda had stopped once more for an honest stop-to-flush. It was increasingly evident, however, that we were up against one now-and-nice dog.

The course finished out of a long bottom to the top of a ridge, and then on to the fadeaway limits of an extensive edge. They took it all together, tails cracking, the pointer and the setter, and it had been a hell of a fine heat.

Lewis and I had stopped together on the crest, watching them away, the judges close behind.

Lewis looked over and rolled his wad to one side of his mouth. "Boy, that dog of yours almos' beat us."

"What do you mean 'almost'?" I said. We grinned broadly. It was powerfully close, I knew, though they probably had us a shade because of the one glitch. Kizzy had been too constantly smooth.

Lewis usually rode only one brace per stake, and that was his own. But Beda had served some notice, and he rode Pat's two heats later.

Billy put her on the line, and she stood there trembling, glancing up at me with those volatile, firebrand eyes that waited to detonate. That said confidently, "Just turn me loose. All I need is the whistle." So I hit it and bawled at her in the next breath, and all you saw was the trail of dust rising, like the tail of a meteor. Then it disappeared over the lip of the draw, and the next time anybody got a glimpse of anything other than her bracemate half-between, she was a merry white dot rocketing into the mouth of the bowling alley.

"*Go ahheaaad, Paaat!*" I sang and laid back at a walk, letting her roll. At ten minutes, what it took to get across the hill, through the bowling alley, and to the top of the hill—by the oak tree where Kizzy had stood on her first find—Pat was wide and away in the distance, taking the far-right edge. The raucous banter Lewis had been carrying on in the gallery dropped like a brick through a rusty bucket, and the little setter had the eyes of every man there.

She neared the outer limit of the course, still burning the remote right edge. "*Yeaoooowhhh,* now!" I whooped at her just before she reached the corner, and she banked the turn like she was glued to a track, and shot on under a happy lick into the next bottom.

We didn't see her for five minutes, before we found her standing in a small pocket to the side of the course, on the rise overlooking the lake. Her weight rested precariously forward on her shoulders, like it had slammed to

a halt there, defying inertia, and she was stretched into the scent, her rear
jacked high. On top of it, her tail stood twelve-straight and stiff as an icicle.
A breeze teased intermittently through its feathers. Billy came tearing up
and took the horses, and I climbed off and walked in, kicked a time or two,
and two birds jumped. Detained in a confrontation of flight feathers and
low-hanging limbs, they finally beat themselves free. *"Whoom,"* spoke the
gun. The setter swelled to her toenails, turning her head slowly as she
watched them away.

In the gallery, there were nothing but murmurs.

I led Pat out, and Billy walked her forward on the course, by the lake.
The day had warmed, was getting warmer. The setter showed no signs of it,
spurning a drink; all she wanted was loose.

It was always that way. She could have sprinted a Sahara hour on the
promise of a dewdrop. Thane was similar. Even Beda, who wasn't quite, I
had to force to stop and drink. They were trained to go, and "wait" wasn't
in their machinery.

Walker Smith would judge them any number of times. In later years, he
observed humorously that "those dogs were so busy they wouldn't even
stop for water."

So we sent Pat on that day as she demanded, and saw her one more
time as the clock expired, just as we topped the final ridge, and caught her
fading out of sight to the front.

"Pick 'er uppp," came the call, and as I cantered to find her, I knew it
was Pat and Kizzy.

But before the fat lady sang, I ran Thane. I grinned when I saw
Clements riding again. Before we broke, he pushed his horse up close to
mine. He had his brace sheet out, squinting at something. Lewis was a spade
too earthy to grasp the Old English sophistication of Thane, or even the less
medieval editions of Thaine or Thayne, becoming the first to adopt a more
plebian version he could carry in his hip pocket.

"Whut's that dog's name?" he blustered.

"Thane," I said.

"What?" he said.

"Thane," I said.

"Thing?" he repeated, screwing his face into a knot. We both broke out
laughing.

He was half joking and half serious. Lewis was a pistol. You couldn't help but like him.

Ever after, anywhere we met, he wanted to know, "When we gonna run old 'Thing'?"

Old "Thing" could lay down a pretty piece of work when he let himself. All-of-a-notion, he decided that day was good as any, and between him, Pat, and Beda, I was happy with the possibility we might win two places.

When the judgment was posted, it was Kizzy one and Pat two. I could see little more separation than the one find versus two, only rarely decisive in a quality trial. Actually, I thought Pat had ranged the more powerfully on the ground. Maybe they thought she ran a little too much. It's a strange thing, the definition of acceptable range in a shooting-dog stake. Strange, you'll find, after you run them enough, as the whims of the man doing the judging and the extent of the grounds. If you take in some all-age trials, you'll perfect that notion. Half or more of the all-age dogs claimed in the world are class shooting dogs, given a recurring opportunity at bigger grounds.

Anyhow, it was a tight stake that day. Pat got in it. Thane and Beda didn't. Though I never understood third. It's hard to win two places in a good stake. You're running against yourself.

I made a point of telling Pat she was second. I wanted to see her bristle. She did her best to seem dispassionate, but I knew better.

The next weekend, she went out, left the course smoking, dug up two sharp finds, and reversed the placements as dramatically as screenplay.

"Damn," Lewis said, off to the side where he supposed we couldn't hear.

Down through the spring and the next fall, they went at each other, Pat and Kizzy. Some days the difference was clear, and others it wasn't, and there was a stretch of two trials when they became so overwrought with the competition the both of them took themselves out of it. But it was a hell of a series, and a standard put hard to the Virginia circuit.

$\sim$ CHAPTER 22 $\sim$

BEDA, MEANWHILE, AS BEDA ALWAYS DID, TRIED MIGHTILY TO RUN with them. I loved her for it. She was a good dog, classy and consistent, had forever the grit but not quite the power. She'd commandeer second or third, occasionally enough. But beating dogs the caliber of her little sister, and Kizzy, left its strain. And then, for a while, it seemed the pressure of it all began to disassemble her.

Where, since maturity, she had been so comfortably smooth and obedient in workouts and biddable in trials, she became, for a time, erratic and obstinate. It was a problem in the making, early on, a big one, and I failed to recognize that as soon as I should have. By the day I did, I was in for an avalanche of trouble, already tumbling downslope and gathering speed.

Gradually enough that I didn't readily notice it, she started selling out of workouts and self-hunting. For only short periods at first, and I'd think she was simply swinging wide, and then she'd pop back out front as usual, and lay on—that it was nothing to worry about. But then the absences grew longer, marring her ground pattern.

I'd go get her, put a check cord on her collar, and reinforce the need to turn, to come around and on when I called. Like she always had.

"Beda, what it is?" I would tease her, caressing her and asking for the rapport we had always known, thinking she would soon correct it on her own. She always had.

But there came the day when I sent her along a grand, long edge, and she took it beautifully to near its end, and I saw her look back over her shoulder to see where I was, and then shoot off into the woods. To be gone for a solid two hours, no matter that I rode and called my head off trying to find her. I get nervous when I lose a dog. There's no greater anathema in my constitution than the thought of losing a dog, of knowing nothing of what came of it, and being left helplessly to wonder the worst—that something that has loved and honored me so dearly, to which I owe every rightful devotion, could be horridly abused and mistreated, and brought never again to trust. Or die, never again knowing love.

The crisis came a week later, when once again on the same edge she pulled the exact trick. Except this time she was gone fifteen hours. I rode two thousand acres, calling and searching more desperately as the time drained by. Finally, as dusk fell, finding no sight or sound of her, I rode to Bill Crews's and asked to use the phone. Abandoning further reserve, I summoned Loretta. I had not wanted to, hoped not to have to. Beda was her dog, her little warrior maiden, and they had adored each other uniquely from the start. She fretted every day I took Beda afield, asked each time her safe return.

"Beda's gone," I said.

There was no answer.

"I've looked everywhere. I can't find her."

There was still nothing but silence at the end of the phone.

"I'm sorry, Retta. I'm sorry."

"I'm coming," she said abruptly.

"Please."

I was at the verge of despair. Past mad, and scared, scared we'd never see her again. So many things you imagine, mostly bad. I thought of all the little ways we loved her. Field trials seemed almost insignificant.

"Bring the radios," I remembered, and placed the receiver back on the hook.

Old Bill was partly undressed for bed, and there he was out in the front yard, tousle-headed, his overalls clinging by one gallows, the cuff of one leg hung over one boot and its opposite down over the other. Looking and calling now himself. He was a kind and caring soul. Every word was delivered with a smile. He believed in the world, old Bill, and all in it.

"I'll fetch one of the boys if we find her," he promised. He wasn't smiling then.

Loretta was there, in fifteen minutes, with Melanie. Mely locked herself in the truck, a brave little girl there in the dark and lonesome, left to stay by the trailer in case Beda should appear and to woman the CB, while Loretta and I took the walkie-talkies and rode the entirety of Corinth. She by car, on the perimeters, and me and the mare by hoof, to its depths.

By ten o'clock, we had nothing, and Loretta started knocking on doors two and three miles distant, some on backwoods paths off the main road, where people lived we knew nothing about.

"No," I said.

"Yes," she had declared.

Many's the time we have thought of it since, the potential danger, but that night there was no consciousness of personal concern, only the resolve to find her dog. I began backtracking, returning again to the edge where the setter had disappeared. Calling, and calling. But there was only the damp and chill and still of the night. Nothing else.

"Where is she?" Loretta uttered helplessly over the radio.

I had no answer. Nor any voice left to call. Or any horse left to look. Dolly was worn into the ground. I could feel her give and sway under me.

A voice came again from the radio. Tiny and taut. "I'm scared," it whispered.

Melanie. So much to ask of an eleven-year-old, who had been warned never to talk to strangers. A truck had pulled partly onto the path that led to where she waited and shrank, while the headlights stared uneasily into the cab, then backed away again.

There was nothing left now, but to return to the trailer. To wait and hope that she would come back on her own. We sat in the truck, in the dark, the three of us, tears in our eyes and no word between us. I couldn't tell Loretta that after so long, I had little hope. I truly thought Beda was gone. That we'd never see her again. The beauty of her face, or the mischief in her eyes. Thought that someone had picked her up after several hours, and God knows how far away she was by now, or that with morning we would find her broken, bloody, and lifeless on the road somewhere, where now she lay alone and lonely in the dark. It was absurd, I suppose, should she be dead, to worry of her as alone and lonely. But love is never slave to reason.

"Please, God," Loretta said in the darkness.

Midnight passed. It was dark as Satan. I would climb out and call again occasionally. Scarcely believing.

"Hyeaaah, Bedddaa, hyeaaah!"

Like rote.

"Hyeaahh, Beda, hyeaaahup!"

My voice just bled away into the gloom. I blew the whistle until my ears rang. Somewhere in the distance, a rooster crowed.

We dozed fitfully. It was one of the worst nights of our lives.

I turned on the penlight and checked my watch. It was only an hour till dawn. I had eyestrain from peering constantly into the darkness. I looked around once more, then slipped off again to sleep. When next I awoke, a woman was screaming.

"Turn on the lights! Turn on the lights! I heard something. Somethin' moved.

"Somethin' moved," she repeated deliriously.

It was Loretta, her face fraught with urgency. Fumbling for the switch, I jerked the headlights on. Hope rose like the second coming.

At first, as all the times before, there was nothing. Then, at the feeble fringe of the lights, a sheepish little setter, begging her way home. We tumbled out and rushed to her. Loretta caught her up in her arms, and squeezed her close, crying and laughing together.

"Beja. Beja.

"Wuttle warrior maiden."

Beda knew instantly she was home free, her tail grabbed a beat, and suddenly she was happy as a lark. I wanted to be mad, but couldn't. It was the happiest reunion of our lives.

I knew, though, it would happen anew. I would lose her all over again. Or rather, she would lose me. We had been lucky this time. Maybe not the next. At the least, it was undoing a good dog. All of our training. She was on her way to becoming a bolting, self-hunting renegade. I had to find a way, before I could safely run her again, to curb the tide. A way to follow and find her when she disappeared. Not a bell or a beeper. She ran too big for either. Obviously she was listening to me call. She knew precisely where I was, made sure she was elsewhere. With a bell or a beeper, she'd just move out of hearing. The little bitch.

At North Carolina State University, in the zoology program, Dr. Phil Doer had a number of natural history studies under way. I remembered that after a week of sleepless nights, as all other possibilities drained to doom. Some of these projects concerned home range and required the accurate relocation of individual animals. From a distance, I knew they had a trick to do that, for everything from field mice to alligators. It was managed by somehow attaching electronic transmitters, some very tiny, which transmitted a faithful radio signal. Once you had the beep, you could meter it audibly or electronically as well on a portable receiver. Some of these Lilliputian transmitting units could even sense motion or its absence, altering the signal at the source to tell you whether the subject was sunning on a log, or out chasing supper. If that wasn't enough, using a hand-held directional antenna that married the signal to the receiver, you could walk straightaway to the varmint if you wanted to.

Peggy's pajamas! It was called telemetry, and I didn't know a wallop from a whirlwind about it just then, but I was about to. 'Cause if you could do it with a chipmunk, then why in hell not a dog?

I called Phil Doer moments after the school bell rang the next morning.

"Pretty simple, really," he said.

"Can you do it with a bird dog?" I asked, all I wanted further to know.

"Well, uh, I don't see why not."

After that, he invited me in and showed me the whole contraption wasn't big enough it wouldn't fit on a horse, and of a moment I had the answer, I thought, to my problem. Only to run into another.

The technology was exclusive as Bob Redford's phone number. A single company in Arizona made the only commercial units tough enough to stand the thunk-and-haul of a moose through a willow bog—about what I figured it'd take to survive an average, hard-driving bird dog—and they sold them only by restricted purchase order to university researchers or state wildlife biologists. Short of impersonation and forgery, the possibilities hit bedrock.

That close, I refused to quit. Where there's a hankering, there's a heifer. There had to be a way.

Jumping in on a cold track, I bawled it hot. The trail led through New Mexico and Nevada, then on through Utah, to a cat hunter in Idaho. The hound folks, I found, had discovered telemetry about the same time NASA discovered the moon. Had been using it religiously on cat and bear dogs for years. Equipment the match and means of Dr. Doer's.

"Better'n monkey shine and molasses," the old boy said roguishly.

Nobody, however—that I could determine—was using it then with bird dogs. Regrettably, it would take ten more years, a lot of beloved and valuable pointing dogs lost and dying, before the bird-dog crowd even became generally aware of the technology. Then another ten top of that before the AFTCA would finally force aside its dotty notions about an iniquitous alliance between telemetry and e-collars, and authorize fly-weight tracking collars in sanctioned trials. Until then, everybody was stuck with bells and beeping collars. The difference between a beeper and a radio collar is the difference between two tin cans and a string, and a cell phone.

I didn't know all that then. Whatever, I couldn't wait that long.

Clandestinely as the message in a moonstone, the cat hunter gave me a name and number in Louisiana. Turned out another old boy in the bayous had finagled a pipeline to the parent company, and was bootlegging alter-brand units for bear hounds as fast as he could build them.

"Bear dogs?"

"No," I said, shaking my head. "Bird dogs. Will it work with bird dogs?"

"Ain't nobody usin' 'em with bird dogs, I know."

"I expect, but will they work? I need to know where they are and what they're doin'. Every second.

"Whether they're piddlin' or pointin'.

"And when I get ready, I need to be able to go to 'em, straight to 'em."

"Do you need to know whether he's p'intin' with his head up or his head down?" he needed to know.

"What?" I said.

"Tree switch," he said. "You kin tell whether he's treeing or just standin' round."

"Uh . . . no," I said, although immediately the possibilities were intriguing. You could tell whether a dog was standing sky-high or goose-loose, if he was jammed against his birds or standing off a mite. Winding.

"Uh . . . no," I decided. "My dogs are stylish enough. I just need to know when they stop and how to get there."

"Easy," he allowed. "Motion switch. Tells you whether he's fartin' or flyin', and how fas'."

"What about when he stops?"

"Flops over after four seconds," he explained, "to a slower beep."

"How fast can you send me one?" I said.

"Tomorrow."

I didn't ask how much. Didn't matter. I've never thought much about dogs and dollars. Just dash and danger.

Three days later, I had in hand a leather-cased receiver about the size of a good book, a plastic collar with an external wire antenna and a bradded-on, steel-encased transmitter about the measure of a box of .22 bullets, and a directional H-antenna about three-quarters of a yard long on a broomstick. I promptly bored a hole in the stick and looped through it a swivel-snap on a hank of rawhide. Then I could clip it on the saddle. Within two months, the mare would mash one flat and lie on another. The electronic wizards had a ways to go on miniaturizing the antenna. But praise glory, I was on the air.

I broke the maiden the day after I got it. Led Beda to the breakaway line, discreetly strapped the transmitter collar around her neck, and hit the whistle. And from the first beep, fell head-over-hamhocks in love with it. Our warrior maiden was wild-eyed as a buck, and I knew once again we were in for mischief. This time it was different. She sailed down the initial edge and whipped into the woods, I clicked on the receiver, and suddenly I had an electronic scout that telegraphed every minute, mark, and motion. The peace of mind was like stepping ice cold under a warm shower.

Purposely that workout afternoon, I set the rebellious setter up for a fall, choosing the same course she had sold out on for the past month. She had a beautiful find in the gallberry head coming out of the creek bottom. A scattered, feeding covey straggled up, she watched them proudly away, I popped the gun and quickly sent her on through the next small block of woods. As expected, she broke out of the pines, caught the long sweep of the forewarning edge, and flew along to its limits. I laid comfortably back, said nothing, just sang to her. The trap was laid. For a moment, after all, it appeared it would be foiled. The little gyp was bouncing along with all intents, it seemed, to handle that day. But just as the far corner was looming, I saw her slip stride almost imperceptibly, throw a glance over her shoulder, and shoot right and gone into the woods.

I rode along quietly, monitoring the beep, nary a peep. I could imagine what must be going on in the setter's head.

"Hmmmhn. Why ain't I hearin' him?

"Never had no problem keepin' up with 'im before."

But the die was cast. She was too sot in her ways to mend. On she flew.

No useless hollering, no wild and ridiculous riding. The mare had to be happy, as we laid back and listened. Listened, said not a peep, and followed the beep. For the first time, I could see what the little bitch had been doing. Cutting a crazy U and backtracking behind me, while I rode on ahead, as she bent in a wide loop around me and deep into the river bottom, to the edge of a swampy thicket where the woodcock lived. Once there, she had been home free. It was like following your elbow to your thumb, and I never thought to go that way to begin with; by the time I would, she was deliriously ensconced in the swamp. To frolic around forever. I could hear her down there now, as the radio signal tattled, beating around in the bushes, pointing, then nosing up timberdoodles.

"Uhhn-huh."

Now I had a trick myself.

Me and the mare slipped along the cap of an abandoned railroad trestle, dropped through the dip of a long wash, tipped along an old sawmill path, and emerged point-blank on top of her as she blundered out of the low bushes.

"*Heyeeee!*" I hollered just as loud as I could.

She'd as well as seen a ghost. Skidding to a stop, she tried her best to get by with a whoa.

Her befuddled mind was splitting quarters like a stopwatch at Pimlico. I could see it in her eyes.

"Where in hell'id he come from?"

Vaulting off the mare, I ran over, grabbed her up, and shook her until her ribs rattled. Not cruelly, just certainly.

Propping her back, I stroked her up and admonished her sternly. After a minute, I walked off a little ways and dug out a peanut. Taking my time to crack it, and then another, leaving her to wonder and reason. She was one chastised setter. Five minutes later, I went back to her, snapped on a cord, reinforced "Come" a time or two, then led her back to the trestle without further accord. I wasn't ready yet, as I would later, to tell her she was my baby.

The rest of the hour, she handled like a dream.

Fifteen minutes, it had taken, to undo a problem months in the making, one that could have cost us her life and loss. One more time, it took for her, after that. To revive the lesson, and accept the Lord. She could never figure how I came to know. Quickly she returned to her old butter-smooth and consistent self, and offered not another problem the rest of her days.

I, meanwhile, had found the Holy Grail. A full-time scout that never lost a dog. An assurance that never again would I worry about losing those dear things in my life. That alone made telemetry worth its weight in gold. I made myself a promise that first day with Beda—all the more after the first day I put it on Pat—that I would never again turn a dog loose without a radio collar. I haven't and won't.

Quickly, I found as well, I had a training partner. Now I could track a dog's pattern, correct a quirk before it became a habit. Know when a young dog went on point, to the second, get to it and handle it in little more than a few heartbeats. Know when an old dog stayed honest, or did not.

A time afterward, the last year before it became a championship, I judged the Alabama Open Shooting Dog Classic with Tommy Mock. Jack and Peggy Herriage were there with some good dogs. Jack was a professional from Texas, a fine one. One day during the running, he invited us by, and I happened to notice on top of a box inside his trailer a telemetry receiver.

When I had him off to a side sometime later, I said, "How do you like your telemetry system?"

He looked at me like I had read the numbers on his bank account.

"How do you know about that?" he wanted to know.

"'Cause I've been using one for about five years," I said.

"I'm in love with it," he confided. "If it was another woman, Peg would shoot me. It's the greatest training tool I've ever had."

So far as I know, Jack and I were the first two people to seriously track and train bird dogs with telemetry. Jack was using it also as a homing device, leaving an extra collar at the trailer when he trained on strange grounds. Then all he had to do was concentrate on his dogs, without caring where they took him. At the end of the day, when he wanted to go home, he simply clicked on the receiver and took himself there.

∾ CHAPTER 23 ∾

BEDA IN THE GROOVE, IT WAS BACK IN THE SADDLE. WASTING NO TIME, Beda won over seventeen dogs at Eastern Carolina; Pat whipped eighteen at Spring Valley. Then together, on a frigid day at Sumter, they claimed the hourlong shooting-dog stake in championship form over the frozen grounds of the Gamecock Club, Pat winning it and Beda solidly in for third.

Five years along, both dogs were nearing the top of their game. Their brother, meantime, was giving me fits. He had developed another hole, wanting now to break off a solid point and circle his birds. God, would I ever get him finished? Ever it was stitch and mend. I put the collar around his waist, as Paul Long suggested, and tickled him a time or so, and got that fixed. Then he started fidgeting at the shot. Wanting nothing more than for me to tap him on, and let him go. He'd let down a little, take one creep step, then another, whining, trembling, and popping his teeth as I returned to him, rather than hiking up rock-solid and proud. It was sheer desire, yet again, but it wouldn't win shooting-dog trials. I worked and worked with him, got him so close. He'd swell up and watch the birds away, wait attractively for the shot. But once it popped, he knew the jig was run. He'd go frizzle-frazzle. Nice he was, so nice, on the ground and on his birds, but on the very top end, he was nitsy as a wool sweater.

A dog has to have it all in top trials. He can't be unraveled at any of the edges.

It bothered me terribly I couldn't get him right. He could have been the third force in a mighty triumvirate, could have won big. He had it *almost* all. I just wasn't good enough then. Or now. He was a man. We had it out man-to-man. Time and again, physically and psychologically, while I labored so to walk the edge, to beg the pledge and save the pride. Occasionally he would be so damned pigheaded that I'd lose my temper for a useless minute. Then, afterward, hate myself for it. Realize it was nothing more than my own inadequacy. In the end, I guess the better man won. He just finally wore me out. I'd still field him occasionally, give him a whirl at redemption. But more and more, it was me and the girls.

Back again to Virginia. Pat and Kizzy. But this time, Beda had her head back together. This time, Beda was waiting for them.

It unfolded at Remington, over the expansive and beautifully configured green hills of Rappahannock. The amateur stakes were run on Sunday that renewal. The boys always threw a pig-picking and a bluegrass breakdown for the handlers on Saturday night. About ten o'clock, about the time the last pinch of pig was exhausted, the band would sail into "Foggy Mountain Breakdown," somebody'd grab a ladling spoon and a washtub, somebody else a harmonica. Enough Jim Beam had passed lips that spirits were full mast. It'd be Billy, and Paul, Jack, and Gary, and Ed, and Huber Ford and Andy, the northern Virginia crew, a few folks down from Maryland, Pennsylvania, or Delaware. Occasionally Gerald Tracy, Norm Basilone, or Henry Caruso. Some effervescent soul would start singing, and then another, until you had a chorus, and from every trailer on the grounds the dogs would yowl—maybe fifty of them—and Lewis would break loose into a buck dance. Somebody else'd start yodeling, and here and there in the dark beyond the fire a horse would blow, while overhead the stars twinkled like moonlight in diamonds, as on the grass underfoot the hoarfrost grew. Between then and the smaller hours of the morning, we'd rerun fifteen field trials again, and wonder toward a few more. Every man would have a wager. And I wish I could do that over tonight. Have it feel like it did then.

'Cause I was proud of my dogs and looking forward to the morrow. I could feel something building down deep inside of me that was more than the mood or the music, a little zephyr of confidence hung on a thread of prophesy, that said tomorrow we would shine.

I remember I didn't sleep much that night, but got up about four o'clock under all those stars, and let my dogs out of the box to be with me. It was numb chilly, but we just sat there, the three of us, until almost dawn, happy with our company. We'd come a ways together, since that May morning and the little white whelping shed behind the house on Chaney Road.

Moments and miles.

The wind was rising steadily, bullying in out of the northwest. It would be howling today, the weather-sayers had threatened. Gusts to forty miles an hour, hard on a handling song. Already it had whisked clean the wispy clouds tarnishing the heavens, and was shivering the trailer in intermittent blasts. We sat in its lee, listening to its lonely wail through the trees on the hillsides.

Whatever I was feeling, I think Beda felt it, too. She seemed more distant than usual. Shrinking from my caress, and staring almost presciently into the night. Dogs—supposedly—don't contemplate the future. Maybe not in weeks, or months, or years. That's a human province, either blessing or affliction. But certainly in days, and hours, and minutes, I believe. Dogs at a trial know most certainly that within the space of practical anticipation they will run. And ready themselves for it in separate ways. Some fret and whine. Others bark and try the chain. A few tuck and tremble. Still others show no visible signs of anxiety whatsoever, while underneath the cauldron comes slowly to boil. But all live for the moment. Beda knew that in a few hours she would run, and tonight there was something different in her. If it had been human, I would have called it resolve.

She took the whistle in the third brace of the morning. You could barely hear it, as she drove away, above the roar of the wind. Overhead, great trees bucked and swayed. On the forward slope, the plumy heads of sedge-grass bowed and bounced in subservient tawny arcs before the will of the squalls. Behind her, a string of riders shrunk deeply into their coats, tugged down their hats, as behind them the broomtails of their mounts streamed in perpendicular digression to their progress. I sat at the head of the belea-guered procession on the mare, knotting the scarf more tightly to my neck, and watching my dog go. She was traveling beautifully, hard and fast, her tail dancing above her back, its silky banner billowed by the breeze and bur-nished by the sun. Out of the protecting shelter of the cover and into the broad wind cache of the open green pastures both dogs flew, and the blast hit them at once, like a stiff-armed punch. The setter raced flatly under it, flinched not a foot, but her bracemate buckled, slowing and looping on a lateral tangent. His handler was reining into the blow, hollering and battling the bluster of the gusts, trying to turn him forward again. Already Beda was far ahead, rounding the first distant corner and catching the long row of cedars at the top edge of the field. Down it she flew, disappearing over the crest of the hill, gone and away.

"*Yaaaahuuup! Yeeeaahh, girrl!*" Doubting she heard, I sang nonetheless. Asking her on. Really, it was a matter of trust now, that she would lay to the front. Check for me at the fringes. My heart was beginning the climb to my throat. God, do I love to see a dog run like that.

But when we reached the peak of the knoll, could see far ahead—a quarter mile across the rolling meadows to the vague, tumbling rush of the creek—there was nothing. And I sat there for a growing minute, then two, searching intensely for her to show at the edges, without sight of her. I looked for Billy in the gallery, could find him neither. Knew he was out. Tarrying no longer, I whipped the mare around and rode with the company of the judge, back along the high edge of cedars, thinking maybe one of us left her on point. Nothing.

I glanced at my watch. The judge read my mind.

"Five minutes," he said. We could not stand ten.

Frantically, I retraced the course forward, glancing ahead to the gallery, hoping to see her to the front. I had to, soon. And then we saw him coming, Billy Blankenship, his black gelding Pretty Boy in a pounding gallop, far, far from the left, along the march of another fencerow, which split away straight as an arrow near the knoll, to carry on and on into the distance.

And then we could hear him at last, yelling with all his might above the assault of the wind.

"*POINT! . . . POINT!*"

We spurred the horses, raced to meet him. Pulling up hard, all three mounts slid on stiff haunches to a halt, whirling and bouncing in a circle at the bit. Hopping, waiting again to go.

"She's standing up the fence row . . . *way* out there," Billy said breathlessly. "To hell and back.

"Had to come back; there wadn' any way you were gonna hear me."

I could have kissed the crusty old fart, overalls, whiskers, and all.

"*Hyiiegh!*" I heeled the mare, left her her head, and she almost jumped out from under me. Loosening the reins, I pulled tight against her neck and let her go, go until she was laid out a quarter-of-herself closer to the ground, and down the offwind side of the fence we blew. Hard behind came

Billy and the judge, and far ahead in the distance, a full half mile on a limb, we could see the faint white sketch of a standing setter. Poised poetically against the scent, the plume of her tail taut in the breeze, little Miss Grace before her court.

Inspiration carried her there, and painted her there, and I'll not forget it as long as I live.

She turned just slightly to look at me, proudly it seemed, and then back, and I walked in and kicked two birds out, and away we all flew, to reach the front. My dog was there long before I was. At time, almost as far as you could see her, she stopped again. For a second find, pretty as the first.

Two braces later, Pat came along, with two finds and a finish that would sell on Broadway. After that, Kizzy. Both did a hell of a job.

There was a time in Pat's heat. She had reached far, far ahead, along a fencerow. Flying. Way high upon the next hill was a small gap in the fence-line, on a hard ninety-degree turn that signaled the switchback of the course. Just as she reached it, I yowled at the top of my lungs.

"Yowwwww nowww!"

Pat never dropped a stride, just whipped left and zipped through it, sailing on. Beda had done the same.

Gary Winall from Powhatan was a young man in the gallery then, on his way up in field trials.

"So damn smooth," he told me later, "how you threaded those dogs through that fence break." And it was, though mostly the dogs, with no great digs from me. They had learned that at Corinth, shooting the breaks along Bill Crews's pasture line.

But that was Beda's day. It was consensus: Warrior Maiden first, Zip Zap second, Roll On Kizzy third.

Lewis hardly knew what had happened, for once was meek as a mission bell.

It was the only time Beda ever beat her little sister on the ground. It was like she was saying, "I count too." Of course she did, and had, after Rappahannock just the more.

~ CHAPTER 24 ~

KIZZY WAS TOO CONSISTENT TO LAY DOWN FOR LONG. SHE WON THE
Region 3 Championship later that year. I scouted for Lewis and was glad to
do it. Birds continued extremely scarce at Hoffman then, as elsewhere across
much of the Southeast, they were dwindling. Sadly, these were the last days
for viable wild-bird trials in the Carolina Sandhills. Already it was a roulette
match. To follow would be a dismal period, when most of the dogs that ran
there had intolerable odds of finding game. Some of the best grounds in the
country, also among the most barren. Almost a decade afterward, faced with
the loss of a century-old sporting tradition, the North Carolina Wildlife
Commission finally consented to the necessity of summer-released, pen-
raised coveys. Much as the directors of the Grand Junction Classic would
submit on the hinge of the millenium. In either case, it would be the salva-
tion of big-time field trialing, but a semblance nonetheless. One more nail
in the coffin.

For us that December day, it was another luckless trip in a major trial,
one that was proving a jinx. Pat ran all over the world—big and forward—
digging up and acing a bevy at eighteen, when only a half dozen dogs in
the whole shebang could claim even a contact. Then purely tore the heart
out of me by lapsing lost for the next half hour. On deer or birds. I never
knew which. The second time straight she had sold out-of-pocket in this
stake. Beda went the hour pretty as perfection, not for the life of her able to
come up with a bird. I hurt with her at time. She had hunted her soul out,
and still did not wish to quit.

Kizzy, with better fortune, managed a small covey in the early minutes
of the hour, then shook her bracemate and completed the clock at her usual
prance and practice. The single stitch in her almost seamless forward per-

formance occurred with sixteen to go, when everybody and his mule, especially Lewis, knew she was waxing the wicker. Laid back and lateral, I saw the sprightly pointer cut south into the corner just before the course switched the same direction, but could see also she hadn't popped through, for Lewis didn't have her. He was a lonesome silhouette out front on his horse, calling. Looking desperately back for me.

It's a hell of a responsibility scouting a dog, one that's a lick and minutes, you know, from a title.

Time was skipping by, tension was growing like a grass fire, and I wanted dearly to go. But you don't take liberties in a championship with twelve left and a dog a whisker west of winning. I whipped further off to the side, waved my hat wildly over my head, and motioned to the judges, was it okay? One glance and I was gone.

"*Hyaagh!*" I hupped the mare, flicked her once on the butt with the flushing whip, and clung on. She sailed five feet over a pine lap and then through the woods, pulled up and danced long enough to set a course down a pulpwood path, and pounded on. At its conclusion, where it opened into a small slash cut, I expected to find my dog. She wasn't there. I circled twice, looking, time and pressure menacing like a guillotine.

"Please, heaven, don't let me lose this dog."

To the east off the slash was one tiny game trail. Through it, me and the mare split the pines. At the end of the diminutive tunnel loomed a small patch of light, but between thee and there lay a legion of tops, crossed like swords over a wedding party. There was little time to tuck, barely time to duck. Limbs cracked and needles flew, as through them we blew. Into the center of another piney glade, on top of one surprised black-and-white pointer dog, who had halted her beating around long enough to check what-and-hell who.

"K-i-z-z-y, what're you doin' in here?" I said gruffly. "*Hey, heel!*"

She was too embarrassed to refuse. I got her in front of the horse, and we slammed again through the pines, back to the path. Hit a hard canter.

"*Git-on out of here, Kizzy! Heel!*" And we took up the road at a gallop.

Five minutes spent, I had her to the front, where Lewis chafed. He could see me as we broke out of the woods, but not yet his dog, his face solemn as a twilight shadow. And then Kizzy topped the rise and he grinned all over, moonlight and madness.

"I's gittin' worried, boy," he drawled.

But there was little damage done, and Larry Moon, who was judging, said out of the corner of his mouth, "I believe if I was winning this field trial, I'd stop now and water my dog."

They didn't want to lose this dog. So Lewis took down his saddle canteen, a gallon jug reinforced with duct tape, and we slowed down another three minutes freshening and tanking Kizzy. Lewis turned her loose again at about two minutes to go, long enough to squall once and have her fade off over the next hill, and the judges to call, "Pick 'er uuuppp." And the persimmons were in the pudding.

Lewis was overjoyed, and I was too, for Kizzy. But sad for us. Things had been going well, and this was a setback. But not for long.

Pat and Beda shot out of that trial like Satan out of a synagogue, winning the next three trials one-two, respectively, including the open money stakes at Cool Springs, in the western Carolina foothills, where once had spoored many an old-time champion. It would pay our way back to Pensacola, and once again we were hot-off-the-pads toward a major trial, the consecutive Sunshine State renewal of the AFTCA National Championship. It rarely came east, but would now for the second year in a row, and was in amateur shooting-dog circles the celestial equinox of hope and happen. A month away and a medley of good workouts under our belt, anticipation grew in giant steps. Just as winter swung hard and decked the fair weather we'd been enjoying, colder than a cobblestone.

For thirteen days reigned snow, ice, and bitter cold. Highs chattered in the teens, lows plunged to zero, and the ground shivered to the frostline. Footing was so treacherous we couldn't even road. The only thing that melted was misery, and it was pooled to my earlobes. I moped uselessly, while hour by hour the fine edge of conditioning we had honed dulled away. By the fifth day, life became insufferable. Cursing, I pulled on long johns, knee-pacs, and a mackinaw and slid to the kennel. Buckling the dogs in harness, I snapped the pull rope to a ring on my weight-lifting belt.

"If you ask me," Loretta vexed, "they're a bat short in the belfry."

"We didn't," I said, and off we went afoot, cross-country. You learn from your dogs. You do what you have to. But you never, *ever* quit.

If it had been deep snow, even, we would have managed a token of defiance, but the ice was impossible. It was slicker than a goat could grapple, and after being jerked on my face a half dozen times, ultimately I surrendered. Given a day or two, I would have mounted another initiative, but by that time my wife had put the fear of Jehovah in me about pulled muscles. So I went back to moping and cussing.

On the eleventh day, Loretta invited me out of the house. For good. No more spaghetti on Wednesday nights. No more bread puddings on my birthday. Don't even think about a Christmas cake next year. Fortunately, before litigation set in, the weather lightened, and we were sleeping in the same bed again.

Remarkably, the reconciliation occurred about the same day I was able to load the mare and setters, and finally take to the field once more. It was a grueling task. The sun peered timidly through a gauzy sky, doing little to frighten away the chill. It was still goose-down cold, barely scratching freezing. The ground was muddy rotten in places from the freeze and thaw, puddled with frigid water, and in others where the shadows collected, perilously occluded by stubborn sheets of hardened ice. It was muck, suck, or slide, the mare slogging and pitching to hold her stride. A couple of times she went to her knees, and I had to climb off to let her buck her way out. On the soaking feathers and underbellies of the dogs, dirty icicles grew.

Devilish as it was, birds were moving. We found four coveys in three hours. The gump of it was, we got little done. All were jumpy, going out well ahead of the dogs before they could reasonably establish a point. But it was running again, and training, and an elixir to spirits worn forlorn.

Pat, largely unaffected by the layoff, went big and fast. Beda, to the contrary, was sluggish, not really herself. I thought it was a loss of conditioning, but a week later Loretta found first show, and our hearts fell. An infortuitous heat cycle would sideline her for the National. It hurt terribly, for all of us. It was an opportunity less in a lifetime that could afford so few. On the frozen and dreary day we left, she reared and moaned at the fence, while Loretta tried helplessly to comfort her.

Life is composed of extremes. Twenty hours and a thousand miles later, Pat and I basked near seventy degrees in robust sunshine. Under the pines, across the open, rolling understory of the Blackwater Forest, the rays glimmered off the shinnery. The air was golden and lazy. Only occasionally rose the flicker of a breeze. From the fragrant green boughs, doves cooed love songs.

Meanwhile, the competition was brutal. I missed Beda, but in honesty, it took Pat's kind of power to win that trial. For forty-five minutes she did. Her ground heat was as bold and masterful as ever one was, and every motion was a statement of style. She was down with a good dog, with no mean race of its own . . . and there had been others . . . but hers was the more thrilling and purposeful. With one stirring find to her acclaim, she needed maybe one more. And that was at hand. Ahead, in a distant, hillside sketch of lespedeza, a bevy was spread feeding. Pat cast far to the right, her bracemate to the left. Across the front, they closed as precisely as the jaws of a caliper into the spoor of the scattered covey. Both dogs arrived in unison, reading the wind, and seconds later we watched as the pointer pulled stiffly up and roaded a few yards to a stop. Seconds later, Pat, circling the cover to grab the breeze, hauled up also. It was a gorgeous stand, both dogs posed expressively upon the hillside.

As we reached them, I saw the judges confer. Moments later, as Pat stood proudly and I dismounted to handle my dog, they called me over. And kicked our world apart.

"As much as we hate it," they said, "we'll ask you to pick her up."

They thought she had seen the standing pointer and should have honored. To this day, I don't. There were occasions when Pat was younger when she had failed to back, for she was hardly given to subservience of any kind. But not that time, for she had become, though reluctant, quite reliable. That time I remain convinced she was totally intent on the birds, and was winding through a line of cover that would have precluded a line of sight to her bracemate.

I told them politely so, but they were unable to concur. I offered no more, for I had been in their saddle. Outwardly, I tried to maintain a semblance of composure, as I walked to Pat's side and stood by her while the opposing handler put the birds up and posted the shot. Inwardly, I was dying. We remained there, alone and behind, while the woods closed round, and the handling song subsided as the trial party faded away, and the world was never emptier. The little setter strained in my arms and asked hard to go, and I could tell her nothing more than no.

But on the long ride home came the awareness that, despite the bad fortune, Pat was getting ever better. She had always had the power, now she was gathering the finesse. Anywhere, any challenge, she was a hell of a force.

Back home and Beda off the bench, we were winning enough that it was nicely becoming a habit, and enjoying each other more than ever we had. It was a special feeling, going off together, excited to the toenails, every one of us. Knowing we could go to any shooting-dog trial in the country, and be up there knocking hard on the door. We weren't big stuff, never thought we were, just a dogged little tribe of homebreds with our caps on straight. But we were proud.

You keep reaching. We had good wins under our belt, quality hour stakes and classics. Though as close as we'd been to winning the big ones—the title stakes—they kept eluding us. It wasn't a matter of deficiency. I knew we were good enough. But it takes more than good to win a championship. It takes karma—a good draw, congenial weather, cooperative birds, the absence or oversight of any one of a half dozen unanticipated hindrances that can throw a winning effort off just enough it slips a-kilter. Still, you've got to be near perfect enough, day in and day out, that on any occasion you minimize the odds. If a dog can do that, and has the charisma to shoulder the best of the best, hope floats.

∼ CHAPTER 25 ∼

THERE WERE A LOT OF GOOD AMATEUR DOGS RUNNING IN THOSE days, many kenneled in professional strings: Calico Calli, Brick Haven Judy, Dynastic, Flair, Selpmet's Big Sam, Dry Creek Button, I'm Jackie, Little Diamond, Tooth Acres Judy, Ramreb Two Dot, Nor-Mel's Bushwhacker, Great Notion, Gateway Trademark, Elhew Knickermock, Roll On Kizzy, Windwalker, State Line Sam, to mention the few. A host of talented handlers at their helm: Bobby Davis, Skip Brown, C. K. Young, Jadie Rayfield, Tommy Mock, Billy Blankenship, Doc Nitchman, Gene Casale, Bob Abric, Norman Melton, John Temples, Frankie Henderson, Dr. Billy McCathern, John Little, Dr. Frank Hines. There were others, a gallant bunch, and you could count on some of them at most any major trial, and most all at a regional or national championship. To win, place, or show in their presence was a sacred feat.

Down through the year, the remainder of spring through fall, we encountered them occasionally. One or two at the time. But then, somehow, the months had worn through, and almost before it seemed the dust had settled from the previous December at Hoffman, it was Thanksgiving all over again, and time for all to gather at the championship for Region 3.

South Carolina had the stake renewal that November. It began the day after the turkey salad expired, over the old Belmont Plantation near Savannah. I had come to love the grounds and, moreover, the rituals. The holding canvassed several thousand acres, and was in its day a haven for Newport financier and sportsman August Belmont, Jr., a portion of his wintering and training operation for his Thoroughbred racing program. It was classically Southern. Stately ranks of whiskered live oaks soldiered and shaded opposing sides of the mile-long, gray-silver avenue to the big house, their great lower limbs spread and drooping almost to the sand, the pewter green of their leaves lending an aura of dignity and antiquity. The mood of lichen on an ancient and weathered gravestone. At their exodus, the avenue of oaks bowed to the gardens and living grounds, and to the imposing presence of the mansion itself. Grecian, whitewashed, and shuttered, its expansive colonnade enhanced on either side by myrtle and magnolia. The carriage path behind took you by the graying hulk of the old barn, and to the regimented rows of adjoining stables.

What gaiety it must have known. Folks in silk or satin, bodice and gown, top hats, long coats and tails, wearing the charm of the Low Country—stepping off fine chestnut horses to a mounting block, handing over reins to a waistcoated attendant, or disembarking from a tasseled surrey, gliding gracefully to the ground on the gentle dip of the springs—climbing the height of stairs to the porch and bowing to their hosts. On the rise of the evening is the delicate scent of gardenia, a waft of honeysuckle, to mingle with the throaty sharpness of bay. And the roast of pig on the spittle. While beyond the threshold beckons the soft yellow glow of the lamps, the murmur and flutter of happy voices, an occasional explosion of laughter, and the lively strut of the fiddles.

I could capture a lot of that, especially late at night when all had retired and I would return alone to the great room, where the fire flickered still. From the broad firebox that could kindle the greater trunk of a tree. To sit in its spell, and think of it not now as the bastion of field trial merriment, which was wonderful enough, but as the ballroom it would have been then. Not all was gone with the wind.

There was adopted that year the running rites of the South Carolina Celebration, held annually over the same grounds. I could anticipate them splendidly. By the time breakfast was spent in the dining room of the old mansion, a sleepy yellow sun would be propped on splayed rays above the windowsill. Outside, under the pines, lazy tendrils of mist would begin their ethereal climb from the lightly frosted grass.

From the distance would come the clean, clarion, two-sided note of a cock quail, asking a blessing of the new morning. Closer by would lift the less assertive inquest of the doves.

All about the venerable estate, people in hats, chaps, and riding boots would be scurrying around in frenzied, last-minute preparation for the

inaugural brace of the trial. Off the colonnade, from the waxy green magnolias, a pair of mockingbirds would trade passionate salutations to the
morning. Dogs would bark anxiously. Horses would whinny, stomp, and
blow, fidgeting under tack heaved hastily aboard and cinched abruptly to
place. Hails, shouts, and summons would grow in a nervous approach to an
eight o'clock breakaway.

In every knot and gather, exhilaration would skip off the air like grease
off a griddle.

Now a team of jennies would draw the dog wagon ceremoniously up
the winding dirt road from the stable to the Big House, the muffled, rhythmic clop of their hooves mingling with the whine and plead of boxed and
ready canines. Off the back portico, as the team stood to a halt, waiting
under rein, the field trial party would amass quickly around it—a host of
ardent folk leading horses at saddle.

To the height of the broad, wooden steps the Trial Chairman would
ascend, to acknowledge the eager throng, announce the Stake and the
judges by his side. Tension would soar.

"Welcome, All, to the seventeenth running of . . ."

At last, with his close, a fervent field trial party would stand fully commissioned to proceed. And in a ritual I will love to my last day, not one foot
hits a stirrup, as a procession of seventy-five field trialers and horses respectfully trod behind judges, marshals, mules, and dogs the eighth-of-a-mile
live-oak avenue from the Big House to the starting point of the morning
course.

"Turn 'em loose, Gentlemen!"

I was excited to my elbows.

But can you imagine that into this promenade waltzed Lewis Clements
and Kizzy? He called me a few weeks before the trial.

"You goin' to the Region 3?"

"Yep."

"Wal, let's us go together."

So we did. I liked Lewis. A lot. And if ever a man could appreciate
Southern tradition, was more a part of it, than Lewis Clements, he has yet
to be inscripted. It was just that he embraced it on a different plane. Kind of
like a game rooster that's misplaced his way to a peacock pen. He can eat
the sunflower seeds, but he'll never breed the hens.

So it's me and Pat and Beda and Kizzy, and old Rod, short for Rodney Dangerfield, a big rangy pointer that Lewis has bartered to run for a friend. "Where's old Thing?" Lewis wants to know every other milepost. "We shoulda brought old Thing." And there are two horses, a few bales of hay, a bag of grain, and a week's worth of chewing tobacco. And up from Early County comes Tommy Mock, with his paint geldings and two or three Elhew dogs, straight off the nest of Bob Wehle's blue hens. All named Buck. And a dozen jars of mayhaw jelly.

It was spontaneous combustion from the moment I introduced them, a raucous collusion of Georgia Cracker and Carolina flue-cured, there under the live oaks by August Belmont's barn. You could hear either one of them a quarter mile.

"What's a Kizzy?" Mock wanted to know immediately, laying a hand on Lewis's shoulder, the shadow of a grin on his lips. Of course, he knew already, for I had forewarned each about the other.

"Boy, don't you ever watch telebision?" Lewis drawled.

"Where I come from, we ain't got no television," Tommy said.

"Wal, if you did, you'd know 'bout Kizzy, and Chicken George, and old Kuna Kinty."

"Kuna who?"

"Kuna Kinty."

"Wuz she from Hawaii?"

"Boy, you ain't got no refinement."

"Besides, hell, I might be braced with *you*. I damn shore wadn' comin' down here with anything named Buck."

There was a pause while both turned opposite directions and evacuated a load of tobacco.

"Kin she jump the broom?" Tommy said.

"Just tell me how high," Lewis declared.

From there every loose moment was driveled until it dripped, left to collect upon the floor of Palmetto panache in one great puddle of hilarity.

I tried hard not to step in it. I was dead serious about this trial. I had to be, from the start. In twelve hours, we had the first brace, Pat and I. I was trying hard to keep my mind right. All else compatible, it's still tough, a first-brace draw. In a trial this big, your performance had to be remarkable. To remain compelling in judicial minds for four days as forty more of the fanciest shooting dogs on the East Coast came behind to throw their utter best at you.

There was more. We were drawn against one of the smoothest, winningest shooting dogs on the East Coast. With already a covey of titles to lengthen her name, Little Diamond was a lithe and light-on-her-feet pointer bitch that knew how to fly. Owned and handled by Dr. L. G. Thompson of Georgia, and cut sharply from the professional string of Eddie Rayl, she was also a paragon of a bird finder. In a legendary performance at the Illinois Open Shooting Dog Championship a few years before, she had matched Ralph Ellison's elite pointer dog Great Notion ten finds for ten in a ground-blazing, bird-riveting altercation that inks the books as one of the most electrifying heats in field trial history. Spilling indecisively into overtime, the contest had raged more than two hours in a callback that still brought no clear advantage to either dog. Finally and reluctantly, the judges were forced to a choice.

She was a daunting hurdle. With stakes this high, you had to worry. But I knew my dog. And sometime in the smallest hours of the new morning, with only pittance to go before their clash, I remembered Dub Watkins, and what he had said to me that first trial at Chesterfield.

"You wanna be down with a good dog. A son-of-a-bitch that leaves on your dollar and forgets the change. One that don't allow you two cents to a nubbin for less than your best."

In memory, I could see Pat glancing up at me from the starting line of every trial we'd ever run. With those powder-keg eyes. Asking me to light the fuse. Never was it shorter than with the dogs she had waged against before—Duke, Kizzy, a handful more. Dogs that had braced her, made her reach deep down inside herself and fan the stem of the flame. Out of the worry came the wisdom. I hoped Little Diamond was tip-top. I hoped she opened with a dare.

Sleepless still, I watched as first light unwrapped the fog that huddled under the nearby pines, that had crept in during the night to color the world gray and shapeless. To give privacy to the doves grieving somberly from the oaks. To render even the imposing presence of manor and barn almost a mystery in a mist. The pregnant air condensed along the limbs overhead, dripping periodically to splatter in big, wet circles into the dust, and upon the hats and shoulders of the half dozen people who were beginning dimly to stir, who collared a semblance of dogs from box to chain to stretch the kinks out of sleepy muscles, and shuffled like ghosts trailer-to-stable to meet soft nickers with breakfast buckets of grain. The nether-mood heightened the anticipation that already lay on my stomach like an unsettled meal.

It was the kind of pain you suffer for love. For the love of being there. When your heart would allow you to be nowhere else to have avoided it.

I got the dogs out, snapped them to the chain, got down on my knees between the two of them. They planted front paws on my thighs either side, and I wrapped an arm each around their shoulders, and we talked together with our eyes. They were both happy. Excited, too. They knew why we were there, and that this was a big one. Beda wouldn't run until the eleventh, though already she trembled with eagerness. I studied Pat. Beneath the smolder in her eyes, she was calm as a cucumber. For a moment more, I had them to myself, and then they both whipped wildly away to raise a ruckus at a mockingbird that dipped by on an expedition to a nearby magnolia tree.

Our reverie would be short-lived anyhow. From the off side of the trailer, I heard a great *hawwwaakkk,* that sounded like gears grinding on a forties Ford, and then a monstrous *pps-tt-oooh.* Lewis was up and stirring. He could raise the rivets out of a mortar bucket.

He had his cap off as he came around the corner, eyelids red and droopy, and scratching his head. There was a lump under his jaw already, from the first chew.

"You ready, Boy?" he thundered.

I grinned weakly and said something hopeful.

"Them shags is ready, Boy, I kin tell."

Then he dug Rod and Kizzy out, and Rod waddled around hunched up and quivering, like he was puckering over persimmon seeds, and soon the air was redolent with steaming fresh dog shit. Kizzy squatted to pee, while Pat and Beda bounced and woofed and watched the show.

Lewis looked around twice to see if there were any women around, then dug out something of his own and watered a box shrub.

"Woooghf." He sidled south to change the wind. "Damn, Rod, you's rotten Boy," he bellowed. Rod, relieved at last, scratched off four or five times with his hind feet, pivoting in a semicircle and spattering the trailer with dirt, dog plaster, and leaves.

So much for a tender moment. Now all I needed was Mock. To egg them on.

"I'm a-goin' up to the house and git a coffee and biskit," Lewis said. "You comin'?"

"Naah, think I'll stay here," I said quietly. Lewis hiked up his britches, rammed the zipper north, crammed in his shirttail, and left.

Peace. Now I could suffer comfortably again.

The minutes raced by. I tried to slow them down, but it was like stopping a windstorm with a screen door. A quarter before eight o'clock, the wagon pulled up to the Big House, and we loaded the dogs. Pat drug me there, her hindquarters pumping, the muscles strutting as chiseled rock. I picked her up and asked her into a box. Latching it, I turned away, glancing at Little Diamond, a box removed. She was a willowy little thing, gathering too, behind the accustomed look of a veteran. All around, people and horses were collecting, cinches were being snugged, curb chains adjusted. The Stake Manager was ordering last-minute details, looking for the marshals. Folks were dragging on chaps. Strapping on spurs.

Lewis came up, leading his horse and patting the pockets of his vest.

"Damn," he said, missing something. I held his horse while he went back to the trailer for more chewing tobacco.

Now the judges were exiting the Big House, making their way in a dignified ceremony down the great flight of wooden steps to the ancient brick walk. Worrying on toughened leather gloves as they ambled in unhurried steps to the mounting block, where an attendant waited with their horses—one a bald mouse gelding, the other a chestnut with a blaze. As they received the reins, the Stake Manager begged the attention of the crowd, introducing them formally, one by one, to the trial party. Then he belabored some of the hospitality courtesies for the gallery to store. Announced officially and welcomed all to the trial.

I looked around. Where the hell was Lewis? Halfway back, hoo-rawing with somebody down the way. I handed him the reins as he blustered his way up.

"C'mon, Boy," he said, "we gonna go win this trial." He said it loud enough you could hear it on the next farm, and I was wishing to God he hadn't.

Tommy made his way through, bringing his paint pony. He winked at
Lewis, squeezing my arm.

"You ready, Boy?"

"I hope."

"Lewis here helpin' you?"

"Yep. Thanks."

"Anytime," he said.

Then the judges were moving off, leading their horses and turning
down the sandy dirt lane under the oaks, making their way toward the
breakaway point for the first brace. The driver slapped the team on the rear
with the flat of the reins, and the dog wagon lurched, then rolled and
creaked into a forward rhythm. The dogs whined and barked, roused to
restlessness by the motion. Trickle by trickle, we fell in behind, the lenient,
dirt-muffled clop of two hundred hooves setting the cadence. It was real
again, the rite and the ritual, stiffening the noose another turn around the
stalk of my stomach.

The warming sun had burned the fog to scattered tendrils. Here and
there, as far as you could see across the open understory of the pines, they
rose and curled in fingers of steam. Pale and sleepy rays painted the air the
color of lamplight, lit the path ahead in irregular splotches of shadow and
gold. Above grew a tint of azure, in a fresh and cloudless sky. In frightened
wingbeats by the edge of an adjoining field, a flutter of feeding doves went
up. Silhouetted and splintering, as the fluted whistles of their apprehension
flickered against the morning peace. Slowly, the world was wakening.

The procession ended roadside, by the beginning of the dawning
course. People climbed on horses, knotted around. I retrieved Pat from the
wagon, grabbing her collar as she charged from the box. She was sky-high,
lunging to go. I handed the lead to Lewis. He whoaed her to the line. She
stood trembling. Beside her waited Little Diamond, propped by her own
scout, quivering as well. The tension sang as Dr. Thompson got a foot in the
stirrup and lifted himself to his saddle. Ahead lay a broad expanse of piney
woods over native grasses, scattered about with clusters of low-growing post
oak and bay. In the distance, beyond the dimness under the trees, the light
lifted slightly, to suggest the sprawl of the first of several large agricultural
fields. It was big country, big enough for a dog to roll out and ramble.

We reined the horses up close, ready for the break. I fingered my whistle, and Pat glanced up at me. The look was so incendiary I winced.

"God-a-mighty, don't let us lose her," I whispered under my breath.

And then the judges said something inciting, and the dogs were gone.

Neck and neck they tore through the pines, fast, front, and wide. Pat lay left, Diamond right, and pop-and-snap they poured themselves into a furious quest for quail. Out of sight now, somewhere out there, three hundred yards on.

"On the far front!" Lewis yelled from behind, lifting an arm and pointing out the setter as she zipped left to center across the distant silver-and-green floor under the trees. She was flying. Rolling to the front, she surged ahead, gobbling up the balance of the pines and breaking far and away onto the edge of the field, just as Diamond appeared again behind her, grabbed the opposite side and dug to catch up.

It would never happen. Both were running inspired races, but Pat clearly had the better of it. The little setter checked once along the edge, doubled briefly and decided no, then on she sped, out the remote end of the field and into the next gamble of woods. On and ahead, always ahead.

"Yeeeaappp, yoooah!"

When I called on her, way out there, she was listening and handling—Lewis hadn't been out once—and inside, my heart was pinging like harp strings. Twenty minutes along, she was one-thirds through a great shooting-dog race. I could feel it, lifting, higher and higher. I'd seen her at her best; this was approaching better. Stylish and strong, she was smooth as satin in Manhattan. There was a part of me loose and soaring above the pines, a part of me strung tighter than Montana barbwire. While I prayed for all to stay together. And the seconds drained on.

At thirty-five, she was pointed, dead ahead. Promised boldly, she stood a few yards inside the cover, just beyond a creek gap. It was as close as you get to a guarantee. I piled off and grabbed the shotgun in a single motion; Lewis rushed up and took my horse. Somewhere behind, I could hear Dr. Thompson, bringing Little Diamond on. I started wide, flushed only a couple of seconds, and up blew the birds. In a wad, between me and Pat. We watched them go, fan out barely enough, had we been hunting, to make it seem real.

"Whoom!"

At the shot, Pat, already to her toetips, stiffened the higher. Jack-and-Jehosefat! You could have counted the chill bumps, I was so elated.

Lewis led her a few yards ahead on the course. I swung onto the mare and never touched a stirrup. When I hit the saddle, I hit the whistle, and Pat was off again like tender-off-a-thistle.

At the three-quarter point of the course stretched a tremendous bean-field. Its daunting edges loomed liked a taunt. It would become a defining challenge of the trial. No matter what had happened the forty-five minutes before, the only way for a dog to ascribe to the championship was to take it in a smooth, fell swoop. Fall in one side or the next, and blister it from the very beginning to the absolute end. Pull off at any stage, and you'd never see Denmark.

Not every dog was asked to do it, only those that garnered this of the three courses. Luck of the draw.

Pat was the first dog of the trial to conquer it, and she took the left edge so immediately you'd have thought the ground was scorched. Little Diamond had hung on somewhere close until now, but thus and there, it was settled. I was three feet off the saddle and so was everybody else—everybody else, at least, that didn't have to beat her—in the field trial party. Because it wasn't just that she did it, it was the *way* she did it. Gleefully, like the shimmer of sunshine across dancing water. There would be a handful of dogs before it was over, including Kizzy, that would do it as convincingly, but none more elegantly.

The course tightened again into the woods in the final minutes. Lewis rode side and drag, but there was no need. Every proper interval, Pat showed merrily ahead.

At fifty-five, she stood again. In light cover, under the pines. She looked certain, and it escaped nobody that this could ice the cake. I clambered off the mare, half stumbling in my haste, and pulled the shotgun free.

We'd never been this close before, to a big one, with the reason still together. And I was nervous, prickled with fear as I walked in. Pausing a moment, I read the find and the breeze, trying to size up the flush. I wanted these birds up and away, away out front of my dog, with little chance of blowing back in her face or over her head, and undoing a performance that was approaching perfection. I played out my strategy, anticipating the rise of the birds with every kick in the grass. But nothing.

Pressure growing, I flushed close and wide, nervous now for a different reason. If birds were there, I needed to move them. An unproductive point at this stage, while not defeating, would be tarnishing. Whereas a good, clean find could be decisive. It's the bane of every field trialer. You flush and flush, until suspense and the strain of the clock tell you not to tarry any further, but still no birds. It was obvious now that time would expire here. We needed these birds.

Pat was still standing tall and tight. Lewis, from the sidelines, was anxiously motioning with body language for me to try again under her nose. I did. Nothing. I ran in a big, broad sweep a widening semicircle. Still nothing. Pat had let down slightly. Only one thing left to do.

Walking back to her, I tapped her lightly on the ear.

"Find 'em, Pat."

She stabbed ten yards forward, jammed again to a stop, before breaking quickly off and whipping birdy, widening lashes through the grass. Ten yards again, she snapped tightly together a second time. For a moment she looked certain, and hope soared. But then the tip of her tail ticked slightly, she fussed a yard or two further, pulled off again, and resumed a frantic search.

"Birds in here, Pat. Find 'em."

They'd been here. No question of that. Pat rarely tolerated unproductives. She jammed the covey too hard. When she said, "There," normally they were. But a great sinking feeling was burdening the pit of my gut that they had left her, running a ways and lifting before we got there.

She tried valiantly. Technically, time had expired. She was running on judicial grace, playing out the benefit of the doubt any good arbiter would afford under the circumstances. A lot more than we could realize was riding on this. But a short time more, and the probabilities expired.

"Pick 'er uu-pp."

The bottom dropped out of me. I called the little setter in, got down on my knees, and gathered her into my arms. I had the feeling we could have won it right there. But win, lose, or draw, she'd done a hell of a job.

"Damn, we needed those birds," Lewis said. "They'da been here an' me an' ol' Kizzy 'ud-a had a job to do.

"Have yet," he admitted. "But it wuz nice, Boy, nice. One thing sure, they gonna remember we'uz here."

I took down the canteen, let Pat lap a fill of water, then roaded her to the dog wagon. Now I could suffer again. Different from the anticipatory anxiety, though the symptoms were the same. A biley, burning queasiness wallowing your stomach night and day. It was the relentless question now of whether we'd done enough. Enough to hold off the thirty-seven more dogs that would strut their best another three days to beat us. I thought about that a long minute, riding along, running Pat's race back through my mind.

They had their work cut out for them.

Tommy rode up, clapped a hand around the cap of my shoulder.

"Good job, Boy."

I murmured thanks, not wanting to jinx anything by exclamation.

He ran his Button dog in the sixth. Got a good, searching race carded, with one pretty find. And I could return the compliment.

The first day drained by. Birds were scarce. Several dogs came up empty. A couple of others, as Pat and Button, posted a single find. None, I thought, had a ground race the power of Pat's. But then, I wasn't judging, and you never knew. More and more, I was wishing I could have produced birds on that second find. There was a long ways to go.

Then, riding back to the barn, Tommy closed alongside. We rode back to the barn together, the three of us.

"I was told," Tommy said quietly, "that Billy McCathern told the judges that it ought to take two finds for a dog to be named champion here."

McCathern was the Stake Manager. "That's ridiculous," I asserted, "from the front end, not having any idea how the birds are gonna go."

"I know, but that's what I heard."

"Wonder whut he'da said if he had a dog in the fight?" Lewis mused. Strangely, he didn't.

We laughed and left it there. Just another thorn in your side.

The last brace before lunch the second morning, Ferrell Snell ran a fine pointer male named Freelance Flip. For the first thirty minutes, Flip was as immaculate as a priest in a prayer fest, laying out smooth and forward, and nailing a feeding covey midway with splash and style. Then, for the next fifteen, truth be told, he wouldn't have won fourth place in a country bird hunt. The day had warmed to hot and dry, and he suffered with the load of it, closing and slacking to gun-dog range. Finally, handler and scout managed to steer him to a small watering hole, and rejuvenated, he mustered to

finish the last minutes of the hour at a tolerable pace and range. And to add, ironically, a second clean find.

"This is gonna get interesting," Tommy predicted.

In the swelter of the same day, Beda and I cast our lot. Against great difficulty, I feared. The sun stood at a pitiless apex, and across the sandy fields, dust devils sprang to race drunkenly about before burying themselves again, as abrupt as they began. The birds would be loafing in the heads and bays, and we had drawn the driest course. I carried an extra water jug and asked Lewis to do the same. The only way you could really cool a dog in such a bake, with the ground parched and little natural water at hand, was to soak it thoroughly to the skin. Several times during the hour. Then, if it drank as frequently and had a better than average tolerance, it could hold the fiendish pace necessary to win a field trial.

Any time you went south you could expect the heat. A midday draw confounded the burden. Given the possibility, Loretta and I had clipped Beda, shearing away the bulk of her coat and feathering, and the dense, silky hair that had clung to her chest and belly. It would help a little. She could never bear it as Pat and Thane, and would run at a deficit. I worried for her. Because she'd not quit—she'd proven that—until it was too late. It was for me to tend.

We drenched her methodically to start, and she went regally for a third of the hour. As pretty as you could wish. But midway, though we had wet and watered her twice, she had shortened and was beginning to labor. She was forcing herself against the growing oxygen depletion of the casts, and had been unable to turn a bird, so I stopped her at thirty-five. Her lungs were heaving and her breath was raspy, so we took no further chance and called it done. Rather, I did, for she fought me, wanting still to go. She looked at me with pleading eyes, asking why.

"Sorry, girl, another day, another draw."

One by one the next two days spun by, and the dogs, but birds remained at a premium. Lewis ran old Rod in the thirteenth, and he did a yeoman job, taking the big field edge in stride. But he came up as dry as the majority on game. So down it came to the last two braces and two great dogs: Kizzy and Jadie Rayfield's State Line Sam. I knew we had to be up there close. Suspense congealed like the skin on a pudding.

Lewis put Kizzy down midway of the final morning, and I helped them every way I could. Ever a threat, she ran beautifully, with gamble and grace. So damn smooth.

"*Yeeeaaaahh!*" Lewis squalled, every dramatic juncture. Pulled the stops, let her roll. He knew the skids were scotched, what they had to do. Kizzy lived to her name. As luck would have it, she ran the same course as Pat, the only other dog to take the vast field edge as charismatically. I only scouted her once, at thirty. She popped ahead on her own, and by forty-five, she had banked a ground heat that marshaled with the best. Everybody with an interest was toed tall in the stirrups.

Tommy cantered up about the fifty-minute mark, flushed and excited. Said, "If that dog points a bird, she'll win this trial."

That really prickled the predicament. I knew he figured his Button dog was up tight, too. Trying to be as honest as I could, as good as Kizzy was going, I still thought Pat's race had more power. But it had been a long beat since the first brace. I hoped they remembered.

Ten, nine . . . seven . . . six. The minutes dwindled to desperation, and Lewis tried every way from Sunday to steer Kizzy to a find. She was hunting her heart in the ground, bouncing off head and hollow, but coming up dry. It would go to the wire. Lewis slapped his horse, wheeled right, and hit the whistle. In the distance, Kizzy caught the cue, laid to starboard, and streaked across the front with the snap of a jib sail, along the hillside where Pat had suffered the unproductive of her second stand. Suddenly she went birdy, and for a cataclysmic moment, it looked like the fat lady would sing. But the drum roll died and the clock bottomed out. It was over.

It fell at last to Sam, running as a bye, odd dog in the field. He was a big, powerful pointer and a proven bird finder. Jadie Rayfield was a cunning handler. They tried. Tried heroically, but it was not to be.

The dust settled to an enigma. The judges had only one dog with two finds, and he had a hole in his race you could have stuck a tank in. Otherwise, it appeared, they had three dogs of championship caliber and birdwork, a single good find apiece. Pat was among them. Clearly the best, I felt secretly. I was not alone. But what would they do?

There was speculation of a callback. Others argued, no, they'd go with Freelance Flip, with the two finds, and pick a Runner-Up from the remaining field of three.

Whatever, the suspense would last the night, because the decision was retired for the evening. It was a long and sleepless night. By morning, Lewis had learned that at least one of the other two handlers had gone to the judges, hoping to impinge the case.

"You got to be up close," Lewis said. "If'n it'uz me, I'd go too. Put a word in."

"I've never been to a set of judges in my field-trialing life," I told him. "Not before the decision."

"Might be time," he said.

I didn't want to. A matter of honor, I suppose. You went out and did your best, and you let it stand for itself. But I didn't want to disadvantage my dog, either. Maybe I needed to declare for her, now as never before. It had been a long time since the first brace. It was early, an hour before breakfast. About the plantation, existence was just beginning to burgeon. It was now. Now or never.

I swallowed hard and did it, for Pat.

I stopped on the back porch, listening for a moment, mustering the will. Aside the muted rattle and bustle from the kitchen, the old manor was empty and quiet. Pushing open the double pine doors, I stepped through the massive door frame into what was once the old gaming room, and moved softly across and into the hallway. I picked my way to the guest quarters, the swish of my pants and the uneasy creak of the floorboards betraying my presence, exacerbating the gnawing queasiness at the pit of my stomach. Pausing again at the threshold, I could hear a murmur of voices inside. I thought maybe to just turn and go, let things be. But my conscience would not allow it. Respectfully, I rapped on the door.

Bill Poe answered, cracking the door, a safety razor in his off hand. Rosy pink and bare-chested over boxer shorts, he was fresh out of the shower and obviously in the midst of shaving. The left side of his face still wore a rime of shaving cream. Behind him, through the breach of the door, I could see Ray Jeffers stirring, equally unclad and indecorous. Outside the context, it would be impossible to understand how two men in such an unceremonious state of propriety could sustain such a presence of authority. Yet I was the one self-conscious.

"Can I beg a word?" I asked.

Bill searched my face a moment, then widened the door. We knew each other casually, of course, but there is the dictum of distance between even the closest of friends, when the one is judging and the other is not.

"Come on in," he said. The concession was polite, but reserved. Across the room, Ray nodded acknowledgment.

I felt like mice leavings on a Christmas pudding. Quickly, I moved to say what I had come for.

"I'm here for my dog," I said. "I know maybe others have been. I could do no less.

"It's been a long time since the first brace; I just ask that you remember."

"Your dog did a nice job," Ray said. "So did a few others. There was the thing of the shot," he added inadvertently.

This is how such things go. You sometimes learn what you hadn't imagined.

"The shot?" I asked.

"You delayed the shot slightly, at flush, on her find," Bill Poe explained, as they dressed.

I said what came first to mind. "Unconsciously. Just let the birds fan out. To make it real. You could have killed a bird."

"Yes," Ray admitted, ". . . you could."

I knew then that it was no real point of contention.

"She was good," I said, "real good, I thought, birds and ground."

"We liked her," they replied.

"Thank you for listening," I said.

They nodded, and I left then. What they would do, I had no idea.

At eight-thirty, the remainder of the field trial party had assembled, just off the back steps of the manor. The officials and marshals of the trial, those of us who supposed he still had a dog in the fight. The timbre was serious. Anticipation of a different kind. Unlike the beginning. Now there were cards on the table and money in the pot.

"We want to see three dogs again," the judges announced. "Dry Creek Button, State Line Sam, and Zip Zap."

I felt my heart leap, behind it the burn of anxiety anew.

"We want it clear," the judiciary continued, "this is for Runner-Up. The title is decided." With that, they turned away.

Tommy was beside me. Not exactly happy. "What did I tell you?" he said.

The gospel, I imagined. For it was reasonably sure now Freelance Flip would be named Champion. On the strength of two finds, certainly not the power of his ground. It wouldn't sit right then. It never will. Nothing personal to dog or man, just the requisite for any trial, and especially a championship: A field trial is both birds and ground, and normally you win it on the latter. A championship-caliber ground heat belongs to be full out, wide and fast. In an hour stake—the normal—not for fifty-nine, not for fifty-eight, but for sixty scratch-and-haul minutes, no exceptions. Do less, and you sanction mediocrity.

But you have to swallow disappointment quickly at a field trial. There was no time to mull and pray. For all remaining purposes, there was a new trial at hand, in a matter of minutes. Whatever we had successfully laid down before was spent. Now it was to go out and do all over again.

One final thing the judges said to us, once the order of running had been established and all had assembled for the initial breakaway: "We wanna see a good, smooth shooting-dog race."

Yep, most times, you win them on the ground.

One by one, the other two dogs ran. Both were formidable. One maybe a hair rough, now that we were down to the hairsplitting, the other maybe a bit handy. Pat was last to run, sent off at high noon. The sun was a brassy furnace in a naked sky, and it was hot as blue-flame hades. She broke fancy and fast, caught the far front, and hung there. Like an ivory amulet, dancing prettily on a string. Canvassing every objective, getting stronger as she went, to hell with the heat. Above the burning sand, you could follow the rent of her travel, rarely by open sight, but by a trail of dust and the snap of her tail. She had a brief absence, only once, and I asked Lewis to lope out and check. Just for insurance. Presently she popped out again dead front, and resumed there. As thrifty as it was thrilling, her ground measure was about as perfect as a shooting-dog race gets, and I knew we were doing what we had to do. Handling like grace follows goodness, she was checking for me, swinging as she needed, but I was still scared to death we might lose her. So many times in the big ones, just below the cap of the mountain, the footing had slipped.

Relief was like the freshened breeze that harbors a summer storm when, finally, after thirty minutes that seemed an hour, they ordered her up. I called her in, against her will, for she was single-minded with desire. Got down off the horse and thanked her for it all—the incomparable ascent of exhilaration, the flight of spirit that ever special day that cavorted somewhere up there in the blue above the wispy green heights of the highest pines. So few times in this old world you are gifted perfection, and most surely this had been one of them.

But then, you never knew. About a field trial.

Immediately I was wishing she might have put a find with such a race, and afterwards Lewis told me he found her standing the one time she was gone. But iffy, flagging slightly, and a little lower than normal. He read it that the birds had trickled off, and brought her quickly on. A wise call, for this really was about ground pattern, and we didn't need the tarry of another fruitless relocation attempt, as in the first series. Though it gladdened my heart that she had dug up birds at the blaze of noon, when so many others hadn't.

Whatever was to happen, it was over now. We had done all we could do.

When all had gathered at the foot of the steps, beneath the colonnade of the old manor house, the Stake Manager moved to fore. In his hand was the slip of paper that settled our fate. I was terribly proud of my dog, knew she was to be reckoned with. Though I dared not even hope, almost, for fear of some last-minute, ambiguous offense to the gods.

Before the announcement, there were compliments and gratuities to attend. Honors were presented to the judges, each called forth now from the customary and respectable distance to which they had retired, to receive farewell recognition and tokens of esteem. Marshals and officials were applauded; accolades accorded to the plantation staff, the stable boys, the grizzled old pilot of the dog wagon. An especially sound round of appreciation rose for the kitchen help, with recorded note of the scratch biscuits, mayhaw jelly, and blackstrap molasses that had graced the breakfast table each dawning. The hiatus from due course served properly to heighten the suspense, and in addition to my now clammy hands was the flush and sweat on my brow. Still I wanted to hope, but didn't, and I'm sure Tommy and Jadie were suffering on the same cross.

There was a pervasive moment further, while the Master of Ceremonies swiveled this way and that to shake a final few hands, before turning again seriously to the front. The conclusion was at hand. I could feel my stomach tightening; I wanted to hear it and I didn't.

Freelance Flip was named Champion. Not unexpected, but it still felt like somebody socked you in the gut.

Tension remained tautest for the unsupposed. For there were two jewels in the crest and three good dogs left in the fighting.

"And this year's Runner-Up, Region 3 Championship . . . *Zip Zap."*

I guess at that time in my life, it felt a lot like I hope it may again some day near its end, something like the Grace and the Glory smiling down in a dazzling aura of gold, with trumpets resounding, and the towering gates of Paradise swinging ceremoniously open to award an entrance you imagined you might never manage.

But there was the big, hammy hand of Tommy Mock, another right beside it from Lewis, and yet another from Jadie, dog men I respected immensely, and there was being handed to me as well a sterling silver platter, all to say it was true.

Would it have been the crown, and others than myself thought it should've . . . Regardless, our Number Six pup had a title.

Right that moment I wanted nothing more than to see her. I hurried to the trailer to get her. She bounced out like she was expected, and we posed for pictures, she and I, beside Ferrell and Flip, and Lewis propped the silver platter alongside, and I'm sitting here now looking at the image, twenty-some years to memory. And ever, it's gripping to relish.

I got on the phone shortly after the ceremony, rang Loretta.

"Throw the sheet off the throne," I said. "We can finally seat the Queen."

We celebrated the next week, the three of us, went to the best steak house in old Raleigh. Retta and I popped a bottle of California Korbel. Even Mely was slipped a sniff, exclaiming gleefully as she hoisted her glass, "Here's to Patty." We took a second bottle home, to the kennel. When the cork went off, a dozen dogs froze to honor the shot. As for the bubbly, the Mistress of Honor, and plainly her court, preferred Kool-Aid.

⟿ CHAPTER 26 ⟿

THE TIMES WE HAD FOR THE NEXT THREE YEARS. THE DOGS AT THE peak of their powers, no force too strong to challenge. We picked our trials—mostly the big ones, the title stakes, or stakes with a blue-ribbon draw, the best dogs on the circuit. Or the wild-bird trials down south, one-hour classics over storied old plantation grounds. Those we relished most. Pat came into season soon after her Region 3 win, opening the door for Beda. She made the best of it, our warring maiden, with gorgeously consistent shooting-dog races and burn-the-timbers-down style on game. She won impressively at Tidewater, aced the field at Rappahannock. Pat got back in time to prevail at Blackstone. Together, they were often winning one-two.

Almost as much as the trials now, we enjoyed the workouts. Enjoyed each other. Gone the days of hack and harrow. The dogs knew perfectly what they were to do, and most times did it, breaking over only rarely to a rebellion of enthusiasm. When they did, the indiscretions were split between contemplated mischief, a stop-to-flush that turned into a hop, skip, and *"ahht-oh,"* when they thought I wasn't looking, or simply a *"Whoops, I forgot,"* when they gambled a step and a whups at shot. Either way, it was humorous. It no longer upended me. For I had them as broke as I wanted them. And discipline needed only be a reminder, nothing more than a word and a lifted finger, or at the worst a pretense of exasperation, one half-hearted shake, and a ride on my shoulder back to the place of disgrace. Maybe I'd make them whoa there several minutes to contemplate the sin, which they detested, before extending amnesty. They'd stand sheepishly for a moment, pretend they were repentant—especially Beda—then a little happy tick would erupt at the end of the tail, like they couldn't contain it, gathering eagerness until the whole of the appendage was cheerfully flagging. A twinkle would grow in their eyes, and the message was "That's about as sorry as I'm gonna git, so tap me the hell on the ear and we'll see about redemption."

Occasionally I would run them together, as before I couldn't dare, to enjoy the brace of them. I held them pretty religiously to a field trial pace, but more and more we'd make it a plantation horseback hunt, for they knew the difference and would always fire explosively for a trial. I started shooting more wild birds over them then. At Corinth, or Oak Hill, or we'd load up and trailer east a few hours to some of the sprawling beanfields of the coastal plain. I'd take Thane sometimes, and we'd make it a threesome. We'd declared a truce in the battle for schooling manners, he and I, at least on the issue of statuary rigidity on shot. And he was a handsome and pow- erful dog, that could still carry a fancy lick. All were about equal on bird finding, but it took some pretty big grounds. I'd prop them up for the break, style them at "Whoa," side by side. Let them stand thirty seconds, just enjoying the electricity of it, while they trembled and stacked like powder over a primer. Then I'd hit them hard with the whistle. They'd hook up, the three of them, not wanting to be outdone, carry plumb out of the country. I'd let them roll, squall about the time they hit the horizon, and God it was pretty, seeing them part abruptly like the prongs on a hay fork, peel off and bend around. To catch separate edges and discrete hunting missions. And always it was Number Six that was fastest and furthermost.

A beautiful thing, three dogs of that caliber, challenging each other to the birds. Moreover, the stand of them, three in tandem, sky-high on game. I had wanted it all my life, the combination of horse, pointing dogs, and gun. When I was a boy, in the late forties, we had a small farm, which strung together with a cluster of others, contributed to a swatch of rolling pied- mont about the tune of ten square miles before you hit the next town. Old- timey patchwork farming, broken only by dirt paths and an occasional graveled road. A few tractors, but still a lot of mules. Folks prized them yet as teams. Milt Thornburg, who lived in the last small clapboard house before our turn, had a couple. Milt was a fine, old man like most of the times, who wore sleeves and garters year-round, under a pair of threadbare but clean country overalls, and kept an unruly thatch of silver hair that poked out over his ears and collar beneath the straw hat on his head. He had a benign tumor on his forehead about the size of a guinea egg, and I tried to remember my manners and not look too hard at it. His wife, Mattie, you'd see usually by his side, in the fields, and I especially recall that in the fall, you'd see her in her bonnet, toiling with a wooden paddle over a great, steaming black cauldron above a crackling fire, coaxing soap from a mix of hog fat and lye.

Milt'd always throw up his hand as we went by, and sometimes we'd stop and pass the time of day. He'd whoa the team and half-hitch the reins over the hafts of the turning plow or hay rake or whatever, pull off his hat, and wipe his brow with a dirty bandanna. Daddy asked him about the mules one time, and he said their names were Ruth and Rhody, and they's old and stone-deaf as a hitching post.

"So deef," he said, "ain't one of 'em heard the other'n fart in twenty years."

There were folks like Milt and Mattie on every farm, and they'd put in a garden plot every year, a few peas and beans, a corn patch, and a small stand of wheat or millet, or barley and rye. What wasn't planted—the edges and fence corners, and ground that was being rested—would grow up in ragweed and briers. Come the harvest moon, they'd gather what they could, leave the rest to frost. Let it go fallow, until spring, when they started over again. Twixt time would come bobwhite in bountiful coveys, assembling to the clarion call of the cocks at dawn, in the fence corners or along the edges at the gather of the woods, slipping back and forth to glean what they'd left. They made birds then just like they made beans, were as hospitable to them as to the rest of their neighbors, and across the sprawl and throw of all the little farms together prospered many a bevy.

About five miles east, as the crow flies, somewhat differently in a manor on a hill, lived Mr. Johnathon Hurley Wrape. J. H., as he was known far and wide. Behind the big house among the white oaks was an even bigger barn, whitewashed as pristinely, and beside the barn a tack room, within which was arrested wondrously the breath of saddle soap and oiled latigo. Along one wall, a dozen plantation saddles were racked in ranks of four. While within the barn were as many stalls, scented by freshly mown orchard grass, to stable the horses that wore them. Blue bloods from Shelbyville that could carry a four-beat lick as gracefully as Astaire waltzed Rogers. Just west, between the barn and sprawling green pastures, were the kennels. A fenced five acres and three dozen barrels to house the big hounds, the Walkers and

Triggs, two dozen runs under a rambling shed roof for the bawling bunch of twelve-inch beagles that could give a bunny merry mischief. And most illustriously, beyond the boxwooded walkway and lifesize brace of pointing dogs pledged forever in bronze, the imposing bungalow with the copper roof and cupola on top that cottaged the quail dogs. Lean and rib-sprung pointers from great latter-day champions like Luminary, John Proctor, Ariel, and Medallion, conditioned whipcord tough and bred to run. Finely honed and feathered setters, who could travel as well, descended from the Ghost, Sport's Peerless Pride, Mississippi Zev.

From his back door, the old man had but to put a foot to the stirrup, whistle away a stout foursome of bird dogs, enjoy the bountiful venue of the little farms. Any one of which welcomed his passing, for he was kind, generous, and well-liked among the folk who lived there, delivering especially upon the eve of Christmas and the New Year gifts from his saddlebags. Or sending around a wagon of warm wishes from his cupboard.

He was about the last of his kind in our part of the country, where once there had been many, and I'd see him ride by, lift a hand. Four fleet dogs testing the fields ahead of the horse. Once, in the distance, I actually saw them stop, near a gallberry head, dead tight in the distance. First one, then another behind him, drawing up until they were stacked against the tawny autumn landscape like the ones I'd seen on the Remington calendar on the wall of the Harvest Milling Company in town. Saw the old man get down, pull his gun, walk up, and take the birds—*whump . . . whump.* And one of the dogs when he released them, running out to punch the grass with his nose, gather up a bird, and recover it to the old man.

How I had envied him, and dreamed endlessly of doing the same, and now finally I was. Maybe I didn't have the mansion yet on the hill, but I had the horse, a good Parker gun in the scabbard, and three spanking-fine dogs. There they were, way out front—pretty as Paradise—and I no longer had to imagine. In ten more years, the country would close down, and my little window in time would fall shut just as his had, and I would have to motor to Georgia or Texas to find what semblance was left. But right then, I had managed the time warp.

How I loved sending them flying along long, diverting edges, Beda right, Thane left, Pat hard out to the fringes. Fast and forward. One folding into the cover, then the next, popping out in turn far afront. Driving on.

There would come sometimes an eclipse of perfection, when the thrill of them would pump my heart so tight it might burst, and I'd shoot an arm skyward and whoop for sheer joy. And when I thought it could get no better, then would come the happy moment I was absent all three, and an anxious reconnaissance found them promised stiffly to birds. Divided equally and proudly over the find, or the one that had stacked first against the birds honored in tandem by the trailing two. I'd slide a leg over and drop to the grass, let go the reins, and jerk the gun from the scabbard. Because Dolly had learned now to ground tie, and I no longer had to worry about her selling off to Bill Crews's gelding.

The dogs would be trembling and taut as tickled harp strings, and I'd slip a couple of shells in the gun, bring it to port. Embrace the privilege of stepping in front of them, and ask the birds away. Out they'd blow, hither and yon, and sometimes when I was as good as my dogs, a neat double would tumble to earth neath a wind-drift of feathers. While behind me, true blue, three setters—well, two anyway, *"Whoa Thing!"*—stood rock solid as Gibraltar, marking them down. And I'd think wonderfully to myself, it had all started that May morning in the little, white whelping shack in the backyard on Chaney Road.

❧ CHAPTER 27 ❧

I WAS GETTING MORE JUDGING INVITATIONS NOW, OPEN AND AMATEUR championships. I took time off to arbitrate a few—the Eastern Open at South Hill, the Region 16 at Albany—but I was hard-pressed to leave my own dogs. We were making good trials regularly together, and enjoying it. Though more and more it was us alone, and less frequently in the company of my wife and daughter. I missed that. Mely was growing up, coming thirteen, and she and Mama were beginning to enjoy going and doing together. Girl things. There was a new Schwinn ten-speed to ride, and new clothes to buy, slumber-overs, and boys—almost—to notice. Addled essence. She'd still go to the closer stakes now and then, to see Patty run, but she was beginning to find wings of her own. I was losing my little girl. The thought of that, selfishly, was less happy than sad.

So we'd travel alone, me, Dolly, and the dogs, about the Carolinas and Virginias, to Florida and Kentucky, Georgia and Delaware, Maryland, Mississippi, Missouri, and Tennessee, and a lot of places between. Loretta always before had the job of keeping me alert, and many was the midnight, coming home, I'd be so tired the road would blur. So drowsy I'd jerk awake, slap a two-handed death grip on the wheel, and wrench the front wheels from the ditch. Sit there for several seconds with the numbing realization I had fallen asleep, warning myself to consciousness with the hot and prickly, stomach-churning admonition of near disaster. Having no recollection whatsoever of the road for the last ever how long, or how I managed to stay on it. Just thankful that Someone had been with me at the wheel. We should have stopped, of course, but once a trial was over, there was the ever-pressing desire to turn for home. So, had we won, we could anticipate and ready for the next; had we lost, we could answer the order of reassuring ourselves back to peak, rebuilding upon several repetitions of perfection.

We won some good trials in those middle years, handsomely, and lost a major few others as monumentally.

Of the losses, at once the most thrilling and disturbing was the Region 3 All-Age Championship the year after Belmont. Disturbing because it was I who blundered, and likely it cost Pat another title. Which was devastating, for, all considered, it was perhaps the gutsiest and most charismatic performance of her life. The venue was Hoffman, in the Carolina Sandhills, and a legion of winning all-age dogs from several states toed the match. All pointers. Pat was the only setter in the stake, and by the luck of the draw, it was the only time ever she was braced head-to-head with Kizzy.

I didn't run Pat in many all-age stakes, and this was the only championship. She easily had the power and drive to do it, had won the qualifiers, but by and large I preferred class shooting-dog stakes on big grounds. Frankly I didn't, then or now, see much difference. Except for the atmosphere and the odds. There were few setters running the all-age circuit then, had not been since the golden-age Llewellins: Gladstone, Sioux, Geneva and La Besita, Eugene's Ghost. Mississippi Zev, Flaming Star, Tishomingo, Mr. Thor, and Johnny Crockett had made them sit up and take notice in the middle third of the century, but since 1970, the longhairs that could hold the mark in the lean-breed trials had run into short supply. John O'Neall, Jr., had an inspiring vision for a landmark program of annual setter awards, to revive interest and challenge among breeders. But it toddled in its infancy. So it was for a setter to prove at the cusp of the eighties, double over, the mettle of a placement in a major all-age stake.

You had to screw your skin down tight just to enter one. Shrug off a few jeers. First person we ran into when we pulled onto the grounds the afternoon before the trial was Parke Brinkley. I was shuttling Pat the few steps from the trailer to one of the kennels. She sauntered down the run, a single setter—and a small one at that—before that fortress of pointers. Like MLK crashing a Klan rally. Didn't bother Number Six a whack.

Parke walked over. We shook hands. He looked at Pat.

"Didn't know you *had* an all-age dog," he said. The remark was thinly slathered with derision, like mustard over apple butter. But then, that was Parke. Often he sold himself for more than his worth.

"Just one," I said, and turned away.

To borrow an old Thoroughbred racing adage, Pat came to that trial "on the muscle." I had been pushing her to a fast ninety minutes in workouts, and she was spending through them with money to spare. In the between times, she was roaded, dragging Thane, Beda, and twenty pounds of logging chain for another hour. Lean and hard in her prime, bottom deep as a well, she was ready to stroll.

It was bone dry, wind-dead, and boiling hot as Lewis and I led Pat and Kizzy to the line, shortly after lunch on the first and sultriest day of the running. The sun glowered down from its zenith through a metallic sky, the air temperature was emblazoned into the upper eighties, and God knows what it was on the ground. Heat monkeys cavorted fiendishly above the sweltering sand, and the thirsty brown leaves slumped on the blackjacks like they were begging last rites. Lewis and I had soaked the dogs in a clubhouse water trough, but the advantage was evaporating almost as quickly as it began.

I'll say it outright. I'm scared of that kind of heat. Get a dog too hot, and rarely does he fully recover again. Pat was strong in the heat, but it can get the best of them. It's possible for a really powerful dog to kill himself before you can slow him down long enough and drench him well enough for his system to recover. I had seen Beda on the edge, other dogs since, did not want to again. Especially my own. I was thinking of all that in the very last moments before we hit the whistle.

But we were here to run, and run we would.

They were away like the gale before a storm. The vista was ambitious, and you could see them roll together before the spurting dust of their stride, side by side for the first two hundred yards. Then, as paper before a blade, they peeled port and starboard on slicing diagonals to the edges, and the power of the little setter started to tell. Kizzy was running big and well, but it was Pat that carried the mail, driving away, opening the margin, reaching to the extremes. Running and hunting. It would be the biggest, most electrifying breakaway of the trial. Under judgment, all-out, all-age, and all-forward, for the first full twelve minutes of the heat. Not just my estimation; a dozen people, opposing handlers, would tell me the same. It was bordering the incredible, and of all the remarkable times she ever ran, I could not remember another more thrilling. So many moments over those years she lifted me sky-high, and every time I'd think I'd seen the pinnacle, the Alps and the Matterhorn, along she would come with another higher. So I shall always remember that special day. That day we scaled Everest.

She came in hot at fourteen—dangerously so. I got down quickly, watered her, doused her fully. Across the way, I could see Lewis down, doing the same for Kizzy. Pat shook nose to tail, and asked away. I sent her. Driving on, she made the first water hole. She was in and out, swimming across, drinking as she went. Touching the opposite bank, she was kicking sand.

It was hot. Sweat was streaming off my brow, burning my eyes and blurring my sight. The mare was white with lather, and we hadn't even broken a fast walk. I dug out a bandanna and mopped down, tied it around my forehead under the brim of my hat. Pat was picking up again, reaching widely forward and searching. Thirty minutes by. Kizzy was punching valiantly as ever, but shortening some. I could see the little setter, well ahead, in a distant corner of the pines, cutting fast across the front into the tawny lane of the open course, and folding on. The gallery was taking notice. She was holding the extreme pace, in that killing heat, and how she was doing it I didn't know, but it was three parts courage. Sheer grit. She was all-age gone enough and showing enough, and there wasn't a scout off hiding her out and resting her in the bushes. When she shot across the front, it was because she had traveled there, and travel she did.

Then, at thirty-five, she was gone. For ten minutes, while I held and scoured the front— *"Yeeahooow, Pa-a-at!"*—and my scout was out combing the perimeter. But neither of us found her.

Until from the rear, someone called, "Dog's right front!" and I saw her coming in from the side, the one time during the race.

I gathered her up, looked to see if she was wet, thinking she had left to find water. But she was not, and I think to this day she was on birds and we missed her somehow. Ten minutes' absence is nothing to worry about in an all-age stake, providing you return out front. The one trip in from the side front wouldn't hurt much. For all she'd done, we were still hard at the door. Problem was, we now trailed slightly the other judge, Kizzy, and the forward party. Quickly, there was a decision to be made.

Climbing down, I watered my dog again, forcing to a climax the thoughts racing through my head. She was whining now, wanting away. Under merciful conditions, the answer would have been instantly crystal.

Heel her tightly against the horse, and haul ass for the front. If there is one cardinal rule in field trialing, it's that—you get back to the front, just as god-damn quick as you can. But it was hot as the boilers of hades, and though Pat was showing minimal effects of the heat, it was taking a toll. How close we were to the edge, I didn't know. Whatever, I was still scared for my dog.

In conscience, I could hear Loretta: "No trial's worth the death of a dog."

I knew we had something going. I knew I had one fine, gutsy little dog, that belonged to have her way with glory. But I could not unduly risk her life, and wouldn't. Rather than endangering her and the mare with a risky and taxing scratch for the front, we'd hunt our way there. Wasting no more time, I clambered aboard, and hit the whistle. Pat tore away, on a line drive for the fore. I knew she would. She knew the game as well as I. With the pace she was going and the ground she was covering, it wouldn't take long to whip the difference.

Laid well out front and flying, she was eating up the distance at the pace of the stake. I could hear Lewis's handling song now, off and on, on the air.

When, *slap-bang,* suddenly there she stood, hard on the fringes, jacked high on birds. I kicked the mare into gear, raced there, judge and my half of the trial party close behind. She was simply perfect—letter perfect— head thrown up and winding a fragile breeze, tail stabbing noon, birds smartly front where she said they'd be. I sorted through the golden sedge, the covey sputtered up russet under the sun, and *whoom!* Swelling to mark the flight, she capped the moment like an exclamation point.

I walked back to where she stood, and she loosened a mite and began flagging happily. I kneeled down and gave her a quick congratulatory caress. "Good girl, Pat," I told her. "You just put the plum in the pudding."

There was a murmur through the little crowd. The tension on the stag-nant air was breathless. Folks were shaking their heads in amazement. In the blistering heat, not only did Pat have a rousing ground challenge going, but in a stake that would wax dolefully shy of bird work, she'd just notched what would prove to be the most persuasive find of the trial.

As complimentary as it was, it had cost us time to the front. Ten min-utes to go, and we were now further than before. I wanted to water her, but there simply wasn't time. Where earlier there might have been a minute or two to spare, now it was imperative. We had to truck hard to the front and finish going away! I thought again of heeling her there, decided no again. I'd send her hard there on her own.

I tapped Pat on the ear, releasing her, but asked her to wait. She was electric now, dancing on hind feet, whining with desire. I grabbed rein and mane, forfeited the stirrup, and swung into the saddle. When my butt hit leather, my mouth hit the whistle. Gone, the little setter. Gone fast away.

"*Yowwwagh!*" I squalled at her, just as loud as I could. I did it only occasionally on breakaways, when we really wanted to sell the goods. She'd give me every ounce.

She was already humping it, but you could see her bunch, like a coiled spring, and give it five times more.

"Reach deep, girl," I said under my breath. "Reach deep."

Courage and class. The hallmark of a great field trial dog, and shunning the sweltering heat, she gave it to us all. Fast, forward, and driving, in five minutes we had gained the front. At time, she was well to the fore, going on. I had to hit a gallop to rein her in.

People couldn't believe it. "I'da never thought a setter could do that," one said. "In pointer weather, at that."

"Damn fine race," said another. "Setter or whatever."

Others said nothing, just rode by with stolid stares, and I figured easily what that meant.

We had scared them, the all-age regulars there, and I knew it. But when all were done late the following afternoon, and the decision was rendered, Pat was not among the winners. I was pretty unhappy over that, 'cause I thought fairly she should have been. I had watched it all and believed she had won outright.

Keith Severin was reporting the trial, and rarely would I do it, but I knew Keith pretty well. I told him straight out and in no uncertain terms after the decision I thought Pat should have been in it. It took him back a mite; he'd never heard me talk so stiffly before. But, truth be told, I was mad. Red-horse mad, like Tommy had been over old Nick at that soppy Region 4 in Kentucky. It was only the second time I ever got really mad at a field trial. The other was when Ralph Ellison and somebody I can't remember were judging at Amelia, and called Beda under a bird, chasing.

Asked me to pick her up. I was looking straight at her. No way she had chased a bird. Until Billy Blankenship, the only one I'd believe, convinced me it had happened, on the off side of the hedgerow where I couldn't see.

Keith sputtered a little, but he's a good man, and he said, "She did a fine job, no doubt of that, but maybe just not quite all-age."

Yeah, and I wasn't quite Jesus Christ.

"She ran plenty big enough," I said. "I just forgot to clip her close enough, right down to the flag off her tail."

Poor Keith, left scarcely else to say, had to bear the brunt of the moment. I was unfair to him. He'd seen neither her find nor the last third of her race. He'd been on the front with Lewis and Kizzy.

Bill Kuser was one of the judges, had watched Pat all of the way. I was stowing my tack into the trailer, getting ready to leave, when he walked by headed to his truck. I couldn't help but ask.

"What didn't you like about my dog?"

Billy never minced any words, and that was fine, because I didn't mean to either.

"Mainly that the other fellow didn't like the fact that she was hunting behind," he said. And I gathered then he had made the argument for Pat.

"You were there," I returned. "You know the story. We'da been up in grace, but then we had that find. After that, she caught 'em and left change. At time, she was out front, going away."

Bill's eyes tightened, and his voice throttled down. "Yeah, but let me tell you something. When a dog gets behind in a field trial . . . has a find . . . whatever . . . any trial—and especially an all-age trial—you get that dog back to the front . . . now!"

It wasn't like he was telling me something I didn't know. But the minute he said, *"especially in an all-age trial,"* I knew I'd messed up. I had left them too much leverage and cost a valiant dog—my own—the honor she deserved. After the short absence at thirty, I should have heeled her directly and all-haste to the front. Would it have stressed her unduly in the killing heat, reduced her reserve to the expense of a sag point? Knowing Pat, probably not. Would she have laid out as strongly in the final minutes or finished as conclusively? Probably. Yet her safety had been my first concern.

Would she have had the find? No. Could we possibly have won without it? No. For each of the two dogs placed, though not nearly so grandly, could boast a single find. Catch-22.

Trials go that way sometimes. You choke a little on the aftertaste, suffer the "if only," and truck on down the road. Learn a little something as you go. In spite of what you may have lost, you get to keep the thing most important—an extraordinary performance by an extraordinary dog.

～ CHAPTER 28 ～

I CELEBRATED A FORTIETH BIRTHDAY LATER THAT YEAR. THE BEST present of all was our first workout of the new season, an unpressured sally with the dogs at Elm Hill. That and the gift of the Canadian front, which had ridden southward behind the sagging jet stream the night before, laundering the air clear and cool. The morning was beautifully blue and sunny, the northwest breeze brisk and fresh. At the tops of the trees, the silver-bellied leaves fluttered keenly against the late-summer sky, and as far as you could see, the fields were riotous with yellow sunflowers and butterflies and goldenrod. A good time to be alive, and we savored it. The dogs went particularly well, considering a first outing. All three went a pretty thirty-seven minutes, Thane to the side a bit, but Pat and Beda fast, strong, and true. To cap the cake, each had a single good find. A hair fussy on the scent, they might have been, in the pungent green grass. A frost would fix that.

The only mischief to mar the mix was a ruckus with a polecat. Weigh in Number Six. Woe to the odorous varmint that dared her path, for given the convenience, she would hunt it out, shake it until the bones flapped. One had, about the end of the first long cast, and she had pulled up, gone fragrant . . . roaded several yards . . . and pointed it convincingly as feathers. I had spurred the mare and set sail, racing to her, anticipating a bang-up covey find. There in the first three minutes. About the instant I arrived, she hauled loose and jumped in.

"Pat! Heyyee!" I bellowed at her, about as successfully as I could order a gum stump.

I rolled off, cursing, charging in to yank her up and restore command. Rounding a corner of briers, I suffered the first stiff volley. It was so thick and fetid the leaves sagged, and I stumbled two steps to a halt, jammed it into reverse, and backpedaled wildly for working distance. The little dog was down on the ground, wallowing and snorting, mustering reserves, and the skunk was cocked on two legs with the muzzle leveled.

I roared again, with the same effect. To hell with it, and retreating another fifteen feet, I let them have it out. Three more assaults and retaliations, and there remained the debate who won, despite the fact that the skunk was defunct.

Pat thought she had, though she now appeared only slightly less disheveled than the enemy, and damn sure smelled no better. She rolled a trio of tight semicircles, muzzle-first in the grass, snorting and sneezing. Then climbed up and shook, looking at me impatiently.

"You ready?" I supposed she said.

With that, she zipped away, to point a covey of birds five minutes later. How? You tell me.

After the main stretch, I put all three dogs in harness and roaded for an additional half hour. "Burning out," it's called in resistance training, a high-rep cardio push at the end of a strenuous strength workout to put a final, nourishing pump into the muscles. By purpose, we finished at the height of the hill, by the old house that overlooked the river. Pulling up under one of the great elm trees, I whoaed the dogs, slipped off the roading gear, and anchored both ends of the rope as a tie-out line. Soon we languished, the four of us, under the company of the tree in the revitalizing breath of the wind, while the mare grazed at will. Lush was the grass, and she would not wander, and for a time we could rest and doze here at peace. The breeze blew fresh upon the hill, and far below, upon the travel of the water, lay the sparking silver shimmer of the sun. I longed with the grace of the moment for Loretta and Melanie, and the picnics of old, which somehow seemed rarely to happen anymore. I guess I had worn them out, my womenfolk, dragging them thousands of miles across a half dozen states. And again, Melanie was growing apart.

As some consolation, I had retrieved from the saddlebags the sandwiches and bread pudding Loretta had sent. I shared with the dogs, and first we made clean work of the sandwiches, and afterwards the whole of the pudding. Soon the dogs were sprawled and asleep, and I lay on my back with my palms clasped behind my head, studying the long, wispy mares' tails that had grown in the sky.

It was a day for contemplation, and there was much to contemplate. The halfway point of my years, probably. A little girl too soon to grow to a young woman. How much, just then, I missed my wife. How great the joy and company of my dogs. How precious, the very gift of life. The miles and moments of the past seven years. Days that had been. For, hard to believe, it had been that long already. Almost. Since that beguiling morning in the little whelping shed out back, when twelve tiny pups had found their way hopefully into the world. And now they were hard into their prime. Holding their own in the fastest of company. Scary. Scary, because time was slipping by, going all too fast, and there wasn't a thing on God's green earth you could do to slow it down.

Why was it you always thought first at such times of all that had passed? Before venturing thoughts of all still to be? Easy enough. Because it was gone. Could never be again. And it had been *good*. That it could be equally so to come was never certain.

But enough of melancholy. You keep on reaching. The new trial year lay ahead. I had pondered long and hard the disenchantment of the Region 3 All-Age Championship the previous spring, how disheartening it had been that Pat had not been awarded the win. All it had served to do was newly center the challenge and reaffirm the resolve. Unique in all the sporting world, the standards for a major pointing-dog trial by horseback. Prescribed only marginally by concept, scarcely by regulation. Wisely so, for the boundaries of human conception are incapable of forestalling the mystery, much less the limits, of superlative canine performance. So it is left to the dogs themselves, and only in the aftermath of their brilliance do we attempt, vainly, to weigh it. That invincible separability we almost hopelessly call "class." That unanticipatable measure of awe at the way a dog, on a given day, in a given arena, surpasses all others, altering to unthinkable heights the premise of triumph.

Normally given to the hands and minds of two mortal men, the judgment can be, and *is*, sometimes inexact. Even when in all good conscience, both men strive for neutrality. You could rationalize on that, of course. That was easy. We'd been close. Titles came tough, and once again, we were close. Very close. When you have judged a while, realize just how thin the separation in the big stakes can be—for only two places in a forty- to eighty-dog field, between the final handful of contenders that emerge as the absolute best, when all were established challengers to begin with—you come to two unassailable conclusions: one, just how difficult it is to win, and two, close counts, and not just in horseshoes. Because you will always know just *how* close you came. As long as you live, you know. When you drive that close to perfection, when the difference is the glint on a gnat's whisker, the consequence is speculative. And every man who had a dog among the top few of the heap knows he prevailed. In most all the ways that really matter, he's right. But no matter how you chew it, it still sticks in your craw. It ain't quite winning.

We would take that, and every time we came that close, every time in my mind we won, I'd be forever proud. I'd award my own titles. And any man who's ever been there, lost blood, sweat, tears, and dog years in the same arena, has done the same.

But the devil with easy. We'd not lie down. We'd knock the hell at the door again. Keep on knocking. We'd gotten a piece of one; we'd work at a piece of another. All said, it was simple as this: You strove for the best—no matter the politics, no matter the peril, goddamn the price—and you never backed up. Championships were the highest calling of the game, and we would hold to the test. I had the dogs. I knew that. They could run and win in any company. They'd proven their worth. We'd go to every top stake we could in the time remaining. They'd earned it. We'd pick a good, timely warm-up trial, hang the topspin on, and ride the momentum into the championships. Whatever the prize, and whatever the price.

$\sim$ CHAPTER 29 $\sim$

AT RAPPAHANNOCK, SPRINGBOARDING INTO THE EASTERN OPEN Championship at South Hill, both dogs were outstanding. Pat won. Beda, closely her equal, could have. The difference was two small steps at shot, on the last of her three well-spaced finds. Against the brilliance of the overall effort, it was the tiniest flaw in an otherwise faultless diamond, but enough to move the judges.

The Eastern itself was disappointing. Occasionally you can beat the odds, but never the gods. Pat had the second brace, against a well-known pointer champion named Arrival, Beda the twenty-fourth against a well-won setter. It was sopping wet the first day of the trial, had poured the night before. I turned Zip Zap loose in the mud and the pelting rain, and she solidly claimed ground acclaim over the pointer, turning in four exciting finds. The last just before time. But she was drenched, the hair plastered to her skin and the rain pounding her in the face, and her style suffered on two of them. In that company, you couldn't give anything away. For over the next three days, the weather would lighten, the skies washed bright and sunny, drying the course to ideal.

We still had Beda to claim the fore, and my hopes ran high in the zest of the clear and crisp November morning. We had driven back up before day, and since it would be only an hour or so before we ran, I had left her in the box. Knowing how much she would fret on the chain. I'd get her out now, give her a brief romp on the cord, let her loosen up and empty out. I'll never forget the defeat or despair I felt when I turned her free of the box, and her tail drooped queerly beneath the level of her back. It was saddening, so totally uncharacteristic of her normal composure, and she was embarrassed with it. Could do nothing to control it, and I concluded at once Fate had visited upon us an anomaly called "limber tail." It was a strange and nefarious malady, of two to three days' duration usually, occurring almost always without warning. While sometimes it might be associated with a prior period of exceptional stress, it could as readily arise at the scarcity of any apparent explanation. A pitiable condition, it robbed its victim of both dignity and cheerfulness.

I looked into Beda's hazel eyes, and it was there, both the letdown and the longing. She knew why she was there and wanted still to run, but it was utterly useless. So I did the only thing I could and scratched her. And hated it so, for us all, but mostly for our Warrior Maiden, for the loss was an opportunity she deserved and could never have again. Before we trailed home, I roaded her for an hour, a small consolation. When her condition continued well into the next week, and a knot swelled midway of the appendage, I hurried her to Danny, only to discover the greater misfortune that her tail had somehow been broken. A forever mystery that sidelined her for a month. Doubly a shame, because that was the last banner year for wild birds at Corinth.

It hurt so much to leave her behind, now more than ever that we had all been so many miles and places together. I missed terribly her evergreen enthusiasm. I think I realized then, for the first time, that when one of us was missing, all was missing. That we could not hope to be together forever. That one day it would never be, could never be, again the same. A happy, happy day it was when she was back, the last day of December.

Workouts during that period were some of the sharpest and strongest of their years. The plentitude of birds was incendiary, like kerosene on kindling. Beda returned fast and complete, went a solid hour the first trip back, pointed three coveys of birds. Quickly she regained a conditioning peak, and I was sending them an hour and a half apiece for a time. They were sewing together some of the biggest, prettiest ground heats you'd ever wish to see, would just raise neck hair every time out, nailing covey after covey with precision and aplomb. Stylish and striking every stand, birds right there, birds up all around them, and not the hint of a letdown. Often three and four coveys each in an afternoon, plus the bonus of a woodcock or two along the way. For the sheer thrill of it, occasionally I'd send them together. They both knew the grounds, of course, would lay out to the max, blister the milk route between bevy haunts—trying to beat each other to the birds. What a time.

With late winter, we rode the South Carolina Classic and the Mid-Carolina and Gamecock Trials into the next Region 3 Shooting Dog Championship. Pat was really big at the Classic, the one we wanted most. Headstrong as a wagon ox a time or so, but overall quite lovely. With a sterling find halfway, she put herself strongly into contention, and was setting the mark, when at forty-five she whipped off a huge cast into woods edge, and didn't as quickly return. I should have ridden to her right then, for I believe she found and pointed another covey—*bang!*—but they up and left her. Because the gallery soon after was hollering, "Birds!" in the vicinity of her exit. I eased that way after a minute or so, as she hadn't returned, threaded a short distance through the woods, and apart from judicial observation saw her following the direction of the flight. I think she had properly stood for a time after they lifted, marking them off and waiting for me, then pursued. I didn't call her back, because maybe we could finesse it by. One of those times you dare the doubt.

But the damage was done, as is usually the case in an affair at that plane. The insinuation, if not the fact, of fault can still swing the judges wide. It was more my fault, again, than Pat's. We had it in our grasp and let it slip away.

Then Beda came along with the fanciest, smoothest race of the trial, just like pulling silk over satin. Not quite as wide as Pat's, but big enough, and seamless. It got better and better, but we could not make a bird. By fifty, I was praying.

"One covey, Lord. Just one." That's all it would have taken.

But it was not to be. How I felt for her. As always, she had given her absolute best. Tried so hard. With a bird, it would have been more than enough.

Though it wasn't the absence of birds that thwarted our bid at the Region 3, held in the Palmetto State also that year, near Pinewood. Both dogs were outstanding. Pat broke like she had yesterday to get to Cleveland—slammed the hammer down—laid out championship caliber and never let up. She was bouncing high, wide, and handsome off all the corners, running so electrically you couldn't wrest your eyes off her. No nonsense, little scouting, and she was doing it all by herself. By thirty, she had two flawless finds. You could have sold tickets either time. One was slapped together so crisply the air crackled, the other flung so correctly out on a limb the tree shook. On both, she was wound so tight the muscles twitched, and when the birds went out and the gun went off, she hiked up to watch them off like she's pricked by a needle. It was the kind of performance that wins trials—big trials—and just past the half, Ernest Newman, who was judging that time with Boyce Talbert, rode up alongside me.

Dapper as always under his Stetson Open Road, Ernest was a fine man, and one of the most respected judges in the nation. I always liked him, enjoyed running under him, but every time I saw him I stifled a smile, remembering another time I was riding before his court and somehow me, him, and my scout all got tangled up in a haphazard bail of discarded army commo wire. All three horses went bananas, their feet in a bind, and for a time we had a rodeo. Ernest was a man of considerable dignity, and the fool horse he was on bucked off his Stetson hat and almost the head under it to boot, and stomped on it. Ernest somehow managed to stay on, and when the dust settled, I got down and retrieved his hat. The crown was flattened, and it wore a big, old dirty hoofprint, and when he straightened it out and put it back on, it sat kinda cross-sided across his head. I imagine he looked like George Pickett might've after the last charge at Gettyburg.

"Be damned," he said. Nothing more. Just resumed his usual patrician bearing as if nothing had happened.

Ten seconds later, his water broke, and we all busted out laughing. It was the only time ever I actually saw him hoo-haw—that is, when he was judging. It was almost as hilarious as the time somebody had a good find at Medway, and the judges and a thirty-horse gallery galloped up and parked square atop a nest of ground-dwelling yellow jackets. For five minutes, you could have sold tickets there, too. Anyhow, I heard Ernest coming, and this time he was in full control.

"I'm liking what I'm seeing," he told me. "I'm gonna give you off, now, to the other man, so he can look awhile."

It was common practice, when you had something really strong going. About then, the nerves began to frazzle. I'd been reasonably calm before; now, as Boyce eased in behind, I was beset with the same old suspenseful plea we could hold it all together another thirty minutes.

"Yeeeooow, Pat!" I remembered again what I was doing, and sang to her.

She was way on out there, scalding an edge. She glanced back, ricocheted off a bay head, shot across the front. Fifteen minutes later, she rang up a third find. I sent my scout out to look for her, and once again it was dug up, right out there where it ought to have been. The birds went up as I was climbing off the horse, and she swelled so high it looked as if she would fly away with them. We sent her on, and my heart was pounding through my chest. Three well-spaced finds and only a few more minutes to go.

There would be a fourth, right before time. Capping a powerful forward cast. She stood by a wild plum thicket—way ahead—shining bright as a new penny from a little opening down through the pine woods. When the covey blew out, they hooked and swung by and over her, and she whirled to mark, back feet firmly in place.

"Pick 'er up."

She'd done a hell of a job, and it would take one hell of another to undo it.

Utterly committed, Beda intended to. Dodging my usual caress, she wanted nothing but to go. There was a steadfast keenness in her eyes: desire whetted to an edge, stropped to a polish. I led her to the line, relinquished her to the scout, and swung aboard the mare. Braced, posed, and ready, setter and pointer traded terse glimpses, each galvanized by the challenge of the other. Muscles bunched, hindquarters gathered, hearts revved.

In body language, Beda intimated she would break left. I wanted her to peel right.

"Beda." I spoke to her, nudged the mare a degree more starboard.

Shifting slightly, cocked so tight she trembled, the setter stared up at me. Watching . . . waiting . . . for one tiny twitch, one little signal to go. While at the periphery, I watched as well—the judges, closing now behind. A mannered pause, a trio of glances, a subtle tip of a hat. Then both whistles blared, and in a violent churn of dust, we were off.

The two dogs locked up, pumping hard for the front, the pointer yipping wildly at the test. Laid to the ground, the trace of their travel billowing onto the sunhewn air like gold dust, they dug far to the fore. At the visible gray-green limits of the course, with Beda gaining slightly the better of it, both dogs rolled right, then faded into the darker shadows under the pines. When next one popped, it was Beda alone. For the hour, she hung there—ever and ambitiously forward—claiming the front. Exquisitely animated, skipping along the edges, swinging the corners like the snap man on a skating line, she could stitch together as beautifully consistent and poetic a shooting-dog race as ever graced goodness, and here it was.

Four times we rode to her, and four times she stood at the edges of the course as firmly and brightly as if she were minted on a silver coin. The birds were right there, and four times when I thumped them out, nothing more than a whisker wiggled. While she jacked up in place and wished them off, and her eyes flashed with lightning when, *whoom,* the gun spoke. Excitement sang through the pines like a night full of katydids, as four times we hustled her back to the front, and on she flew. I could feel the tension running through me, pumping my veins hot. I couldn't remember a time both dogs had been more spectacular on a single occasion. When it counted like now.

Seven minutes to go. She was still laying grandly forward, if anything, stronger. Better.

"*Go ahheeaaad, on!*" I hollered an encouragement, pushing it past the lump in my throat, drawing out the song. Behind it, I sent the urgent, rolling peal of the whistle. Pleading, meanwhile, beneath my breath: "Do it, girl, you can do it. Take it on home."

The setter was driving on, reaching into herself, building for a finish. I could read the body language, sense the utter determination. She tried so hard. I was so proud of her I trembled, so proud the tears were rising in my eyes.

"Do it, girl, do it," I kept whispering, in my heart, where no one could hear.

On she grew, farther and farther, and from the corner of my eye, I could see both judges, glued to her like a peregrine to a pigeon. Until, at last, she disappeared, distantly ahead.

But then she was gone. At time, she was gone. Didn't pop out ahead. And I could feel the fear leap to my chest. The judges pulled up, to watch and wait. The message was imperative: "We need to see her." And in the scant few minutes of grace allowed, we rode frantically for her, I and Ed Turner, who was scouting for me, until the horses were blown and ropy with lather. While my mind was pounded by the old hammer . . . "You can win with any dog but a lost dog."

Beneath my legs, I could feel the mare's sides heaving. She was spent, but I ask her again, glancing at my watch and whipping back out of the cover to where I could see the judges, assuring myself they were still sitting their horses, waiting in the distance. And finally, on the third backtrack, when all seemed lost and Dolly could be pushed hardly longer—with only moments to spare—I found my dog.

"PO-INNNT!" To the top of my lungs, I hollered. *"PO-INNNT!"*

She was buried into the secret of a bay head, under a single, great live oak, in a small swale that sagged between the pines. Just off the right fringes of the course. Standing, though she had been there a time, as proudly as a pauper in a palace.

"Got you, Beda," I said softly, to assure her I was finally there. There was the faintest tick at the extreme of her tail, before it stiffened again. About now, Ed came tearing up, and just further I could hear thudding hoofbeats, bringing the judges and the gallery.

I climbed down, pulled the shotgun. Examining again the find, I started briskly from a left oblique, widening as I went and booting the brush. Beda was regal, high and taut, with her nose locked to the breeze in her face. I figured the birds were out a piece, given the time it had taken to find her, and they were. Just as I stepped clear of the bay, the covey lifted from the short grass and fern, at the far end of the depression. A fog of birds, maybe eighteen or twenty, and Beda took one small step for a better vantage, to intently watch them off. After the shot, I walked back to her, laid the gun aside, and only after I kneeled beside her did she finally let down to accept my caress. I was reeling with the brilliance of her hour. And particularly with its climax. What a sterling piece of work!

I styled her again, rubbing her flanks and crooning to her, thinking back to the day Loretta had held her up as a little calico puppy, and said, "This will be Beda . . . little warrior maiden."

"But we might not keep her," I had said.

My God. What if we hadn't? If we had routinely sold them at the measure of seven weeks, it would have been done.

I tapped her on the ear, released her, called her to heel. She bounced a time or two, shook nose to stern, happy with herself. Grabbed my pant leg. Mischievous still.

We were a pretty jubilant crew that evening. There was a day to go before the trial was concluded, and you never counted biddies before the eggshells cracked, but we had served fair notice. I had both horses, Dolly and Maggi, had ridden every brace. With a half dozen passionate years of horseback trialing now under my belt, I had judged weekend stakes and open championships. I knew what it was about, and I knew what they had. I'd been there, rode hard and back. If ever we were beating the door down at a championship stake, it was now. Pat or Beda, either or both. Both placements would be a miracle, even if they had earned it. But barring something absolutely spectacular on the morrow, they could take their choice. Pat, as ever, had the edge on pace and power; Beda, big enough, had a butter-smooth and fancy shooting-dog race. Both had been exquisite on their game. The difference was gnat's whiskers. As brutally objective as I could be, both were better than anything else I'd seen. One of them had to be in there.

We suffered through eight or ten more dogs, and a couple were pretty nice. Still, in my mind, none had cleared the bar. I was trying to fight it down, but couldn't. A whopping lump of exultation was building in my gullet.

Can you imagine, then, the disappointment when the winners were declared, and neither Pat nor Beda was named? They say you never really recover from heartbreak. I'm here to tell you twenty years later, it's true.

A step on one find, they said of Beda, when later I asked, and she moved on one bird, they observed of Pat. One step for better vantage on a mark, a whirl to mark flight. Their only debatable "faults." If you're looking for something hard enough, I guess you can find it. I told them then—one of them, anyhow, the fellow deserved to hear it most—what I'll tell you now: "Against the whole of what they did, and the dogs you named, that's about as consequential as the mole on Michelangelo's ass." And we loaded up and went home.

It was becoming harder to reconcile, the disenchantment of the big trials. I suppose everything's proportional to the investment and intensity you put into it, and it's hard to adequately express the passion we put into those years. Maybe I'll borrow, this time, for I love the line, from Elton John. We lived them "like a candle in the wind." And when they were exhausted, for me most particularly, I guess, all was spent but the wax.

That year, especially, was disappointing for Beda. So many grand performances, and so many times I felt she should have won but didn't. Pat beat her some, 'cause most trials you just about had to win twice for two placements. Which we did, enough to tell. But the last trial of the season, at Central Virginia, Beda absolutely blew them away. Four sparkling finds and a razor-sharp race. Took it all. Beda "Blue."

About the time your spirit was parched, it rained again.

~ CHAPTER 30 ~

WE PUT THAT WIN IN THE BANK, CALLED THE ACCOUNT CLOSED FOR the year, and opened the doors to spring. Never was its coming more resplendent or mending. The woods lines blushed with buds, bursting into mint green leaves. Doves soared into exultation flights against an egg blue sky, crooning vespers from their shabby, little stick nests among the pines. Bees droned a happy tune, on air misty gold with pollen, and the first of the large yellow swallowtails worked the newborn apple blossoms. From the treetops, high upon the vines, wisteria ripened in cloying purple clusters, the flowers showering at the slightest push of a breeze. April showers begged May flowers, coaxing the pansies to lift their pretty little faces, and along the winding path to the garden, the old-fashioned iris swelled and popped into delicate petals of lavender and wine.

Days were soft and sunny, nights full and fragrant, sweetened by jasmine and honeysuckle, lilac and sweet Betsy. Meadows sere and spent grew lush and green. The mare rarely lifted her head, even at a whistle, from the tender young grass. Whippoorwills returned almost to the back stoop, to roll in the winter's wood ashes. With the rise of evening, you could hear the welcome whip-start of their song from the woods edges by the pastures, where fawns gamboled alongside feeding does with big, nervous eyes and twitching tails. The fern basket on the side porch a wren now claimed home.

Life was light. Living was easy.

In May, the pups—we still called them that—celebrated a seventh birthday. Loretta baked a bread pudding with raisins, for that was their very favorite, and upon it put seven lighted candles. Pat and Beda came up to the big house, toenails clicking anxiously on the kitchen floor, while Loretta lifted out two ample pieces, each to a paper plate. I proxied a wish and blew out the fire.

"Happy birthday to you, Happy birthday to you," Loretta was singing as she set the plates down in front of them. Melanie and I joined, exaggerating when it came time for the "... *many more.*" The pudding was long gone, of course, before the song, but we've been careful to do such silly, little things over the years.

"Off to the kennel," Retta announced, whisking up the dish and a soupspoon.

There Thane, Ben, and Jill wriggled as eagerly, once the pudding was disclosed. And we sang again. Before we finished, Joe Montana had not only scoffed up his pudding, but was yowling along. Then we delivered a slab of pudding to everybody else in the kennel, capping the celebration, and hoping we might do it many times more. To Mama Cindy, November's Calling, went a double portion. Always there was the thought of the tiny, white shed in the backyard of the house on Chaney Road, and the morning it all started.

The summer that followed was the third hottest in Tarheel history, muggy and oppressive. On and on it sweltered, without a shower of reprieve. Days upon days of blue haze and high nineties, stale, stagnant air, and drought. Leaves withered and yellowed on the trees, dried and dropped before their time. Creeks dribbled to a trace and trickle. Ponds retreated to mud holes. Wells dropped dead. Through the long, sultry nights drubbed the combustion of irrigation engines, as relentlessly as the rasp of the cicadas, until at last even the source water evaporated to dust, leaving the crops prostrate in the parched and blistered fields.

We suspended our off-season roading program that year. The normal cooling grace of first light and the initial hour of dawn was absorbed into sticky nights of unbending misery, and the mere hint of the rising sun incinerated to sweat and stifle the slightest exertion. Dangerously so. Stubbornly, we pushed through it for an inaugural few airless mornings, but the going was so heavy and threatening, I worried for the dogs. Especially Beda, ten minutes into the haul heaving so cruelly her lungs might burst, refusing to quit the harness but looking up at me from eyes desperate and bloodshot. My clothes would be sweated to my skin, my heart pounding to the drumbeat of hell with the simple labor of breathing, the mare drawn to a dirty white lather. It was wicked.

So we swore off, until latter September. One side of me worried about it: the concession to conditioning. The other, at least at first, was relieved. I, and I think really all of us, were a little ragged from the grind of the previous trial season. It felt good to let go for a time. Later I tortured myself with that, too. A commitment is only as good as its courage.

Loretta provided the square sense of the thing. "Would you gain a dime," she asked, "to gamble a dollar?"

But after three boiling, insufferable months, when at last September arrived, there was scant relief in sight. Nothing of hope for the sag of the jet stream that usually ushered in the first freshening swill of cooler Canadian air. The opening day of dove season was perhaps the most miserable of my experience. It was an honest ninety-eight in the shade, absent the faintest breath of a breeze. We shot over a field of green, unpicked cotton, spackled with croton weed. I crowded under the shelter of the thickest plants, gathering what meager protection the leaves offered from the scorching search of the sun. It was like huddling in a sauna under a clammy wool blanket. Soaked and steamed, I oozed from every pore.

Aside from the sweat and swelter, the shoot was grand. The doves fogged in all afternoon, craving the tiny, black ticklike seeds, and even in the face of a considerable barrage refused to relent. Though the sun beat me light-headed, and it took two days and two gallons of Kool-Aid to rehydrate.

Meanwhile, the quail dogs sequestered into the dark cellars they had dug under their houses, hassling the laborious hours away, and hoping for something they could recognize as hunting weather. Sprawled and floppy, they'd roll only their eyes to watch me by, offer a feeble tail beat or two and a makeshift apology. "I'd get up . . . really I would . . . but I'll be beggin' your pardon, cause it's too damn hot, and this cool, black earth feels like blue heaven under my runnin' gear."

It was Thursday morning, the third week of the month, before an obstinate artic blitz broke the scrimmage line of the entrenched heat, kicking the hateful swelter tail-over-teakettle back to Central America. Throughout the darkness of the evening before, the stiff northwest winds gathered and grew, roaring their pent-up rage and pummeling the trees, ripping through the drought-tindered leaves until swirling shards littered the stiffening air. The skies were swept clear and the night deepened, and stars pulsed like white coals. While beneath it all, the coolness swelled, as water seeps upon broken and thirsty clay. Dawn broke clean and chill, and the natal rays of the sun touched the tops of the trees as purely as gold, the leaves cut against the laundered blue of the sky as chastely as lace against satin. I walked out of the house into the new morning, and it was like climbing out of a grave and finding life again.

Autumn had arrived, and it didn't matter a hang-or-a-however what the calendar said. Your heart told you so.

"Whoooohaw!" The neighbors four-square over registered my joy.

From the kennel, the setters were going crazy, one great jubilant frenzy. Relief was as infectious as whooping pox. I hurried the length of the kennel, offering a hand to each in turn, whooping again to egg them on. Everybody was on hind legs, bouncing and barking, begging to go.

It took thirty minutes to catch up the mare. She was running and bucking in the pasture, ebullient as a broom-tailed filly, snatched up into her own delight. Finally I seduced her to halter with an apple. Prancing and fidgeting, she stole the blanket twice with her teeth while I tried to bargain the saddle on.

"Hey, horse." I slapped her on the neck with a riding glove.

Happy mischief. She knew full well what she was doing. Setting the blanket back in place, I turned to get the saddle, and she dumped the pad a third time. After this I cross-tied her. She walled her eyes and afterwards attempted to nip me.

I figured I'd ought to ride her down a mite before I hooked on the dogs, so I set her on the path and clucked her to a fast walk. Holding her lightly but diligently against the bit, she hit a brisk, collected four-beat as electrically as Satchmo could march into "When the Saints . . ." Yet full of herself, she broke from the path to the shoulder of the main road at a lovely lick, and took the two miles to the sneeze-town of Shoofly and return in jig-time. All the many occasions, it's still hard to describe . . . just how splendid it felt then racking down the road butt-in-the-saddle of an easygoing walking horse on the first crisp day of fall—your breath on the air, with October and a new field trial season hard ahead, a mount so fleet but silk smooth you could sip hot tea on the fly. Something like a magic carpet ride, I reckon, to the proper side of a rainbow.

We roaded for a solid hour, regardless that the dogs hadn't been in the harness for three months. They were eager for the work. Pat seemed hardly affected by the layoff. Muscles knotted, she lay into the pull with the spare-nothing expenditure she always invested. So much that on the opposite side of the haul, Thing, brawny as he was, had to scratch and strain to even his end of the load. While Beda drew between, vigorously fighting to hold the middle. Tails stood like rapiers, pumping in rhythm with every lunge, eyes flashed lightning bolts of determination, and periodically I could feel Dolly brace against the force of their collective strength. When the sixty minutes were used, none of the three were spent. Pat was on her toes, fixed on the horizon and taut against the leather, Thing cocked a leg and peed jauntily on a bush, and Beda strained to reach a monarch butterfly. They'd be a hair sore for a day or so, but trivially. It was a propitious start, something to get excited about.

It was when I climbed down to undo them from the harness that the difference came to light. Beda had gotten a hindquarter over her tether cord, so I routinely reached down to throw her leg back over. When I stood, there was a slight smear of blood on my glove. First I thought it was the tale of a small cut or scratch, from a stem or stob. It happened most every trip. But thirty seconds later, it hit me, the weakening, intuitive feeling you get from a sudden revelation. The feeling deep in your stomach that you're right, though the fact is yet to be substantiated.

"Beda." When all were kenneled, I stepped into the run with her and Pat, and called her to me. "Whoa, girl." I asked her to stand while I untied my bandanna, balled and dabbed it against the bulb of her gender. Blood again. First show. She was just into season.

I swore automatically. A bitch in season was forbidden by the AFTCA to run in a one-course trial, and permitted to compete in a continuous-course stake only if its officials judged it to be fair to all competitors. A female in season has the disturbing propensity to drive every male dog in a trial to an abstracted slaver. It's like Halle Berry in a Bond-movie bikini, doing a pump-and-grind on the thirty-yard line before the kickoff of a high school football game.

It meant we were three weeks on the bench, with the first trial of note to commence at the end of the second. Disappointing, to say the least.

I walked to the house, announced it to Loretta. She got this empathetic look in her eyes and trooped to the kennel, to see her warrior maiden. Girl stuff, I guess. She was gone awhile.

When she came back, she bore a query.

"Did you look at Pat?"

"No." With the tone of the question came the presumption.

"Pat *too?*" I said.

"Oh, yes," she said.

My heart sank. A double whammy. No great surprise, for we knew the two were close, always tracking one another. But a swift poke to exalted spirits. Here was this grand and gorgeous September day, with autumn coming down, a fresh trialing season looming, and the world by the tail. While Fate dropped by to shackle a ball and chain to our ankles.

I pined for a night and finally decided since it had to come, best it be now. Rather than dead center of the competitive season, or in spring, when several of the classics and championships ran. We could still condition, work hard, and toe the line by late October.

But there was a larger dilemma, and its time had come.

"If ever we are to do it, it needs to be now," Loretta vowed. "She's solidly seven. It's dangerous to think further."

$\sim$ CHAPTER 31 $\sim$

WITHIN THE MIRACLE OF EVERY TRULY REMARKABLE DOG HOVERS THE mortal hope that greatness might replicate itself. That blood will tell; that, moreover, the blood of two great dogs in union may bind so eccentrically as to create a sensation the equal or better than either or both. Though occasionally it approaches close, rarely, if ever, does it happen; not equivalently, and I think the reason for that is beyond human quantification. Thankfully so, or it would never be so special.

But always there is the hope, and always there must be the attempt, for it is the only way we are granted to perpetuate to any sustainable degree such a precious and individual gift of divinity.

So that we are left to stand in surrogate for the greatest of our dogs—for the grand privilege of their mortal journey—to assure, in paraphrase of the Blood, Sweat, and Tears song I have always loved: "And when I die, and when I'm gone, there'll be one pup born ... in this old world to carry on ... to carry on."

We had thought to breed Pat before. From the time she reached five. We had talked of it many times, always to an impasse. We knew we would have to give her up one day, that we wanted a part of her to have and hold close for the rest of our lives. It was the only way. I was infected incurably, I believed, by field-trialing fever. There was simply nothing else, and I wanted dearly to have young dogs coming on the equal of those then. Even so, I knew how special Pat was, that likely I would never enjoy another so extraordinary. Again, and ever, there is hope. The only thing you have is the hope.

Oppositely comes the apprehension. First and foremost for the health and welfare of the dam-to-be, and afterwards for the well-being of the potential litter. Eight or nine years of age is quite late for breeding most females, for they are broaching the fault lines of their physical being: the increased risks of mammary cancer, irregularity of ovulation, amplified possibility of uterine infections, diminishing metabolic efficiency, and weakened litters. To name the prominent few. Litter size tends to diminish, along with milk production. Most maiden females are bred at three or four. Seven was on the conservative side of caution.

Mostly I worried about the effects of maternity on such a bold and flighted spirit. You could never be sure of the residual. Some intrepid bitches are hardly affected. After weaning, they quickly regain all the fitness and fervor, returning to their winning ways with no discernible extraction. Others, distracted at the top of their game and dampened by the hormonal roller coaster, never again manage the same exquisite plane. At five, Pat was only rising to the height of her powers as a trial contender. The fires of her desire for birds and heels raged as fiercely as when she was a puppy, but the hunt and blistering ground pace had been honed and practiced, molded to charisma and game savvy, intelligent search and polished manners. I hadn't wanted to lose any of that. So we had deferred the decision, fearful of stalling the wings of fortune. Now, at seven—even two years on—she was still approaching the pinnacle of her promise. I could see it, feel it. She was winning, and we were challenging the best and most demanding trials. The hardest and sturdiest dogs in the land. The gamble was costlier than ever.

Seven come eleven. There was little time to debate. In the throes of the dilemma, Loretta and I faltered once, averting our gaze and reflecting for moments on our own. When next our eyes met, the answer was complete. If ever a dog was superbly fit, mentally hard, and rock tough, it was Zip Zap. We'd will the risk.

"But who?" Loretta wondered.

I had three heroes in the world along then: John Wayne, the "Duke" of Western movie fame, whom I lionized for every red-blooded, cowboy American value he ever stood for; Secretariat, the incomparable, Triple Crowned chestnut stallion by Bold Ruler out of Somethingroyal, most compelling champion ever to grace Thoroughbred racing; and a gallant setter dog out of Hurtsboro, Alabama, named Bozeann's Mosley, who was setting the English pointer kingdom onto its contentious ear.

Providence rehearsed twice along the way to staging the heroic saga of Bozeann's Mosley, the greatest David-Goliath story the world of major-stakes field trialing has ever known. For you could say it originated fifty-eight years to fore, on September 1, 1923. When a burly baby boy was born to Pierino and Pasqualena Marchegiano in the burg of Brockton, Massachusetts. Christened Rocco Francis, the world would know him as Rocky Marciano, arguably the bravest professional heavyweight boxing champion ever to toe the ring. 49-0. That's all you have to know about Rocky Marciano, only boxing champ ever to retire undefeated. A noted sportswriter of his day observed, "If you locked all the heavyweight champs of all time in a room, Marciano would be the one to walk out."

Rocco Marchegiano rose from post-Depression poverty, from the sooty dust of the coal mines and the vinegar-stenched curing ovens of the New England shoemaking trade—by sheer grit—to become a venerated national prodigy. In 1943, during an army stint, a bully taunted him into entering a camp boxing tournament. His rough-and-tumble altercations with the toughened urchins of a coal town stiffened him through. He pounded the bully senseless and won the contest, too. Lacking the speed, style, and finesse of the big-name boxing champions, but wielding a never-say-die will of steel and the rage of a lion, Marciano turned professional, taking on organized boxing and the best comers of his day. In a whirlwind succession of gargantuan clashes from the fifties, he solidly KOed, among others, Joe Louis, Jersey Joe Walcott, and Archie Moore.

Marciano was a story that couldn't have happened. But it did.

Fact is no stranger to fiction. Fifty-three years later, simile would shine again.

This time, a down-and-desperate actor named Sylvester Stallone would happen along with one of the most appealing underdog epics ever to play on film. Perhaps not so ironically, it sprang again from the pugilistic world. Inspired by a bout between an unknown named Chuck Wepner and Muhammad Ali, in which Wepner went the distance, Stallone hacked out the screenplay for *Rocky* in only three days. Its protagonist was an unheralded, apathetic but lovable, backstreet-boxing bum named Rocky Balboa. His quest, wholly fortuitous, became the implausible dream: the heavyweight boxing championship of the world. Looming was the arresting aura of the big-time boxing establishment and the grandiosity of the titleholder: motormouthed, lightning-fisted Apollo Creed. In a gory marathon slugfest,

Rocky is bloodied and decked by Creed time and again, struggling by iron
will each time to his feet, to ultimately return the reigning champion the
beating of his life, and narrowly miss the title by a split decision.

The story of Rocky Balboa captivated the nation, the screening awarded
best picture for 1976.

The similarities between the ascents of Rocky Marciano and Rocky
Balboa and the rise of the setter champion Bozeann's Mosley are drawn
from tracing paper.

In the egalitarian and elite all-age stakes at the dawn of the 1980s—the
National Championship, the National Free-for-All, the great prairie trials,
and particularly the premier futurities and derby championships, *les trés
meilleurs* of American pointing-dog trials—setterdom got little respect.
Granted, in the sixty-odd years since the golden age of Sioux and Geneva
and the early Llewellins, there had been occasional longhair champions who
kept the torch afire, dogs with the astounding flair and verve to carry any
day in any company. Dogs that had risen fearlessly to hold at bay the menacing label of mediocrity. Tishomingo, Wonsover, Mississippi Zev, Johnny
Crockett, Mr. Thor, Flaming Star, to name the few, were so superbly gifted
they would not be denied. But the phenomenon lapsed infrequent. In
majority, it was an exclusive world, and for better than a half century, the
sovereignty of the English pointer had reigned supreme. None but the English setter found any hope to challenge it.

By entry alone, the numbers of pointers running in any major stake
overshadowed the setters manyfold-to-one. That was simply the arithmetic
advantage. The hurdle was far more substantial. It had been wagered, and
tested, that the English pointer was the consummate trial athlete of the
pointing-dog universe, perfectly suited mentally and physically to the
always demanding, sometimes brutal hardships of the great horseback trials.
The aura of its collective excellence was the bully on the block.

There was an Apollo Creed arrogance about it, a swaggering, condescending boast that lay on the air and got in your nose. A foreboding presence that taunted and teased.

It took a hell of a setter to fray the odds. It was like sending Daniel into
the lion's den, and forgetting to warn the Lord.

In January of 1981, Loyd and Ruth Bozeman were peripatetic
Illinoisans—Loyd an upland bird hunter—who happened to harbor at John
and Pat O'Neall's famed Alabama setter kennels. It was here that Mr. Thor

and many another stellar longhair earned his way. Loyd and John had founded a friendship, and Loyd would frequent and help about the kennel, greatly taken with the panache of the blue-blooded setters that also, at the time, called the Hatchechubbee grounds home.

Soon Loyd longed for a pup of his own.

In the same wish, on February 24, a little chestnut-and-white male setter pup was born to Amos Mosley and Thor's Sweet Moriah in the township of McKinney, Texas. His daddy was famous and his mama good-looking, and of the six pups in the litter—four brothers and two sisters—his was to be the name written in the stars.

None other than Fate knew it then. Actually, the little male that would be the most charismatic young setter sensation in trialing memory was the breeders' third choice for the Bozemans. But the same stroke of augury that brought them together at the triumph of weaning became the voice of prudence in Loyd Bozeman's head.

He knew little, really, of field trial dogs, had never owned or handled a field trial dog in his life. Much less had he a basis for choosing the best of the six seven-week-old prospects. Except that the breeders were proposing the one quite confidently.

But *"Care,"* a voice kept whispering to him, and scarcely he knew why. When it became evident that the two females were spoken for, Loyd heard himself saying, "Then we'll take the rest of the litter."

On that impulse, destiny was borne.

Almost from the beginning, even at four months, Loyd recalls the male pup that would be his great friend and shadow as benignly different.

"He never really acted like a puppy. There was this strange distinction and maturity about him. He was never helter-skelter or silly. Always laid-back."

"With one exception. When you took him hunting, he was explosive."

Loyd didn't have a horse, but there was an old golf cart on the place. He'd run Rocky from that.

Oh, yes. Loyd named him Rocky, 'cause he never quit. After another who wouldn't either, Rocky Marciano.

From the golf cart, Loyd noticed more and more that he laid out to the right places, that you couldn't put the pup behind. Field trialers dream about that kind of innate sixth sense in a dog. Then his head spun twice, and Loyd found himself and Rocky one auspicious day running out of Collier Smith's kennels, 'cause Collier was handling some of John O'Neall's field trial dogs. Here was Herman, Collier's dad, looking over his shoulder. "The Little Fox," they called him, one of the most celebrated old-time professionals in the game. The Herman Smith who had piloted the immortal setter champion Flaming Star to fame.

"I'll have to borrow a horse," Loyd said meekly.

"You take this one," Herman offered, "an' I'll take Old Blue."

So they turned Rocky loose on "The Ridges," a vastness of rolling hills not far from the kennels.

"An' Blue was kind of crippled, couldn't hobble along too fast but on three legs. I rode up front," Loyd remembers, "handling my dog. Rocky was running far, fast, and wide, hitting every head and hollow. Always sailing on to the front. On out there . . . huntin'."

"Herman was somewhere behind. Ever' now and then, I'd think I'd hear Old Blue, a-puffin'. Finally, Herman managed to catch up, switch his horse up next to mine, and Blue was in a soapy lather, tryin' to keep up with me and Rocky.

"An' Herman sorta punched up Old Blue one last time, leaned over across the saddle, and his face was flushed red an' there was a shine in his eyes, and he was 'bout as short on breath as Blue.

"And he said, 'Boy, you've got yourself a great one!'

"So we started going to trials, puppy stuff first. I'd borrow a horse, and off we'd go. Anything ever I asked, Rocky would deliver. He was Open Puppy of the Year for the Tri-State Circuit off the blocks.

"He loved to run and hunt, but mostly he wanted to be with me. Everywhere we went, he was my shadow. I never put a lead on him. The other dogs would be lunging and whining wildly on a tie-out chain, huffing and choking against a cord. He'd walk placidly by my side until his turn to run.

"I could leave him by the truck, ask him to stay—and he wouldn't like it, but he'd be there. Whatever time it took, he'd be there when I got back."

Though God and mercy, he was a firebrand when Loyd turned him loose.

It was in his derby form that Rocky showed his steel. Whatever notions anybody ever suffered that Bozeann's Mosley was a pampered homebody short the mustard for the big time were obliterated forever by the cloud of the young setter's dust.

It was like the theme song from Stallone's movie, "Gonna Fly Now," 'cause the pup literally did.

In fall of 1982, less than two years old, he posted notice with a prestigious third-place win in the Kentucky Derby Classic.

"Gonna fly now, flyin' high now . . ."

By the following spring, he was all but unconquerable.

On the horizon loomed the Devil's Quadrangle, the four greatest derby tests in the land. Four idealistic championships—strung from the pitch and roll of the Deep South piney woods to the vast, sultry stroll of the prairies—that in tandem tried the mettle of young, major-stakes, all-age hopefuls as nothing other. It was the incontrovertible province of the pointer. For as long as its history, English pointers had dominated. So utterly it was presumed.

Rocky took it apart like a tornado demolishes a single-wide. Coming out of nowhere, prevailing so stunningly that the collective breath of the field trial world caught in unison. A veritable juggernaut of speed, strut, and style, with bird savvy astonishing in one so young, he won the Georgia Championship what-and-away, punched out the pointers in the All-America as overwhelmingly, missing by mouse whiskers, as Runner-Up, titles in the National and Continental. To this day, he remains the only pointer or setter derby *ever* to win or place in all four trials.

Rocky would ascend to twenty-six major-stakes wins in the cast of his career, including four titles and three Runner-Ups, against the best of his time, bar none. For years during and afterward, he would reign as the all-time setter sire. Notwithstanding the life-threatening bout of ehrlichia that robbed him of competitive faculty for a great hunk of his prime.

In fall of '83, with Pat near the crest of her powers and the question of a breeding on our lips, Bozeann's Mosley was a national phenomenon. I loved him as I loved Pat, for the very gift of him. For his undying spirit. For the day-in, day-out, ever-to-keep inspiration of him, same as Big Red or the Duke. I loved him for running the Valley of the Shadow—like we all must come times—for bracing the Apollo Creeds of the world, and emerging a shining star.

"Rocky," I told Retta. "Rocky . . . or no other."

I got on the phone, didn't quit, until I caught up with Loyd Bozeman. He and Rocky were on the way back from Saskatchewan, where Rocky had just beat the punishing winds, sleet, and freezing rain of the prairies to claim Runner-Up honors in the Border International.

"We can meet you in a few days," Loyd agreed, "in Moline."

Pat sat by me on the cobbler's bench during the call. "We're goin' a-courtin'," I told her. She looked up and her tail thumped.

"Doesn't the boy usually come to the girl?" she wanted to know.

"Not this one," I said.

"We'll see," she vowed.

It was a happy little trip. On a shout and a shoestring. Just she and I.

We laid in a week's worth of loaf bread, beans 'n' weenies, sardines, and Vienna sausage, fifty pounds of Purina dog chow, and threw a crate in the back of the truck. Doubted we'd need it, 'cause Pat rode shotgun front seat of the cab. We hassled through the Carolina Piedmont, puffed up the Blue Ridge, stopped in Maggie Valley and chased a groundhog or two fore we reached the rugged step of the Tennessee Pigeon River country. There was a kindly little state park there the first night hard by the river, with not a soul else about. Just us and the big owls, insisting to know "Who," and the gushing tumble of the water. From there it was on into the bluegrass meadows and horse farms of middle Kentucky. All the pomp and property of the Thoroughbred legacy. I promised myself we'd piddle there on the way back.

The second night we slept in Indiana. At another small woodland park. I think it cost us four-fifty. Actually it was nine dollars a night, but the park manager liked bird dogs. He had had a setter once, and another since, and we remembered them together. He asked me about Pat, and she offered him her eyes while we talked. We pointed grouse for a while, cast about for a time after plantation quail, and wondered over gray partridge in Montana. By then the sun was dying, the last mellow rays pooling the scarlet and gold of the gums and poplars, already adorned in October colors. The hues were warm and cordial, close and comfortable like the company of a good friend. Still we prattled on, until dusk was closing, and he needed to find the missus and home, wishing us Godspeed and good seed on our mating trip. I lifted a hand as he drove away. We promised each other a hunt we never made.

Pulling the chop box out of the truck, I found a match and kindled a fire. A timid curl of blue smoke climbed the chilling air, and then a little blaze erupted under the fatwood I had brought from home, licking its way up through the sticks I gathered. Soon the orange flames were whispering and cheery. Opening a tin of pork 'n' beans, I bent the lid back and snuggled the can against the fire; did the same with a tin of Vienna sausage. That assured, I pulled loose a couple of slabs of bread from the loaf. Leaned back on an elbow in the newly fallen leaves and ventured a bite. Pat had polished off the Dinty Moore beef stew I had poured over her dry food, was crunching softly now on the kernels. The night songs grew, the singsong rasp of the cicadas monotonous and piercing if you dwelled on it. Summer was at ebb, frost at hand; perhaps they knew. At the edge of the diminishing yellow meadow, a whippoorwill fired once, then twice and thrice—on a half note— like a Model T that caught, but didn't crank, on the first several turns.

Then the ignition engaged, and he hit his stride. *"All-is-well, all-is-well."*

Alone again with the night. Hide nor hair in sight. It felt right. Pat had finished supper, was sitting raptly beside, begging a mouthful of the smoking beans I spooned lustily to mouth. The eight-track of Marty Robbins in the dash player of the truck had reached "El Paso." The Spanish tones of it floated gently through the open window of the cab, onto the concerto of the dry flies and the drawn-out *ke-yannnks* of the toads. The fire popped and sparks flew, swirling in profusion against the coal black darkness, as a salvo of live coals was launched in meteoric arcs.

"We'll make Illinois tomorrow, girl," I told the little setter. "Moline, even, by late afternoon. Won't that be loverly?"

She studied me tentatively.

"Rocky . . . remember?"

She glanced away. "We'll see," she said again.

She was definitely approaching full bloom. The soft maiden assertion of her sex pouted to the size of a large, ripe strawberry, the tiny drop of fluid at its tip altered a rich straw-orange. When I tickled the make of her thighs, she was beginning to roll her tail stiffly one side and the other, opening the invitation. More and more, the idea of puppies from her and Rocky was escalating to an ardent wish; I hoped their meeting married well, and that out of it would come another three pups something like Pat, Beda, and Thane, and we'd ride merrily on down the road through another era.

I remember, too, shuddering slightly that night against the concurrent thought that one day Pat would be gone. And Beda. Dolly and Thane. The whole of it. Except for me and the pups. More than ever I wanted these pups.

Abruptly upon our reverie, and the peace of the evening, rose the guttural, repetitive thud of a motorcycle engine. It grew louder and louder, thumping brusquely against the pavement of the meandering little avenue leading into the park, bringing with it the measured, white sweep of a headlamp. On the motor grumbled, until the whole damn Harley pulled up with it. On its back was a burly, rough-chiseled hamhock of a man in black leather coat and chaps. So indistinct was the figure that it took a second or two to make him out against the night. Rakishly upon his head sat a Greek seafarer's cap, about his burly neck was knotted a red bandanna, and a leather bracelet laced each brawny wrist. Below the hem of the cap, long, dark hair billowed over his ears and spilled across his back.

Pat was up and rumbling in her throat, the hair roached along her back. My hand found the Walther pistol in my pocket.

The man sat for a moment longer, measuring his surroundings, then killed the throb of the bike. Stillness permeated like the sound of death.

"Hello the Camp," he ventured boldly. "Noticed your fire. It looked friendly."

"Is," I said.

He unzipped his jacket and an ample belly spilled out.

"Manny Bishop," he said, thrusting a hammy palm across the fire.

I accounted for myself and Pat.

"Setter," he observed. "My grandpap had setters."

He noticed a loose stump at the edge of the woods, fetched it, and rolled it on its side for a seat.

"Don't reckon you'd share some of that vagina sausage?" he asked, pointing to the can by the coals.

Grinning, I passed him the can by the lid, with the three remaining sausages. By that time he had fished his knife out of his jeans, immediately stabbing one of the juicy links and shuttling it to his mouth. "Ummhmn," he smiled, "almost good as the real thing."

"Where you headed?"

"Illinois."

"Where you from?"

"Pennsylvania."

"Keystone Country," I affirmed.

"All day long," he laughed.

His face was rough but unthreatening, the reflection of the fire travel-ing his eyes when he spoke. He finished the last of the sausage. I knew he was still hungry. Opening another can, I pushed it to him.

"Obliged," he said, nudging it with the blanched toe of his riding boot into the glimmering coals.

Pat had recovered her dignity, advancing a couple of steps to sniff his jacket, then stepping back. The man stabbed another sausage, took it off his knife, and handed it to her.

"Here, girl. Believe this came out of your cabinet."

Pat took his offering. She had relaxed now, accepting him. If she did, I did.

"You're a few clicks from home," I said, as he checked to see the sausage was warm.

"And you," he observed.

"Goin' where?" I asked.

"Dakota. Got a friend in the Hills." The Black Hills, I assumed cor-rectly.

Our talk heartened while he ate his sausage and some light bread and chased it with a swig of my Kool-Aid. I rationed him a couple of Loretta's homemade oatmeal cookies for dessert. He had been in Nam, at the spear-point of the Tet Offensive. I asked him much of it, for a reason, and every vivid thing he told me had its special horror. I had always felt bad about Nam, and I was feeling it especially in the person of Manny Bishop. I don't know now, didn't then, never will, how he came to be there that night . . . but he was, and the cost was a lot more than empathy. As horrific and unpopular as it was, Nam was my war. The bill to my generation for the never-ending price of freedom and national honor. And I hadn't gone.

It hadn't been for dodging. Facing draft in the mid-sixties, and with a career just out of port, I opted for the reserves. Artillery. In '68, my unit was full alert, at the highest level of training, next slated to go. But never did. I would have. Often wish I had. Because to the end of my days, though I have an honorable discharge for that troubled period of our history, I'll never stop feeling a touch negligent. Never mind that Jane Fonda and half the young people in the country were hung out against it, the Country had chosen that we should go. And I would have. I believe there is obligation and honor to the country you live in, particularly one so uncensored as America, that cannot be abandoned behind freedom of speech. That personal convictions aside, to each of us is charged a price and time to fight for the liberties we enjoy. Others have paid it. So should we all.

Manny Bishop made me feel inadequate that night, a little less than American.

"How much of life did you lose?" I asked him after a while, adding a stick to the flames.

He looked at me.

"More than ever I can reclaim."

I reached across the glow of the fire, and this time he accepted *my* hand.

"Thank you," I said.

I have always figured, so strangely it happened not so long after the war, Manny Bishop and that night in Indiana was my personal cost for Nam, extracted from the latent coffers of my conscience. Whatever, the penalty was exacting.

When finally our conversation dwindled, Marty had gotten through some half dozen rendings of "El Paso." We all three got up to pee, and I turned off the tape. When we came back to the fire, Manny dug out a harmonica. He was good, and for the silence of another hour, it could have been reverie at Gettysburg. Sweet, lingering notes that bartered in the silence for your heart. "Lorena," "Shenandoah," "Dixie," "Jacob's Ladder," "Battle Hymn of the Republic" . . . my Lord, how they completed the night.

Manny Bishop left as impulsively as he came. He told me how best to negotiate Bloomingdale and Peoria, for he had been through there many a time, and after midnight, a car turned into the camp. I could see the stab of headlights once again as it made its way slowly along the path through the grounds.

Manny got up, looked at me earnestly, and rolled the Harley into the trees. Into the deep, secret shadows of the moonless night. In a moment, the car stopped by my truck. An officer of the Indiana Patrol got out, set proper his trooper's hat, and approached our fire. Again the hair rose across Pat's withers, and she growled. This time she never let down.

"Have you seen anyone here tonight?" he wanted to know. "A beefy guy, five-ten maybe, on a motorcycle?"

"No," I said.

I don't *know* that Manny Bishop was the one he asked after. And then again, maybe he had murdered somebody. But I doubt it.

What I do know is that I crawled into the back of the truck with Pat that night, and once we had settled and she had snuggled against my armpit, muzzle on my shoulder, I felt as thankful as I ever have for simple freedoms. Above all, the liberty of peace: a placid sunrise, a day of hope, and an unthreatened night. The choice to climb in a pickup truck with a little setter dog and set sail halfway cross the country doing damn well as you will, with the civil assurance nobody's going to stop you—waylay you and question why. A lot of good people had suffered or died for that.

Sometime in the lingering darkness before dawn, I heard the leaves stir as Manny wrestled the Harley out of the woods, the faint whisper of the tires as he pushed it back onto the path. Then a vacant quiet, shattered by the roar and rumble of the engine, and its dampening, thudding mumble as charily he left.

I never saw or heard from him again.

The setter and I stirred before day. The morning was chilly. You could watch your breath fog. The sky was yet dark, deep, and clear, punctuated by the glimmering silvery prickle of the stars. By the meadow, the whippoorwills lingered at work. We shared a cold camp, a banana, some raisins, and a bowl of Special K. In the last obsidian minutes preceding the gray wash of dawn, a meteor laced the sky, the fiery lesion of its passing healed almost as swiftly as it appeared. Immediately ensued a gulf of emptiness, translated by the distance to home.

By midmorning, we made Lincoln's Land. I thought again of Loretta, wished she were there. Charlie Pride was on the radio: "Kiss an angel good mornin', 'n' luv her like the devil when you git back home." Pat was alert, up on the seat, tail popping, checking out the incoming traffic. Up to Bloomingdale, on and bear a bit left to Peoria. Finally, the last leg to Moline. By then Pat had bored, was sprawled asleep across the seat with her head on my knee. The tall cab of a Peterbilt pulled by, commanding the inside lane. The driver glanced down into the truck, smiled through a carrot red beard, and traded a thumbs-up sign.

We got there before we thought, early afternoon, checking into a Howard Johnson near the airport. Immediately I called Loyd, and established a time midmorning next for the rendezvous. The excitement was cresting now. I was confident Pat was at the peak of estrus, and Rocky was only a few short miles across town.

The rest of the afternoon was spent in a restless doze. Come dinner time, I sallied to the restaurant and got a great carry-out platter of fried clams. Pat and I divided it back in the room while we watched, peculiarly, a segment of *Roots* on TV, the epoch of Kizzy and Chicken George.

"Wonder what ol' Lewis is doin' tonight?" I said to Pat. "I heard he's gonna breed Kizzy, too."

"Do tell." She shrugged.

"'Spect who could take who with both you swole up like a tick?" I said.

No reply.

I don't guess I slept two hours in ten that evening. I was excited. Just plain happy and wired. Pat got to go out three or four times to pee, need or not. The clock dawdled until the minutes crept by at the speed of a sloth. The darkness outside the windows lapsed interminably. I wondered if it was morning yet in Cincinnati. Hell, I hadn't waited this long for Retta to decide to be married.

Finally I think I wore myself out. Ironically, when daylight ultimately came, I was asleep. But not for long. I woke to the bare gray suggestion of dawn, and it scorched my senses like the blare of the noontime sun. Throwing the covers back, I sprang out of bed. Pat cracked one eye to see why. She was rolled out flat on her side like a rug. I pulled on my pants, and she got up yawning, sitting back on her haunches and parking out like a walking horse, stretching mightily to fore, then rocking her balance to her front toes and extending stiffly one hind leg and next the other. Ready for duty, she wagged her tail.

I reached over and tickled her right thigh. She glanced at me over her shoulder. Her tail rolled provocatively right, then as suggestively left.

"All's left is the red dress," I said. "And today, your name is Lolita."

She stared out the window, at the sparrow on the sill.

At last the time drew near. When the clock spun somewhere close, we left an hour early. Off the circuit and biding in Illinois, Rocky lived in a pleasant little Middle American house in suburbia. Following Loyd's directions, we found our way there. With all the notoriety he had received as a stud already, I expected a shingle out front. But the only announcement was the number on the mailbox. I rolled the truck to a stop by the front walk, and attached Pat to a check cord. She was high and happy, worn with the hiatus and yearning for a fast, hard sprint.

"Not today, little lady. Powder your nose. We've traveled a thousand miles for illicit interstate commerce. No flinching now. Before we're arrested, let's get on with the thing."

"And if you don't like him, God forbid, at least suffer the effort."

"We'll see," she said, looking past me. She was a broken record.

Women, dogs, horses, or sprig, you never know with females. Of any species. Unless they're willing to be paid for it, you rarely expect easy. Despite the common misperception of the mongrel bitch on the street, a half dozen males waiting a turn, dogs are not naturally promiscuous. I think this to be especially true with blue bloods, the more so with bold and dominant individuals used to their way. Like their human counterparts, it frequently takes more than hormones to heat the hatch. I've known gyps at the pinnacle of estrus, so hot they'd wear a grin silly as a goose, lesbianize any other female handy, to be willing toward only one male in a kennel of ten. One chosen sire, to whom she'd offer herself like a Harlem hussy, with whom she'd ball the jack at the drop of a donut, while she put fang and the fear of God in any other that dared look at her.

In later years, I would spend thirty-two hours once on a breeding trip to the Florida Panhandle, to carry Kate, one of the finest gun-dog females I have shared life with, to stand to another stud of national repute. My heart was set on it. Problem was, it was my heart, not hers. Shrieking and raging like a banshee, she refused to accept him, doing anything possible to rip him limb from limb every time he nosed close. In general mien, she was the kindest, gentlest, most compliant bitch I have ever known, but she would have nothing of him. Finally, sustaining a nasty rip from a frenzied canine tooth trying to hold her, I gave it up. The only thing left, aside from artificial insemination, was forcible rape.

She looked at me with wounded eyes, asking, "Always I could trust you. Why are you doing this to me?"

I couldn't. It tore me apart. *Nothing* was worth a cleft between us. Sickened with the whole affair, I didn't try to find a vet. I forfeited a thousand-dollar stud fee and came home.

Two days after, in her home run, she accepted Ches, a kennelmate, as completely as Guinevere fell to Lancelot. She had courted him before we left, hadn't wanted to leave him then. Of the five possible sires in the kennel, *he* was her only. Destiny shot an arrow into the mix as well. The litter was the best Fate ever bred.

Loyd Bozeman came to the door that day at the bell, a tall, lanky man with a kindly face and a welcome that was grown in south Alabama. He was a gentleman; maybe he gleaned that there, too, and I liked him from go. I immediately looked for Rocky by his side. Pat stood on the cord by mine, nose at work, testing his britches.

"Rocky's out back," he explained, reading my mind. "Didn't want him to get overcorked and blow the bottle. Before I could meet your girl."

He stooped to Pat, offered a caress. She met his eyes, tail flagging softly.

"Hey, girl." He studied her a moment.

"Come on through," he invited, rising.

"She's beautifully made, easy on her feet . . . sculpted like a gymnast," Loyd said, glancing back and forth as we wound through the house to a small, fenced backyard. Pat was mildly interested. I, otherwise, was almost queasy. Flush with the heat of anticipation, and numb with awe. The way you feel when you're about to meet somebody bigger than life, somebody who lifts your spirit on his wings. I could sense my heartbeat, rushing toward the brink of phenomenon. And there it was, as we stepped out the back screen, in the flesh.

Rocky came running from a corner of the little courtyard. He was a statuesque setter of medium build, lightly marked and ticked, a rich chestnut-orange on white. From his right ear rose a triangular patch that narrowed at its apex to mask one eye. Tight on his toes, he was square of shoulder and deep of chest, with legs lithe, straight, and clean. Placed gracefully over them, his gait was poetic, his stance tall and lean. To that extent he was handsome, though not extraordinary. It was the sense of him that differed. Not what you saw, but what you felt. Above all was the esoteric air of eminence, a smoldering, impervious, irreproachable aura, the same keen, self-possessed bearing of assurance as the eagle.

Touching nose to Loyd briefly to anchor his affection, he measured us from hazel eyes cool and level, absent the least edginess or anxiety. Instantly his interest peaked with Pat. He knew well, by now, his role. Approaching her, they touched noses, then Rocky sidled to the side. Pat shifted stiffly, locking in place, considering him. Despite the ploy, there was play in her eyes.

"I'll hold Rocky," Loyd said, collaring the now eager male, "see if maybe she'll make the move."

I undid the snap from Pat's collar. She traipsed nonchalantly aside, squatting to pee. Raking with her hind legs as she finished, she kicked a small explosion of dirt and grass into the air. Cutting her eyes as she went, she piddled a coquettish semicircle back to Rocky.

Sniffing his shoulder, she danced away, then back. This time she smelled the very maleness of him, touching her nose to his sheath. Rocky wriggled with his urgency, asking liberty from Loyd's restraint. Loyd turned him free.

He moved instantly to Pat. She danced away. He pranced to her shoulder, asked again. Both setters danced and chased, then closed again. This time Pat stood for a moment, waiting. Rocky moved behind her, licking the heat and cleft of her. She rolled her tail aside, begging the more, until he mounted her and she felt the probing of him, causing her to dance away again. But she wanted him, waiting again for him to come. She looked at me once, past a panting, goofy grin.

"We'll see," I teased.

This time his tongue caressed the swollen and steamy seam of her longer and more vigorously, and she stayed, arching herself to his advance. Climbing to her back, Rocky locked his forelegs around her body, clutching her tightly, struggling and pumping. Then he shuddered violently in hard, short strokes for several seconds, and it was done.

Their tie lasted twenty-three minutes, and we all were elated.

Two minutes afterward, Pat resumed regularity as if nothing had happened. Rocky, meanwhile, walked in weak-legged circles, hassling, spent but happy.

Pat glanced at him. "He got paid for this, *too?*" she asked.

It was a good, natural breeding, obviously at the peak of Pat's cycle. Loyd and I were hopeful about it, agreeing there was little need for a second breeding.

But there was this strangeness about it, too. A certain sadness. I wanted puppies, badly. But it was the first and only time that Pat ever surrendered. To anybody or anything. And I had placed her in its path, at the only time she was vulnerable. Maybe it's crazy to think about the thing that way, maybe it's just the fickle way I'm made, but I did. When an indomitable spirit bows once in a lifetime, that's poignant. Maybe it's the pure marvel of it. Only one force on earth could make it happen. But it was as always. In love, as in war, she excelled at anything she did.

We stayed one more night by the airport. I hauled in the old Remington 17 typewriter that traveled with me, and worked off another installment of a story overdue. Then Loyd came by to bid us farewell, and we talked for a time about dogs and trials, and what life would not have been to the either of us without Pat and Rocky.

At sunup, Pat and I were off for the long trek home. With nowhere to hurry, no schedule to meet. If the trip there was brim with anticipation, the return was one of peace. We stopped where whim wished, at every roadside beckon. Late in the afternoon, we pulled into the backcountry for a jaunt across some big Illinois prairie. Not a farmhouse in sight for miles. Cast by her spirit like a stone from a sling, the little setter flew to heart's content, so distantly once she was no bigger than the glint of light in a diamond, and as capricious. I sang to her, and she rolled on, on and on. Teetering on the very edge of infinity, it seemed. It was beautiful and scary together, for what should I lose her fifteen hundred miles from home, with all we had past and so much of hope ahead? At the same time, my soul soared to the clouds, fear weighted my insides to the ground, until on the far corner of forever, she banked and turned, and sailed for home. Back to my summons, high and happy.

We stopped at the little parks again. Ate from a can. Dreamed by the fire. In the maiden light of each new morning, we wound our reverie up into our bedrolls, and turned another several miles toward home.

In Lexington, Kentucky, we meandered through miles of bliss and bluegrass, by stately alabaster mansions on high distant hills, beyond long gravel avenues defined by rambling white fences that inscribed perfect rectangles around all the pretty horses. Farm after manicured farm under a clean, blue sky, pledged to Southern heritage, and the legacy and pageant of the Thoroughbred. Here and there we lingered by the side of the road, sitting together on the hood of the truck and sponging up the glory. Reveling at the caper of the horses. Pat seemed as engrossed as I. With the great stallions, obvious by their pride and parade, prancing about their dedicated paddocks on stiffened legs like the very ground was hot. Bursting and bucking into powerful, headlong gallops across the rolling green turf for the sheer declaration of it. With plump and glistening mares, and the broom-tailed colts of the year gamboling on toothpick pinnings along beside them, bunching intermittently for wild, frolicking flights of play three and four at a tear.

I thought to myself several times that Claiborne must be near. Where the Great One was standing. Secretariat. Wondering if simple and starstruck wayfarers like ourselves ever got to see him. It seemed only remotely possible. Yet here we were, in this inspired moment, at the locus of the dream. We had stretched for a lot of things in the last seven years. Maybe one more. Suddenly it seemed imperative. To seize the chance.

"There's only to try, Pat," I told the Number Six setter, "only to try." All else, she had willed me that.

Clambering into the truck, we drove to the Kentucky Horse Park. I begged Pat onto the cord because I didn't want to leave her unguarded in the parking lot, and we walked to the gate. We had to wait in line while the ticket sales cleared, and then I up and asked the cashier in the idle moment where Claiborne Farm was. And she said, "I don't know, but if you'll go over to the barns where they keep the exhibit horses, somebody there should be able to tell you."

So we sauntered over to the stables, and there was a groom under the hallway of the first barn burnishing a gleam into the coat of a gorgeous little Morgan mare. There was also a Catahoula leopard cur mascoting on a hay bale, and Pat gave him the stiff upper lip and a curdling snarl when he strutted over to say hello. The Catahoula was attempting frisky, and Pat was about to erupt into a blistering rage. Right away the groom left off the mare, grabbing the cur roughly by the collar and dragging him into an empty stall. I felt bad about it. I had forgotten, in the adventure of the mission, I had a dog in heat.

"Sorry," I said.

"No difference," the attendant replied. "He'd like to. But he's harmless. Hell, he'd need a hobble in a whorehouse."

"Claiborne Farm," I said. "Can you tell me how I get to Claiborne Farm?"

"You don't, I doubt. Past the season. They've likely closed for the year."

I felt my heart sink.

"Been here a month ago, and you could have probably got in on the regular tour. Anyhow . . . Paris," he said. "Not far. 'Bout twenty miles up the road."

He could see I was crestfallen.

"Why you wanna go?"

"Secretariat," I said, looking him directly in the eye.

I wasn't sure what we'd do next. Probably drive to Paris. Might as well be France, I guessed. But I was a ways from quitting. I thanked him and we turned to leave.

"They got a reception and security gate at the entrance," the horseman added. "Always somebody there. Number's in the book."

"Hell, give 'em a call." He pointed to the phone booth end of the hall.

Probably ought, I thought. Still might go there, even if they said no. Argue the case to the bench, before we accepted the verdict. There'd never be this time and place again. Not like now.

I looked through the book and found the number, while Pat eyed a barn cat.

"Whoa," I cautioned.

The ring tone buzzed four times before an answer. A woman's voice. Really on the wings of a wish, I hoped it might be Penny Chenery.

"Hello, Claiborne Farm," she said. I felt my heart quicken at the words.

I told her who I was, where we had been. Two thousand miles, just me and my dog. That we were passing through and couldn't leave without the call. Was there *any* possible chance I might see Secretariat?

"We're past the normal tour season and closed for the year," she said, words I was dreading to hear, "so there's really no one here to show you through. I'm sorry."

The inflection of her voice with the last two words was assertive. The door was closing. I got down on my knees then, at the last of my means.

"Ma'am, I got three heroes in this world: John Wayne, a setter dog named Rocky, and your horse. Maybe you've had a hero of your own sometime."

There was a precipitous pause. I thought I could sense a quiet smile. "Come on out," she consented. "We'll see what we can do."

"Thank you," I said, with all the sincerity I could convey.

Into the gray stone columns that marked either side of the road leading into the farm were set metal placards that, in understated nobility, announced, "Claiborne Farm." Beyond, the paved narrow lane fell away to a vast green bottom speckled by sunlight and shadow. Dotting its journey were sycamores, maples, and oaks, donned gaily in early autumn colors. Beneath them, here and there along the path, yellow leaves had fallen, like gold coins spilled from a pouch. As far as you could see, the little avenue meandered, between undulating hills and great heritage oaks inside long white fences that guarded lush green pastures. About them the brood mares were feeding. Dapples and grays, chestnuts and bays.

Some three hundred yards beyond the entrance, the reception and security office soldiered the first great bottom, an inauspicious and arresting citadel of stolid white block. Around it waited two long, black stretch limousines, and beside them milled a gaggle of foreigners, Arabic in turbans and robes. Oil sheiks, I supposed, somehow invested in the Thoroughbred trade. Their uniformed chauffeurs stood by the open doors of the limos, while the royals and attendants migrated back and forth to the security station, closing briefly in small knots and jabbering and gesturing passionately. The whole reeked of money, station, and privilege.

I was a pauper among kings. My wealth was not so easily seen. We pulled up and parked right alongside the shiny limos, polished to the sheen on a crow's wing, in our faded old Chevy pickup. The oil sheiks glared at us. But not the three men sitting on the stone wall to one side of the building. They were in work clothes and appeared as if they belonged to the farm, grooms and stable tenders, maybe. They were conversing warmly, and laughing in quiet, respectful tones. The look they gave me was far more appreciative.

I stepped out of the truck, attired in worn Levis, a navy Henley, and western work boots.

"Back, girl." Pat was crowding the door, wanting out as well. I rolled the window up partway so she couldn't jump through, then, with a nervous look around, started to lock the door.

"We'll watch after her," came an offer from one of the men sitting on the wall.

They knew I was a little lost. I think they liked the look of the old truck and the fact I had a dog in the cab. By nature, I guessed they were kinfolk.

"Thanks," I said, and crossed to the door of the office.

Stepping inside, I addressed the man at the counter. He called to a young woman at a desk in a side room. I wish I could remember her name. I'll never forget her face and kindness. She stepped with grace and bearing to the counter.

She was disarmingly attractive, thirty-something.

"John Wayne, huh," she said. "And Secretariat, I believe I know, but I'm unfamiliar with the dog."

"Bozeann's Mosely. They call him Rocky. A young dog, revelation on the field trial circuit. Won in the four biggest derby championships in the country."

"Kinda like the Triple Crown?" she asked, laughing. God, she was engaging.

"You could say that," I said. "How did you know who I was?" I wondered.

"It wasn't hard," she said.

Reckon not, I thought, among the Arabian Knights in the lot.

"Secretariat's groom will be here shortly. He's on his way up from the barn."

And there it was. I couldn't believe my ears. It was actually going to happen. One moment I was captive to the suspense, hanging by my nails to a root over the sheer plunge of a cliff, and the next she's reaching over and pulling me up.

She smiled, amused by my incomprehension.

"Thank you," I said again. It was very little. But what else could you say?

"You can wait here," she added, motioning to a chair, "or outside if you want, under the trees."

"Outside, I think." I had to get somewhere I could breathe. I opened the door and started down the steps.

"Let me know, please," she called, "when you're ready to leave."

I nodded.

My heart was thumping like an eave drip on an oil drum. I could feel the *throb-throb-throb* of it in my fingertips. Not the Pope, not the President, not even Linda Evans . . . This was Secretariat.

Pat was dancing on the seat of the truck, wanting to be with me. I offered a hand through the window, consoling the root of her ear. Five minutes later, I noticed a long, lanky man in a plain white shirt and khaki work pants, approaching at a purpose up the walk. There was nothing particularly different about him, but somehow you just knew.

The receptionist had prompted him who to find. He crossed directly to me, glancing at Pat, and our old truck.

"Like to see Secretariat?" he said with a smile.

This couldn't be happening. But it was. I left Pat, once more, in the kind hands of the Samaritan on the wall, who reassured me again she would be waiting upon my return. Accompanying the groom, past a small wooden gate and down an interior walkway, I strolled intimately through Claiborne Farm. Its world was mine alone. Mellow afternoon sunlight flickered through the trembling lace of the trees, dancing in shadows along the pleading ribbon of the path. Across the distance, through fleecy white clouds in a brilliant blue sky, it fell in long lemon fingers that relaxed and retracted across broad green pastures. Scattered about were majestic maples and elms, and great oaks, and a mockingbird was singing its heart out from atop the cupola on a nearby breeding barn. Sifting down in soft golden showers, the colored leaves volunteered quietly to the breeze. It was like the passage to a palace, the esplanade to a throne.

We talked amicably as we went. Of Big Red. I learned the little, happy things about him I had yearned to know. By the path upon our left drew a small stud barn. Before the dark recess of an oversized stall stood a massively framed door, closed for the top half by cast-iron lattice and below by rich red mahogany. Otherwise, the barn was spotlessly clean and brightly whitewashed. The stall smelled sweetly of fresh orchard grass and lush alfalfa hay.

"He's in the paddock," I was told, "but this is home."

My attention was already transfixed by the gleaming brass placards that ran the mahogany height of the door. In ordered progression, beneath his name, they heralded the timbre of greatness: Bold Ruler x Somethingroyal, Winner, Triple Crown—Kentucky Derby, Preakness, Belmont Stakes, 1973. The sheer power of it left me trembling.

A few steps down the path, and my senses were assailed anew by the glimmering eminence of his stablemate: Spectacular Bid, Triple Crown, 1978. Two of the most charismatic horses that ever ran, under the same barn. This could only be a dream, and I would wake soon, to have it vanish, like a bubble upon the air.

On we ambled down the golden path and among the trees, a hundred yards more, until the oaks bowed to the open pastures. A series of five-acre paddocks crisscrossed the near hill. He was in the first. Standing as you would expect, at the furthermost end of the pasture, majestically atop the crest. He was mostly in shadow but silhouetted against the brighter canopy of the trees, on his toes, tall and proud, looking at us. Even at the distance, I could feel his energy singing through me like a current of jubilation. He took two bold steps forward, stopped again, staring. The he tossed his head in hauteur and burst into a full gallop. To us, he blazed, suddenly out of the shadows and into the burning glow of the sun, the flash of his coat copper and red, shards of turf flying high with the beat of his hooves. His tail was cocked and flying, and he rolled his great neck, turning his head jauntily one side then the other. Three white socks and the diamond blaze of his forehead flared, as here he came, the greatest horse that ever ran. We stood at the gate, watched him come, the pounding of his hooves like the thud of cannonballs. Until he slid to a stop at ten feet, showering us with grass and earth.

He was big. Not so tall as some, but thick and deep, and massively mus-cled. Not the lithe, sculpted Pegasus he was as a three-year-old, but the proud, imposing specter of a mature stallion. He pranced and reared, then settled, ears pricked, the look of the eagle in his eyes. He was rare and royal, and he knew it. On the cheekband of his richly burnished leather halter was another shining brass plate, and upon it was one overpowering word: SECRETARIAT.

"What's going, Red?" the groom said to him.

The big horse tossed his head again. The tall man opened the gate then, and stepped inside the paddock, snapping the lead to the stallion's halter. The

horse settled at the neck stroke and voice of his handler, and the man laid
aside a need for a nose chain. Then the groom led him out, and he stood gallantly there at touching distance, the greatest Thoroughbred that ever lived.

My nose was burning and my eyes were welling with the sheer
supremacy of him, and I couldn't move or speak. I just stood there, rooted
to the earth and numbed to the senses. Trying to comprehend the incredible
privilege.

When finally I could, I said two words. "He's magnificent." And he was.

Since, I have met presidents, dignitaries, celebrities, and kings. Only
Secretariat was mightier than the myth. His was the greatest presence I have
ever known.

For perhaps ten minutes, I was man-to-man, shoulder-to-shoulder with
the big fellow. I don't think I said a thing else for the whole of it. I was pris-
oner to his power. Point-blank I studied every chiseled muscle, the breadth
of his barrel, the sheen that traveled his rich chestnut coat like the migration
of sun-and-shimmer over water. Never once did he abandon his bearing.
Not once did he appear anything less than he was, the consummate champion.

I ventured a few pictures. He stood as regally as he had in '73 for the
plethora of media images, the *Time* magazine cover: head erect, ears
pricked, eyes rapt and gazing into the distance. He turned once, with that
air of nobility, and stared directly at me for several moments—King that he
was—bidding, "Hail, knave. What ask you of my court?" A picture, my
Lord, and boldly I snapped it. It was impolite, but it helps me always to
remember him that way.

At last, I surrendered my welcome, and Big Red galloped freely away to
regain his vigil upon the palatial crest of the hill. As I left, I took my eyes
away from him once, turning them to the next knoll. On it stood Spectacular Bid, striking as well, the bay of his youth creamed to dapple gray.

Pat greeted my return to the truck. Our Samaritan was yet at watch
from the wall, one foot up, elbow on a knee. I crossed to thank him and he
nodded. He was a while ago from Lafayette County, Tennessee, near Grand
Junction. His great-grandfather had once held land adjoining the Ames
Plantation. We talked dogs for an earnest minute, and relieved of duty, he
departed to attend again the Claiborne mares at the brood barn. I opened
the door to the cab. Pat reared to my chest from the seat, and I laid a hand

behind either ear, kneading the union of neck and stoop. I was reminded again, the more after seeing Secretariat, of her own rarity. For it welled in her eyes as in his: the hazy concession to affection, but greater, the crystal ascendancy of confidence.

Keeping my promise to our benefactor at the reception desk, I stopped in to say good-bye. There would never be an adequate way to thank her, but I tried. We passed a few last pleasantries, and I started away.

"He was here, you know," she said.

"He . . . ?" I said, turning.

"Wayne."

I smiled, and closed the door softly behind me.

Through the Pigeon River Gorge, back through the smoke-blue haze of the Smokies, we made for Carolina, anticipating again the gentle hills of Granville County. We spent the last night at the same little haven by the Pigeon River, and my sleepless thoughts tumbled along as nomadically as the gurgling waters. It had been a grand trip, much more than I could have imagined, but my heart was ready for harbor. It would be good to sweep Loretta and Melanie up in my arms, to kiss my wife deeply, to feel them warm against my chest, to see the rest of my dogs again. To once more be whole. Patty was anxious also. The protracted idleness was chafing her will. She was as restless as my mind. Two hours before dawn, we broke camp, turned the old truck back onto the main highway, and pointed it home.

"Hang on, Patty-cake," I told the setter. "We're off for gone."

CHAPTER 32

NO HOMECOMING ON EARTH IS MORE JUBILANT OR GENUINE THAN the welcome of a dog. After a soaring gathering of wife and daughter, we went immediately to the kennel. All saw us coming, and the din was stupendous. Beda danced against the fence in delirium. There was a depth of ecstasy and devotion in her eyes, as I cupped her muzzle in my palm, like the sounding of a well. Like the grip of a whirlpool, drawing in your soul. Jill, Gabe, Hank, and Ben. My beloved Mama Cin'. Even ol' Thing. All bouncing, barking, and bubbling for joy.

> *"When Johnny comes marchin' home again, Hoorah! Hoorah!*
> *We'll give him a hearty welcome then, Hoorah! Hoorah!*
> *The men will cheer, the boys will shout,*
> *The ladies, they will dance about . . ."*

You'd have thought I was the largest hero in history, home from war.

We turned them all out, into the kennel yard, and for thirty minutes had a plain old, backwoods Baptist reunion. Pat was as happy as the rest. After a lot of butt sniffing and posturing, she bounded into the run with Beda, as always they had kenneled together, since little puppies. Tell me not that dogs are incapable of longing, loss, or affection, one for the other. For the next few days, they were inseparable. We'd see them from the house, lying together in the comfort of the sun, the muzzle of one over the shoulder of the other. Or grooming turn-and-about, caressing with a caring tongue each other's faces.

That first night we were back, I sat up past midnight with Loretta, regaling the trip. She wanted every detail of Pat and Rocky, since I had only meagerly advised her by phone of the ardor of their tryst. Afterwards, she ran to get a calendar to scout out the time, mark off the days. Indexing with her finger, she counted them off aloud, under her breath ... one, two, three, four ... thirty-five, thirty-six ... fifty-seven, fifty-eight, fifty-nine ... sixty-one, sixty-two ... She paused, as in surprise. Joy brightened her face.

"November twenty-third. Thanksgiving. Maybe even Thanksgiving Day."

She looked at me. "How right would that be?"

The prospect was perfect. What a blissful gift of faith, sixty-two, sixty-three days and puppy breath. Puppy scamper. Little fragile, wet, blind, pink-white, whimpering and twitching hunks of fur that sprouted in three weeks to fierce, little blue-eyed lovers and warriors with quick, warm tongues and needle teeth, that licked you in the mouth, that fought and tumbled, that bunched tight, backed and barked, and spun around like wind-up toys.

"If she caught," I said.

"She did," Loretta said.

"You know?"

"I can tell."

Oh God, here we go with the intuition again. By now, I was a believer.

She looked at me with a purpose.

"Yes, I know. Stay close round Thanksgiving."

I told her of the unbelievable private showing with Secretariat. Every delicious, incomprehensible morsel of it. Most of all, the overwhelming, almost indescribable feeling of him.

"He was right there," I said. "An arm's length."

"I could have touched him."

"You didn't?" Retta asked incredulously.

"No."

"*Whhy?*"

"I couldn't," I said.

Her eyes were a question mark.

"The strength of him," I said.

There was a silence, that grew to an imperative. I had thought about it long and hard on the lengthy trip home. For it had been something of an enigma, even to me. Finally I had been able to pose it to myself, in ways that approached the feeling.

"If, after searching with abandon for fifty years . . . ," I said, "in the moment you were given to discover the rarest and greatest ever of diamonds . . . it was lying there, eye-level, so grand and brilliant it was numbing . . . could you touch it?"

She looked at me, questioning herself. Still she said nothing.

"After witnessing the battles . . . at the height of his heroism . . . had you been given the company of Braveheart, William Wallace of Scotland . . . found yourself standing suddenly beside him . . . could you touch him?"

"No . . ." she said.

I returned her gaze. "That's the way it was."

We settled into living again, counting the days. Beda was soon out of season. She and Thane shouldered the roading harness, and we toiled back toward the top of the mountain. Until we climbed to a conditioning peak again. Ben, Jill, and Gabe I was taking out regularly, for the gunning season was close to hand. Cindy was getting up in age now, beginning to suffer the toll of the years, but I'd always take her along, too. She still whined to go. I'd give her thirty minutes, then an hour. She'd brave along, still with flashes of the old dash and style. Her nose was nevertheless strong. She couldn't cover the same ground, but if a bevy was handy, she could nail it as positively as ever she would.

A few days before Pat and I had left for Illinois, to mark my forty-first birthday, I had set the cornerstones for a log house on a small, green knoll overlooking the pond. Always it had been a goal to build one, from scratch. Here and there, between the dog work, I picked up on it again. Built a gin pole so I could lift the heavy logs to height as the walls grew higher. For the next four years, I would cut and snake logs, scoring them with a chopping blade and hewing them square with the broadaxe. Shaping the dovetails onto the ends. I retreat to it now—twenty-three seasons later—to gaze at the picture of Pat, Beda, and Thane over the mantle, the field trial memorabilia of their era on the wall, before a blaze in the stone fireplace, the first ever I laid. Remembering wistfully that autumn, the fall of '83, when all the pieces were yet in place, and so joyfully we looked forward to Pat's pups.

During October then, while Beda and Thane hardened in the harness, and Pat grew, I pulled away only long enough to judge the Central Virginia and Virginia Capital Stakes. By the end of the month, with Pat on the bench, we were just back to the pink, ready to crusade again. It had been so hard to leave Pat behind, harder yet for her. Though for a happy reason, it was as if an essential piece of me was missing.

At Corinth, we were finding wild birds with pleasing regularity. Beda and Thane were relishing that. Beda, especially, had made good use of it, chalking up stand after scintillating stand. Every workout, her stamina was building, her pace and style keening. We looked hard toward our first trial. When, just as our warrior maiden sharpened to a razor edge, mishap loomed.

Routinely, we left for the flat grounds the thirtieth of the month, for an hour zinger. I planned to send Beda fast and hard. Probably road her to hold the peak, but not run her again until the Blackstone stake just a short week away. Dawn woke to pastels of pink and yellow, on air freshly chilled and breezy. By eight o'clock, the morning had washed clear blue. Here and there at the skirts of the sky, gray-white in the sun and gnarled and knuckled like arthritic fingers, stood the empty limbs of the maples. Shorn of their flamboyant beauty save a last few blood drops of scarlet, it was left to the more dignified burgundies of the oaks and cured tobacco-gold of the hickories to color the woods lines. About the fallow corners and pockets of the fields, still a week from first frost, ragweed prospered rank and green. It was the sickness of the crops, pale and jaundiced in the rows, the succumbing of the gum leaves, liver-splotched and withering as an old man's hand, that gave melancholy testimony to the last of summer. While November waited in the wings, hours from her curtain call.

Beda took the whistle like a mainsail grabs the wind that fine autumn morning, and fast and far she flew, and when she reached the distant parabola of a cast, and banked for the front, I'd hit her with another shrill blast and on she'd roll. We were running the big fields leading to the chute into the railroad track bottoms, and it was huge, open country that challenged heart and soul. I let her go, kept the mare at a easy shuffle, and watched her lay out and swing along the distant edges as I might a bird on a wing. She was fit and fine, going swift and hard, with no letup. Twenty, thirty, forty-five minutes into the heat, the same, and God was it pretty. Nearing the woodland funnel into the railroad trestle, I began gathering her up.

"*Whaaaup, yooow, Beda, whuup!*"

She knew the march. It's one of the loveliest things in dogdom. Way on out there, she slowed, then glanced over her shoulder for orders just as she reached the crux of edge and funnel. I hooted again, swung the horse sharply starboard, and she shot right . . . into the woods. I stopped for a moment, listening for the train, but all was clear. When Dolly made the path and I could see down the funnel, Beda was clicking merrily out the far end, across the tracks, and into the network of small beanfields and thickets that bordered the creek bottom.

Reaching the tracks, we could ride the railroad trestle for a half mile before the next bold turn of the course. As the gravel and cross ties churned and clopped under the mare's hooves, I searched through the chain of little fields ahead until my eyes burned. No Beda. Two hundred yards more of the same, and my instincts were screaming. We'd ridden her by. I heeled the mare off the tracks, and we caught the field edges, loping back. Five minutes later we found her, just a faint wash of white deep in the shadows of a switchcane head. She was stacked up straight and hard, acknowledging me with only one slight tick of her tail as I piled off, grabbed the gun, and threaded my way in to flush. She had worked those birds almost fifty yards into the thick, briery cover, and pinned them dead tight between bush and water in the cane head. A beautiful piece of work. The covey fumed up out of the dry cover in a sputtering rattle, one cock whipped hard across, and I made good the chance to drop him. Beda watched him fall, hoisted to her tiptoes, and straining against her will, steady but dying to go. I crawled through to her, tapped her on the ear, and gave her leave. She bounced out and back, circling me once, proud of herself.

"Uh-huh," I said.

I asked her for the Bob, and she complied, then shook herself hard and looked at me, "All right, Boss Man, turn me on outta here and let's git on a'ter anuther."

"Good business, Bedja," I said, grabbing and jostling her ruff.

I was loving her, every exciting moment of her. Weaving our way out of the thicket, I whoaed her, climbed on the horse, and fingered the whistle. She was gone before it blew.

Two minutes for the hour, there was not enough time to take the big river bottom swing.

"Yooowwwh, now!" I shot her left, on a shorter errand, to check the partridge pea patch by the garden of a tenant shack. Nobody home, I thought, as I rode through and no Beda.

An hour-ten now. Time to get her up. Seconds later, she crossed the broomsedge corner ahead, and I hailed her up and called her in. I rode to her, trimming the distance to half. She came prancing, and I climbed off the horse, got down on a knee then and waited for her. Realizing my purpose as she neared, she dropped to a reluctant trot.

"Sorry, girl, jig's up."

"Nice round, Beda, nice round."

She grinned at me, and her tail whipped the broomstraw. Then, in the midst of happiness, my veins ran cold. Heavy splotches of crimson defined her tracks in the grass, and there were thick and sticky brownish smears on my chaps where she had reared briefly to place her forepaws on my knee. Glancing with dread, I found the source. The setter's right forepaw was wet and matted. Quickly I picked it up to check, and one of the pads was sliced deeply in half. By broken glass or a sharp tin around the shanty. The fresh blood welled thick and red, overran, and dripped into and out of my hand.

I took her head in my hands and looked into her eyes. She was still smiling, wagging her tail, as if nothing were wrong.

"Oh, Beda." I dropped my forehead to her own, and stopped there for several moments. The tragedy of it was devastating, for in the instant I saw it, I knew she would not make the Blackstone Trial, nor maybe another to come. Pad cuts are forever to heal. And why Beda, so brave as she was, against whom so much had interfered?

"Dammit!" I shook my head, and cursed the luck.

The blood was pouring. I unknotted my bandanna and wrapped it several rounds about her paw. Almost immediately, it was soaked through. Gathering her in my arms and jamming a foot in the stirrup, I reined the mare, laboring us up and over the saddle. It was home and an anxious while later Loretta and I got the bleeding under control.

A pad cut was the lesser of a blue-dozen things, temporarily debilitating, dire, or dread, that could halt the promise or curtail the career of a field trial dog—by one day or all his days. After a while, you hover in apprehension of each and every one of them. So much of greatness is good fortune, and many a gifted dog has been stricken even in its prime by mishap or malady that foiled what seemed the guarantee. The window of opportunity for a dog, at best, is so short; the blow, if it comes, so utterly discomforting and confounding. A field trial dog is a warrior, and a warrior will not quit.

In this, the courage of a great dog knows no bounds. The annals of the game attest to incredible triumphs of desire over adversity, even injury. But all that lives has a limit. All is flesh and bone. A trial dog, at peak condition, is one of the most superb athletes in creation. All the so, as superhuman as he is, he must still be sound to prevail. Fate, against many odds, must allow him that.

In the rank of things, a cut pad would heal, I told myself. But still it robbed us. It was one chance less.

Two weeks and two trials passed with both Pat and Beda on the bench. Thane and I trained on. Mostly we went hunting. He was a whale of a big-going bird dog, but still nitsy after shot. The battle of our wills had taken its toll, and I had given up ever getting him finished with the stand-on-after-the-shot flair it took to win the good trials. It was a tragedy, really; he was such a great dog in most all respects. I accepted the failure as mostly my own, and to this day, it hurts. One, that I wasn't good enough, and two, that he was deprived of the competitive opportunity. But we had a hell of a good time shooting quail, when the only judge was the one in my saddle.

∿ CHAPTER 33 ∿

MEANWHILE, THE COUNTDOWN CONTINUED FROM HERE TO MATER-
nity. By November 1, thirty-six days into the watch, Pat was already showing. Filling out like a ripening melon. Not so long ago a weanling herself,
little Number Six was about to be a mama. We were elated, and the promise
of puppies again became the priority of our lives. Preparations accelerated in
earnest. I put the finishing touches on a new whelping box; hammered
together a new wire puppy-run-on-legs, with a hinged top, that could be
appended to the big, green doghouse that would host the maternity ward.
Loretta laid in the various tinctures, salves, ointments, and accessories
demanded by motherhood, some baby formula just in case, a special set of
soft terry towels. Melanie, a tall and slender lass of thirteen now, acknowledged accountability for the medicine kit: the antiseptics, the cotton and
swabs, the antibiotics, scissors and tweezers, and thread. Hopefully there
would be small need of it, but all would be ready.

By disposition, Pat had changed not at all. On Loretta's orders, I had
been roading her separately, to avoid the stress and strain of the other two
dogs. In all likelihood an unnecessary precaution; still, we would suffer no
chances. The little setter had softened not the least; she fought and scratched
against the harness every step. In her eyes still smoldered an explosive suspense, like powder begging to be ignited. That I was glad for, as I could not
shake a degree of concern that a whelping might mellow her.

We didn't field trial that fall. By November 7, Loretta's birthday, Beda
was back running on four good feet, but the growing excitement of Pat's
pups-to-be consumed the total of our aspirations. Forty-two days now.
There was a swelling sense of family, and togetherness. Little of parting. I
didn't want to drive to Kentucky, or Oklahoma, or Jersey that fall. I wanted

to be home. On Loretta's Day, the bunch of us loaded up and went to Elm Hill, picnicking like earlier times by the old mansion under the trees, high on the hill above the river. There was the same wistful, silver shimmer on the water far below, which ran restlessly along for a time only to effervesce and vanish, like a wish hurrying along to gain its destiny. Behind the one grew another. Gulls milled in white circles about the tailrace of the dam, shrieking shrilly and diving to pluck glimmering minnows from the foaming pool that caught the gurgling water. The sun gentled down from a sapphire sky, and on their stems, the painted leaves twirled and fluttered before a cool and freshening breeze.

After we had eaten, we lounged on the hill, the dogs on the tie-out chain and us on our backs, side by side with a clasp of hands behind our heads, in the cushion of the deep green grass. Loretta had blown loose the wish from the thirty-nine candles on the cake, and now it had joined the others on the river below.

"So what did you wish?" I asked, my eyes closed to the caress of the sun and the wind.

"As always," she said, "safe passage. For us all. Little puppies safely into the world."

"Another like Patty," Melanie added.

God, let it be, I thought.

Loretta stayed with a book, beneath one of the great trees on the hill, while Melanie and I ran Beda and Thane, and roaded Patty. Melanie rode Dolly, and I Maggi. After the dust settled, we handed the gundogs a whirl. Gabe and Ben and Jill. Ecstatic, they were giddyap and gone five minutes before they came in and settled to the hunt. Sunset we saved for Cindy. The horses were given their means with the grass, aisling along and blowing softly, munching four bites to the step. While the three of us mounted a slow, careless walk by the river, the world about us the color of the purple-mauve glow across the western sky, the old girl hobby-horsing along happily to the fore. It was a gentle day.

Forty-seven, forty-eight, forty-nine . . . The days crept by like molasses traveling a cold slab of marble. While anticipation stacked to a fever pitch. Pat grew bigger and bigger. Beda stronger and stronger. Thane stubborn and stubborner. We started bringing Pat into the house more, to offset the boredom away from the field, and to defray the anxiety whenever the rest of us left to train. I suspended her roading program for the duration. Wanted to take no further chances. Her weight had ballooned from a hard-in-the-harness thirty-six to a portly forty-four.

Beda, Thane, and I held the course. Birds were at a comeback at Corinth, one of their better years. The last tolerably good one there. Or most anywhere in Carolina, except a few places still in the coastal plain. Wild quail were coming onto hard times throughout the South. The message was plainly on the wall. The decline in home coveys—the disappearing geniality the few miles down the road, to a neighbor's welcome and four to seven coveys an afternoon—ranks among the most disheartening losses of my life. But that year, things were as old. Nothing like the fifties, nor the middle seventies even, but pleasing. Enough to train a dog. It was like a fire that had died to its ashes, when one last flame flickered, enjoying a trace of fuel and oxygen for a brevity, but doomed to die.

We made the best of it, sensed it was fragile. Both dogs were turning in some good bird work. Beda was Beda again. Running with flair. Leaving smoke in her tracks, chalking up the flawless finds. One, particularly, in the Stay-a-While Thicket, an ornery Satan's Garden of head-high, matted brier, slash, and dense saplings. A bevy was regular there, betwixt a small bean-field and swamp. The dogs pointed them any number of times, especially Pat. Often the only way I'd find them was with the telemetry system. Flushing was hell. I'd come out bloody as a hog killing, rarely moving the birds. They'd hoof it through that mean cover, never fly. I threw rocks, my hat, the gun. Didn't matter. They knew better. So me and the dog-that-done-it would get down and crawl out, and I'd take him fast and on, and guard for the doubling back, so we didn't get back in there again that trip. Once a week was more than enough.

But Beda had them that day, dead-to-daylights, to hell and back in that punishing cover. I actually glimpsed the birds, skulking off single-file through the briers, like a squad of tiny camouflaged soldiers.

Fifty-five, fifty-six . . .

Every time we made home, I'd hurry to the house, to see of Pat's progress. Ask of Loretta, had there been any change?

"What do you expect?" she said.

"I don'no, anything."

"Nope, not even anything."

Disappointed, I'd drop to my knees—Pat-level—comparing with measuring eyes the differing expanse of her beam.

"Except I felt a puppy move," Loretta added, the fifty-seventh day.

"You didn'!"

"Did too."

"That's not fair." I had both hands underside of Pat's bulging abdomen, trying my best to feel something kick.

Pat looked at me strangely. "Gittin' a little fresh, aren't we?" read the note in her eyes.

"I don't believe it," I said, moving my hands slowly back and front.

"Believe what you will," Loretta said, folding another towel.

Women are so damn important when it comes to babies.

I moved the breakfast table aside, anyway, and set up the whelping box in the kitchen. Just in case.

The next day—fifty-eight into the march and one before the holiday—Pat grew finicky, picking at the cooked liver and playing with her dry food. Déjà vu. She waddled between the kitchen and the living room couch like a constipated duck, at the speed of a turtle. It was pitiful in a respect. I know, pregnant is beautiful. Still, I tried to picture her in my mind as she looked kicking dust, about the time she hit the quarter-mile mark, on the bowling-alley breakaway at Amelia.

Thanksgiving morning, November 24, 1983, debuted solemn and wet. It should have been first light, but it wasn't. The night outside the beaded window was not even charcoal gray. On the roof, you could hear the steady patter of the raindrops. Loretta and I lingered in bed, her head on my shoulder, the soft warmth and texture of her hair and naked body paradise against my own. Neither of us had spoken for a time.

"It's close," she said. "I can feel it."

Ahhat-oh.

"Better you check."

Reluctantly, I drew myself away, felt my way downstairs. Pat had spent the night on the dog bed by the whelping box. She had shown some restlessness the night before, so we had denied her the bedroom, excusing the caution. I could hear her tail thumping before I turned on the kitchen light. She labored up off the dog bed, tried to stretch, and wobbled to greet me.

"Hey, girl." I kneeled and stroked her head, and the length of her sides. There was the same trace of restlessness in her eyes, and queerly, a new softness, too. But neither hid the evergreen independence. Suddenly it was all sad again. My mood swings on the Zip Zap–and–puppies issue were something I imagine as menopause.

"I'm all to blame," I told her.

"Well, not *all*," I wanted her to say. "I was hot to trot."

But she didn't.

I stood and took a long, careful look at her. Nothing seemed different than the evening before. Until I looked around the room. Then my heart leaped. The papers in the whelping box were torn to shreds.

Loretta appeared then, rounding the corner in her blue velvet robe, tossing free her long hair with the aid of a hand. She read the excitement in my eyes.

"She's bedding," I said. Her eyes lit.

"I thought maybe."

Retta took her turn on the floor with Pat. Her appraisal was sympathetic. She checked the food bowl. And the clock. Seven o' seven. Pat hadn't eaten.

Nine thirty-seven. Even after I had taken her out to pee, the little setter was anxious. She curled in the whelping box, seeming to know that it was the locus of her dilemma. Shortly afterwards, she was up again, leaving an accident on the kitchen floor. Taken outside once more, she was whining and scratching with the urge to go.

When we returned, Retta had spread aside the maternity kit, and wakened Melanie.

I was feeling queerly. Not at all like I had felt with Cindy. I should have been hold-your-breath happy, and I was, but I wasn't. Suddenly I was scared. What if some bad thing went wrong? Things could. Somehow with Cindy, it hadn't seemed that way. Pat was the dog of my life. And I had exploited her one and only weakness, was putting her through this.

Nine thirty-eight. Pat was frantic, tearing papers in the whelping box. Panting and whining.

"She's going into labor," Loretta pronounced, moving to standby. The apprehension washed over me in a prickly heat. Melanie looked about as pale and petrified as I was. She was sitting on the edge of her stool, both fists clenched against her mouth.

The sweat popped on my brow. It was like Gabriel raising his horn in one wing and Satan poised with his pitchfork in another.

Pat was shivering, whining, and licking herself.

Then, at nine forty-five, Sherman marched into Georgia. Her water broke.

It was like somebody was holding my arms and I couldn't move. Though I wanted, I couldn't do a thing to help it.

Nine fifty-six. Pat was lying now, whining and pushing.

"Contraction," Loretta said.

I think I was having it. I couldn't altogether understand why it was affecting me so.

Nine fifty-eight. Pat was up again, hurting, whining, panting, tearing papers.

Ten eleven. Contractions. Several in a row. Melanie was white as a sheet, Loretta calm as a refrigerated cucumber. There are times I especially admire women.

Ten twelve. A tiny opaque sac appeared. Pat chewed and burst it with her teeth.

Ten twenty. Contraction, then panting.

Ten twenty-three. Another. Pat was shoving.

This was forever. My knuckles were bloodless, where the bend of my fingers clutched the slat of a chair.

Ten thirty. Pat had quietened, was straining, pushing. One little foot emerged.

Ten thirty-eight. Feet. The right number of them. Tiny hips and little female things.

Finally, ten minutes later: *whooosh*. At the end of a fifty-two-minute journey into the world, a complete little girl emerged. There she was, whimpering and spanking new. Firstborn. A comely little lass, though a bit slick and soggy. A classic tricolor, her only body markings, aside from the ticks, the full black mask and the fawn of her cheeks. She was beautiful.

Though still attached to the umbilical cord, and now Pat was truly frantic, whirling and whining, slinging the pup this way and that. Hard against the whelping box, the legs of a chair, the corner of a cabinet. It made you wince with every thud. Loretta was trying without success to calm her. It was chaos. Scary. You never know what to do: let nature make its course or intervene.

The puppy, bumped violently to and fro, was yelling it head off, and Pat was whining and whirling, trying to reach her, and the result was ever worse. Melanie was crying, and even Loretta's face was taut with concern. I was beyond myself, coming to pieces. Scared hot and sick over Pat, wishing I'd never bred her, wishing I could take the whole of it back sixty-one days and do differently.

The puppy thudded against the wall and screamed again.

"She's gonna kill her!" I yelled to Loretta, while I looked on helpless as a man, looking to her to do something.

She did. She ordered me out of the ward.

"Go feed the horses," she demanded.

Gladly. I was hot, weak as sunstroke. Sweating and nauseous. A man's got no place in a birthing barn. No place at all. Not this one.

Then, just as I was leaving, like a wave that spends itself in a foaming rush of surcease, Pat's anxiety subsided and the mother took over. Settling back into the whelping box, she quietly chewed the cord in two. Loretta lifted little Number One, now freed of ordeal, and removed her to the nursery box of warm, fluffy towels over a hot-water bottle. She was yelling nonetheless, for life was rough, she must surely have thought. But the soothing warmth of the towel quieted her, and for the first time in more than an hour, peace prevailed.

I still had to leave. Had to get out into the wet, cold air. I took my hat off and turned my face to the sky, and just stood there for a time, letting the rain beat down. Afterward, things were better. I fed the mares, and no sooner was it done than I wanted to go back again. To the house. To the kitchen. To the unfolding joy of little puppies. I wasn't weak or sick any longer, just impossibly happy.

Life had traveled the circle, all the way from Cindy and Johnny and the little, white shed in the backyard on Chaney Road. Seven years were gone to do it.

Now there was urgency in my step. I hurried to the back door, jerked off my raincoat, and made my way softly into the kitchen. I could hear nothing at first, then the faintest, tiniest whimpering. I looked to Loretta and then Melanie, and both smiled, and Loretta pulled aside the flap of the blue towel that covered the nursery box, and therein were two bitty puppies. Curled together and twitching, like you do when somebody taps your kneecap. One of them was liver-orange and white, like her papa, and the other—I looked closer, turned to Loretta and returned her smile—had a cute little sing. Tricolor also, half-masked, chance would have it he'd be the only male, and we'd have to give him a strong name—like Sir—to put up with all those females.

Loretta held up three fingers. Our firstborn was with Pat in the whelping box, yelling again for a different reason and searching madly for a nipple. Wherever did nature learn so about such things? Reassuring me, Pat looked up and wagged her tail. It beat twice against the box, and suddenly I was so very glad we had gone to Illinois to meet Rocky, and that I was fast becoming a granpaw.

Four through Six arrived easily. Four and Five favored Rocky, and Six, as we held our breath, slid into life speckled heavily black and tan on white, like—well, like a speckled pup. Intently we looked for a rump spot, but Fate had decreed it elsewhere. A cute little affair, she looked like she belonged on an episode of *The Little Rascals,* and the name that would fit her best was Sixer.

It was one thirty. Loretta put me and Melanie on nursing duty, delivered Pat a small bowl of chicken noodle soup, and started Thanksgiving. It had arrived already, twice over, but there was now the matter of celebrating for sure, and all the good food. The yams already steeped in the oven, and the room reeked perfectly with the aroma. Soon there would be the wholesome yeasty mingle of freshly baked oat bread, the peppery-and-butter-basted waft of the roasting turkey, the heady heaven of the ham, the side-meat-and-bacon pungency of the green beans and corn, the sugary spoor of the tomato pudding, and the spicy hallelujah chorus of the punkin pie.

All this and puppies, too. Our platter was full.

A dark cloud of despair soiled it all. Number Seven was stillborn. A perfectly formed little girl, a black patch set jauntily over each eye, she arrived headfirst with not a sign of life. Perhaps she had suffocated in the canal in the course of the extended labor. Perhaps her tiny heart had stopped beating. What had taken back what almost she had been given? I worked desperately for an hour, clearing her nostrils, trying to breathe for

her, rubbing and massaging her chest, shaking her. Praying. Doing everything I could to beg for her life.

Until Loretta lay her hand on my shoulder, and said, "It's not to be."

No life is more tragic than the life that can never be. All that might have
been, all of joy it could bring, buried before ever it lived. Not even the
euphoria of the seven that would survive, to love and be loved, to jump and
play and run and hunt like the wind . . . not the homespun completion of the
holiday, not the many blessings it gave occasion to tally . . . nothing could
remove the pall of sadness that descended as drearily as the gray, rainy day.

Eight and last was marked a daddy's girl. We'd have to send word to
Loyd and Rocky. She came along two hours later—a buoyant, little
thing—in the bleakest hour of the day, just after night had fallen. When we
thought all was said, all was done. She was proof that faith must float, that
trust can brighten the darkest of nights. We called her Hope.

Now that it seemed all were assembled, we dug out our list of names
and christened those for whom it had not happened spontaneously. When
we finished, in order of birth, there were Meg, Flare, Sir, Tina, Frecks, Sixer,
and Hope. Duly, we recorded them in the Kennel Log, the equivalent of the
family Bible. Number Seven we would not be allowed to keep, and on the
morrow I must dig a tiny grave, for all time, alongside those of Bess and
Mutt. There would be three now. Today, too many years beyond that dismal
task, there are nineteen.

Gathered around Pat's small family, we saw Thanksgiving through to its
midnight that year. Emotion wafted joy to sorrow and back again. Of all
the blessings we counted, mostly we were glad for each other.

When finally we retired, I couldn't sleep. I was dead tired and emotion-
drained, but my mind churned on. The tragedy of Number Seven would
not be shaken, and I wondered to the quick if *that* was the puppy, the *one*
destined to be the make of her mama. Then I would think of the remaining
seven, and if I lay completely still, didn't even rustle the covers, and held my
breath for a few moments, I could hear Pat stirring, and the tiniest whimpering from the kitchen below. Could know that much was warm and
right. At last, as Seth Thomas sounded three, I turned the blanket aside,
slipped out of bed, and made my way downstairs.

The storm had passed and the sky had cleared, and the silver wash of a
harvest moon spilled through the French doors and bathed the whelping

box, mama and puppies, in moonlight. There was a Michelangelesque quality about the little scene, an inspirational ambience of Madonna and child. I
left the room otherwise in darkness and pulled a chair close. Pat was
stretched peacefully on her side, a puppy suckling at every spigot, except
that a couple had gone to sleep at the watch, dozing and twitching but still
adamantly anchored to the table. All were happy, all was well. It was obvious that Pat had adopted mothering as wholeheartedly as anything else she
took a mind to, the terrifying ordeal inflicted on Meg, the firstborn,
notwithstanding. She rolled her eyes to me and thumped her tail, but made
no further effort to move.

"*Good* girl, Pat. They're beautiful. Tell me which one will be you."

Her tail thumped again.

I studied at length every puppy. On each tiny shoulder was borne the
family honor, and no doubt each would bear it with pride. The quest of the
past seven years had been the most thrilling of my life, I was as smitten as
ever with it, and now here was Promise, born anew. Pat had given me that,
as so much of the rest.

Every day, December to New Year's, brought little revelations of joy. By
December 6, misty blue eyes blinking open. Four seventeen after midnight,
eve of the twentieth, the ungodliest wailing. Eerie . . . shivering . . . like a
lament from a sunken grave. Sixer, escaped from the whelping box, deciding as quickly she wanted back in, and complaining to the warden from the
kitchen floor. Sprung again twice, before dawn. Turns out, there was an
accomplice. Hope was boosting her along.

"Pupper breaf." Scrap and scamper. Dreadful little barks and growls.
Even after we moved them to the kennel, to the puppy run, in the taut stillness of the night we could hear the fury of their battles. *Miz* and might,
Meg dominated all—on the premise, I suppose, from the pounding she took
getting into the world, that life was tough so you had to be tougher. Sir
stood the only one to buck her, that or be henpecked six-over. On for seven
wonderful weeks it reigned: Puppy Stuff. Catch Mama's Tail, Sneak Up 'n'
Nip Brov'er in the Ass, Run-and-Go-Pounce, Tag and Seek, You're It, Back
Up 'n' Spin, Pop-Went-the-Weasel, Pinned Ja', and Bite-Your-Little-Sing.
Play like the devil. Nap like an angel.

Tell me, please, that once they happened, those tiny pawprints in the
sand. Time has washed so many of them away. Too soon, the little spirits that

left them were weaned, off to leave larger ones on their own, and there are days when my mind is a desert, and those too are gone. Days I marvel, could it all have been real? Then, you could touch it. Each small life was true.

There were minutes lapsed to hours when Loretta, Melanie, and I lay in the grass, serving as cordilleras of conquest, upon which their tiny adventures were cast. Minutes, then hours, we just watched them gambol and grow. Minutes turned hours when we wanted to scotch the wheels of time. Knowing as they grew closer to us, some were also growing away. Weaning would bring the familiar agony: a bittersweet fusion of anticipation and ashes. I looked greatly forward to having Pat on her own again, to see her flying once more across the fields. How wonderful it would be, bringing on the puppies. But parting with one of those tiny lives was like ripping another chunk from your heart, and wondering could it go on beating.

Ironically, Sixer left first. To live with our dear and longtime friends Sam and Nida Giddens. It was hard to leave go Number Six. We wouldn't have, to anyone else. Sixer was not only the Number Six puppy, but, more, the sleeper in the litter. We were more uncertain than with Pat at seven weeks as to what she would be, and were they to have a pup, it was the wish of Sam and Nida that they start from a weanling. In field trial promise, I tottered at that stage between Meg, Tina, Sixer, and Hope.

"We probably shouldn't let her go," Loretta said of Sixer.

I bit my lip, and purely from the field-trialing vantage, thought nervously the same.

"If the odds were never we would see her again, I couldn't."

In the end, we let her go. We probably shouldn't have, but we did.

Through the back window, I can tell you that true to karma, she proved of tremendous nose, exceptional charisma, and obvious ambition. One of the two best, maybe *the* best, dog of the litter. She was never seriously horseback trialed, but adorned with "Pat," the name of her mama, she honored it superbly as a gun dog for long and happy years.

Tina went to Ed Emerson, setter man and field-trialing friend from northern Virginia, about the same time. I loved Tina. Tina was my sweetheart. She was a sweet and pretty miss, an exquisite blend of flash and fancy. Kinda like the highlights that flare and shoot like sparks through a glass of port when you raise it to the sun. Pretty is as pretty does. You could see the tinder of it already, in her frolic. Even at her delicate age, it was there, as well, about her poise on a bird. But we wanted her to have every chance and felt that Ed would provide it. He did, though Tina was later sold as a gun dog. Who knows would Fate have wrought differently had we kept her.

To Gene Hogge, some months later, we entrusted Hope. She was the most difficult decision of the three. First, because of her birth order in the litter, triumph after tragedy. Two, she was an alluring pup, with a merry carriage, an eye-catching gait, and the dash to go with it. A goodly amount of bird sense, an endearing personality, the desire to run; all were reasons to keep her. But, mainly it was heart-wrenching because she adored Loretta, and Loretta cherished her. The rapport between them was rare—even for puppies, who love everybody—from birth. To Hope, Loretta's lap was the door stoop to heaven, and she ascended there, by any means, with every opportunity. So vaunted, the two of them would converse at length, eye-to-eye, no word spoken, fathoming as lovers the wellsprings of their affections. If there was a stick to be retrieved, it was returned to Loretta; a bug to be pounced, only should Retta be close to watch; birds to be chased, then most boldly at the bidding of her mistress. The love between them deepened with every day.

Loretta cried for a week after Hope left. When memory resurrects their parting, she cries still.

"I wish we had kept her," she said to me, only this morning.

I held her, looked into her eyes, at the gray in her hair.

"I wish that, too," I said.

Love so pure should never be parted. Why I allowed it to happen, I ask myself, and find no acceptable answer.

No disrespect to Gene. Gene was, and is, another respected field-trialing friend from Virginia. He only interceded upon our beckon. Like Ed, he would give her the chance we desired. But it could not happen today. We are incapable of doing it again.

Meg and Hope topped our short list as the promise of Pat, but from the hour they were born, Meg worked to make every modicum of life for her youngest sister a living horror. Domineering beyond exception over all her siblings, most especially she demanded subordination and terror from Hope. Merciless and relentless, she exacted her spite; we tried, water hose and hand, to stem it. But there was little we could do short of separating them to diminish the torment. Hope was a gentle soul; Meg was hell-up-the-hedgerow. The more we attempted to intervene, the deeper Meg's disgust. So vehement and vindictive was her hate, there was enough to last a lifetime.

Loretta gave up Hope so she would have the chance at wings of her own. It was Loretta's decision. She did it of love. Gave up hope and kept the pain.

Hope was campaigned for a time on the Virginia circuit. She died at nine, of a uterine infection.

On Meg, Little Miss High and Mighty, we hung our dreams.

I tore myself away for seven days, at the honor of a judging invitation. Tommy Mock was Stake Chairman for the Region 16 Shooting Dog Championship that season, which drew sixty-seven dogs, over Blue Springs Plantation near Albany, Georgia. So I went down to share the judicial duties with Bud Stone from Missouri. I loathed to leave the dogs and the pups, but what a privilege, the wild-bird fest. Blue Springs was, and is yet, legendary for quail count, and that year was nothing short of astonishing. It was one of those halcyon occasions when riding to cover one find, you'd see another huge bevy lift wild from deep in the hollow, and another from the far hill. Just sit there numbed by the awe of it. Over the course of six hours and twelve dogs the first day, we moved fifty-nine coveys; thirty-four for the first three braces! Every bird hunter and field trialer should have the freedom of seeing that once in his life. Even in those days of accelerating depletion in wild-bird numbers across most of the Eastern Seaboard, there they existed in riches. Thank God for those few bastions where foresight, fortitude, and fortification allowed it still to happen.

When the feathers settled, we named Hook's Bounty Hunter Champion, and Giveaway Penny Runner-Up. Bounty Hunter would go on to additional renown, not so noticeably by win record, but as a landmark pointer sire.

Occasionally I would hear, in years after the Region 16 title, a despairing remark about his performance record, to the effect that that was the only thing big he ever won. As if there were doubt he could have won that one.

Well, first, it was maybe the only championship, but not the only good trial he ever won, and even had it been, Mister, he won that day at Blue Springs as convincingly as a dog could. He was fleet, fine, and fancy, and he laced those plantings and piney woods with driving casts that banged the corners and rimmed the fields. Every move he made said, "Give me your attention, *right here.*" When he said he had birds, there were no bones about it, and they blew up where he told you they would. No dog wins a championship as a fluke. The competition is too keen. All said, he was a good dog that was sought for his prepotency by some of the best breeders in the land.

Region 16 and Blue Springs and that plethora of wild quail pumped me tipsy as a mockingbird on pokeberries. Home couldn't come fast enough; I was burning to get the dogs back in the field, to see the pups, and to get to a field trial. Rain, sleet, snow, or shine, gun dogs, puppies, or trial contenders, my training log says I didn't miss a day for the next three months. It is said all things diminish with familiarity. Not then. Not for a long time more.

~ CHAPTER 34 ~

IF EVER THERE WAS HESITATION THAT ZIP ZAP WOULD SURPASS maternity sans zeal or blemished, it was obliterated by the afterdraft of her momentum. Back in the harness the day after the pups were weaned, and four pounds over fighting weight, she hit the leather with a resolve that would buckle a Missouri mule. Even Thane could not anchor his side of the threesome, drug to and fro at his least sister's will, with poor Beda struggling in the yaw between them. Pat setting the pace, it was tough training. Grueling. Never had I seen her fight it so. Three sessions and five days later, all were hardening, and Mama was knotting again with muscle and two pounds lighter. One week to the day after she shouldered the harness, I propped her up at the opening of the peach orchard course at Corinth, swung over the mare, and hit the whistle—blowing her free for the first time since spring.

It was like slapping a rifle primer with a roofing hammer. You could almost feel the gust of her departure as she broke, and thick, wet splotches of mud hit my face from the power of her exodus. Five minutes later, I saw her pop for the first time two hundred yards to the front. Oh, God. Zip Zap was back. I've never walked on water, but I've soared among the clouds. There was the old, crisp, happy bounce, which needed only the polishing of a few more workouts to sparkle as demonstrably as ever it had; there was the hell-and-haul-horse devilry of her desire; and there was the bring-on-the-world courage—so much I loved her for.

"*Yaaaapppph! Yoooo!*"

She swung the far corner at my song, like the last kid on a whiplash chain. Tearing to the front and through the woods, she slammed into point at the make of the ragweed head that capped the hill and bordered the orchard. It was a known covey location; she was there waiting for me, standing like a dreaming-chair wish.

"Got cha, Pat."

Swinging off the horse, I thrashed out the cover, but no wings. Pat had loosened, was ticking lightly, asking on. I tapped her on the ear, and she shot twenty yards head-high into the breeze, then cut a tight couple of figure eights and stiffened, swelling from a crouch to full height. The running birds started staggering up from the slope ahead, one wad, then another, blustering through the dry blackjack leaves like a horse blows suddenly through his nose, followed by a stutter of stragglers. At the shot, Pat was one notion short of going, but didn't. She could still mark the birds, a fleet and consolidated trace of gray now against the lighter gray stand of the trees, banking, lifting, then dropping abruptly into the tawny obscurity of the hollow at the base of the hill. I waited until they had settled, then walked to Pat and tapped her, "Go," and led her out of the cover.

"My sakes, little lady. You *do* know how to stage a comeback," I told her. I was on my knees, and the setter danced back and reared to my arms. She was happy as an urchin in an ice-cream line.

Released, she shook herself hard, then begged on to the habit of the course.

Three minutes more I sent her, for a total of twenty, just enough for a zinging finish, then persuaded her in. She wanted more, but no use yet, the excess of it.

Beda, too, went a sharp, fast twenty, posting a nice woodcock find just before time. She had added a pound or so herself in the recent hiatus. But she hadn't shown it.

"Pretty tight, Chubby," I told her.

Three days later, I sent them both for thirty, three days after that for forty-five. By early February, they were turning a good, exciting hour. Alternating for diversity between Corinth and Elm Hill, every time out they were gobbling up a swatch more ground in the same expenditure of time. Once, then, I sent them together, which only a few times I ever did. One dog of that caliber is most all you can manage. But it would jack them tight if really I wanted to. Usually they'd lock up, go too big, run ragged on the handling response. That day they split the difference, Pat bullish and stronger on the ground, Beda the kindlier and one-up on bird finds. Steadily we closed on a conditioning peak, with solid and stylish bird work. Soon, now, there would be need of a trial.

By the Ides of March, both dogs were hard and svelte again. We were wearing the old confidence. Pat was as good, probably the better, than ever she was. The same unconquerable powerhouse on the ground, savoir faire on her birds. Beda was true-blue, fashion and flare, consistent as a Rolex. Tidewater would be the icebreaker. Trials were the test. They might be perfect in practice, but the minute they toed that first breakaway, look out. After so persistent an interruption, it would be like jostling nitro.

True to the trust, from the instant we made the familiar turn into the Amelia Management Area and the gravel crunched under the tires, they knew they were at a field trial. Both exploded out of the dog box, each almost pushing by me.

"Hey, now!"

Managing to collar them on the grab, I clipped them to the stake-out chain, and their eyes burned like hot cinders. Beda took the shivers and shakes so fiercely her teeth rattled, and even Pat, normally way cool until travel time, was on her feet, barking and tail-popping.

"Oh, God," I observed, "there'll be hell weathering this one."

I was righter than I knew. What followed was a catastrophe of calamities.

Bill Blankenship was helping me. Beda almost took him off his feet at the line; once he recovered, gathering and propping her up, she resumed the tooth chattering. She left hard enough at the whistle to set a grass fire. The dust was flying, then I got caught up in the excitement and threw in a Lewis Clements squawl. Billy scowled at me like I's one shake short of popcorn, and Beda left the country. Topping the far hill going into the bowling alley, about as far as you could see before the land fell away, she had left her competition in the valley, and was on and going away. I swung the mare to avoid a woodchuck hole; the next moment I looked, Beda was skidding into point at the brink, and when she hauled up, you could see just the top third of her flag ramrod stiff above the drop of the hill.

High as my dog, I nudged the mare in the ribs, asking her SOS to go cover the find. After the first fifty yards, I remembered I was supposed to be somebody now, not some "Willie off the pickle boat," as Ruark was wont to say, and pulled her back into an easy canter. To let the judge, Billy, and the gallery catch up. Into the valley, we lost sight of the standing setter, and

310 _____ ZIP ZAP

it was only when we topped the next crest that all could see she waited as proper as Peggy, like she was set in concrete. I relaxed a bit about then, pulling the mare back into a flat walk, exuding confidence and to allow everybody, particularly the judge, the full advantage of my dog. Little was I to know, but this allowed the pointer in the mix time to catch up, too. So that, in the few seconds we all arrived, he finally pulled ahead and was delighted at the sight of Beda as well. So much that he thundered in past her and blew the bird away.

"*WHOA!*" His handler bellowed like he's trying to stop a plow mule berserk up a corn row. Then twice more.

Figuring she was entitled to a piece of the parade, Beda stuttered two steps, and I had to holler "*Whoa!*" too. When I got off, got up there in front of her and shot, she decided she deserved another step. Leading her out, I had to look at Billy, and he was back there grinning and shaking his head. I tried to help it, but I grinned, too. It just hurt more and didn't show. Billy led our warrior maiden forty yards down the course, I tapped her with the whistle again, and a minute down the road she accomplished an "accidental" flush. Slamming brakes innocently to mark flight, she looked around, appraising the damage as if she were an insurance adjuster. It was an Academy performance. Problem was, the wind was in her nose.

Nothing to do but I lifted a thumb to tell the judge I'd pick her up. When I got her collared and in the harness, Billy was laughing again.

"You're 'posed to be helpin'," I muttered.

A few yards back, on the ride in to the clubhouse, he got this one more shit-eating grin on his face and pointed to the tree where he'd tacked up the sign back in our first shooting-dog year: "Gaddis' Folly." And busted out laughing, the clabbered old fart.

Beda was fast. Pat was like a Tomcat off a carrier deck. A scintillating race and four fashionable finds later, she had set the standard for the stake, enjoying upon the fourth stand the same bracemate assistance as Beda had, but *staying*. We were in the driver's seat, trying to keep the last twenty seconds between the shoulders, when she hauled up when I wish she hadn't, posing picture-pretty for the fifth time. On my way to her, four birds lifted on their own dollar. I knew it was going to happen . . . you just know . . . Pat swelled . . . one, one-thousand, two, one-thousand, three, one-thousand . . . then chased like a puppy to collect the change.

Blankenship's dog broke over at Blackstone about two weeks later, hauled a covey into a foreign county. I sure was glad.

At Central Virginia, the dogs were still wound too tight for a smaller trial. Pat, not three minutes down, rooted out a bird and tried her best to collect tailfeathers. Didn't even try to point. I couldn't believe it. Yanking her up, I set her back and reminded her she was supposed to stay.

"I thought we passed puberty seven years ago," I said. She looked at me cockeyed, a jowl over one tooth. "You don't say . . . ," she allowed, clearly all I'd ever get out of her on the matter.

Then Beda went big and beautiful, laying down a heart-banging ground, a nice divided find off the first bend, a back that could have played on Broadway—the only time her running partner was ahead the whole heat—and a stay-and-stylish flush through shot on a second, all-her-own stand. The whole shebang was promising as a stock option before one last bird got up and flew square back into her face. Her front feet bounced and settled, that was the all, and she caught it—*thunk*—in her mouth, like a shortstop. Oh, it was intriguing . . . also disqualifying.

Sister, sister.

For the final rite of spring, Mike Winchester had a winning, snow white setter out of Belle-the-Devil named Dance Fever, Dee for short, and we teamed for the Region 2 Championship at Smyrna, Delaware. It went poorly for all of us, not the least that we were drawn late in the stake and had to wait several days before we ran, nor that it rained like "well, hell, it could be Kentucky" the day we ran, or that we couldn't buy grits gone-or-found, but most especially the Baltimore Turnpike up and back. It was six lanes, I think—hell, maybe eight—north or south, and the whole time we were on it, the gale warnings were up. Cars and semis were roaring by close enough to spit on, side, front, or rear, horns were blaring, buildings towered every side, and there wasn't a rest stop, shoulder, or blade of grass in sight for seventy miles. Plus you had to drop a quarter every ten miles, the price of enjoying it all.

I passed every foot of it my hands glued to the wheel, my mind split between "Where on God's earth would we put two gray-coats, a truck and a trailer, two horses and three dogs if we have a breakdown?" and "Please, Lord, get this Southern child back to hog jowls and hoecakes, and on Marse Robert's grave, he'll never venture north of Virginia again."

God, I wish we'd won the War.

To dismiss the whole issue, Pat ran in the driving rain on Sunday, last day, last brace. Puddles stood in the fields the size of small ponds. Mud sucked at each lick of a hoof. You couldn't see a hundred yards for the fog and gloom in any of four directions, and chilled and soaked, the liberated quail were flightless and dying by the dozens. We had Pat at ten, looking good in spite of all, but she was too much for the conditions. Fading to the front, she went a-glimmering at twelve. Two hours it took to find her, and in the short-of-breath between, I wished we'd never come.

Beda, in similar conditions, beat herself, it must be said. On wet, fickle birds that couldn't lift to wing, but ran around on the ground in powerless temptation. Breaking over, she took two disparaging steps while I chased ridiculously around for a persnickety judge trying to get something to fly.

Mike and Dee fared better weather-wise, and the white setter had an admirable trip, finding twice. Though not enough, quite, to broach the stake.

When we left, it was still raining, and the sun didn't cleave the clouds until we were a hundred miles from home. I've never been happier to see the Carolina line.

"Turning these dogs loose at a trial right now is like shootin' that damascus gun in the corner," I told Loretta two nights later. "I'm about scared to pull the trigger. Those six months off didn't help."

"Pat might argue with you about the 'off,'" she countered. There were three puppies about the floor dividing a blanket. Two more, across her lap, were sectioning a sock.

"Well, whatever, they're jacked tighter than a Daisy pump gun."

"Thought you liked 'em that way," she said.

"Well, I do, but they've gotten plumb sneaky about it. Beda, that is. Pat's just Pat, up sky-high."

"She won't take those two steps in a workout," I fumed, after a pause.

"Who?" Retta said innocently.

"Beda," I said. "You *know* who. *Your* dog."

"Not 'Ja-Bwee,'" she defended.

"Letter perfect for two months. Take her to a trial, and she wants to do the Texas two-step."

"Too big for her britches," I declared.

Loretta was grinning. Finally, I smiled back.

"Ain't so damn funny when you're on Broadway," I said.

"Oh, I don't know," she said. "I think it's pretty groovy. What, they'll be eight next month? Kinda like turnin' sixty and hang-glidin' the Matterhorn."

I had to admit it warranted humor.

I heard the muted rattle of a key in a lock, the quiet double-swish of wood against a jam. Soft footsteps across the kitchen floor. Melanie, coming fourteen, out on a school night with a girlfriend and sneaking in the back door.

"You're gittin' too big for yours, too!" I hollered through the house.

There was a titter, then a "Hey" at about the volume of a titmouse. Seconds later, she had gained the sanctuary of her bedroom.

"We need to put a tracking collar on that girl."

A week and a workout later, off the line at the Virginia Capital trial, Pat was Zip Zap—the consummate eruption of presumption and panache. Reaching the same precarious boil, this time she kept the lid on the pot. I had seen it now many times before. It was almost as if she made the conscious decision to win. Barring onerous breaks of Fate, it seemed almost that simple. When she decided to win, she would.

In a stellar stake, she slammed the door on the competition so hard, the backdraft blew the pictures off the wall. Three decorative finds and a big, perfectly patterned ground. It wasn't just exciting; it was electrifying. It was the epitome of the trialing aura, the attraction of a great dog at the height of its ability. I, the judges, the gallery—it was like we were caught up in a magnetic field, an assortment of particles captured and aligned to the will of its spell.

Still, again, after the hundreds of times now I had seen her perform—in training or in trials—she gave me pause for awe. I didn't want to pick her up. I wanted to run her on. On and on. Never to quit. I try now to see her in my mind's eye, the way it was. I can't. Not quite. Not really.

So deeply that hurts.

In the afteryears, Billy Blankenship—with all his face-to-face honesty—would say: "Gaddis's dogs could take themselves out of a stake about as fast as he could put 'em in, but when they had the ends together, the storm's comin', git the cow in the barn."

I've always taken that as a compliment. 'Cause that's the way I wanted them.

Not that it was always comfortable. Beda, at that same Virginia Capital trial, exercised the option. After a blistering breakaway that propelled her wide and handsome, she swelled up on a first find before the initial five minutes had expired. She had those birds some ways back. The wind was stiffly into her face, teasing the feathers on her ears and rippling the plume of her tail; standing in a spot of brilliant sunlight and otherwise surrounded by shadow, she was leaning angularly into the blow. Altogether, it was a rousing sight.

Striding confidently in, I put three quail to wing, fired the shot, and the warrior maiden did her regular-lately fancy version of the two-step. That quickly, we'd spent our entry fee.

One thing she hadn't counted on: Trialing Code of Gentility or not, there comes a time; I had an option of my own. Picking her up off her feet, I shook her hard and set her back, right there in front of God and Judge Norm Basilone. Then I walked back out in front of her, ask her what part of "Whoa" she didn't understand, and shot again. This time she stayed.

The incredulous look on her face said it all: "I *never* thought he'd do that *here.*"

After that, she believed again, and the problem resolved itself. The following Sunday at Blackstone, she carded three immaculate finds and wowed the stake. Bringing to mind another of the oldest and wisest adages in dog training: It's never the severity of the discipline, but the timing of it.

On the wings of strong respective wins, we traveled the Shenandoah up to Culpeper the end of April, for the Rappahannock Trial. The air was mountain fresh and the hillsides were mint green with newborn leaves, and our spirits were as clean as the sunshine spilling down from the laundered blue sky. The last trial of the '83–'84 season, we thought to make the best of it. Pat and Beda were cresting a peak, and we decided to run both the amateur and open shooting-dog stakes. The dogs were saying, "Do it," and though, in truth, the better of the amateur events were competitive as the money proceedings, once and again I relished going horn-to-horn against the pros.

Zip Zap could have won any contest in the country that day. She took those rolling, northern Virginia hillsides to the extreme, gliding the far caps of the ridges like the sparkle of the sun that dances across moving water. With that and three hair-raising, dug-up finds in each dispute—the first in the Open Stake standing about as far ahead as you could see, across the ribbon of a roiling stream, sky-high and higher, the closer we got—she clinched both stakes, as charismatically as Reagan carried America at the time. It was a high, hallowed day. I pitched off the mare at the end of the course, the second round down, my heart pounding with the force of her finish, dropping to my knees in the lush, green grass as she started back to my hail. My senses were so full I was trembling, and vision blurred as the tears grew, from the thrill of her. My Lord . . . how many times had she given me that? Straight in, she reared to my chest, and there was the joy of life truly lived in her eyes. The kind you hope for, at least once, before you die.

Though Beda, for reasons unknown, ran beneath herself that day—did not gain a place—that nor else could mar the occasion. For weeks, it sustained a luster, like the sheen of moonlight on fine silk.

~ CHAPTER 35 ~

THANE, PAT, BEDA, JILL, BEN . . . EIGHT GOING ON NINE NOW. ANOTHER birthday past in lives far too short. At the end of May, to underscore that, their sire, Johnny—Johnny Crockett's John—died. At fifteen years. He was in our kennel at the time. Side by side with Cindy. We ran their grandpups on the twelfth, and Meg, emerging swiftly now, found and pointed a quail. Johnny died the next day. When someone has given you something so very special, you wish, never more than in the vacuum of their passing, you had been able to give some extraordinary thing in return. Words of thanks over a grave are never enough. Maybe the quail Meg pointed was.

The thing most to mind was that the first piece of a hallowed era had fallen away, and after we had buried Johnny, I went back to the kennel and sat with Cindy for over an hour. Stroking her softly, considering the gray on her muzzle, and the pensiveness that had grown in her eyes. We were still hunting, she and I; for a season more, I hoped. But deep inside, certainty shuddered, with the inevitable awareness that too soon, other pieces would be lost as well.

"Time's to the hourglass," I told Loretta that evening. "I think with Pat and Beda, we've been to the last of the smaller trials. Even the best of them. From here, we'll go only to the big ones."

"You've been selective for a long time," she said.

"Yes," I said. "With what's left, all the more."

"They're still strong?" she asked, concern in her eyes.

"Yes."

She was thoughtful for a minute.

"But not you?"

"Yes," I replied, my gaze dropping.

I looked up again. The question was yet on her face.

"So long as my dogs," I said.

Another long, smoldering summer lay ahead, till we could go to *any* trial again. We reinstituted a roading program, thinking it important to continue to work on the mass and suppleness of aging muscles. Honestly, I could perceive no weakness. Both dogs sustained the peak of their prime. Pat was the explosive juggernaut she always was, Beda still chiseled and hard. Their desire was unflagging, their endurance tenacious. They were as fit as ever they were. It was just Johnny's death, and the message it bore. That served to make me cautious.

In the meager cool of the mornings, we would run the pups. Six months old now, Meg and Flare continued the battle for top honors, challenging each other with wind sprints. The dust would fly. Frecks and Sir, not so competitive, hunted birds and butterflies. Took the time to smell the roses. All were teenage crazy, giddy with joy. So were we, when we were with them.

During June, I finished the sill and sleeper grid on our log cabin, laying up the initial two wall logs. For the first time, after all the scratch work, dragging up and skinning the logs, the result encouraged a house. Stripping to my underwear to advantage the sweat, I toiled with the broad ax through the baking, sticky days, hewing square the rest of the logs. Through July and August, the structure grew, until it became time to raise a gin pole—a mule days' tripod-and-pulley arrangement of pine poles—by which the last of the heavy logs could be hoisted and eased to place at the height of the walls. Loretta womaned the Fergy, which supplied the lifting power, while Melanie chanted the cant of the logs, and I sat astraddle the wall, waiting to maneuver them into place. With much hollering between us, each was guided into the dovetailed marriage at the corners that bound them into the walls.

At long last, September loomed more than a wish, and our first free-to-fly workout was at Corinth on the sixteenth. So good it was to be afield again. I gave Pat and Beda fifteen minutes, watching as they slugged it out with the intense heat and humidity. Each reached fast and wide, withered no more than slightly, and were hard put to quit. When Dolly rounded them up, tongues were lolling, and they were hassling heavily, but the happiness flapped about their eyes like sheets in a March wind. Both pointed once, at the spoor of quail, though I could never flush the birds from the dense milo, lush soybeans, and high green grass. I wrote either dog a credit for the benefit of the doubt.

After we ran the big dogs, we loosed the puppies the first time in front of the horse. There were three distinguished judges, and the log entry from that excursion attests each pup was ranked on a four-point scale against eleven performance factors: pace, range, animation, intelligence, heart, self-confidence, desire, tractability, tail carriage, heat tolerance, and stamina. Meg carried the colors, nudged by Flare, the difference in sustained pace and drive. Course, Flare was stopped by a butterfly for two full minutes, staunch but ultimately not steady. Flare, that is. Frecks, lovable, little freckled-faced kid she was, had a generally good time, not troubling herself about it. Sir fired in spurts, always one careful eye on the mare. When the grasshoppers settled, not a lot had changed, but all was a ripping good time.

"Mine's," Melanie said, grinning, when she gathered up Meg and loaded her into the trailer.

Year to year, it seemed, the meteorological records kept falling. October proved brutal, scorching and dry, one of the most oppressive in Carolina history. Little matter, it appeared. By midmonth, Pat and Beda were pointing birds, going great guns for forty-five minutes, and wanting more. Though I had watched and thrilled to her through many seasons, Pat was inspired to run and reach as rarely I had seen her; it seemed that the premise of all her years sought to prove itself as never before: in the power and poetry of her going, the savvy of her quest, and the consuming expressiveness when she found and stood. But it was a miserable bunch of mischief. The days burned on, baked in Hell's Kitchen, singed and blackened by the heat. The ground cooked to a fine, powdered dust, billowing in abrasive clouds from the horse's hooves to climb into your nose and throat. Heat devils rejoiced over the withering cropfields, and the river was throttled and wasted to a few smothering, green pools where even the rough fish suffocated. As surely, the birds dried up as well. It was the beginning of the end for good times with wild quail at Corinth. For the rest of that year and those to follow, we would struggle to get enough done for the bigger trials. I worried about the younger dogs coming on. Times there, or elsewhere, would never approach the halcyon days we had known.

Beda began to endure unproductives, in a manner never she had before. It was desire brought to frustration. So badly she wanted and needed a find that she would point in places she had found many times before, but the birds would not be there. Maybe they had been; I could never be sure. I think she was trying too hard. The telling degree of uncertainty in her stance and the indecision of her tail would beg the question. The torture of the heat was dragging at her, too. Her pace and range were flagging. She would go until she dropped; of course, I never let her. It was here, against the teeth of such adversity, that Pat pressed on, in staggering displays of steel and stamina. Pushing herself on and on, refusing to relent, hunting . . . hunting, and finally finding. Reluctant to even pause a moment, between the rows, for a drink of water.

Once she had gone an hour-twenty—without a find—and still she battled on. I found her at an hour-thirty, tacked proudly to the wily old bevy in the Stay-a-While Thicket. She caught them before they hoofed it to the creek. It must have been a hundred degrees. So hot the mosquitoes sought the white bellies of the leaves. But so sweet the triumph. Those birds got pinned, by God, and I fired a 20-gauge salute at their tailfeathers, the once if never before.

On to its death gasp, October suffered and parched in the throes of ninety-degree days that lodged near the century mark. Autumn was an enigma, a fantasy of false promise, something told but not to behold. Hell sweltered on. The ogres of summer cackled and stoked the furnaces, and life shriveled to subsistence. Never, before or since, has there been its equal. The month we looked forward to most was a disappointment. A betrayal that always before we could trust. The Canadian fronts that brought the renewal of the chill breezes were turned back before the resistance of the Bermuda highs. Frost never painted the leaves. They yellowed and browned and failed to fall, clinging and curling about the stems like a desiccated corpse drawn to a fetal position before it expired. October died in its infancy, as a beautiful young girl with rosy cheeks that never got to live. Affected by dread disease, her color bled to a death pallor, and she lapsed a cruel shell of her normality, scarcely recognizable. It was a dreadful thing to those who knew and loved her as she was. A matter of relief and regret when mercifully she passed.

In the marginal comfort of first light, we worked the puppies on liberated birds. All were scent-pointing now, holding for several seconds until I approached, then taking wings for a ride and bouncing like a gazelle at shot. Meg and Flare were still the sharpest overall. Frecks was going to be a bird dog. Sir was yet deciding.

I looked for the trial potential in Meg and Flare. The same I saw in their mother at their age. They were snappy, pretty, not running much yet, letting off a bit when they got hot. Pat would have died first. They were young, though. We'd leave the jury in the box.

On through November and the first half of December—with a few days off to judge the Eastern Open at Elm Hill—we slugged on, working toward the National Amateur Shooting Dog Championship, to start at Belmont two days after Christmas. We pulled off Corinth, switching to other grounds, trying to find running room and a few wild birds. In the absence of the quail, the dogs were forced to dig in, encountering woodcock in what was left of the swampy bottoms. Woodcock are lovely to hunt, but flit and flop; they can undo the polish on a field trial dog like a floozy in a fraternity closet.

Hot it remained, too, and sticky, on and on. Indian summer was given to a trail of tears. Despite all, Zip Zap was the strongest, surest, prettiest ever she'd been. Coming nine, she was still ascending, coming to an all-time pinnacle. Beda, also, looked very, very good. She had trouble with the heat, but was turning an imposing hour-fifteen, posting two or three sparkling woodcock finds every time down. Given the break of a good draw, she could go the distance, and buy your attention doing it. I had tremendous confidence going into this trial, formidable as it was.

To heighten the happiness, Meg gave me a present two weeks before Santa Claus. She began to run. Big, fast, wide. Flare, too, on her heels, and there was little difference. Except that Meg would catch an edge, test her speed, lay on. And never coast. Shades of Mama, and Lord I was thrilled.

"Want me to put a bow on that?" Loretta teased, knowing how I was elated.

"Yeah," I said, "how 'bout blue?"

Loretta and Melanie helped us off, in the small hours, the morning after Christmas. When all was loaded, including Dolly and the dogs, the good-byes said, and the tears shed, I climbed into the truck and sank behind the wheel for a moment, readying for the eight-hour drive to Savannah.

I wanted to leave and I didn't.

"Stay," Loretta said.

"Go," I said, as quickly.

We gazed at each other a moment. Melanie was standing by.

"You know I can't," she said.

"Do I?"

"Yes." She shook her head, pursing her lips. "Not like we used to. Melanie has school, and I have Melanie . . . I just don't want to leave."

"Heck with school. The both of you go."

"No," she said after a moment.

"Has so much changed?" I asked.

"Yes."

I thought about that.

"Melanie doesn't want to go anymore. She's finding her own wings, and before she flies, I want to spend all the time with her I can. It's pretty precious.

"Different with men, I guess," she offered behind a sedate smile.

It was, and it wasn't, I supposed. It hurt, what she said. The more leaving her. And it was a plea, I knew. But there was still the thing at the rudder of my soul that said I had to go. As always it had. Starting the truck, I pulled the shift into gear, looked one last time into her eyes.

"Love you," I said. She nodded, her cheeks glistening.

Home and harbor receded in the mirror as we pulled out the drive. The sky above was deep, dark, and clear. Among the glittering stars, I searched, and found again the one that wandered.

Drought and heat had reigned insufferably over the whole of the Southeast for the entire masquerade of autumn. We reached Garnett near sunset the evening of December 26, and shortly afterward discovered the plantation a maelstrom of swelter, dust, and humidity. At least provocation, the thirsty soil boiled and hung to the air like talcum powder, and the bay bushes looked as droopy, brittle, and belly-up as if they'd been baked before a fire. Pleased to find our customary spot by the kennels unoccupied, I pulled the truck to a stop under the huge live oak tree that stood a giant among its neighbors. We had sheltered there when Pat won in the Region 3. By the time I got the horses and dogs staked and fed, night was falling. Twilight had the asthmatic breath of August: close, thick, and stifling. All evening, dust billowed, dogs barked, and horses nickered, as the field trial party poured in, growing in a sweep of headlamps and a glare of taillights around the sleepy, old mansion. It was just past midnight, when all had calmed.

Hellos to a few old friends, and I was in bed by then, in back of the old Chevy, anticipation prickling my insides with the hope of the morrow. We had shared a big can of Dinty Moore beef stew, the three of us, while Dolly crunched grain. All was hale and happy, without the least shudder of the misfortune that would arrive with the morrow. Life loves to do that, it seems. Lull you into an impervious period of faith, only to shatter you with a lightning bolt of treachery.

It accomplished its purpose well. I was totally unsuspecting. Up before day, I woke the dogs out of the box, snapped them to the chain to pee. Nickering, Dolly asked me about breakfast. I threw her a pat of hay, and invited her to a bucket of sweet feed. It was just breaking light; the doves were moaning from the boughs of the pines. The mockingbird in the magnolia off the colonnade was hitting another chorus of the same tune he'd garbled since midnight. I listened hard for a covey call, off somewhere in the distance, and after tense, lengthy seconds was rewarded. It was warm, though, summer muggy. The last of December, and winter was as limp as summer in drag. Most important, Pat and Beda were on-their-toes happy—tails high and popping—hot with the notion of competition. Pat squatted by a palmetto clump, lifted, and scratched stiffly with her hind feet, sending the sand flying. Beda barked, whined, and lunged against the chain.

"Hey . . . hey . . ."

I got down on my knees, one in arm either side, roughhousing with them. They wriggled playfully against me, rolled to the ground, climbed up and shook. Spirits were high. I wanted this for them, the chance at another big one. With good fortune, there'd be a couple more, but nine years down the pike, you figured to look back over your shoulder. There were a lot of mountains back there, and we had climbed them all, and now there were just the few more we yearned for out front. The success of field trialing at the pinnacle, as with life at large—dog and man—is not that you win every time, because you won't, but that you win enough to know in your heart you were good for the challenge, to know of yourself that you will *never* quit, but die in the trying. We were good for the challenge.

Give us this one chance, Lord. This one and a few big ones more, before time forfeited the test.

Pat reared to my chest, looked far across the pines, wanting to go. It was about an hour yet, before the Stake Chairman would announce the breakaway, the marshals would call up the dog wagon. We'd walk down the dirt avenue to the breakaway. Pat had the last brace of the day; it was a good draw. There'd be only the two hours in the box after noon. Beda wouldn't run until the twenty-eighth, the corresponding match on the morrow. Just to humor Number Six, and myself, too, I set her down, squared her feet, and styled her up. She stiffened, dead serious, cutting her eyes to me. All I had to do was light the match. Everything about her two months to this very minute said she was ready, the best she'd ever been. My heart was thumping at the mere anticipation of it. I knew she was right to put on a show.

I lifted her rear off the ground, set her back, nudged her forward. She was tail-top plumb and tight as Dick's hatband. Then I tapped her suddenly on the ear, and she spun around, jumping up and nipping me for teasing her. Affording Beda equal time, I applied the same treatment. When I tapped her loose, she whirled, barking, and engaged Pat. They stood face-to-face, rear-up, head-down, and bouncing on their front legs, yapping furiously at each other. Dogs do that when they're happy and excited.

Standing, I glanced at my hands, starting to wipe them on my pants, but noticed a moist smear of red. Blood. Only slightly concerned, I figured it must be from some small scratch on one of the dogs. Head to toe, at first I could find nothing . . . was about to dismiss it as insignificant . . . when I noticed a trite and similar discoloring on the fine feathering of Pat's hind leg. And in the space of a mortifying moment, I knew. *First show.* She was coming into season. I felt the nausea swell in my gut like I'd been punched on a full stomach. No, God, this couldn't be. By calendar, we were a month to the good; there'd been no sign.

Another shudder hit me. Pat and Beda not only kenneled together, they almost breathed together. Physiologically, as one was affected, so was another. Quickly, I examined Beda, only to find to my horror she was just coming in as well.

My knees were weakening, and I had to find a seat on the fender of the trailer.

I said it again: "This can't be happening."

Waves of heat rushed my head, sweeping me to the brink of illness. Here we were at the biggest trial of the year—of any year—with Pat at the prime of her life, at nine years and counting, and both dogs in season. The mere chance at a National within a canine lifetime was no more than once or twice, because it moved—east to west, the distance as foreboding as impractical. And *both* dogs were in season.

I wanted to roar with desperation, but I couldn't. I was too numb with the injustice.

Pat was braced with a male dog—of course Fate would decree it that way—and the AFTCA rules allow bitches in season to start only in a continuous-course trial, which this was, but only if it is deemed fair to the other competitors by trial officials. Though this was barely first show, day one at worst, too early almost to warrant canine notice, head-to-head against a male dog wouldn't possibly be deemed as fair. Reeling already with the prejudice, now I was horned by the dilemma.

Should I say anything, or not? Nobody knew it. Unless somebody got down on their knees and wiped with a Kleenex, it was way too early to tell. Beda, fortunately, was braced with another female, so she was allowed to run. But Pat. And *why* Pat? I knew, had seen it time and again. At the whistle, Pat would be gone so far and fast, there'd be no chance for bias. So what should I do?

I wanted sorely to run Pat. For Pat. She had earned this. She was the best she'd ever been, and saying that with Zip Zap was akin to Babe Ruth stepping to the plate and pointing to right field. This trial had felt right for three months. I knew and believed in her, more than ever I had.

At end, I did the thing I should never have done. Were it to do again, I'll tell you squarely: I'd go the other way. Because the trust that in the face of such unfairness, life would be fair, was ill ventured. At the time, under the conditions, I couldn't have cared less about the possibility of personal sanction, but I did not want to risk the possible disadvantage—slim chance that it was—to another dog. From the first day I loosed a dog in a field trial, I viewed the game as a rite of gentility and honor, and pledged that I would pursue it that way. Should circumstances ever combine so grievously as to prevent that, I'd quit.

As I recall, Charles Young, of the South Carolina Association, was the Stake Manager for that trial. Charles was a good and fair man. So I went to him and posed the problem, proposed the solution, and begged redress.

"I'm doing the only thing I can," I told him, "for my dog and for the sake of making right a terrible wrong. I know you understand.

"Skip Brown has an identical dilemma. The weather for the extent of the trial is forecast as uniform; all the other extraneous influences on the trial are reasonably the same. I believe strongly that my dog and Skip's can be run together, can be provided the chance to compete, without being unfair to any other dog or handler.

"Leave the position of the braces undisturbed; switch bracemates. Have male with male, female with female. That leaves the option to the other handlers of running first day or second. The females take the alternate."

Charles had listened. "I don't know," he said.

"Do you agree the rules provide the discretion?" I asked.

"Maybe."

"Then understand. I'm formally and respectfully appealing for the consent of the officials. Asking that it be explored, considered, and granted."

"I know it's important to you," he said.

"You don't know how much," I replied.

I thought the proposal fair then, as I do now. Fat in the fire, all was left was the wait.

Leslie Anderson, secretary of the AFTCA, was in attendance. The answer was no.

Beda and I tried, though it was hard to have my heart in it, Pat nine years old and prohibited from her chance. I wanted to turn the truck toward home that first day. But Beda deserved her try. I was so proud of her. She had everything going at the end of the half hour, an imposing ground, two fine finds in a stake scant of bird work. She fought the heat and won, ran strong for the hour. Our Warrior Maiden. But she grew obstinate in handling response the last quarter of the heat, and her pattern lapsed a bit too erratic for that discerning a stake. She did that sometimes when she was coming into season. A good job, nonetheless.

Billy McCathern rode up after she ran, had a good word. He'd seen Pat run, as well, many times since she was a pup.

"Shoulda let her run," he said. "He'da never gotten close to her."

Moments and miles. We packed up and came home. I believe now as I believed then, as I will believe to the day I die. Had Zip Zap run that trial, she would have won it.

~ CHAPTER 36 ~

THAT INCIDENT ROBBED A LOT OF STEAM FROM OUR ENGINE. MINE, AT least. It was a time we could never have again, at a time I wanted it most. By then, I was used to adversity and episodic unfairness in trials, but the degree of that occasion I have never resolved.

Punish me, never my dog.

But there were puppies waiting at home, and for many weeks, with nothing big in trials on the horizon, we took to the field and had a rollicking good time. Meg and Flare were burning the ground down now, reaching and flying. All the puppy exuberance, which ignited like brush before a spark. Meg was all-out every time, going bigger each fling, spending herself recklessly. On birds, she slapped hard into point, stood so taut she shivered. Flare was as fast, as exciting on game, but give her a long edge and she'd back off the throttle here and there. Coast a bit. Meg would never. More and more, I could see her mama in her.

Pat and Beda, meanwhile, enjoyed the woodcock at Corinth. A meager few quail we continued to find there, or anywhere within a reasonable motoring distance. So we beleaguered the timberdoodles, often charting, between the two dogs, nine and ten finds in two hours of horseback time. There were a lot of large, lowland bottoms along the river corridor, and the woodcock conventioned there, to auger for earthworms in the mud. I held the dogs tight-to-honor, and they remained true to the core, stylish and steady. Often, in the thickets, they'd hold ten to fifteen minutes, waiting, but they knew I was coming. That was my part of the trust. As a reward for their loyalty, I would shoot a bird or so for them along. We stayed the course, but let ourselves enjoy each other, too.

The third week in January, there were no woodcock to find. January 21
of 1985 remains the most frigid in North Carolina history. All day the
twentieth, the ropy gray skies coughed snow, in swirling flurries agitated by
stiff northwest winds. The thermometer dropped like a rock through a win-
dowpane, and when it stopped in the small hours of the new morning, the
mercury shivered at minus ten. Ponds froze solid in a matter of hours, offering a scale to how solidly the river bottoms were iced and crusted. Locked
out of the larder, the woodcock packed bags and sold for Louisiana. For
three days the north winds keened, until the chill stood thirty below. Old
Man Winter, surly as a carbuncle on a cocklebur, had icicles in his beard.

In the Midwest, I suppose, it would have been business as usual, but for
a Southerner—man, dog, or horse—it was mean weather. All we could do
for its duration was keep the ice knocked out of the buckets, pile in more
hay for bedding, and carry hot water from the house. When finally on the
afternoon it had alleviated enough you could stick your head out the door,
when the sun poked out and the winds shifted, loading up and heading out
was like climbing out of a grave. Most amazing, we pointed six woodcock
and a covey of quail. New birds, I guess, the 'cock railing in just in time
from New England. How is it they know?

Beda had five of the woodcock, all perfectly handled finds. So sharp.
She enjoyed it, and I did as well. She, too, was the best of her life. Four days
later, she was singing around the railroad course, and after stopping for
another tip-top woodcock find in the bottom, she hauled up in the next little laid-out weed field on the hill. Covey scent. The wind was in her face,
and she tossed her head up and stiffened, roaded about twenty yards and
froze to point, gorgeously committed. I got off, and the birds stuttered up
dead ahead, about forty yards out. Lifting in place, eyes blazing, she watched
them away. So nice.

A dog man never tires of that, like m'lady never tires of diamonds.

By March, Meg, at a year and four months, was close to the measure of
her mother then, not quite the top-end fire and drive, but awfully nice. A
lot of snap, so consistent, forward and classy. Elegant on her game, when she
wasn't giving the meadowlarks a fit. She was showing the promise she was
born for; you can win a lot of trials with that kind of constancy. Flare was
persevering bravely, too, but finding herself outdone when I would set them

to challenge now. It seemed to bother her, aggravating the weak points. She would pause in midheat, unraveled, as if to ask, "What do I do next?"

One last chance at a big one for the season. Midmonth, the Region 3 Championship would run at Camden. Pat and Beda and I worked heart and harness to be ready. The dearth of wild birds was damaging. We went to Corinth on the sixth, Elm Hill on the tenth, an antediluvian tract in the coastal plain on the thirteenth, and found but two wild coveys the entire stretch. The deprivation failed to satisfy the high edge of desire, leaving a residual of explosive tension that no amount of liberated bird work could salve. It was the same kind of frustration you find in people who yearn for and are unable to find one unsubstitutable thing. Once you have known it, nothing else in life is so exciting or fulfilling. It can create a void of intensity when you try to transfer the passion to something inferior. Wild-bird dogs are no different.

Beda was of concern as well. Abruptly, in the last three workouts, she had not been herself. Her bird work and pattern were exquisite, but her power on the ground had diminished. Just enough to remove the patina, the high-end effervescence, the ultimate five percent of the magnetism that puts a field trial dog over the top. Loretta worried nights, beefing up her nutritional regimen with hamburger, liver, honey, and soy. Pasta loading. Nothing seemed of help. The last workout before we left, she ran as if she didn't feel good. She had a great covey find, one of the two for the period, but on a backcast. It was not Beda, and we debated whether to run her in the trial. But chances at the major contests were so few, and she was reaching the slope of her career, so we acceded.

The Region 3, like every other trial that season, was grueling. The heat was wicked, the air thick and stagnant. Underhoof, the dry, sandy loam powdered to boiling clouds of dust, while above, the fuming eye of the sun glowered from a brassy sky. Laying up, the birds withdrew to the cool of the low-ground thickets. Scenting conditions bordered on the impossible. You pushed yourself and you went—sweating and thirsting, digging and panting—because that was the demand of the quest, and it was in you to want it. The enjoyment, on such occasion, was not in the doing, but in the conquering. The pushing through, finding in yourself the something down deep that hauled you up by the galluses when your britches sagged, and pumped in the determination that made you stick. That gave you the dying resolve to fight the thing out, not back up, and find the high, far edge. To reach the places that seldom few go. Dog men manage that, at the courage of their dogs.

So we dug into the test at Camden on the strength of blood, grit, and gravel, trying mightily to make something happen. But Beda grew quickly hot, fell to pull-and-haul, and of worry for her, I watered and relegated her to harness at little more than the twenty-minute mark. Just not her kind of conditions, even at her mightiest, and I could readily see she labored below par.

Pure and simple, Pat was power. I'd seen her go bigger, and faster, but not much . . . and under the swelter, on the ground she was equal or better than the handful of dogs that were tough enough to weather the test. Including the first-year dogs, to whom she conceded seven years now. She had a thrilling find at twelve, another at twenty-five. Once again, we stood on the last hill before Paradise, gazing into the Promised Land. When— three minutes to go—she pulled up for a third, misread the scent in the dormant air, and started to flight two quail that loitered under a call box. Damn the pretense of the thing, but faced with it, she locked-to-flush as she should . . . then took the two small steps—about the time the judge got there—that drove the nail into our coffin. I hadn't bothered to caution her. Maybe I should've.

The famine of wild-bird work over the past months had earned us that. The stab of it burned like a hot knife. My heart sank, and I sat limply on the mare. Where was the justice? That we should be so close again, but all the far.

Above it shimmered another remarkable effort by a truly courageous dog. "It's all right, Pat," I told her, and it was.

In the big trials, you try to put the pieces into an intricate jigsaw puzzle, and every one is different, and every minute the board keeps shifting, and if so much as one little fragment is missing or out of place, somebody else will find it and put it together faster, smoother, and better than you do. The dogs have some pieces, and the handler has some pieces, and luck is proportioned most of all. The big stakes got in your head, stuck there, and were hard to get out. Every time we ran one, I was left to wonder, Was I as good a handler and trainer as my dogs were competitors? The answer was no. You asked yourself, Did I help them or hold them back? Sometimes you held them back . . . because the margin of tolerance was zero. Sometimes, even, I asked myself, Did Pat deserve more than I could give her? Should I have sold her to the professional who wanted her derby years ago? He was a major national force. But the answer there was no as well.

With Pat, as any great dog, there was a part of her that lay beyond the bonds of emotion. She never let you there. She couldn't. Something outside her guarded that. It was the center of her mystery and power, as the undivined, shadowy secret of a beautiful and beguiling woman. As essential to her being, as it was necessary to her magic. So you were ever thankful for it, though never you could reach it.

Within the approachable territory beneath, there was our love for one another. As nowhere else it could have happened.

∾ CHAPTER 37 ∾

SOMETHING STRANGE TRANSPIRED THAT DAY AT CAMDEN. IT WAS AS IF our world were made over. Maybe it was like you have traveled with the love of your life, hurled along by mutual wanderlust, through the most exotic, exciting, and enticing galaxies of the universe. And one day, years afterward, when the foremost of your dreams have all been searched out and explored, even though you left a piece of yourself in each and every realm, you find that the kingdom most comforting, necessary, and precious is the one that lies simply between the two of you, that it will abide and flourish wherever you put it. That much otherwise is unnecessary. That never could you have reached it with anyone else.

Maybe I'd seen the elephant by then. Pat and Beda, even old Thing, had taken me there. And maybe, now and then, I'd want to go back. See it again. Maybe it was finding, as in most arenas of life, the greatest rewards are within. Maybe it was that you can only do a thing with someone one first, incomparable, and defining time, but spend a lifetime trying vainly to do it over again. Maybe it's that after a while, things get in the way of the love. Draw you so far away it's distilled and wrapped up in tangents separate from where it belongs.

I drove the several hours home after that trial, resolved that we'd seen a lot of what we'd set out to in field trialing, and that in the doing, I'd discovered a lot of wonderful places I'd hoped for and never been. Of them all, the one most completing was the one between the three of us—the simple privilege of the journey together—so that now we'd been, we knew what we were made of, and no impulse of life could take that away. The thrill of the dogs was still existential, but heightened by dimension, and validated by exacting standards of judgment long since meted and proved. It was a most special place, this we had reached between us, and it was unnecessary to travel six hundred miles to find it. We could go there anytime, *anytime we were together.* The thrill and pageant of a field trial I would love to the end, but no longer, I found, were they life-and-breath fundamental.

It hardly seemed possible, but I enjoyed the dogs more than ever after that. We came home happy to be there, never stopped by the house—called Loretta and Mely "Hello"—and went straight to Corinth. Turned loose, had a hell of a good time. Found a half dozen woodcock, and three scattered quail. Next day I had the puppies out. I needed Pegasus to keep tabs with Meg; she flew from start to finish. Hers was a future bright and beautiful. Then on May Day, Loretta, Melanie, and I worked the whole kit and caboodle—puppy to matriarch—on liberated quail. We wanted them to enjoy one last fling on birds before we dug in for another endless, sultry summer.

Cindy stood feeble, but fast, to a cock bird. Her tail below her back, a pitiable caricature of what proudly she had been. She was deaf, both eyes clouded with cataracts, the mantle of silver-gray cast upon the once velvet fawn of her muzzle like windblown snow. But I shot the bird for her, and she lumbered awkwardly out to get it, and delivered it as honorably back.

Loretta and I could only look at each other. The sadness was deeper than words.

The last entry of my field trial log from those treasured days is bittersweet, dated October 27, 1985. As the scores of times before, we went to Corinth. Corinth was home, and this was a homecoming. I had been working Meg and Flare through September. Now it was Pat and Beda's turn. It was to be, again, just the three of us. They'd been seven months in the kennel, and Pat turned fifty-seven star-bound minutes without even breathing hard. She covered half the flatwoods course, and handled two coveys with an expressiveness that left my heart pounding. Simply unbelievable. She could go to any shooting-dog trial in the country and reign close to the threat she'd always been. She loved it so.

Beda, to the contrary, was sluggish and slow. Her demeanor continued to convey the troubling malaise that had marked her going the past spring. Always so beautifully she had gathered up the ground, as light and deft on her feet as a wind-tuft of thistledown. Now she labored, and the gaiety of

her gait was tarnished by a discordant lumber. Had it not loomed so illogi-
cal for a dog sustained for fitness, that remained imposing of muscle and
carriage, I might have accorded the condition to age. As it was, I worried it
might be something more.

The memory returns an overpowering sorrow, that welled more deeply
than ever I'd known. Her competitive days were at wane, and I had enjoyed
her beyond telling. Number Two. Our little warrior maiden. Sheer spirit
and residual prowess predicted yet her success in the smaller stakes. But we'd
been there. No longer were we content with that. Numb with hurt, I could
feel her era hurtling closed. I wasn't even sure, now, we would go to
another trial—Pat and Beda and I. I was wrestling long and hard with that.
But it was still nice to know we could.

I got off the mare and sat with Beda a long time that day—till near
sunset—on the porch of the old, gray tenant shack that stood not far from
the bend of the river. Among the feathery heads of the broomsedge, that
burned a misty, molten gold beneath the mellow rays of the smoldering
sun. In the place where once some people named Copperfield had lived and
loved. Near the corner where the little setter had staunchly held a first
covey of wild quail, when she was nothing more than a speckled pup.

Don't recall we said anything. Only that we sat side by side on the old
porch, happy to be together, and sensing where we'd been, and that at the
very deep of dusk, a single bird—maybe from that very same covey—
pleaded plaintively for reunion.

I found myself tired and troubled then. Part of it, of course, was Beda's
decline. That night I told Loretta of it. That I didn't think she could run the
big ones competitively any longer. I think, really, Retta was happy with the
thought of having her home.

"Pat's a different story," I said. "We could win some more trials."

"Is that important?" she said.

I turned to her, knowing it was a pointed question.

"It's important for Pat.

"She was born for field trials."

"She was born to run and hunt," Loretta said.

"A lot of dogs are that.

"It's more.

"She's one in a thousand. She loves the game."

"And you?" she asked.

"And me what?"

"Do *you* still love the game?"

I glanced away. "You know I do."

A minute trailed, nothing said, trust demanding truth.

"Maybe not as completely as when we went to those first South Carolina trials with a green mare and a box full of puppies."

I smiled, and she smiled back, waiting for me to continue.

"When you and Melanie . . . we all went."

"Good times," she said, threading her arm through mine.

"You don't go anymore," I said.

"No."

"It's changed," I said after a moment. Maybe *it* hadn't. Maybe I had.

"Going without Beda can't be the same," I said.

"Meg's in the wings," Loretta observed.

"She's nice. Real nice," I agreed. "She can win . . . win big . . . win a lot.

"She needs the chance."

You start talking about a thing, and you start to find out more about it than you knew. It was that way then.

"Pat can go," I said again.

"If you want to," Loretta said. She knew me almost better than I knew myself.

It had been building for some time. The divided territory in my heart. At the crux of it was the ebb of this most beautiful season of my life. I was forty-five years old, and I think I'd learned enough about living by then to know that never again could there be another that could feel the same, or be the same. That there could be other grand dogs in my life, but that each would be as individual as night to day. That never again would there be Pat and Beda and Thane, me, Loretta, Melanie, and Dolly, the exact thrill of those first trials, and how it had felt together. How breathless it was when first we won. What a season of pride whenever we won.

There would never again be something so peerless as Pat, a spirit more buoyant than Beda's, nor a time in the afteryears of my life when I could muster the same intensity, the same binding, consummate passion that I gathered that first time. All that was given was more than was left.

"One great dog, one good woman, one good horse," the old dog hands say. "*Once . . . in a lifetime.*"

When you pursue field trialing at its highest levels, amateur or open—breed, develop, train, handle, and campaign your own dogs—largely by yourself, which is the march as only many of us would have it, the commitment can be no less than supreme. There is time for nothing else. It's a lot like a mail route, except there are no holidays. It has to happen: on schedule and regardless of else. Rain, snow, shine, or sorrow, the show goes on. Otherwise, you'd as easily stay home, because even with good dogs, you'll rarely succeed. You go against a force that has had the pink of opportunity and the attention of order and discipline, and if you expect to be noticed, you have to give close to the same.

So you promise yourself to priority. Sacrifice here, so something can happen there.

Relentless, the regimen of conditioning and training; endless, the hundreds upon hundreds of miles; merciless, the birds to buy, pens to build, kennels to tend, tack to mend, feed to lay in.

A lot of desire it takes, to prod the passion, all driven by the dogs. When the tide ebbs, when there've been one or two special dogs, for one special time, and you find it fading, know it can never be again, the obsession stalls. It's like inside you the trade winds die. There's still the ship and still the sea, but no longer the song in your sails.

"Maybe I'm a little tired," I told Loretta.

There was more. With it a twinge of guilt. The world is full of fascinations. Destinations near and far. You travel the journey of your heart. For some, the voyage is short. Satisfied near the harbor of home. Within the contentment of one place, or one thing, for a lifetime. For others, the going will be far. There will never be enough. Of places, or things, or lifetimes.

I was restless with yearning. So many things and places wild and wonderful in the world, and I wanted to see them all. Places, again, I had been, and those I had not, and all the little islands of anticipation that lay between. Those distant and strange as a dream, others familiar as a backyard memory. For twenty years, from back-pasture gun-dog gatherings to national championships, I had given my all to field trialing. As intensely as anyone ever could. I still loved it . . . would always. But there was not another twenty years in me to give, not to the exclusion of else and all.

There was too much wanderlust. Too much wonder, of what new color was the elephant, over the mountain.

Dogs and birds would always be foremost in my heart, and always there would be homecomings. When my soul would occasionally wander too far and grow sick for home, there would be the necessity of gathering it up and anchoring it again on constant ground. The dogs and birds would always be there. Home could not be home without them. Home was in my heart.

Loretta had said nothing, was waiting for the more.

"There are things I miss. I haven't been deer hunting, turkey hunting . . . duck hunting . . . grouse hunting . . . in ten years. I haven't seen kudu in Africa, the bears on Admiralty Island, pigeon or perdiz in Argentina . . . stag in New Zealand. Partridge . . . in Spain.

"Kilimanjaro, the Selous, the Sierra Madre . . . not even the Rockies.

"I want to.

"There'll not be enough time.

"There might not even be tomorrow."

"Then you should," she said, even as she searched my eyes with her own. Giving me to know again why I loved her so.

"Will you go?" I asked.

"My heart's with home," she said. "You wish for the butterflies that embroider the islands of Costa Rica; I look forward to the swallowtails that decorate the apple blossoms in our orchard. The ones we planted when we moved here.

"I would not want them to come and find me gone."

The melancholy in those last words, the anticipation of rending heart from home, caused me to wince inside. However deep the longing, in the moments before you would leave, there is always the ambiguity. The self-reproach. Ever the danger you might never come back.

"Maybe I'll go some," she said, "but mostly I'll be here waiting, with the dogs and horses.

"Hoping you won't be gone too long." There were tears in her eyes.

"They'll miss you, you know," she said after a pause. There was the deeper inference as well.

"You, Melanie, and the dogs will always be first," I vowed. "It's not like I'll leave for months. Just for a time."

"How will you do it?" she asked. "We're not rich, I believe."

"I have no idea," I said.

"So when do you leave?" she said, smiling. I kissed her and offered the obvious.

"Not tomorrow."

～ CHAPTER 38 ～

I NEVER RAN PAT IN ANOTHER FIELD TRIAL. SHE COULD HAVE GONE until she was thirteen. She was still hitting the lick. It was me, somehow, that never gave in to go. I ran Meg in a few derby stakes. The very radiance of her begged the chance, I could not deny it, and she won them all. Here was the ship and there was the sea. Why, then, was there not, still, the song in my sails? The depth of it I can't explain. For that year and many after, I was content to retire from the pressure, the race and the grind. To aspire elsewhere. To christen myself again in the quieter waters of a friendly hunt, where Beda and Thane . . . all of us . . . could go together. Where the four of us and the mare set an easy pace and a happy course a few miles from home, circumscribed by neither limit nor judgment outside our own. Where, anytime we wanted, we could invite Meg and Flare or another few friends along.

Life fled on. The nights were long and the days were short.

We lost Cindy the next autumn, beloved Beda the one after.

For weeks before she died, Cindy barked mournfully in the night. At the cusp of a new morning, we would hear her from our bed. Her plea would rise, one sorrowful, disconnected lament after another, settling to the cadence of a death drum. For hours it would continue. So sadly you would lie there searching your soul for its meaning, until the tears arrived to tell you. When first she started, we'd go to her, hurry to the kennel to determine the matter. But there would be nothing. Nothing beyond the merciless toil of age upon her already emaciated body, which we were hopeless to remedy. We could only listen the more helplessly, as the time grew short, and she knew it, as did we. Did she grieve for years gone? Beg for beginnings or plead for the end? Finally, God in heaven, there came the peace.

It was not age, but anguish, that took Beda. She fought it with utter determination to prevail, as always she had. Tried so hard. Even at the last, when she grew pitifully frail. We fought it together, but despite the sum of our resolve—and finally, our prayers—the hideous thing defeated us. Now that I could put prejudice with pattern, I could see it had been lurking for a long time.

For more than a year, ever since that last Camden trial, she had not seemed herself. Most days, she was beautifully Beda. Running with the flash and fire of her prime, her spirit too optimistic to yield. Though others, as the cruelty grew, when she appeared less than herself . . . remiss, quite, the power and passion. It worried her, and on those days she would dig the deeper. I know now that it hurt, know what courage it took to continue as she did.

The health checks, bloodwork, revealed no abnormality. Still there was the inference, and still there was our fear. Until one dark day early in January of '87, worrying the cockleburs out of her coat after a hunt, I discovered a small, hard swelling on her left leg, just above the paw. I figured it a transient thing, not so different from any other of the bumps and bruises in a pointing dog's fare. But a month later, it had not subsided, and we felt the mounting prickle of apprehension.

With intuitive dread, we took her to Dr. Lynn Elliot, a young and conscientious vet who had earned much of our trust and respect during her first year of local practice. Again, the blood workups and chest radiology found nothing of alarm. But her examination of the swollen nodule on the leg was grave.

"A tumor, I fear," she said, after a time. "Fibrous . . . hopefully benign."

Loretta's face was bloodless and taut. I remember the heat and queasiness at my gut.

"I'm afraid we're facing a biopsy," Lynn continued. "If you can leave her with me tonight, we'll do it first thing tomorrow. I'll get it off to the vet school. We need to know better what we're dealing with."

"You're a happy girl," she told Beda, stroking the setter's flank.

Beda acknowledged, tail flagging. She stood genially upon the stainless steel table. Her spirit unwavering, no qualms about the next minute, the next morrow, the months on to forever. She could not know, or fear, what lay ahead. Happy, always so happy.

I look back now at the bland, blue paper of the pathology report and can only recall we were about as lifeless when we received it. How joyful still Beda was as Loretta sank to the floor, met her at the wardroom door, buried her face in her coat, and gathered her into her arms. I remember the setter looked up at me as she might in the minutes before a trial, life and expectation in her eyes. And that I was wrung devoid of brightness, as a washcloth could be wrung of water.

"A fibrous, malignant tumor," the reporting pathologist decreed. A "fibroblastic osteosarcoma," the more vile and apposite description. "We don't have a lot of data on this type of malignancy. But the likelihood is that it's secondary, and the primary tumor is growing from the bone."

"There's some suggestion," he wrote, "that this type of osteosarcoma is less aggressive than the classical or long bone condition."

"It means maybe we have some time," Lynn interpreted.

Neither of us could form the question with words, so we both asked with our eyes.

"Dr. Richardson at State says, nominally, two to four months."

There are no words in the language adequate to the hopelessness and heartbreak we felt at that moment. Loretta, most especially, and I tried to hold her and ease the sobbing, but Beda had been the orbit of her affection from almost the first moment she was born. You reach for the small, special bits of joy that have defined a life at such times, and I could remember Loretta cradling her in her palms that first morning of her existence in the tiny, white shed on Chaney Road.

Crooning "Lookat t-h-at f-a-c-e," and hoisting her for me to see, all dressed out like a calico kitten.

"Beda," she had pronounced. "This will be Beda . . . little *warrior maiden*."

"But we might not keep her," I had said.

She had looked at me forgivingly, through the instincts of devotion. "We'll keep her," she had vowed.

A second opinion confirmed the worst. Two options eventuated: Do nothing, or surgically remove the offending bone.

Loretta collected herself, wiping the tears from each eye with the back of a hand. "What does that mean?" she managed.

Dr. Elliot dropped her eyes. "Take the leg," she said.

"Would you pull the wing from a bird?" Loretta asked me somewhere in the long, long night that followed. I needed not answer.

Beda had been a blissful free spirit, the most unfalteringly cheerful dog I had ever known. She still was. We'd spit in the face of the Devil, wrestle the fate of this damn thing to the grave in the ground, but we'd not take that away from her. Not by the sake of her trust would we affront her with the insult of worrying around on three legs and a hip socket.

Beda was with us that night, and many others, before the end.

"When it's time," Loretta told the adoring setter, "when you can no longer be happy . . . we'll give you wings again."

There followed a time of amnesty. While on the surface there was gladness, beneath there was dread—knowing it was unreliable, yet praying it to last. On through spring, throughout the summer, we went afield most every day. Beda and Pat and Dolly and I. Even in the sweltering drag of July and August, we arose well in break of dawn, drove midst a billowing shroud of fog, to be on our grounds at first light. We'd run the maiden hour of the morning, while the air was cool, and upon the cornstalks the purple morning glories slept. Then be happily home again as the crows harangued the hawks, their raspy din an ignominy to the hushed, struggling rays of the newcoming sun.

Though for me, each was bittersweet, Beda looked forward to those trips with the inexhaustible passion she always had, running with glee. But as the months passed, the swelling at her leg advanced, at the march of a wicked and unbendable foe. Until the external expression of it had metastasized the size of a mango, blood-gorged and purple, burdensome and grotesque. Until God knows what further evil seethed at the bone. Until it drew her ribby and gaunt. Until it robbed her of appetite, her physical ability to defend. Still, when I went to the kennel, ever she would beg to go. Defiantly I wrapped and taped the hideous thing when we ran. To little good; spitefully it renewed the siege, bruising and tearing against the brush, weeping and bleeding. And still, with the final reserves of her spirit, the brave and determined little setter drove it aside.

September came, and the roadside ditches were bright with sunflowers, and among them monarchs flitted. With morning, you could find your breath upon the air. Spiderwebs glistened across the verdant green meadows, appearing as silken veils set with silvery diamonds of dew. At the woods line, the leaves of the sweetgums smoldered blood red, as the cloak of the poplars gilded to gold. Of evening, a hunter's moon gleamed boldly from a star-flocked sky, and the bay of hounds could be heard from the hollows. October was in reach; you could almost touch it, the breath and blaze of fall. It was a season of excitement, of anticipation and yearning.

Beda felt it as we all did. I could see the faith in her eyes. For all her life, it had been the harbinger of another trialing season, the coming of brisk weather, hunting days for sure. But she was failing fast now. Reaching still for what she had known. Beneath the flame of her hope lay the telling wick of her pain. It was growing and would no longer subside. Fight as she did she could not prevail. Finally came the day she was happy no longer.

In the somberness of a mid-September Saturday, we held her in our arms and watched her away. As horridly as it hurt, we had given back her wings.

Alone, I loaded the mare and went to Corinth that afternoon, rode to the little, grizzled sharecropper's shanty by the river. On the moldering porch boards, I sat as Beda and I had that day not long before. How utter and profound was her absence. I tried, one-upon-another, to remember every day of her life. Every joy, every sorrow, every triumph, every loss. Nothing could diminish, or salvage, the privilege we'd known. On past the sunset, deep into dusk, I lingered. Straining to hear in the silent, rising loneliness the pleading of a single bird from the covey once we knew. But there was nothing. It was gone.

Humpty Dumpty sat on a wall . . . We were a team: Dolly, Pat and Beda, Thane and I. All for one, one for all. Now Beda was gone, and nothing on God's green earth could put it together again. Nothing I could buy, beg, borrow, conspire, or steal. For a time, I would have done any or all. Months passed, and the more I knew, the more I understood why no longer I could feel again the way I had. Because it was never so much about the field trialing as it was about us.

Without the part, there could no longer be the whole.

For the first time in more than eleven years, Pat and I took the field without her. It was hard. We'd been inseparable. Empty as I was, Pat was the much or more. Convince me dogs don't grieve. She and Beda loved each other. They had not only trained and trialed together all the years, but weathered all of life together, too. From the hour they were weaned, they were mutually devoted. Many's the day I had stolen to the kennel, to catch them sleeping at peace in the sun, the muzzle of one cradled on the shoulders of the other. Or to find them grooming, sister thou sister, tender the care. The nights nearing the end, when we had kept Beda close to us in the house, we could hear Pat howling softly from the run. Sad, so unmistakable and sad, the loneliness.

You hold to hope, push yourself on. Nothing really heals. Time runs the river, carrying away the tears; the grief is only diluted, in an unseen ocean of fears.

Pat and I recovered ourselves where we always had, at the crossroads of the hunger and the hunt. The clouds parted and the sun burned through, and what was left of life found meaning again. When I was ready, Pat was there waiting for me.

Golden, the following five years. Pat was a force. If I sent her, she could reel off an hour and a half in front of the horse, and still jam your heart in your throat. On till she was sixteen, she faded but little. Zip Zap to the end. It was only in her last year that her body conceded the haul her spirit would not.

What times we had between. She and I alone now mostly, from the horse. Usually in torrid, hour sprints. Three heats a day. She knew the pressure was off, but would never relent. She couldn't, any more than a river can avoid its plunge to the sea. The drive was in her, escalating every trip to an adventure, and we coveted each as if it were the last.

We'd load up before day, trailer two or three hours to some antebellum farm on the Carolina coastal plain, where you could still scratch up a few wild birds. She loved it when I shot them for her, relishing every retrieve. All the years I'd shot very sparingly, just enough to jack the dogs tight. Now she could anticipate a fetch every find, and it drove her even harder. It was a timeless thrill for me as well. Even now, I can remember almost every stand . . . how good it was to climb down under the long, pale rays of a newborn sun, how grand it was to pull a shotgun from a saddle scabbard, how the birds came up, the thrill of bringing a nimble double gun to shoulder, the smell of gunpowder mingled in the earth scent and mist of a chill December morning. The *thump* . . . swing . . . *thump* of two quick shots, the satisfaction of feathers adrift on the breeze, the blaze in Pat's eyes at the fever of the send and retrieve. After the facsimile of field trials for so long, where you spin through the motions—now here it was, coming real. Like a dream wrung gray and white, that suddenly bursts into vibrant, living color. So evocatively your heart sings. A picture you can step into. Somebody calls, "Action!" and the scene breathes true. A plantation bird hunt, on a smooth-stepping walking horse, behind a big-going pointing dog that is also a field trial champion—the closest you could come to it, at least, in 1980s Tarheelia. And it was all our own.

It commanded my spirit so completely that many days I would don a shooting coat, vest, and tie, under a old felt hat. Tug on jodhpurs and knee-boots. Let my mustache grow out until it kinda curved down and twisted up a bit each end. Should I meet James Avent or Hobart Ames somewhere along the pike, I'd not care to appear ungentlemanly.

It was fun to dress back. I was born too damn late anyway.

"This is worse than turkey season," Loretta complained, wincing at the intrusion of the alarm clock that announced four o'clock about every other morning. Though always she was up, building sandwiches and tucking in dog treats, wishing us off. As we pulled out predawn, just like in the trialing years, sometimes for two or three days at the time.

Pat would ride with me in the cab, no longer serving duty in the dog box. She thought that was the greatest, nose-prints and ears-in-the-wind a-going, curled dead-to-the-world against my leg a-coming.

"Rare, special days," Retta would say, coming or going.

Oh, my God, but they were. And we both knew there could be just so many.

We made good a long-standing promise to Danny Allen, breaking off now and again from saddle leather to shank's mare, to just old-fashioned, ragweed, pea-patch, and blackberry-head bird hunting.

"I've got to hunt over this'un," Danny had said, the day he had plucked her from the chasm between the Here and the Hereafter, a puppy nearing death from the extreme anaphylactic shock reaction to a wasp sting.

And he did, as did also my old friend Jim Dean, though truth be told—despite all accounts contrary of great and impassioned horseback field trial dogs amicably dampening the burners to a walk-along, bird-hunting pace—Pat was never a comfortable foot dog. The flames licked too high. Turned free, she had only one mission. The one God and I had set her to, from the day she was born. Go. Go hard, fast, and far, go until she couldn't

anymore, go until she found birds. I would never have thought to hack that
out of her. You couldn't have. It would have been like demanding the
sparkle from a diamond. But we had some big foot tracts, huge beanfields
and cut-over grounds you could walk all day if you cared and never cut
your track. We'd put the telemetry collar on her, and set her fly. She'd blister
the edges as far as we could see, and when we couldn't anymore, I'd keep up
with her on the radio receiver. Harbor and habit, she knew where the birds
were, every bevy; if she didn't, she soon would, so that when she pointed,
we'd hoof it to the find. As long as the birds stuck, she'd be there.

What grand, happy times.

Inexorably as the shadows that build toward the advance of evening,
those last few, joyful years stole by. With their lapse—hard as it was—we
were reminded that not even a force so formidable as Pat was infallible. That
despite the many occasions of her younger years that would have declared
otherwise, eventually, all of life is mortal.

Even so, it was only late in her sixteenth year that the knotted muscles
ran limp and lean, that her carriage sagged, that her face grew old and tired,
and her pride seemed to flag. We still went to field, though with less fre-
quency. As, ever more, her spirit was imprisoned in a body that could no
longer answer its will.

In the first month of her seventeenth year, it mounted one last fling.
One last challenge, flung against eternity. I had left the gate to the kennel
yard ajar, and Pat found its fraction of freedom almost the moment I let her
out of her run. I yelled, but it was too late. She was through it and gone. It
might as well have been the breakaway at Belmont. All day I called and
called, called until I couldn't anymore. Knowing the while it was futile, for
her hearing was all but gone. All day I traveled the woods and the fields,
looking for a track, a trace, some hope or sign, until my legs cramped and
my lungs ached. While Loretta drove the roads, searching. Wanting, as horror pictured, not to find her.

I wore myself out on foot, came home, saddled the mare, took off riding and looking anew. As hour upon hour, the emptiness grew. First the
frustration, then the despair, finally the tears.

Over and over, my mind screamed, No, God, please. Not after all the
years. Not Pat. Not this way.

All I could think of were the many near tragedies, the times as a derby she was lost and found at trials, the times death had grabbed and missed. Only to lose her like this, at seventeen.

After nine hours, we truly thought she was gone. It was too long. She was too gone. I could envision her running, and running, and running, until at last, somewhere we would never find her, her heart failed. Maybe she wished it that way. Maybe destiny willed it that way. We would never know. I recall that the sunset that afternoon was rarely beautiful, which only amplified the sadness. Dusk draped the day like the cloak of doom, and nightfall brought the greatest swell of despondency I have ever known. It was like the well of my soul was being pulled lower and lower, soon to run dry.

We had closed our circle of hope to home, the immediacy of the kennel area, the recognizable little corner of the world she had known so long and so well. It was all of faith that was left. Exhausted, we stumbled along over the near and far of it, calling hoarsely, one, then the other. If now we were to see her again, she must find us. Had she been younger, more complete of faculty, maybe. As was, with each passing minute, the prospect loomed more doubtful.

It was our half-dozenth trip back from the cabin and the pond when, in the faint reach of the flashlight, we caught the dubious glimpse of white. It was one of those cataclysmic flights of phenomenon, when your eyes disbelieve, but your heart shouts it's true. It was Pat, and we ran to her, falling on our knees and gathering her up in our arms, laughing, crying—together—thanking God and All of Creation for her return. She was so completely spent, she tottered and trembled, could hardly stand. Eyes rimmed-red, brier-torn and bloody. I knew she had been running and hunting the entire space of her absence.

"Oh, Pat . . ." It was all either of us could say.

She was happy with herself, happy as I remembered her at Rappahannock, at Hoffman, at Blackwater . . . the scores of places between . . . when her heart climbed the heights of her spirit, and rejoiced there together with the triumph of her soul. Like a flourish at a flag raising.

It was the last special thing—of so many—that Pat gave us . . . to hold on to, to the moment seven months and seventeen days later when, after dinner on that last evening of the year . . . Loretta looked at me with fearful eyes, and confided, "This morning, I heard a rattle in her throat."

On that premonition, we made our way to the kennel. And it was on that evening I dug her grave.

"I spent all the years," Loretta said, "watching . . . Pat, Beda too. Trying to memorize every wisp and curl. Knowing there would come the day I couldn't."

EPILOGUE

I DON'T THINK IT'S POSSIBLE TO BREED A GREAT DOG LIKE PAT. I MEAN
. . . I think you can plot and plan, pore over pedigrees until you've climbed
every branch in the tree, seek the counsel of every pointing-dog breeder in
America who's produced the privilege of a truly exceptional dog, breed the
best to the best, and throw straight sevens between . . . yet not inevitably
produce a Rocky, a Luminary, or a Palamonium. Yes, I know that every
extraordinary dog eventuates from the corporeal union of a good sire and
dam. But never with a guarantee. And always very scarcely. And ever with
an ethereal element of wonder.

After Pat, it is as easy for me to believe that with tidings of each tiny
new arrival upon earth, the Angel of Genesis requisitions from the Ware-
house of Life a small, luminous ingot. That from the vast and voluminous
shelves of a great repository, upon which glow innumerable orbs of light,
the Keeper randomly selects. For he is ancient and blind, and he is only the
instrument of destiny. It is not for him, but for the Lord, to see. That of the
thousands of bright sparks that line each shelf, each capable of bestowing
life, only a few can confer the gift of greatness. Only a very few burn blinding hot with genius. That these few, unlike the others, are given to burn for
eternity. So that they cannot be passed on, and must be relinquished before
mortal flesh is again returned to dust. To one day, who knows where or
when, be selected again. Never more than once in our lifetime.

It is similarly reasonable that those of us who receive them, through the
gift of a dog that incites our spirit as can never another, somehow know.
Come finally to expect. That in the hours nearing the end, the Angel of
Exodus shall arrive as well.

Softly to say, "It's time, old girl. Time to give it back."

Much has changed in the many years since. Two autumns after Pat left, we lost Dolly. On an October day that opened splendidly, belying the tragedy that lay beyond its dawning, I left the house in darkness . . . made my way across the creek . . . to take up a deer stand on a neighboring hill. It was the bare gray of day when I heard Loretta shrieking from the barn. I slid, fell, jumped out of the tree, ran all the way home. The brave chestnut mare, who had carried me so many miles, to so many moments, lay cast in her stall. She had left during the night, gone on, alone.

Gone, too, ol' Dub Watkins, and Duke, and Bob Lindler. I suppose it was fitting that long before they passed, Bob and Dub shared a big dappled horse named Tombstone, 'cause between the three they planted many a field trial competitor. That Dub, even after he got too old and decrepit to fork Tombstone, still had the wherewithal to mount a golf cart and work his dogs. That Bob, through his last days of dreams and delirium, held to the quest for one more big-going puppy, such that to his honor and name, the South Carolina Field Trial Association dedicates annually a Puppy Classic. Gone, sadly, as well, Verle Farrow, and with him much of Old Virginia. Departed, also, old Jake Vaughn, not a field-trialing soul in the Dominion gray enough to remember who doesn't miss his ardent occurrence at an Amelia breakaway.

Mr. Graham Dean's no longer with us, nor Ben or Luke and Storm, or Thane and knock-'em-dead Dax, or cute little Suzy-Q, gone to join Jake and the rest in the Elysian Fields. Meg, Pat's firstborn, surviving until 1999, came to be one of the top two or three gun dogs of my life.

Secretariat's mortal remains are buried at Claiborne. His spirit races on, the all-time best, in the Stake of the Ages.

Parke Brinkley is in the Field Trial Hall of Fame. Billy Blankenship, who deserves to be, is not. You wouldn't notice. He's still winning regularly at seventy-something—crotchety as ever, just better at it. Skip Brown, some years after weathering the Kentucky rains, found brighter days with a big-going setter named Commander's Casey Jones, the only longhair ever to win the Amateur Invitational Championship at Grand Junction. Frankie Henderson, who campaigned Calico Calli, a setter, back when, switched allegiance, partnering with Dick Quackenbush to establish a pointer dynasty. Young Gary Winall, not so young anymore, head-to-head against the pros in the open stakes with his Mohawk Mill dogs, is one of the winningest, most charismatic amateur trainer-handlers in the country.

My old friend Norman Melton and I still meet now and again, turn a puppy loose. We do a lot of remembering . . . dogs and days. Tommy Mock, as Norman, commands national respect as a dog hand, is widely sought as a field trial judge. Tommy maintains a fine wild-bird lease on the Flint River near Camilla in South Georgia, and a plantation shooting-dog string that harks back to old Nick. I usually meet him there once a year, with my own string. We're about as gray now, Tommy and Norman and I, as the Spanish moss that crepes the live oaks, and most as old. But we're still pals—will ever be—have a hell of a good time, running and remembering horseback dogs, shooting a covey rise now and when.

Little Diamond was elected to the Field Trial Hall of Fame in 1983, the year after Pat triumphed over her in the Region 3 Championship at Belmont. Bozeann's Mosely, "Rocky," still . . . and likely forever . . . the only setter to gather Champion or Runner-Up titles in all four major derby championships, was likewise honored in 1997.

We still go to Elm Hill on occasion, the great-grandpups and I. But even there, it's hard to dream anymore. The magic has been taken too long for granted, by a world that considers itself too sophisticated for sentiment. The old house molders in ruin. Gone the great portico, the ballrooms, the gardenias and the lilacs, the jasmine and the jocundity. Gone the magnolias. Stoic and abandoned, the lonesome old elms.

At Corinth, our mainstay, Mister L. B. is failing, but hanging on. He stops on his one-mile loop from the house to the heart of the farm—his best buddy, an old blond cocker, on the seat of the truck beside him—to wish me well when I'm there, and hows-about the young dogs and the horses? The two boys forge on. Ernie shoulders ninth-generation trust for the farming operation, given almost wholly now to the golden leaf, clinging to tradition to the end. Frank, after an unpredictable courting eternity, finally tied the knot with Cathy, uniting Averett and Crews. They live on the Crews side, near the grand, two-story clapboard homeplace that Dolly and Pat and Thane and Beda and I always passed, making the round along the old Henderson & Oxford railroad line that skirted the low grounds and wound across the Tar River. Old Bill Crews, patriarch of the clan—who was raised up there—is gone a-glimmering, silhouetted along the tracks, somewhere in the morning fog that blankets the river bottom. I miss him most, his bright smile and blue overalls. Hickory-faced old Madison Pitts,

I'm happy to say, trods on, a mile across the hollow. Beneath the bark, he's always a fine old man.

There, and most elsewhere throughout the South, the wild quail are all but gone. The demise has continued, and I realize now—ever the more— how fortunate we were. Even as late as the seventies, to find the wild birds we did. How essential they are to exciting true brilliance. We struggle now, I and the young dogs, to sustain the fire, and too often are brought to fail.

We brave on . . . still go to a trial or two each year . . . but mostly I labor with the guilt that I can't give them even half the chance their grand-mother had. There's the thing of the birds, and then there's me. The fire's grown cold.

I think of giving it all up sometimes, and then I think again. I still love the game . . . more than the game, the marvel of the dogs . . . always will.

I've been to Africa now, Alaska, Argentina, seen a lot of wild and won-derful places about this old world. I've shot sand grouse in Tanzania, perdiz on the pampas of Cordoba, driven birds about the Isles, woodcock and grouse in Quebec, Gould's turkey in Chihuahua, searched up a lot of other critters, big and small, in a plethora of places between. I've beheld the Rockies, scaled the Sierra Madre, pondered the snowcapped peaks of the Andes beyond the pale green plains of Patagonia. I've fished, fresh and salt, from the Madison and the Gods rivers, through the Costa Rican Pacific, to the Rio Grande of Tierra del Fuego, the last island on earth. I've tasted point-blank the metallic fear of a Cape buffalo, been awestruck by the majesty of a kudu bull, known face-to-face the might of a coastal grizzly on Admiralty Island.

God willing, there'll be far more.

But above all, and despite the grave in the ground, Pat lives on.

There's a portrait of her in the foyer, by the door, and I spend a moment with her each and every time I go out and return upon the world. Over the mantel at the cabin hangs a picture of Pat, Beda, and Thane in their first shooting-dog year, standing longside a weathered rail fence, and locked on tiptoes into a stiff, divided find. It's testament that once, this all was real. Under the shed—beside the old, rusted '71 Chevy truck that saw us to Illinois, is a Nissan Turbo Z car, one of five thousand, a fiftieth-anniversary model. Upon its stern it bears her name. Zip Zap. I had the plate before I had the car. When I get on it—I mean really shower down on it—it's almost as fast as she was.

Each morning I begin my writing day, I tap in her name. Close my eyes for a few seconds, try to remember her as perfectly as she was. A pounce on a bug, a trembling stand on a butterfly, a faint fleet blur, fading far to the front.

She was the one constant in an inconstant world—she still is—and much that I am, much of what I can ever hope to be, I owe to her.

Time and again, she taught me that "impossible" is merely the dare of a dream.

MIKE GADDIS was born in Asheboro, North Carolina, on September 15, 1942. Among his fondest recollections are Sunday afternoon storytelling sessions on the porch of the ancestral home place, near the small farming community of Cedar Grove. Following in those footsteps, he has been telling his own stories professionally for forty years.

Associate Publisher and Senior Editor for *Sporting Classics* magazine, Gaddis has traveled much of the world in search of hunting and fishing adventure. Through feature articles and his highly regarded column, *First Light*, he has delighted readers with affecting tales from the sporting life.

From early childhood, sporting dogs—terriers, beagles, hounds, retrievers, pointing dogs, and spaniels—have been constant companions, field and hearth. His first book, *Jenny Willow*, published in 2002, has been widely praised as one of the best hunting novels and dog stories ever written.

PRAISE FOR GADDIS'S
Jenny Willow

"A heartwarming, compassionate story . . . an endearing read."
—*Publishers Weekly*

"*Jenny Willow* covers a lot of country: the frontiers of human and canine courage; the mysterious geography of the heart; the high, lonely places where honor resides; and the steep paths that lead there. Powerful and unforgettable, a stunning debut, and a remarkable achievement."
—*The Pointing Dog Journal*

"Good dog tales are legion; great dog novels are rare. With *Jenny Willow*, Mike Gaddis enters the select company of such writers as Donald McCaig. Read it!"
—Steve Bodio, author of
The Edge of the Wild and *Querencia*

"Few, if any, readers of *Jenny Willow* will soon forget this work by Mike Gaddis. One of the top 25 dog books of the last quarter century."
—*The American Field*

"The only problem with this book is one encountered before, the inability to put it down for a moment before reaching the satisfying conclusion."
—*The Discriminating Shooter*

"A great story, detailed and moving with characters and places every bird hunter has known."
—*The Checkcord*

"Destined to become one of the classics of modern literature."
—*Spartanburg Herald-Journal*

"It is a treasure, *Jenny Willow*, a rare find in an age seemingly bereft of truly talented hunting-story tellers, and one no self-respecting sporting library should be without."
—*The American Hunter*

"A commendable story, one that may even make you look forward to growing old."
—*All Things Quail*

~ ALSO AVAILABLE FROM

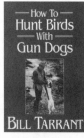

GUN-DOG TRAINING POINTING DOGS
Kenneth C. Roebuck
$18.95, HC, 192 pages, 5 x 8

HOW TO HUNT BIRDS WITH GUN DOGS
Bill Tarrant
$16.95, PB, 192 pages, 6 x 9

SPEED TRAIN YOUR OWN BIRD DOG
Larry Mueller
$19.95, PB, 256 pages, 7 x 9

TARRANT TRAINS GUN DOGS
Bill Tarrant
$19.95, HC, 224 pages, 6 x 9

TO THE POINT
A Tribute to Pointing Dogs
Dale Spartas & Tom Davis
$40.00, HC, 176 pages, 233 color photos, $8^{1}/_{2}$ x 11

TRAINING A YOUNG POINTER
How the Experts Developed My Bird Dog & Me
Joe Healy
$19.95, HC, 144 pages, 6 x 9

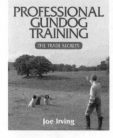

PROFESSIONAL GUNDOG TRAINING
The Trade Secrets
Joe Irving
$36.95, HC, 192 pages, color photos throughout, $7^{1}/_{2}$ x $9^{1}/_{2}$

GUNDOGS
Their Learning Chain
Joe Irving
$21.95, PB, 224 pages, 6 x 9

FIELD TRIALS AND JUDGING
Charles E. A. Alington
$24.95, HC, 136 pages, 6 x 9

STACKPOLE BOOKS ❧

**THE COMPLETE
GUNDOG TRAINING MANUAL**
James Douglas
$31.95, HC, 148 pages, 7¹/₂ x 10

**GUNDOG SENSE
AND SENSIBILITY**
Wilson Stephens
$26.95, HC, 192 pages, 6 x 9

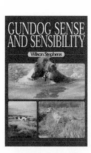

GUNDOGS
Training & Field Trials, 16th edition
P. R. A. Moxon
$26.95, HC, 148 pages, 7¹/₂ x 10

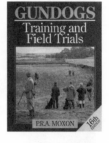

GUNDOG TRAINING
Keith Erlandson
$24.95, HC, 254 pages, 5¹/₂ x 8¹/₂

HEY PUP, FETCH IT UP!
The Complete Retriever Training Book
Bill Tarrant
$29.95, HC, 512 pages, 6 x 9

**WORKING POINTERS
AND SETTERS**
David Hudson
$29.95, HC, 176 pages, 8 x 10

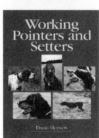

**TRAINING THE
POINTER-RETRIEVER GUNDOG**
Michael Brander
$24.95, HC, 176 pages, 5¹/₂ x 9

PROBLEM GUN DOGS
How to Identify & Correct Their Faults
Bill Tarrant
$16.95, PB, 192 pages, 6 x 9

**GUN-DOG TRAINING
SPANIELS AND RETRIEVERS**
Kenneth C. Roebuck
$19.95, HC, 192 pages, 5 x 8

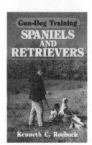